This book is a guide to the development of E and Modern periods. Beginning with an over early English syntax, it gives a unified account of the grammatical changes occurring in the language during this period. Written by four leading experts in English historical syntax, the book demonstrates the ways in which syntactic change takes place and how these changes can be explained in terms of grammatical theory and language acquisition. The authors draw upon a wealth of empirical data and through a series of well-selected case studies they cover a wide range of topics including changes in word order, infinitival constructions and grammaticalization processes. This invaluable introduction to the significant changes in early English syntax will appeal to students and researchers in historical linguistics, theoretical linguistics and the history of English.

OLGA FISCHER is Professor of Germanic Linguistics at the University of Amsterdam. She is author of *Syntactic Change and Causation: Developments in Infinitival Constructions in English* (1990) and has co-edited *Form Miming Meaning: Iconicity in Language and Literature* (1999). She is also a contributor to the Middle English volume of *The Cambridge History of the English Language, volume II: 1066–1476*.

ANS VAN KEMENADE is Professor of English Language and Linguistics at the University of Nijmegen. She is author of *Syntactic Case and Morphological Case in the History of English* (1987) and co-editor of *Parameters of Morphosyntactic Change* (1997).

WILLEM KOOPMAN is Lecturer in English at the University of Amsterdam. He is co-author of *A Key to Better English* (1990) and co-editor of *Explanation and Linguistic Change* (1987).

WIM VAN DER WURFF is Lecturer in English Language at the University of Leiden. He is co-editor of *Reported Speech: Forms and Functions of Verbs* (1996) and of *Negation in the History of English* (1998).

CAMBRIDGE SYNTAX GUIDES
General editors:
S. R. Anderson, J. Bresnan, D. Lightfoot, N. V. Smith, N. Vincent

Responding to the increasing interest in comparative syntax, the goal of the Cambridge Syntax Guides is to make available to all linguists major findings, both descriptive and theoretical, which have emerged from the study of particular languages. The series is not committed to working in any particular framework, but rather seeks to make language-specific research available to theoreticians and practitioners of all persuasions.

Written by leading figures in the field, these guides will each include an overview of the grammatical structures of the language concerned. For the descriptivist, the books will provide an accessible introduction to the methods and results of the theoretical literature; for the theoretician, they will show how constructions that have achieved theoretical notoriety fit into the structure of the language as a whole; for everyone, they will promote cross-theoretical and cross-linguistic comparison with respect to a well-defined body of data.

The Syntax of Early English

OLGA FISCHER
ANS VAN KEMENADE
WILLEM KOOPMAN
WIM VAN DER WURFF

EDINBURGH UNIVERSITY LIBRARY
WITHDRAWN

CAMBRIDGE
UNIVERSITY PRESS

PUBLISHED BY THE PRESS SYNDICATE OF THE UNIVERSITY OF CAMBRIDGE
The Pitt Building, Trumpington Street, Cambridge, United Kingdom

CAMBRIDGE UNIVERSITY PRESS
The Edinburgh Building, Cambridge CB2 2RU, UK   http://www.cup.cam.ac.uk
40 West 20th Street, New York, NY 10011–4211, USA   http://www.cup.org
10 Stamford Road, Oakleigh, Melbourne 3166, Australia
Ruiz de Alarcón 13, 28014 Madrid, Spain

© Cambridge University Press 2000

This book is in copyright. Subject to statutory exception
and to the provisions of relevant collective licensing agreements,
no reproduction of any part may take place without
the written permission of Cambridge University Press.

First published 2000

Printed in the United Kingdom at the University Press, Cambridge

Typeface Monotype Times NR 10/13 pt   *System* QuarkXPress™ [SE]

A catalogue record for this book is available from the British Library

Library of Congress Cataloguing in Publication data

The syntax of early English / Olga Fischer . . . [et al.].
    p.   cm. – (Cambridge syntax guides)
    Includes bibliographical references and index.
    ISBN 0 521 55410 1 (hardback)
    1. English language – Syntax.   2. English language – Old English, ca. 450–1100 – Syntax.
    3. English language – Middle English, 1100–1500 – Syntax.   4. English
    language – Grammar, Historical.   I. Fischer, Olga.   II. Series.
    PE1369.S96   2000
    429′.5 – dc21   0–023266   CIP

ISBN 0 521 55410 1 hardback
ISBN 0 521 55626 0 paperback

Contents

Preface

In the course of the 1980s and 1990s, historical syntax in general, and English historical syntax in particular, developed into a thriving field of research. Much of the credit for this renaissance must go to the advent of sophisticated models of language variation and of linguistic theory. It is perhaps in the domain of syntax that modern theoretical work has most clearly sharpened the traditional questions of historical linguistics, leading to a surge of novel and interesting insights. Happily, this interest in theoretical questions has gone hand in hand with a continued interest in philological matters and, perhaps even more importantly, the creation of ever larger and more sophisticated computerized databases. For these reasons, it seems a particularly felicitous moment for a textbook to appear in which questions concerning the historical syntax of English are consistently addressed from the perspective of a model of syntactic theory.

The model of syntactic theory adopted in this book is the one known as the Principles and Parameters framework. This has important consequences for the way in which we view historical change. In the Principles and Parameters framework, the focus of investigation is the grammar internalized by the native speaker rather than the language output. Consequently, we will attempt throughout the book to make a distinction between language change and grammar change. In the first chapter, we outline the view of grammar change that we try to establish in the book, and set out our arguments and methodology for making the distinction between language change and grammar change. Chapters 2 and 3 are devoted to descriptive overviews of the most important features of the syntax of Old English and Middle English respectively. The remaining chapters are case studies emerging from our own ongoing research into Old and Middle English syntax. In each of these chapters, we present and discuss the relevant facts, giving a structured and critical appraisal of the results accomplished in work done on each case in the literature, substantially including our own research results cast from the perspective of grammar change. Thus, it is attempted in each chapter to strike a balance between theoretical argument and historical detail.

The choice of topics was dictated by a simple consideration: we have tried to make a combination of those among our research topics that are currently of interest, and that would make a coherent book. The case study chapters contain, first of all, three chapters on closely related word order phenomena. Chapter 4 is on the position of the finite verb. In Old and Middle English, the position of the finite verb was determined by a rather complex version of the Verb-Second constraint that is a characteristic of most Germanic languages. This chapter gives a detailed discussion and analysis of this phenomenon and its loss. Chapter 5 is on another classic of word order: the loss of OV word orders. This is essentially about the position of the non-finite verb. It has often been observed that Old English had many OV orders, which were lost in Middle English: the chapter reviews the evidence and pursues an analysis in current theoretical terms. Chapter 6 is on verb–particle constructions, or the rise of phrasal verbs. For Old English particle + verb combinations, a good case can be made that the position of the particle corresponds rather precisely to that of the non-finite verb (in an OV order), whereas that of the verbal part follows the processes governing finite verb placement. Thus the chapter makes crucial use of the results of both chapters 4 and 5. With the general changes in word order as treated in chapters 4 and 5, the verb–particle combinations came to be reanalysed as fixed lexical constructs. Chapters 7 and 8 are on developments in infinitival constructions. Chapter 7 is on the rise of infinitival constructions with a lexical subject, such as *I believed him to be innocent*. It is argued that an important factor in this development is the loss of OV word order as discussed in chapter 5. Chapter 8 is on the rise of the so-called *easy to please* construction, whose development is also closely interrelated with word order developments. Finally, chapter 9 is on two cases of grammaticalization in the history of English from the perspective of grammar change: the rise of periphrastic *have to*, as in *I have to do my work*; and the historical development of sentence negation. Contrary to much work on grammaticalization, it is argued in these case studies that our specific and theoretical notion of grammar change yields an interesting perspective for these cases.

This book aims at an audience consisting of advanced undergraduates and beginning graduate students. It is suitable as a textbook for a specialized undergraduate course, and lecturers and students alike should find it of help in delineating topics for research essays, and paving the way toward thesis research. Although we have attempted to clarify theoretical issues as they come up in the discussion, some background in the Principles and Parameters framework will make it easier to put the case studies in perspective. For individual use, the book should be of interest to both language historians and theoreticians, and may be seen as a guided tour through the most relevant literature on the empirical topics under discussion.

We are grateful to Kluwer Academic Publishers and the editors of *Neophilologus* for permission to reprint the appendix on *have to* in chapter 9, and to Mouton de Gruyter for permission to use the appendix on infinitival constructions in chapter 7.

We owe a debt to several people, editors and kindred spirits in our quest for increased knowledge of and insight in the historical development of English. Judith Ayling, formerly of Cambridge University Press, initiated the project with us, and her efforts were later taken over by Kate Brett and Andrew Winnard. David Denison and Anthony Warner wrote encouraging referee reports in the early stages, which advanced the whole project a step. David Lightfoot has given us various rounds of comments which have helped considerably in sharpening the issues and tightening the discussion. Richard Hogg gave positive feedback on the whole manuscript. Finally, Liesbeth Visser provided student feedback on chapters 4 and 5.

Editions used

The editions cited in this book are listed alphabetically under their abbreviated title. Citations of Old English texts are taken from the Dictionary of Old English Corpus (apart from *ÆCHom* I where Thorpe's text is cited) with the line references and short titles employed by the Dictionary of Old English (Healey and Venezky 1980). Unless otherwise indicated texts are cited by volume/book, chapter, page and line reference where applicable.

The following abbreviations are used:

ASPR   G. P. Krapp and E. V. K. Dobbie (eds.) 1931–53. *The Anglo-Saxon Poetic Records: a Collective Edition*, 6 vols. New York and London: Columbia University Press

EETS   Early English Text Society, Original Series

EETS ES   Early English Text Society, Extra Series

EETS SS   Early English Text Society, Supplementary Series

Alex   *Alexander's Letter to Aristotle* in S. Rypins (ed.) 1924. *Three Old English Prose Texts* (EETS 161), pp. 1–50. 2.3

Ancr.   J. R. R. Tolkien (ed.) 1962. *The English Text of the Ancrene Riwle, Ancrene Wisse, CCCC MS 402* (EETS 249). By folio and line. 3.15, 3.63

Ancr. (Nero)   M. Day (ed.) 1952. *The English Text of the Ancrene Riwle: BM MS. Cotton Nero A.xiv* (EETS 225). 3.34, 6.46a, 6.42a

And   *Andreas*, in *ASPR* 2. 7.23iii

ApT   P. Goolden (ed.) 1958. *The Old English 'Apollonius of Tyre'*, London: Oxford University Press. 5.38

Arth.&M.   O. D. Macrae-Gibson (ed.) 1973. *Of Arthour and of Merlin I: Text* (EETS 268). 3.23

Audelay *Poems*   E. K. Whiting (ed.) 1931. *John Audelay: the Poems* (EETS 184). 8.79

Ayenb.   R. Morris and P. Gradon (eds.) 1965–79. *Dan Michel's Ayenbite of Inwit*, corr. and repr. (EETS 23, 278). 3.31, 5.57, 5.59

ÆAdmon 1   Admonitio ad filium spiritualem, in H. W. Norman (ed.) 1848. *The Anglo-Saxon Version of the Hexameron of St. Basil . . . and the Anglo-Saxon Remains of St. Basil's Admonitio ad filium spiritualem*, London. 7.8a

ÆCHom I   B. Thorpe (ed.) 1844–46. *The Sermones Catholici or Homilies of Ælfric I*, London: Ælfric Society. 1.21a,c, 1.22b, 2.2, 2.5b, 2.6a, 2.17a,c, 2.26b, 2.28, 2.29a, 2.32, 2.33a, 2.34a,b, 2.36a, 2.38a, 2.39d,f, 2.40a, 2.47, 2.50a,b, 2.54a,c, 2.61b, 2.68, 2.71c, 2.77, 4.4, 4.5, 4.6a, 4.12, 4.15, 4.19, 4.22, 4.24, 4.33, 4.34, 4.35, 4.36, 4.39, 4.40, 4.50, 4.55a, 4.59, 4.67, 4.71b, 4.73a,b, 5.5, 5.7, 5.16, 5.18, 5.19, 5.20, 5.23, 5.24, 5.26, 5.28, 5.31, 5.40, 5.46, 5.48, 6.2a, 6.5b, 6.14, 6.17b, 6.20b, 6.28b, 6.29b, 6.32, 6.35, 7.1, 7.15a, 7.21iia, 8.46, 8.53, 9.23a, 9.24

ÆCHom I, 17(App)   P. Clemoes (ed.) 1997. *Ælfric's Catholic Homilies: the First Series* (EETS SS 17), pp. 535–42. 7.21ia,b

ÆCHom II   M. Godden (ed.) 1979. *Ælfric's Catholic Homilies: the Second Series* (EETS SS 5). 2.9b, 2.19b, 2.24, 2.30, 2.38b, 2.39a, 2.48, 2.51, 2.52, 2.54b, 2.61a,c, 2.62b, 2.76a, 2.78a, 2.79b, 3.8, 4.43a, 4.68, 5.15, 5.17, 5.21, 5.27, 5.33, 6.18b, 6.28a, 6.31, 6.39d, 6.43a, 6.45, 7.8c, 8.28, 8.43, 8.81, 9.5b

ÆColl   G. M. Garmonsway (ed.) 1947. *Ælfric's Colloquy*, 2nd edn., London: Methuen. 2.5a, 4.9, 7.18b

ÆGram   J. Zupitza (ed.) 1880. *Ælfrics Grammatik und Glossar*, Berlin: Weidmannsche Buchhandlung. 7.15b, 7.17

ÆHom   J. C. Pope (ed.) 1967–68. *Homilies of Ælfric: a Supplementary Collection* (EETS 259, 260). 1.22c, 2.7a,b, 2.12a, 2.25, 2.33b, 2.49, 2.64, 4.44, 4.46, 4.69, 4.70, 5.8, 6.13, 7.21iiia, 9.21, 9.23b

ÆLet 2(Wulfstan 1)   First Old English Letter for Wulfstan, in B. Fehr (ed.) 1914. *Die Hirtenbriefe Ælfrics*. Bibliothek der angelsächsischen Prosa 9, Hamburg: Henri Grand. 2.39b, 6.29a

ÆLS   W. W. Skeat (ed.) 1881–1900. *Ælfric's Lives of the Saints* (EETS 76, 82, 94, 114) (repr. as 2 vols. 1966). By life and line.1.21b, 2.12c, 2.15b, 2.20b, 2.31, 2.53, 2.67, 2.71b, 3.6b, 4.42, 4.43b, 4.47, 4.55d, 4.71a, 5.12, 5.22, 6.3b, 6.10a, 6.11, 6.20a, 6.36a,b, 6.44, 7.21iiib, 7.22a, 9.26a,b, 9.27a

ÆTemp   H. Henel (ed.) 1942. *Ælfric's De temporibus anni* (EETS 213). 7.7a

Barlam   J. C. Hirsh (ed.) 1986. *Barlam and Iosaphat* (EETS 290). 5.64

Bede   T. Miller (ed.) 1890–98. *The Old English Version of Bede's Ecclesiastical History of the English People* (EETS 95, 96, 110, 111). 2.18b, 2.37a, 2.57, 2.58, 2.59, 2.62a, 2.65, 4.61, 6.6a, 6.39b,c, 7.18a, 7.21iib, 7.23iva, 8.41, 9.14, 9.16A1

Ben.Rule(1)   E. A. Kock (ed.) 1902. *Three Middle-English Versions of the Rule of St. Benet* (EETS 120). 4.79a,b,c

Beo   *Beowulf*, in *ASPR* 4. 1.27, 2.10a, 2.22a, 2.55, 5.35, 5.36, 9.10a, 9.28, 9.29a,b, 9.note14

Bo   W. J. Sedgefield (ed.) 1899. *King Alfred's Old English Version of Boethius' De consolatione philosophiae*, Oxford: Clarendon (repr. Darmstadt 1968). 1.22d, 2.12b, 2.45, 2.69, 2.70a, 2.76b, 3.6a, 3.20, 3.86, 4.18, 4.48, 5.13, 5.25, 5.39, 7.7b, 8.40, 8.47

ByrM   P. S. Baker and M. Lapidge (eds.) 1995. *Byrhtferth's Enchiridion* (EETS SS 15). 6.38b

Capgrave *Chronicles*   P. J. Lucas (ed.) 1983. *John Capgrave's Abbreuiacion of Chronicles* (EETS 285). 5.60, 5.62

Caxton *Paris&Vienne*   M. Leach (ed.) 1957. *Paris and Vienne translated from the French and printed by William Caxton* (EETS 234). 3.41

Caxton *Knight of Tower*   M. Y. Offord (ed.) 1971. *The Book of the Knight of the Tower translated by William Caxton* (EETS SS 2). 5.77

Cely Letters   A. Hanham (ed.) 1975. *The Cely Letters 1472–1488* (EETS 273) By letter and line. 3.3, 5.63

Chaucer   L. D. Benson (ed.) 1988. *The Riverside Chaucer*, 3rd edn. Oxford: Oxford University Press. 3.2, 3.4, 3.27, 3.32, 3.33, 3.35, 3.36, 3.44, 3.45, 3.46, 3.47, 3.48, 3.50, 3.51, 3.52, 3.53, 3.54, 3.55, 3.56, 3.57, 3.58, 3.59, 3.62, 3.65, 3.66, 3.67, 3.73, 3.75, 3.79, 3.80, 3.89, 3.90, 3.91, 3.93, 3.94, 3.96, 5.3, 5.55, 5.56, 5.58, 5.69, 5.83, 5.84, 7.12, 7.19a, 7.28, 7.note16, 8.67, 9.8, 9.11, 9.34a,b

Cloud   P. Hodgson (ed.) 1944. *The Cloud of Unknowing and the Book of Privy Counselling* (EETS 218). 8.59, 8.73, 8.74

ChristB   *Christ*, in *ASPR* 3. 6.note2

ChronA   The Parker Chronicle. MS A, in C. Plummer (ed.) 1892–99. *Two of the Saxon Chronicles Parallel*, Oxford: Clarendon. 2.9a, 2.19a,c, 2.21b,c, 2.27, 2.41, 4.10, 4.16, 4.53, 5.1

ChronB   MS BL Cotton Tiberius A.vi, in B. Thorpe (ed.) 1861. *The Anglo-Saxon Chronicle*, London: Rolls Series. 6.34

ChronE   The Peterborough Chronicle. MS. E, in C. Plummer (ed.) 1892–99. *Two of the Saxon Chronicles Parallel*, Oxford: Clarendon. 1.6, 3.60, 4.75a, 4.76a, 5.2, 6.42b, 6.47, 6.note12

Conrad *Lord Jim*   Joseph Conrad 1949. *Lord Jim*, Harmondsworth: Penguin. 6.49

CP   H. Sweet (ed.) 1871. *King Alfred's West Saxon Version of Gregory's Pastoral Care* (EETS 45, 50). 1.23b, 2.4, 2.6b, 2.8b, 2.11a,b, 2.13, 2.16, 2.17b, 2.35b, 2.40b, 2.43, 2.44, 2.46, 2.62c, 2.70a,b, 2.78b, 2.79a, 3.26,

4.7, 4.14, 4.25, 4.26b, 4.49, 4.54, 4.55b, 4.64, 4.71c, 5.4, 5.9, 5.11, 5.30, 5.32, 5.50, 6.3a, 6.4b, 6.12, 6.15, 6.18a, 6.19, 6.20a, 6.38c, 6.39a, 7.23ii, 8.37, 8.52, 9.9a, 9.25, 9.27b

Cursor Mundi   R. Morris (ed.) 1874–78. *Cursor Mundi* (EETS 57, 59, 62, 66, 68). 1.26b, 3.74, 3.82, 8.57, 9.12

Destr. Troy   G. A. Panton and D. Donaldson 1869–74. *The Gest Hystoriale of the Destruction of Troy* (EETS 39, 56). 3.13b, 3.92

Dives&Pauper   P. H. Barnum (ed.) 1976–80. *Dives and Pauper* (EETS 275, 280). 3.17, 3.19

Dryden   M. E. Novak and G. R. Guffey (eds.) 1970. vol. 10: (*Plays*) of *The Works of John Dryden*, Berkeley: University of California Press. 5.81

EARLPS   K. D. Bülbring (ed.) 1891. *The Earliest Complete English Prose Psalter* (EETS 97). 4.78

El   *Elene*, in *ASPR* 2. 2.22b, 3.68

Gawain   J. R. R. Tolkien and E. V. Gordon (eds.) 1967. *Sir Gawain and the Green Knight*, 2nd edn., rev. by N. Davis, Oxford: Clarendon. 3.97a

GD (C)   MS C, in H. Hecht (ed.) 1900–07. *Bischof Wærferths von Worcester Übersetzung der Dialoge Gregors des Grossen*, Bibliothek der angelsächsischen Prosa 5, Hamburg: Henri Grand. 4.38, 5.49, 6.20a, 8.26, 8.34

GD (H)   MS H, in Hecht 1900–7. 6.4a, 8.35

Gen&Ex   R. Morris (ed.) 1865. *The Story of Genesis and Exodus* (EETS 7). 3.37, 3.71

Gower *Confessio Amantis*   G. C. Macaulay (ed.) 1900–01. *Confessio Amantis* in *The English Works of John Gower* (EETS ES 81, 82). 1.17a, 3.14, 7.29c

GuthA,B   *Guthlac*, in *ASPR* 3. 7.8b, 8.38

Havelok   G. V. Smithers (ed.) 1987. *Havelok*, Oxford: Clarendon. 3.7a,b, 3.61, 3.97b

Hoccleve *Jonathas*   F. J. Furnivall and I. Gollancz (eds.) 1892–98. *Hoccleve's Works: The Minor Poems* (EETS ES 61, 73). 1.17b

HomS 17(BlHom5)   Blickling Homily 5, in R. Morris (ed.) 1874–80. *The Blickling Homilies* (EETS 58, 63, 73) (repr. in 1 vol. 1967), pp. 55–65. 2.23

HomU 19(BlHom8)   Blickling Homily 8, in R. Morris 1874–80, pp. 97–105. 2.35a, 4.13, 4.51

HomU 20(BlHom10)   Blickling Homily 10, in R. Morris 1874–80, pp. 107–15. 2.15a

HomU 42(Nap 52)   Homily 52, in A. S. Napier (ed.) 1883. *Wulfstan*, Sammlung englischer Denkmäler 4, Berlin: Weidmannsche Buchhandlung, pp. 275–6. 7.22b

HomU 46(Nap 57)   Homily 57, in Napier 1883, pp. 291–9. 5.14

Imit. Christ   B. Biggs (ed.) 1997. *The First Translation of the Imitatio Christi* (EETS 309). 7.9a

Jacob&J   A. S. Napier (ed.) 1916. *Jacob & Iosep: a Middle English Poem of the 13th Century*, Oxford: Clarendon. 3.9

Jn(WSCp)   John (Cambridge Corpus Christ College MS 140), in W. W. Skeat (ed.) 1871–87. *The Four Gospels in Anglo-Saxon, Northumbrian, and Old Mercian Versions*, Cambridge: Cambridge University Press. 9.16A2

Jud   *Judith*, in *ASPR* 4. 7.18d

Jul   *Juliana*, in *ASPR* 3. 7.18f

Ken. Serm.   *Kentish Sermons*, in J. A. W. Bennett and G. V. Smithers (eds.) 1968. *Early Middle English Verse and Prose*, 2nd edn, Oxford: Clarendon, pp. 213–22. 4.75c, 9.33a

King Horn   J. Hall (ed.) 1901. *King Horn: a Middle English Romance*, Oxford: Clarendon. 3.28, 3.29

Lanc. of the Laik   W. W. Skeat (ed.) 1865. *The Romans of Lancelot of the Laik* (EETS 6). 3.64

Layamon *Brut*   G. L. Brook and R. F. Leslie (eds.) 1963–78. *Layamon's Brut* (EETS 250, 277). 3.49, 7.25a, 7.26a,b, 7.29a, 9.13

Lch I(Herb)   Herbarius, in T. O. Cockayne (ed.) 1864–66. *Leechdoms, Wortcunning and Starcraft of Early England*, 3 vols. (repr. 1961), London: Holland. 8.44

Lch II   Bald's Leechbook, in Cockayne 1864–66. 7.23i

LibSc   S. S. Getty (ed.) 1969. *An Edition with Commentary of the Latin/Anglo-Saxon "Liber scintillarum"*, dissertation, University of Pennsylvania. 8.31

Lk(WSCp)   Luke (Cambridge Corpus Christ College MS 140), in W. W. Skeat (ed.) 1871–87. *The Four Gospels in Anglo-Saxon, Northumbrian, and Old Mercian Versions*, Cambridge: Cambridge University Press. 9.5a

*LS*7 (Euphr)   Saint Euphrosyne, in W. W. Skeat (ed.) 1881–1900. *Ælfric's Lives of the Saints* (EETS 76, 82, 94, 112) (repr. as 2 vols. 1966), vol. II, pp. 334–54. 4.6b, 4.52

*LS*8 (Eust)   Saint Eustace and his Companions, in W. W. Skeat (ed.) 1881–1900. *Ælfric's Lives of the Saints* (EETS 76, 82, 94, 112) (repr. as 2 vols. 1966), vol. II, pp. 190–218. 8.42

*LS*14 (MargaretAss)   B. Assmann (ed.) 1889. *Angelsächsische Homilien und Heiligenleben*, Bibliothek der angelsächsischen Prosa 3, Kassel: Georg Wigand, pp. 170–80. 7.note6, 9.10b

*LS*17.1 (MartinMor)   Saint Martin, in R. Morris (ed.) 1874–80. *The Blickling Homilies* (EETS 58, 63, 73), pp. 211–27. 6.16

*LS*20 (AssumptMor)   Assumption of Mary the Virgin, in R. Morris (ed.) 1874–80, pp 137–59. 6.17a

*LS*23 (MaryofEgypt)   Mary of Egypt, in W. W. Skeat (ed.) 1881–1900. *Ælfric's Lives of the Saints* (EETS 76, 82, 94, 112) (repr. as 2 vols. 1966), vol. II, pp. 2–52. 8.45

*LS*29 (Nicholas)   Saint Nicholas. Dictionary of Old English Transcript. 7.18c

*LS*32 (Peter&Paul)   Peter and Paul, in R. Morris 1874–80. *The Blickling Homilies* (EETS 58, 63, 73), pp. 171–93. 6.30, 6.43b

Lydgate *Troy Book*   H. Bergen (ed.) 1906–10. *Lydgate's Troy Book* (EETS ES 97, 103, 106). 3.30

Malory *Works*   E. Vinaver (ed.) 1947. *The Works of Sir Thomas Malory*, 3 vols., Oxford: Clarendon. 3.24, 3.25, 3.39, 3.40, 3.72, 3.83, 3.85, 7.25b, 7.27, 7.30, 7.31a, 7.33b

Mandev.   P. Hamelius (ed.) 1919–23. *Mandeville's Travels* (EETS 153, 154). 3.70, 3.78, 3.95

MAngl   Mappula Angliae, C. Horstmann (ed.) 1887. 'Mappula Angliae', *ESt* 10, 6–34. 8.56

Manning *HS*   F. J. Furnivall (ed.) 1901–03. *Robert of Brunne's 'Handlyng Synne'* (EETS 119, 123). 3.87, 8.84

Mart 5(Kotzor)   G. Kotzor (ed.) 1981. *Das altenglische Martyrologium*, Abhandlungen der Bayerische Akademie der Wissenschaften, Philosophisch-Historische Klasse, Neue Folge, Heft 88/1–2, München: Bayerische Akademie der Wissenschaften. 7.23ivb, 8.27, 9.9b

Met   The Meters of Boethius, in *ASPR* 5. 4.26a, 4.37, 4.63

Mk(WSCp)   Mark (Cambridge Corpus Christ College MS 140), in W. W. Skeat (ed.) 1871–87. *The Four Gospels in Anglo-Saxon, Northumbrian, and Old Mercian Versions*, Cambridge: Cambridge University Press. 4.41

MKempe   S. B. Meech (ed.) 1940. *The Book of Margery Kempe* (EETS 212). 3.38, 6.42e,f

More *Dialogue of Comfort*   L. L. Mantz and F. Manlay (eds.) 1976. *A Dialogue of Comfort* (vol. 12 of The Complete Works of St. Thomas More), New Haven: Yale University Press. 5.66, 5.67

Mowntayne   J. G. Nichols (ed.) 1859. *The Autobiography of Thomas Mowntayne*, London: Camden Society. 9.36

Or   J. Bately (ed.) 1980. *The Old English Orosius* (EETS SS 6). 1.22a, 1.23a,

2.20a, 2.22a, 2.26a, 2.29b, 2.36b, 2.37b, 2.56, 2.60, 2.61d, 2.66, 2.76a,
4.8, 4.17, 4.20, 4.23, 4.55c, 4.60, 4.62, 4.65, 4.66, 5.6, 5.10, 6.2b, 6.5a,
6.6b, 6.10b, 6.33, 9.7

Orm   R. Holt (ed.) 1878. *The Ormulum: with the Notes and Glossary of Dr.
R. M. White*, 2 vols., Oxford: Clarendon. 3.22

Paston Letters   N. Davis (ed.) 1971–76. *Paston Letters and Papers of the
Fifteenth Century*, Oxford: Clarendon. By letter and line. 3.18, 3.84,
5.65, 5.76, 7.19b, 7.29b, 7.31b,c, 7.33a, 9.16B1

Phlebotomy   L. E. Voigts and M. R. McVaugh (eds.) 1984. *A Latin Technical
Phlebotomy and its Middle English Translation*, Transactions of the
American Philosophical Society 74, part 2, Philadelphia: American
Philosophical Society. 9.16B2

Phoen   *The Phoenix*, in *ASPR* 3. 2.10b

Piers Plowman B   G. Kane and E. T. Donaldson (eds.) 1988. *Piers Plowman:
the B Version, Will's Visions of Piers Plowman and Do-Well*, rev. edn.,
London: Athlone / Berkeley: University of California Press. 3.97c

Poema Morale   J. Hall (ed.) 1920. *Selections from Early Middle English
1130–1250* I, Oxford: Clarendon, pp. 30–53. 9.35a

PPs   The Paris Psalter, in *ASPR* 5. 8.29

PPs(prose)   J. W. Bright and R. L. Ramsay (eds.) 1907. *The West Saxon
Psalms*, The Belles Lettres Series, Boston: Heath. By psalm and verse.
4.45

Rel.Lyrics   C. Brown (ed.) 1914. *Religious Lyrics of the XIVth Century*,
Oxford: Clarendon. By lyric and line. 7.9b

Rid   *Riddles*, in *ASPR* 3. 7.18e, 7.21ia,b

Rolle   G. G. Perry (ed.) 1866. *Richard Rolle de Hampole: English Prose
Treatises* (EETS 20). 4.80a,b

RRose   in L. D. Benson (ed.) 1988. *The Riverside Chaucer*, 3rd edn, Oxford:
Oxford University Press. 2.77, 8.78

Sat   *Christ and Satan*, in *ASPR* 1. 6.38

Sermon   *Testimony of Thorpe*, in A. Hudson (ed.) 1993. *Two Wycliffite Texts:
Sermon of Taylor, Testimony of Thorpe* (EETS 301). 5.61

Shakespeare   S. Wells and G. Taylor (eds.) 1986. *William Shakespeare: the
Complete Works*, Oxford: Clarendon.

Solil   W. Endter (ed.) 1922. *König Alfreds des Grossen Bearbeitung der
Soliloquien des Augustinus*, Bibliothek der angelsächsischen Prosa 11,
Hamburg: Henri Grand. 2.18a, 2.42

SSecr   R. Steele and T. Henderson 1898. *Three Prose Versions of the Secreta
Secretorum* (EETS ES 74). 3.5

Stanzaic Life of Chr.   F. A. Foster (ed.) 1926. *A Stanzaic Life of Christ* (EETS 166). 7.9c

St.Juliana (Bod)   MS. Bodley 34, in S. R. T. O. d'Ardenne (ed.) 1961. *Þe Liflade ant te Passiun of Seinte Iuliene* (EETS 248). 6.42c, 9.33b

St.Juliana (Roy)   MS. BL Royal 17 A xxvii, in S. R. T. O. d'Ardenne (ed.) 1961. *Þe Liflade ant te Passiun of Seinte Iuliene* (EETS 248). 1.26a

St.Kath.   S. R. T. O d'Ardenne and E. J. Dobson (eds.) 1981. *Seinte Katerine* (EETS SS 7). 3.76, 6.42d, 6.48b

St.Marg.   F. M. Mack (ed.) 1934. *Sainte Marherete* (EETS 193). 6.46b,c, 6.48a

Sward   *Sawles Warde,* in J. A. W. Bennett and G. V. Smithers (eds.) 1968. *Early Middle English Verse and Prose,* 2nd edn., Oxford: Clarendon, pp. 241–61. 3.16, 4.76b, 9.35b

Syr Tryamowre   A. J. Erdman Schmidt (ed.) 1937. *Sir Tryamowre: a Metrical Romance,* Utrecht: Kemink. 8.77

Tale of Beryn   F. J. Furnivall and W. G. Stone (eds.) 1909. *The Tale of Beryn* (EETS ES 105). 8.64

ThCap2 (Sauer)   MS. Bodley 865, in H. Sauer (ed.) 1978. *Theodulfi Capitula in England: Die altenglischen Übersetzungen, zusammen mit dem lateinischen Text,* München: Wilhelm Fink. 7.11, 8.30

Trevisa *De Proprietatibus Rerum*   M. C. Seymour et al. (eds.) 1975. *On the Properties of Things; John Trevisa's Translation of Bartholomaeus Anglicus De Proprietatibus Rerum, a Critical Text,* Oxford: Clarendon. 8.71

Trevisa *Polychr.*   C. Babington and J. R. Lumby (eds.) 1865–86. *Polychronicon Ranulphi Higdin, Monachi Cestrensis: together with the English Translation of John Trevisa and of an Unknown Writer of the fourteenth century,* 9 vols., London: Rolls Series. 9.16A3

VespHom.   MS Cotton Vespasian A.xxii, in R. Morris (ed.) 1868. *Old English Homilies of the 12th and 13th Centuries* (EETS 34). 6.40

Vices&V   F. Holthausen (ed.) 1888–1921. *Vices and Virtues* (EETS 89, 159). 3.13a, 4.75b, 4.76c, 4.77, 6.41a,b, 9.35c

WBible   *The Earlier Version,* in J. Forshall and F. Madden (eds.) 1850. *The Holy Bible . . . made from the Latin Vulgate by John Wycliffe and his Followers,* 4 vols., Oxford: Oxford University Press. 3.10, 7.20b

WCan   R. G. Fowler (ed.) 1972. *Wulfstan's Canons of Edgar* (EETS 266). 2.63

WHom   D. Bethurum (ed.) 1957. *The Homilies of Wulfstan,* Oxford: Clarendon. By homily and line. 2.8a, 2.21a, 2.39c,e, 5.29

Wooing Lord   R. Morris (ed.) 1868. *Old English Homilies* (EETS 34) pp. 269–87. 3.69, 8.55

WPal.   G. H. V. Bunt (ed.) 1985. *William of Palerne: an Alliterative Romance*, Groningen: Bouma. 3.21

Wycl *Clergy HP*   in F. D. Matthew (ed.) 1880. *English Works of Wyclif* (EETS 74), pp. 359–404. 8.60

Wycl *Feigned Cont. Life*   K. Sisam (ed.) 1921. *Fourteenth Century Verse & Prose*, Oxford: Clarendon, pp. 119–28. 4.81b

Wycl *Leaven Pharisees*   in F. D. Matthew (ed.) 1880. *English Works of Wyclif* (EETS 74), pp. 1–27. 8.58

Wycl. Serm. (Arnold)   T. Arnold (ed.) 1869–71. *Selected English Works of John Wyclif*, 3 vols., Oxford: Clarendon. 7.20a

Wycl. Serm.   A. Hudson (vols. I, III) and P. Gradon (vol. II) (eds.) 1983–90. *English Wycliffite Sermons*, Oxford: Clarendon. 4.81a

1

Language change and grammar change

1.1   Introduction

Ða com of more under misthleoþum
Grendel gongan, Godes yrre bær;
mynte se manscaða manna cynnes
sumne besyrwan in sele þam hean.   (*Beo* 710–13)

These are four lines from one of the earliest Old English texts, the famous heroic poem *Beowulf*, which was composed over one thousand years ago. This piece of language, indeed Old English in general, is almost completely unreadable without specialized training; the most an unskilled reader will recognize is a few words still around in the language, like *of* and *under*. A word-by-word translation is: then came from moor under misty cliffs / Grendel go, God's anger bore / meant the foul-foe of-the-men / one trap in hall the high. An idiomatic translation into Modern English is: 'Then from the moor under the misty cliffs came Grendel, bearing God's anger. The foul foe meant to trap one of the men in the high hall.' Leaving aside phonological and lexical differences, which are not our concern in this book, it is not difficult to spot differences in sentence construction between these four lines and the present-day language. For instance, the word order *Then came from the moor . . .* is at best a stylistically marked option in present-day English, and the word order with the finite verb in initial position in line 3 is ungrammatical: *meant the foul foe . . .* Other differences are the combination of the verbs 'come' and 'intend' with a bare infinitive, as in *com . . . Grendel gongan*, and *mynte . . . besyrwan*. A further difference is the word order of the nominal group *sele þam hean* 'hall the high'. Beside these, the language of *Beowulf* has a system of cases and of verb endings, and there are various other syntactic differences apparent from these four lines of text. Many of these differences will be discussed or touched upon in the chapters to come, though not all of them, for it is not the aim of this book to give an inventory of the syntactic changes that have taken place in the history of English. This is a task that is best left to handbooks, such as the various volumes of *The Cambridge History of the English Language*, which contain excellent and extensive digests of the work that has been done. The approach in this book will be different, in that we pursue in detail the nature and causes of a number of cases of syntactic change in the history of English. The approach that we shall take in doing so is inspired by theoretical work in the vein of Chomsky's Principles and Parameters approach to syntactic theory. Looking at historical developments from this generative perspective has important consequences for our view of syntactic change, since it means that we will focus on change in grammar as conceived of in the Principles and Parameters approach, rather than on language change.[1]

In this introductory chapter, we explicate our approach and its consequences in the realms of syntactic theory and philology. We first sketch the basic ideas underlying the generative approach to syntactic change, and show how its emphasis on the grammar of the native speaker as the object of study both sharpens and complicates the study of historical change. We will also discuss some important recent contributions to the study of English historical syntax from perspectives other than our grammar-focussed one, to achieve a more comprehensive view of the syntactic changes in the history of English that we discuss in subsequent chapters. Section 1.2 will be on grammar change from the Principles and Parameters perspective; section 1.3 on grammar change and language change; and section 1.4 will concentrate on methodological issues and presents a discussion of problems that historical data pose for the linguist in general, and the generative linguist in particular.

1.2   Historical change, language acquisition and the Principles and Parameters model

1.2.1   Language acquisition and grammar change

The general framework for the study of syntax adopted here is Principles and Parameters theory. This is not one single set of ideas or theoretical notions, but rather an approach to the study of language. Its nature is perhaps best captured in the following quote from Chomsky:

> The study of generative grammar has been guided by several fundamental problems, each with a traditional flavor. The basic concern is to determine and characterize the linguistic capacities of particular individuals. We are concerned, then, with states of the language faculty, which we understand to be some array of cognitive traits and capacities, a particular component of

---

[1] For introductions to generative syntax, we refer the reader to Radford (1997) and Haegeman (1994).

the human mind/brain. The language faculty has an initial state, genetically determined; in the normal course of development it passes through a series of states in early childhood, reaching a relatively stable steady state that undergoes little subsequent change, apart from the lexicon. To a good first approximation, the initial state appears to be uniform for the species. Adapting traditional terms to a special usage, we call the theory of the state attained its *grammar* and the theory of the initial state *Universal Grammar* (UG).   (Chomsky 1995: 14)

It follows from this characterization that in this perspective on the study of language, the object of study is the grammar of the native speaker, to be understood as one language learner's choices for her native language with respect to the abstract parameters that are part of Universal Grammar (UG).[2] One of the core aims of generative grammar, then, is to solve what has come to be called 'the logical problem of language acquisition', i.e. the question how it is that the language learner is capable of constructing a mature grammar of her native language in a surprisingly short time, and on the basis of impoverished evidence. The evidence available to the language learner consists of the speech output of her language environment, which contains many performance errors, and little to no evidence about ungrammaticality. It seems that the role of correction by parents in the language acquisition process is very limited indeed, as illustrated in e.g. McNeill (1966). The starting point for the answer to the logical problem of language acquisition is that the human language capacity, the 'initial state' or 'UG' as Chomsky and Lasnik call it, is a highly structured system of abstract principles and parameters, the values of which are filled in by the language learner on the basis of exposure to the language environment. This system is called Universal Grammar and is assumed to be part of the genetic endowment of the human species.

If we consider historical change from this perspective, it follows that the focus of investigation is on grammar change rather than on language change. This distinction is crucial and has important ramifications for how we approach historical change. The distinction between grammar change and language change correlates with the distinction usually made in generative approaches between a speaker's *competence* (knowledge and understanding) and *performance* (what the speaker does with that knowledge and understanding). The competence of the speaker, grammatical or otherwise, is reflected by what she knows about her native language. An important method for obtaining information about this grammatical knowledge is by eliciting a native speaker's wellformedness judgements. There may be a considerable

---

[2] Following frequent practice in the literature on language acquisition, we refer to the language-learning child as *she/her*.

discrepancy between competence and performance. Whereas competence is supposed to constitute the steady state referred to by Chomsky, performance very often reflects that steady state imperfectly, and is influenced by factors such as slips of the tongue, tiredness, boredom, external distractions and, as the case may be when working with historical data, factors that are beyond our reach, such as the possibility of a piece of written performance like a manuscript being a late copy of a copy of a translation from Latin, written in winter when the scribe's fingers were cramped by frost, with a quill that was badly in need of sharpening, while the candle was running low. What we aim at when we study historical change from this perspective is to isolate from the set of historical data, which comprises historical written performance material, those data that reflect changes in the competence of speakers, changes in grammars.

An implication of this view of grammar change is the notion that the process of acquisition of the grammar of the native language is the main locus of change. Data from language change are of particular interest to this approach because, as Paul Kiparsky first put it, they provide a window on the form of linguistic competence (Kiparsky 1982). Instances of change can show something about the grammars of languages, because we can get a clearer view of a partially hidden abstract system when it changes from one state to another. This in turn may throw light on the precise way the theory of grammar should be formulated.

The idea that we should look primarily to language acquisition for explanations of syntactic change has evolved with increasing emphasis since it was first formulated explicitly in this context in David Lightfoot's *Principles of Diachronic Syntax* (1979). In that work, Lightfoot reacts strongly against ideas about language change in terms of drift and teleology, and the notion of diachronic grammar, which were popular in the 1970s. Such notions presuppose that language change follows, even across many generations, a predestined direction. This, according to Lightfoot, cannot be right. Each speaker constructs her own grammar afresh. The language learner does not know anything about the history of her language, and hence cannot follow any predestined process. Lightfoot argues that the language learner is endowed genetically with the ability to construct a grammar of her native language on the basis only of the speech in her language environment. Example (1) (dating back to Andersen (1973)) illustrates this:

(1)

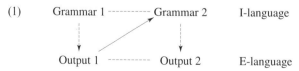

If we see output 1 as the speech of the parent grammar (their E-language, or external language), what this diagram shows is that the language learner constructs her grammar (grammar 2) on the basis of output 1. Crucially, this happens without reference to the grammar of the parent language, since the learner has no access to that. The relationship is between output 1 and grammar 2; there is in principle no relation between grammar 1 and grammar 2. On such a view, there is no (direct) relation between the grammars of speakers, often called their I(internal)-languages, whether they belong to the same or to different generations. There is therefore no ontological basis for such notions as drift, teleology or diachronic grammar, since they presuppose that the language learner recognizes a change in progress as part of a master plan spanning many generations, to which she conforms. There is indeed no theory of change, since change is by definition synchronic, and takes place as each new language learner constructs her grammar.

There are, nevertheless, many long-term changes which often seem to follow a particular direction. This is the kind of change that inspires notions like drift and the emphasis on diachrony found in the work of grammaticalization theorists. For example, Hawkins (1990: 102–3) talks about 'diachronic universals' ('regular diachronic drifts'), and states that 'The causes of these drifts are various and constitute part of the theory of language change'. Because grammar change takes place in the acquisition process, it is a fallacy to analyse such phenomena as essentially diachronic. We discuss this more closely in section 1.3, and devote chapter 9 to a discussion of some case studies of long-term change.

Lightfoot (1979) gives an explicit methodology for work on syntactic change, which has the important quality of being falsifiable by virtue of its being explicit. Lightfoot argues that each language learner constructs her own grammar in an optimal fashion within the bounds set by the principles of UG. In his (1979) contribution, he assigns a major role to the *Transparency Principle*, a principle of grammar that requires derivations to be minimally complex, so that underlying structures are as close as possible to their surface structures. It is intended to minimize opacity in the derivation. In the course of historical development, a construction or category may acquire a number of marked characteristics through independent developments such as phonological changes, the loss of morphology and changes in word order. An example of this would be the precursors of the present-day English modals. The history of the English modals will be considered in greater detail in the next section, since it provides a good illustration of Lightfoot's view of syntactic change as well as that of others that will come up in the course of this and following chapters.

1.2.1.1 The history of English modals

Let us start with the standard assumption that in the present-day language, modals are auxiliaries, verbal function words. They occur as finite forms only, and in conjunction with an infinitive form without *to*, as in *I will do my homework*; *she might be going to the party*; *you can go to the party*. Syntactically, they function essentially as sentence modifiers: *I* in *I will do my homework* is the thematic subject of the predicate *do my homework*, not the subject of *will*. *Will* expresses future time reference, which is evidence that it is not a lexical verb. In the present-day language, modals lack inflections for person (first, second, third) or number (sg, pl), and although they have forms which reflect a present/past tense distinction historically, like *will/would*; *can/could*; *may/might*, these do not now necessarily mark a present/past distinction: for instance, the choice of *can/could* and *may/might* may reflect degrees of politeness, as in *can/could you pass me the salt?* or degrees of confidence of a positive reply as in *may/might I borrow your gold fountain pen?*

In the Old English period, modals had many more characteristics typical of lexical verbs. Evidence for this is that they could have objects and tensed clause complements, and, though they were part of the special class of so-called preterite-present verbs, they had a wider range of verbal inflections, including endings for the subjunctive mood. Lightfoot (1979) discusses the chain of events through which the Old English 'premodals', as he calls them, changed to the present-day modals as a paradigm case of a catastrophic change, a grammar change from one generation to the next. This account has been the subject of much criticism, not all of it justified: for instance, Plank (1984) argues that the history of the modals is a case of all graduality, but Warner (1990; 1993) shows that there is an abrupt shift in the behaviour of the modals in the early sixteenth century, although this is not a case of grammar change in the sense of a parameter of grammar being reset. Rather, to the extent that there is an abrupt change, it is a change in the lexical properties of modal verbs, the modal verbs being reanalysed from main verbs of sorts to auxiliaries, i.e. grammatical markers of mood.

The account in Lightfoot (1979) recognizes the following changes affecting the modals:[3]

(2)   a. Modals lost the ability to take a direct object. According to Lightfoot, this seems to have been complete in Middle English (fifteenth century) with the exception of *can*, which was a good deal more resistant (seventeenth century).

---

[3] Lightfoot adds a fifth change to this list, based on a highly theory-internal word order argument. We have omitted this for the sake of clarity.

    b. Most premodals belonged to the inflectional class generally known as 'preterite presents'. The notable thing about this class is that the third person sg did not have the usual -*eþ* ending. Gradually, all the non-premodals of this class were lost. As a result, the premodals became a morphologically unique class.

    c. Because of phonological similarities in the endings, the opposition between present and past as one of tense, and indicative and subjunctive as one of mood became increasingly opaque, so that the present and past forms and levelled subjunctive forms acquired separate modal meanings.

    d. There were changes connected with the rise of the *to*-infinitive. In Old English, the premodals were never followed by *to*. The *to*-infinitive was firmly established in the course of the fourteenth century, except with premodals. Lightfoot concludes from this that at this stage the premodals were already beginning to be recognized as a separate class.

Following these changes, the premodals came to function as a separate class inflectionally, syntactically and semantically. Evidence for this is that the premodals (now modals) ceased to display a number of typically (main) verbal characteristics:[4]

(3)   a. They ceased to occur as infinitives.
        b. They could no longer occur with -*ing*-affixes.
        c. They could no longer occur in clusters.
        d. They could no longer occur with *have* and with -*en*-affixes.

According to Lightfoot, the modals have now acquired too many exception features to be learnable as lexical verbs. The Transparency Principle then predicts a reanalysis; the form of this reanalysis is constrained by other principles of grammar, and in this case the premodals changed into a different word category: that of auxiliaries, grammatical function words. In this view of the history of modals, the premodals were verbs and in one fell swoop underwent a radical categorial reanalysis, changing into modal auxiliaries.

    While much of the ideology of Lightfoot's approach (1979) still stands, the Transparency Principle has proved to be an undesirable and superfluous addition to the theory of grammar. It is undesirable because it has no possible formal characterization like other principles of grammar, as it is not clear what opacity in a derivation really is. Also, it is implicit in the way Lightfoot illustrates the Transparency Principle that reanalyses are only forced as the result of accumulating exception features. This is not necessarily correct, as we will see below. Roberts (1985) argues that the Transparency Principle is superfluous

---

[4] The changes listed in (3) should be seen in perspective: the four changes reduce to one, i.e. the loss of nonfinite forms. But it is not the case that the modals before the reanalysis occurred in nonfinite forms on a large scale, and some of them (*e.g. may, must*) never had any nonfinite forms, as discussed in Warner (1983).

in that its results are incorporated in the parameter-setting approach to language acquisition formulated in Chomsky (1981). This will be explained further below.

1.2.2   The Principles and Parameters model

Work in the Principles and Parameters model has dominated the generative scene since the development of Chomsky's 1981 theory of Government and Binding (GB). In GB theory, UG is organized in terms of a number of subsystems or modules, which interact with each other. One important subsystem is the theory of Government, which started life as a structural recasting of the notion of government in traditional grammar. Thus the head of a constituent, say a verb or a preposition, governs its complement in a constituent structure. A second subsystem is the theory of Binding, which defines the grammatical conditions on the reference of nominal constituents: anaphors like reflexive pronouns obligatorily refer back to (are bound by) a subject antecedent in a local domain such as a tensed clause, so in *John likes himself*, *himself* is bound by *John*, but in **John expects that Mary likes himself*, it isn't. Pronouns may refer back in the discourse, but not to a noun phrase in a local domain. Full noun phrases have their own reference.

Subsystems of grammar consist of quite general principles and of parameters. Parameters define the dimensions along which languages may differ from each other. As an example, we will consider in some more detail the theory of Case, which is closely related to the theory of government. Consider the following bits of constituent structure (VP is a verb phrase, PP a preposition phrase, IP an inflection phrase in which inflection for tense and agreement is 'coded'):

(4)

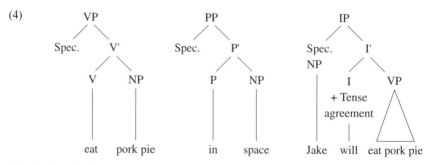

The basic principle of constituent structure is that each constituent has a head (V in VP; P in PP, I in IP etc.) with lexical properties determined in the lexicon. Heads are governors. Some heads are also case markers. In present-day

English, verbs and prepositions assign object case to their complements; a tensed I-head assigns nominative case to the subject, which is in the specifier of IP. Thus, for present-day English, Case is an abstract notion, since morphological case is visible only when the NP in question is a personal pronoun (*he/him, she/her*). Case theory consists of the following general components:

(5)   a. *the Case Filter*, which stipulates that each NP must have one and only one case
        b. an inventory of heads which are possible case markers
        c. a definition of ways in which case can be assigned

(5a) is a good example of a principle of case theory, and is universal. In (5b) and (5c), parameters come into play. Suppose that UG makes available a possibility of case marking heads, but not all languages use all options. A difference between Old English and the present-day language is that where the present-day language has the case markers as in (4), Old English has adjectives added to this inventory; adjectives may take complements that have dative or genitive case, an option that was lost in the course of the Middle English period. Contrast the Old English (6a) with Modern English (6b) and the impossibility of (6c).

(6)   a. þeah   hit þam cynge   ungewill   wære
           though it the king (D) displeasing was
           'though it was displeasing to the king'   (*ChronE*(Plummer) 1097.22)
        b. though it was displeasing to the king
        c. *though it was displeasing the king

A complicating factor here is that adjectives combine only with dative or genitive case, typically lexically selected cases. This brings us to (5c): there are at least two ways in which Case can be assigned. It is assumed that in present-day English, Case is assigned exclusively under structural conditions such as those in (4) above. But lexically selected cases appear to be different: they are probably specified in the lexical properties of the head, and therefore lexically associated with that head, rather than purely structurally determined. Also, the option of having lexical case probably presupposes that the language in question is able to signal those cases by means of morphological case endings. Languages differ, then, in the extent to which they have lexical cases. If we consider the loss of case marking by adjectives in Middle English, there are at least two ways of formulating the grammar change that must be associated with this loss. The first could be that adjectives like *ungewill* in (6) dropped out of the English-specific inventory of heads that were case markers, which would be a change involving the inventory of case-marking heads; the second could be that English lost the typically lexical cases dative and (objective) genitive, probably because the Old English system of morphological case marking was lost. Since dative and genitive were the cases combining with adjectives, adjectives ceased to be case selectors. The change would then be a change in the ways in which case could be assigned. The latter view is the more interesting one. It is certainly the one with the most general validity. Dative and genitive cases did not only cease to combine with adjectives; the dative and (object) genitive cases were lost generally, with the loss of morphological cases, as we will see in chapter 3.

In a parameter-setting model of acquisition and change, the task of the learner is to decide, on the basis of the evidence in her language environment, how to fill in the values for the various parametric options allowed by UG. Choosing the values for the parameters for any particular language is the main task of language acquisition. With respect to the changes in Case marking by adjectives discussed above, we could say that in the Old English period, the language learner was able to incorporate lexical Cases in her grammar because the system of morphological case distinctions (in combination with some other properties) enabled her to learn a distinction between structural and lexical Cases. This is what, according to Roberts (1985), makes the Transparency Principle superfluous, since the nature of the acquisition process is such that the optimal grammar will be chosen. Roberts (1985, 1993) also suggests an explicit parametric account of the history of the English modals. While subscribing to Lightfoot's story of the history of modals as essentially a change in word-class resulting from the loss of specific main verb characteristics, Roberts shows that in addition, this categorial reanalysis interacts with and is furthered by other instances of grammar change, such as changes in verb placement, and changes in the system of subject–verb agreement. This makes it clear that the historical fate of the English modals was not necessarily shaped as a random accumulation of exception features, leading to a change in category forced by the Transparency Principle. The changes affecting the modal verbs interacted with other, independent changes.

1.2.3   More on language acquisition and grammar change

The general spirit of the Principles and Parameters approach to language acquisition and grammar change should be clear by now: language-learning children, on the basis of a richly structured innate UG, construct a grammar of their native language on the basis of the language they hear being spoken around them. There is no consensus in the literature on how children proceed to do this, and this lack of consensus makes itself felt in acquisition-oriented work on grammar change. In the following subsections, we give a flavour of the kinds of debates that currently dominate the scene, which really revolve around two interacting issues: the nature of the language evidence which is the potential input to the acquisition process; and the question of what it is that children actually do with this potential input: do they construct a grammar which matches this input as closely as possible? Do they create fragments of grammar that are later put together and may then turn out to be (partially) conflicting? Or do they keep an overall grammar in mind during the process? With respect to any case of grammar change, this leads to the question of what the change in the language environment is (to the extent that it is observable in our historical data set), how this is caused (if that question can be answered), how it triggers a grammar change, and how in turn the grammar change is reflected in the data set produced by the next generation. We will now review some of the literature with these issues in mind.

1.2.3.1 Degree 0 learnability and robustness

In the course of the 1980s, there was increasing emphasis on the question of how the language learner comes to set parameters in a different way. With this development, it has become important to appreciate the nature of the triggering evidence for the language learner. Lightfoot (1991) emphasizes very prominently that we should try to find acquisition triggers for the resetting of parameters, i.e. we should try to formulate clearly what the changes in the language environment are that induce the language learner to set a parameter differently. Such evidence must be robust, Lightfoot argues; in Lightfoot 1997, he quantifies this robustness as: exceeding a threshold level of thirty per cent of the potential of environments. An additional constraint that he formulates on the robustness of evidence is that it should come from simple, unembedded clauses. This is called *degree 0 learnability*. The rationale behind it is that the language environment of the learner consists largely of main clauses. They should therefore contain the evidence for the resetting of a parameter. Hence, if a language change formulated as a parametric change has to appeal primarily to embedded clauses for evidence, this does not qualify as an appropriate explanation for that change, according to Lightfoot. For example, modern Dutch is a 'Verb-Second' language, which means that the finite verb occupies the second constituent position in any main clause, and the first constituent position can be of any category or function: subject, object, adjunct, NP, PP, AdvP etc. Some examples are given here:

(7)   a. Jan *heeft* gisteren   het boek aan Marie *gegeven.*
          Jan has   yesterday the book to   Marie given   (subject NP-first)
       b. Gisteren *heeft* Jan   het boek aan Marie *gegeven.*
          yesterday has   John the book to   Marie given   (adverb-first)

c. Het boek *heeft* Jan   gisteren   aan Marie *gegeven*.
   the book has   John yesterday to   Marie given   (object NP-first)
d. Aan Marie *heeft* Jan   gisteren   het boek *gegeven*.
   to   Mary has   John yesterday the book given
   'John gave the book to Mary yesterday.'   (indirect object PP first)

It has become standard to assume that Dutch is an SOV language in the sense that objects precede the non-finite verb in surface word order. In main clauses, some constituent is moved to the specifier of CP, and the finite verb is moved to C, as in the following abbreviated structure:

(8)

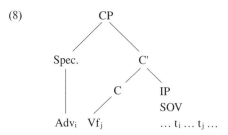

First-language learners acquiring Dutch have to work out that in main clauses the first constituent position is a category-neutral one, a topic position rather than, say, a subject position, and that this position is followed by the finite verb, regardless of the structure of the rest of the clause. Since the input from the language environment contains many clauses which are subject-first, the crucial clue for the language learner should come from those clauses which are non-subject-initial, i.e. sentences like (7b-d). According to Lightfoot (1999: 153), statistical counts for Dutch, German, Norwegian and Swedish show that simple main clauses are subject-initial in about seventy per cent of the cases. The conclusion is, then, that the thirty per cent of non-subject-initial clauses suffice to trigger the Verb-Second grammar of Dutch, and that a threshold of robustness need not be more than thirty per cent. There is nothing magical about this number, but it should give an idea of what Lightfoot means by robustness.

1.2.3.2 Input matching

Robin Clark and Ian Roberts (1993) offer an explicit perspective on the relation between acquisition and change in 'A computational model for language learnability and language change'. According to Lightfoot (1999), their approach to language learning is essentially what is called an 'input-matching' one: the learner, endowed with UG, constructs grammars and evaluates those grammars with respect to the input she hears in the language environment. In principle, all possible grammars are available to the learner.

Clark and Roberts propose, following Clark (1990; 1992) that *genetic algorithms* provide a computational model of learning for a principles and parameters theory. In their words:

> Genetic algorithms model the basic process of natural selection in the biological world: how certain patterns of genetic material are more adapted to their environment (i.e., fitter) than others, and hence tend to reproduce at the expense of others. Our account of language learning is analogous: the input text is the analogue of the environment, and so 'fitness' means consistency with this; parameter settings correspond to the genetic material of the biological world (and so a whole grammar would be a genome). Successful combinations of parameter settings 'reproduce' (i.e. contribute to the formation of new hypotheses about the target grammar) at the expense of others. In this way, the learning mechanism gradually eliminates 'unfit' hypotheses (those that are not consistent with the input text) and arrives at a single fittest grammar. Since nothing in the approach requires this grammar to be consistent with the one that underlies the input text, learners may arrive at final-state systems that differ from those of their parents; this, in essence, is our solution to the logical problem of language change.   (1993: 303)

Clark and Roberts propose that parametric change typically occurs when, because of various factors (phonological changes, morphological changes, etc.), the input data do not unambiguously force the setting of certain parameters to a definite value; several alternative grammars can adequately account for the input stream and so the choice of grammar cannot be uniquely determined on the basis of the language environment. This can happen when the evidence presented to the learner is formally compatible with a number of different and conflicting parameter settings. Clark and Roberts suggest that in such a situation the learner 'will turn in on itself, abandoning external pressure, and rely on its own internal structure to select from the alternatives at hand' (1993: 302).

This model of language learning assumes, then, that learners match all the potential values for each parameter against the language environment. Only those that fit the input data are then combined into larger grammar fragments, which are again matched, until one grammar is arrived at. This presupposes two important and contentious notions: the first is that this approach is highly UG-driven, in the sense that the learner actively explores all the options potentially offered by UG. This is in stark contrast to the approach in Lightfoot (1991), which gives pride of place to how the language environment triggers the acquisition of new parameter values. Clark and Roberts, on the other hand, postulate that the learner herself fuels diachronic change when confronted with a situation where the input is inconclusive. Thus, there is not necessarily a direct trigger in the language environment, merely a situation of indeterminacy that the learner resolves with an appeal to UG. This is a situation not allowed for by Lightfoot, and it remains to be seen if that is correct for all language change.

A second contentious feature of this approach is that it assumes that the learner tries to match the input from the language environment in full. We will now briefly look at a case study by Alison Henry (1997), in which both these contentious issues play an important role. Henry studies syntactic change in progress in Belfast English imperative constructions and observes that, from one generation to the next, children ignore some of the positive evidence that they receive and adopt a grammar which systematically deviates from the parent grammar. Belfast English is undergoing a remarkable syntactic change in imperative constructions; the oldest of three generations has two types of imperative constructions, one with and one without inversion:

(9)   a. You sit down
         b. Sit you down
         c. Sit everybody down

Henry shows on the basis of a number of distributional criteria that the proper analysis of inverted imperatives in what she calls the 'Unrestricted Inversion' dialect has the finite verb in the C-position, much as in the Dutch Verb-Second constructions discussed above.

(10) $[_{CP} [_C \text{Sit}_i [_{AgrSP} \text{you} \ldots t_i \ldots \text{down}]]]$

This is the only construction left in Belfast English in which lexical finite verbs move to C; other contexts have *do*-support here. In the dialect of the oldest generation, when the verb is passive or unaccusative (i.e. where the subject is the underlying object), the subject may appear in AgrSP, as in (10), corresponding to (11a–b), but it may also remain in object position, as in (11c–d):

(11)   a. Be you picked for the team
         b. Be you going out of the door when they arrive
         c. Be picked you for the team
         d. Be going you out of the door when they arrive

(11c–d) are analysed as follows:

(12) $[_{CP} [_C \text{be} \ldots [_{VP} \text{picked you for the team}]]]$

The middle generation also has inverted imperatives, but they are now restricted to constructions with passives and unaccusative verbs:

(13)   a. Go you away
         b. Arrive you on time
         c. Be picked you for the team
         d. *Eat you those vegetables
         e. *Run you around the room

Distributional evidence shows that the structure of inverted imperatives in what Henry calls the 'Restricted Inversion' dialect is quite different from those in the Unrestricted Inversion dialect. Where the structure of (9b) is as in (10), that of (13a) is as in (14):

(14)   [. . . [$_{VP}$ go you away]]

In other words, the only inverted imperatives now left are the ones we have in (13a–c), analysed as in (14): movement of lexical finite verbs as in (9b) analysed as (10) is no longer possible.

The transition from (9)–(12) to (13)–(14) is an interesting one, for a variety of reasons. With respect to the issues at hand, its most significant aspect is that the learners of the younger generation must have been exposed to a significant number of inverted imperatives during the acquisition process (perhaps imperatives are the most frequent type of sentence addressed to small children). They indeed arrived at a grammar which accommodates the superficially similar verb-first construction (13a–b), but the relevant sentences have a different structure, that in (14). Henry argues that this happened because some other aspects of the grammar militated against constructing a grammar in which lexical finite verbs move to C. This implies that learners made a UG-driven choice, ignoring part of the input data (the Unrestricted Inversion data), and accommodating another part of the input data (inverted unaccusatives) in a way compatible with the rest of the grammar.

Henry argues on the basis of this that the task of the language learner does not seem to be to set the parameters corresponding to all the data in the input. Rather, children select the grammar, from those made available by UG, that can accommodate the majority of data in the input, and may ignore other data, unless they are quite robust. Thus children can adopt grammars different from those of their parents, and be major contributors to language change. It is interesting to see that Henry's approach, like that of Clark and Roberts, is a strongly UG-driven one, where learners are assumed to run their UG-options by the language input in a continuous process of hypothesis creation and verification. Where the approaches differ is that, contra Clark and Roberts, Henry explicitly argues that learners leave part of the input unmatched.

1.2.3.3 Cue-based learning

The latest contribution by Lightfoot to the ongoing debate about language learning and change is Lightfoot (1999), in which he adopts ideas from some of the most recent work on language acquisition (the reader is referred to Lightfoot's book for references). He argues against the input-matching approach: on the one hand, because it assigns too large a role to UG; on the other, because learners do not always match the input, a point that was discussed above in connection with Henry's work. Lightfoot pursues some recent work that argues in favour of what is called 'cue-based learning'. Where the cue-based child perhaps differs most sharply from the input-matching child is that the cue-based child does not explore all the parametric options that are made available by UG. Rather, the cue-based learner remains true to Lightfoot's earlier triggering experience, where the trigger now feeds into cues. We may think of cues as pieces of structure, little grammar fragments, deduced by the learner from robust pieces of degree 0 evidence in the language environment. As an illustration, we follow up the discussion on robustness above. The reader will recall that the trigger for acquiring the Verb-Second grammar of languages like Dutch presumably consists of the subset of main clauses introduced by a non-subject. What children have to learn is that the structure of those sentences is something like in (15), where XP can be a range of different phrases:

(15) $[_{CP}$ XP $[_C$ Vf $[_{IP}$ SOV]]]

Lightfoot (1999: 152–3) argues that the cue for the learner is that a robust number of main clauses begin with an arbitrary phrasal category. The account for why this is accompanied by movement of the finite verb to C must come from a UG condition saying that material in Spec,CP must be licensed by a lexically filled C. This is because the learner cannot know that movement of the finite verb is obligatory, since she does not have access to ungrammatical data: she does not hear sentences with [XP . . . Vf] that are marked with a star. This part of the account must therefore come from a UG condition. Hence, the trigger is, according to Lightfoot, the thirty per cent of main clauses beginning with XP, to which the learner assigns a piece of structure, the cue:

(16) $_{SpecCP}$ [XP]

This is an abstract representation of a partially analysed syntactic structure. A cue is, therefore, an element of I-language, which in turn feeds into parameter settings. Thus, the child gradually builds up a grammar, following a learning path. One point that is less than clear in this approach is that Lightfoot assumes that there will be a robust trigger in the language environment, hence a cue, for all and any of the parameter settings. One may reasonably wonder whether this is always true, and what the learner does if this is not the case. The latter situation is the very one that Clark and Roberts are concerned with: situations where the input is inconclusive; this is, according to Clark and Roberts, precisely when learners invoke some default value dictated by UG, or 'turn in on themselves', as they call it.

1.2.4   Synchronic variation and grammar competition

In the first few sections of this chapter, we outlined the generative approach to syntactic change in terms of the resetting of parameters. Of primary interest in this view are clusters of changes, like those in the history of the modals, which are analysed by Lightfoot as the result of a single under-lying change (a categorial reanalysis from verb to auxiliary). In the scenario of changes sketched by Lightfoot, this kind of change is typically abrupt. The emphasis is on discontinuity, which follows from the fact that its focus is on the moment of grammar change rather than on the gradual change in the lan-guage environment. Generative work on syntactic change is often criticized for its emphasis on abruptness, which does not in general sit well with the surface graduality of language change. Let us evaluate as an example the changes involving case marking by adjectives discussed above. Adjectives in Old English could take nominal complements with dative or genitive case, and this option was lost in the course of the Middle English period. English generally lost the dative and (object) genitive cases, typically lexically selected cases. This would be a change in the ways in which case could be assigned. Verbs, adjec-tives and prepositions could no longer assign lexical cases. Supposing we look upon the availability of inherent case as a parameter, we might assume that this parameter was reset in the second half of the thirteenth century.[5] But after that date, examples of adjective + object will still be found, side by side with adjective followed by a PP. The examples in (17) illustrate this:

(17)   a. and tok   hem   out that were him lieve
           and took them out that were him dear
           'and took out those that were dear to him'
                                        (Gower *Confessio Amantis* 2.3395)
        b. This man to folkes alle was so leef
           this man to people all   was so dear
           'This man was so dear to all people'   (Hoccleve *Jonathas* 170)

If reanalyses are as radical as suggested, this situation is unexpected. This is also a problem from a theoretical point of view. One of the core ideas in the parameter-setting model is that when a parameter is set by the language learner, it is set once and for all. It then becomes a problem to deal with forms that suggest the opposite setting of the parameter. Forms that suggest the older parameter value, in this case the possibility of assigning lexical case, should presumably be handled by the learner in terms of some kind of adap-tive rule. But it is questionable whether a restrictive theory of grammar should

---

[5] Arguments for this can be found in van Kemenade (1987), chapter 6.

allow adaptive rules that say the opposite of what the parameter says. We see then that there is considerable friction between the parameter-setting model of grammar change, which basically emphasizes discontinuity, and the fact of synchronic variation between older and newer forms in the language.

In ongoing work by Anthony Kroch and his associates (e.g. Kroch 1989; Pintzuk 1991), a view of synchronic variation and change has been developed which deals to some extent with this friction. The idea is that speakers are in a sense bilingual speakers of their native language: they acquire more than one grammar, and these grammars can differ with respect to one parameter setting. In the case at hand, they would have two grammars, which differ in that verbs, adjectives and prepositions can assign lexical cases in the one, and they cannot do so in the other. These grammars are in competition; there is a period of variation between the two, and eventually only the newer grammar remains as an option. Grammar change, according to Kroch, generally follows an S-shaped curve as in the diagram (18), in which the rate of occurrence is plotted on the y-axis, the time course on the x-axis: the change takes off slowly, then gathers momentum and there is a period of sharp rise, followed by a gradual petering out when the change nears completion:

(18)

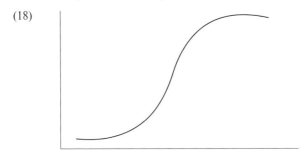

An important feature of modelling change in this way is that it allows the linguist to track clusters of changes. As noted above, grammar change is often seen on the surface as a cluster of changes spinning off from the grammatical reanalysis. It is then to be expected that changes in such a cluster occur at the same rate. Kroch (1989) calls this *the constant rate hypothesis*. Conversely, we can say that, if a cluster of changes follows the same quantitative curve, there is an argument for saying that the changes are grammatically related. Kroch (1989) illustrates this in an interesting way with the rise of *do*-support in the early Modern English period: having reworked the quantitative data gathered by Ellegård (1953) and established that the various contexts in which *do*-support is being established (negative sentences, various types of questions) follow the same curve of change, he presents his hypothesis that in the grammar, *do*-support replaces movement of lexical finite verbs by showing that their curves of change are each other's converses, as in the following idealized graph:

(19)

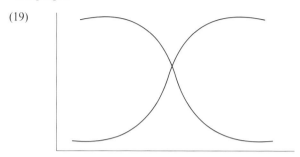

By showing that *do*-support and the contexts in which the lexical finite verb is moved have a complementary distribution, one gradually rising at the expense of the other, Kroch shows the analytical power of the constant rate hypothesis as a statistical tool in tracking down grammar change. Work from this perspective is currently expanding, due to the increasing availability of language corpora that allow for syntactic research.

It should be noted that this framework is primarily interested in synchronic variation between older and newer forms that is parametrically determined; it is designed to monitor the time course of change; in and of itself, it has very little to say about the motivations that push any particular change forward.

A good deal of synchronic variation is not conditioned by grammar-internal factors. Language contact of various kinds and social factors are other important sources of synchronic variation. Here again, we make a distinction between grammar and language, or I-language and E-language: language contact and social factors are facts of E-language; these may trigger grammar change because they change the language environment and hence may change the input for the language learner. But they are phenomena that can be distinguished from grammar change itself.

1.3   Grammar change and language change

So far we have discussed the notion of grammar change, as distinct from language change, concentrating on the acquisition process as the locus of (abrupt) grammar change. We have occasionally mentioned the friction between such an approach and the graduality of language change observable in the data. In this section, we want to broaden this perspective and discuss some literature that is mainly concerned with language change. In doing so, we have two reasons. The first is to clarify further the distinction between grammar change and language change that we make in this book; discussing other approaches will put in relief what we want to achieve in the following chapters. The second is that important work has been done from a variety of perspectives on constructions discussed in this chapter and elsewhere in the book, with which we compare and contrast our approach here. The scholars whose work we will discuss would shrink from making a distinction between grammar and language, hence between grammar change and language change; indeed they probably feel this is wrong in principle, and shun the abstractness implicit in the notion of grammar as we see it here. In 1.3.1 we discuss work on the history of the modals in English, formulated from various lexicalist perspectives. In 1.3.2 we discuss work on impersonal constructions in Old English in which it is argued that lexical changes take place on the basis of surface similarities between uses. In 1.3.3 we discuss the kind of long-term change called grammaticalization, and suggest how grammaticalization as a phenomenon can be made compatible with our approach.

1.3.1   Prototypes and notions

In section 1.2.1.1 a summary was given of the basic changes affecting modal verbs in the history of English. Lightfoot (1979) believed that these set the scene for a radical change in word class from main verb to auxiliary. Anthony Warner and John Anderson have each tried to arrive at a better understanding of the nature of word classes and the changes in the modals, along the way refining the cataclysmic story told by Lightfoot to one that emphasizes graduality. The result is a more diffuse approach to syntactic categories, and hence to changes in word category, one that accommodates the diffuseness of the language facts in a manner that is sharply different from what is customary in the Principles and Parameters perspective.

Warner (1990; 1993) extends the theory of semantic prototypes formulated by Eleanor Rosch to grammatical categories.[6] At the heart of Rosch's approach is a general theory of human categorization, in which categories are defined in terms of opposing clusters of properties and in which certain groups of properties may be more central or prototypical, others less so. Warner's assumption with respect to word classes is that classification is done by grouping relevant similarities and differences. A word class such as 'verb' exists in opposition to other classes, so that a group of properties typical of one class (for verbs, this

---

[6] Surveys of this approach can be found in Rosch (1978; 1988).

would include a system of verb endings) stands in opposition to the group of properties typical of another. Within one class, properties tend to correlate with each other. A particular class need not be completely homogeneous: some elements belonging to it are in the core of the class. They are then called proto-typical, having all the characteristics of the class. Among verbs, these would be the lexical verbs with a full system of morphological inflections and syntactic complementation patterns. Other elements may be less precisely defined: they lack some properties typical of the class. Warner argues that the Old English modals give evidence of being such a less precisely defined category: they are lexical verbs, since they have the possibility of taking nominal complements and tensed clause complements. And they have a wider range of inflections than their present-day counterparts. But they are not prototypical lexical verbs. Evidence for this is that in some constructions they behave much like the present-day English modals in not having a subject of their own and being sentence modifiers. With respect to the morphology, Warner also shows that some of the modals (the precursors of *must* and *shall*) occur only as finite forms as early as the Old English period (contra Lightfoot 1979). Thus, they are verbs in Old English, but not prototypical verbs. From the early Middle English period on, the verbal properties they had became less and less prominent, witness the changes observed by Lightfoot summarized in (2) and (3) above. The modals lost their prototypical verbal properties (nominal and tensed clause complements; further loss of verb inflections) and came to be largely used as sentence modifiers in conjunction with bare infinitives. The categorial reanalysis advanced by Lightfoot now takes on a different guise: in Warner's view this is not a radical reanalysis. Rather, the modals shifted from being a peripheral verbal category, to being a separate category Auxiliary. From the time that this happened, the differences in syntactic behaviour between main verbs and modals became more prominent. Likewise, the precursors of the auxiliaries *have* and *be* acquired more auxiliary properties, and *do* was established as a dummy auxiliary. In Warner (1993), this account feeds into a detailed treatment of the development of the morphosyntactic properties of English auxiliaries from the perspective of Head-driven Phrase Structure Grammar. Comparing this account with that of Lightfoot, we see that Warner treats the changes in the modals as gradual, and much of the graduality is in the nature of the categorization of the modals; the shifting morphosyntactic and semantic properties are a reflex of this.

Anderson (1993; 1997) has developed a theory of notional grammar in which categories are defined in terms of the notional components P(redicative) and N(ominal), the first being associated with categories that define situations, the second with categories that define things. The most basic categories are finite verbs, which are simply P, and nouns, which are simply N. Other categories are more complex and consist of hierarchical combinations of the two basic categories. Nonfinite verbs would be characterized as P;N (the semicolon indicates that the left term, P, dominates over the one on the right, N). Adjectives are P:N (the colon indicates that the terms on the left and right are mutually dependent). Espousing a view of the historical development of the modals very similar to Warner's, Anderson analyses the development as a type of categorial change called *realignment*.

On this view, all Old English verbs are of the category P, as they all occur as finite verbs. Although Anderson recognizes that some modals lack nonfinite forms in Old English, he assumes that this does not require a distinct subclass. All Old English verbs potentially have nonfinite forms and are thus also characterized as P;N. In the course of history, this category has been diversified: the situation in present-day English would be as in (20).

(20)	{P}	{P} & {P;N}	{P;N}
	.	.	.
	.	.	.
	.	.	.
	verbs 1	verbs 2	verbs 3
	modals	other auxiliaries	main verbs

Modals have become restricted to finite use only. The auxiliaries *have* and *be* are both finite and nonfinite. Main verbs are basically nonfinite, as there are constructions such as questions, in which they cannot occur as finite verbs.

The main difference between treatments such as those by Warner and Anderson on the one hand, and that of Lightfoot on the other, is that in Lightfoot's restrictive theoretical framework, word categorization is a clear-cut thing, and therefore a change in word class is by definition an abrupt one, with the abruptness reflected in the syntactic behaviour. Fuzziness is, in such a context, a phenomenon of language rather than of grammar. In the approaches by Warner and Anderson, this distinction between language and grammar is not made; fuzziness is something that is accommodated in the overall approach, and in the case at hand, it is clear that word categorization can be non-clear-cut. Graduality can thus be accommodated in the framework itself, and therefore the relationship between the data and the theoretical model is more straightforward.

1.3.2   Surface similarities

We touch here briefly on an approach to change in the lexical properties of verbs that is primarily concerned with the diffusion of change. This should be viewed against the general background of the theory of *lexical diffusion*. Like many ideas on language change, this was first formulated for phonological change and goes back to Wang (1969). The core insight is that any change spreads gradually over the forms to which it can potentially apply.[7] Such a view is also relevant for syntactic constructions that are keyed to the lexical properties of heads, such as passives, impersonals, and constructions with predicative adjectives as discussed above.

David Denison (1990) suggests that an analysis in terms of lexical diffusion is appropriate for the Old English impersonal verbs. 'Impersonal' is a cover term for a class of verbs that describes a certain cognitive/mental experience of being unvolitionally involved in a situation (for more details, see also chapters 2 and 3). In the syntax, this is expressed by the lack of an agent subject. A famous and much-discussed verb is Old English *lician* 'like', which is often regarded as the prototypical impersonal; another example is *ofhreowan* 'rue', discussed in Anderson (1988). It is argued by Fischer and van der Leek (1983) that these verbs each systematically occur in three alternative constructions which derive in the syntax from one underlying construction.[8] This basic construction has no syntactic subject and the two NPs are a 'source' NP (or 'cause', 'theme') usually associated with genitive case, and an 'experiencer' associated with dative case. Fischer and van der Leek suggest that the syntactic system allows a NP with either of these roles to appear in subject position, where it receives structural nominative case, as in (21b) and (21c). The examples are from Anderson (1988).

(21)   a. him   ofhreow þæs mannes
            him/them (D) was-pity the man (G)
            'he felt pity for the man'   (*ÆCHom* I, 13.192.16)
         b. Se mæssepreost þæs mannes ofhreow
            the priest (N)   the man (G) was-pity
            'The priest took pity on the man'   (*ÆLS*(Oswald) 262)
         c. þa ofhreow ðam munece   þæs hreoflian mægenleast
            then was-pity the monk (D) the leper's   weakness
            'Then the leper's weakness caused pity in the monk'
                                                          (*ÆCHom* I, 23.336.10)

The disappearance of the impersonal construction in (21a) in the course of the Middle English period is ascribed to the loss of inherent case and to the fact that the subject position becomes obligatory in the later period. On this view,

---

[7] For a very interesting application of this view to early Old English sound change, see Toon (1983).

[8] Anderson (1988) suggests similar basic structures (subcategorization frames) for impersonals, but distinguishes three types rather than one, which does better justice to the differences that exist between the various semantic groups of impersonal verbs.

the change in the impersonals is closely related to other changes taking place in the grammar.

Denison (1990) argues that this is an undue simplification. Not all impersonal verbs fit the above framework of genitive source and dative experiencer, and not all verbs appear in all three surface structures (as noted also by Anderson 1988, and as shown in detail in the work of Allen 1986, 1995). Moreover, Denison argues that the notion 'impersonal' extends to more verbs and phrasal combinations than have been recognized in the literature so far. An example is the verb *secgan*, which can be used impersonally as in (22a); other examples involve verbs that belong to the semantic class of impersonals, and which similarly take a dative experiencer (such as (22b), with *derigan*, semantically similar to *scamian*), or appear in combination with a true impersonal (22d), but which nevertheless *obligatorily* take a nominative subject, unlike the 'true' impersonals of (21):

(22)   a. swa hit her   beforan sægð
          as   it   here before   says
          'as mentioned above'   (*Or* 9.70.19)
       b. swa þæt þæt fyr   ne mihte him   derigan
          so   that the fire (N) not-could him (D) harm
          'so that the fire could not harm him'   (*ÆCHom* I, 37.570.9)
       c. se   cyning þa sona   swiðe þæs   fægnode
          the king (N) then at-once greatly this (G) rejoiced
          'the king at once rejoiced greatly in this'   (*ÆHom* 22.333)
       d. oððe forhwy hi   ne mægen hiora   ma   scamian þonne
          or   why   they(N) not-may   them (G) more shame   than
          fægnian
          rejoice
          'or why they may not be more ashamed of these things/themselves than
          glad'   (*Bo* 30.68.14 cf. Denison (1990: 124))

According to Denison this indeterminacy and synchronic variation make it hard to fit the impersonals into a constrained syntactic analysis. To account for the subsequent development of the impersonals, Denison invokes the notion of 'gradience' or 'serial relationship', and shows how, by lexical diffusion, the 'true' (subjectless) impersonals slowly adopt the characteristics of the pseudo-ones such as those in (22). This explanation takes account of all the raw data, and involves no idealization (as the analyses by Anderson and Fischer and van der Leek do), and in that sense it may be more accurate. But it is not in any way clear from Denison's proposal that it has anything to say on the directionality of the change in impersonals: a change via gradation may go one way or another. In the analyses of Anderson and Fischer and van der Leek, the structure of the grammar in which the impersonals figure determines the path of development.

We do not wish to deny that the language environment may change as a result of lexical diffusion, and thus a grammatical reanalysis may be triggered by surface similarities. Indeed, this is illustrated by the case histories in chapter 7, involving the so-called ECM constructions, and in chapter 8 on 'easy-to-please' constructions. Not all syntactic changes will necessarily have deep causes. But a path of change such as that of the impersonals can only be accounted for if we view them against the background of the grammatical structures which constrain them. It is therefore sometimes necessary to allow for some idealization with respect to the raw data.

Some linguists go as far as to say that most change proceeds by lexical diffusion, e.g. Aitchison (1991: 95–8). While there are plausible cases of lexical diffusion in the syntax, like those referred to above, this cannot be right. There are many syntactic constructions which are not tied to particular lexical elements, usually involving clause-level syntax. An example of this is the phenomenon of Verb-Second, which is discussed in detail in chapter 4; another example is the case of *have to* discussed in chapter 9. It is extremely unlikely that such constructions are influenced by lexical elements inside the clause.

1.3.3   Grammaticalization

The term 'grammaticalization' seems to have been coined by Meillet (1912), who defines grammaticalization as the attribution of grammatical character to an erstwhile autonomous word. The best-known and most widely discussed example of grammaticalization in the history of English is the sequence of changes through which modal verbs like *can, may, will, shall, must* were transformed from a set of verbs that were somewhat special main verbs to the finite auxiliaries that they are in present-day English. The main developments were discussed above in section 1.2.1.1. The result of this sequence of changes was that the modal verbs became grammatical function words, markers of mood: using Meillet's definition, we could say that they were grammaticalized from main verbs to modality markers.

There are two ways in which the term 'grammaticalization' can be understood. The first of these is the one originally intended by Meillet: it refers to an empirical phenomenon that is widely attested in language change, and it covers cases such as the development of the English modals. Some more cases of grammaticalization in the history of English are described in Rissanen, Kytö and Heikkonen (1997), and in chapter 9 of this book. Particularly well-known cases in the history of the Romance languages are: the development of determiners like French *le, la* from the Latin demonstrative pronoun *ille* (see, for instance, Vincent 1997 and references cited there); the development of the system of future verb endings, such as French *chanter-ai, chanter-as, chanter-a, chanter-ons, chanter-ez, chanter-ont*, which developed out of Latin constructions with an infinitive followed by a form of *habere* 'have' (this is described in detail in Benveniste 1968). What all such cases have in common is that some full lexical item develops into a grammatical function word or morpheme. This is particularly clearly the case in the Romance future tense marker, where the marker becomes a bound morpheme. This entails that the lexical item in question loses a good deal of its lexical meaning, a phenomenon that we also saw above in the history of the English modals. A second characteristic is that the change is very often a gradual one, spanning across a long period of time. A further characteristic is that such changes seem to be 'unidirectional': it is often thought that once a process of grammaticalization sets in, it leads inexorably to its completion.

The second way in which the term 'grammaticalization' is often employed is to refer to a particular approach to the study of language. Indeed, it seems reasonable to characterize this appoach as 'grammaticalization theory'. Grammaticalization theorists take the phenomenon of grammaticalization as part and parcel of language, and are primarily interested in the cognitive mechanisms that drive grammaticalization. They tend to stress the long-term, diachronic aspects of this type of change; indeed they speak of diachronic processes, and emphasize that language is a changing object in time. This approach is not readily compatible with the one adopted in this book. Our approach is essentially synchronic, with the emphasis being on the grammar of the speaker/learner. Since learners build up their grammars afresh, they do not take account of 'processes' that started long before their lifetime; they proceed on the basis of the language spoken around them. Long-term processes like grammaticalization therefore pose an intriguing problem for a synchronic approach such as ours, and this is why we devote a separate chapter to it. We will be primarily interested in the evidence available to the learner at each stage in a series of synchronies, at the same time confronting the question of why it is that such change nevertheless tends to be unidirectional across the generations. Part of the answer must be that UG preferences of the sort advanced by Clark and Roberts drive grammaticalization. We will discuss this in detail in chapter 9, and illustrate with several case studies.

1.4   Methodology and the role of data

In this section we turn to the status of data in historical language research. Historical data require a consideration that is different in many ways from that of modern synchronic data. Before going into this, let us briefly consider the role of the latter in generative syntactic research. It was noted at the outset of this chapter that the aim of generative grammar is to arrive at a characterization of the highly structured system of principles and parameters that is assumed to be part of the human language capacity. Hence, generative grammar is interested primarily in data that reflect the native speaker's grammatical *competence*, rather than actual language use, termed *performance*.[9] Grammaticality judgements are therefore the most important source of data for the generative syntactician working on a contemporary language. This can be complemented by investigation into language use, which is often based on research in data corpora of spoken and/or written language, though not many generative syntacticians do so, precisely because these do not reflect the competence of the speaker and are therefore not of primary use. Generative syntacticians are largely what Fillmore (1992) calls 'armchair linguists', who sit down and reflect on their grammaticality judgements, as opposed to 'corpus linguists', who look for data of language use in corpora of various sorts.

The student of historical language data from a generative perspective is faced with a completely different situation. Grammaticality judgements, reflecting the competence of the onetime native speakers, are completely lacking; we have access only to the products of historical written performance.[10] The text material available is moreover very diverse (including various kinds of poetry, legal documents, homilies, saints' lives, prescriptive grammars, inscriptions, translations from Latin) and contains many performance factors that are in whole or in part hidden behind the mists of time. Another problem we are faced with is that it is not always possible to find texts suitable for comparison for the different historical periods. With respect to the history of English, we can safely say that the texts written in Old English are mostly formal texts, written in the standard Old English literary language, the West Saxon *Schriftsprache*. In varying degrees, these texts are influenced by Latin, either directly (in the case of glosses and translations) or indirectly (homilies, saints' lives), or are influenced by the ancient habits and constraints of the Old Germanic alliterative four-stress line (poetry). The language adopted in these genres is different and sometimes hard to compare with that of the Middle English texts, which comprise, for instance, a rich array of colloquial poetry, and other religious texts beside homilies, which are very different from the Old English ones. Quite apart

---

[9] For further discussion of this contrast, we refer the reader to general introductions to generative syntax, such as Haegeman (1994) and Radford (1997).

[10] The reader is referred to Lass (1997) for thought-provoking discussion and meta-discussion of the source material for the historical linguist.

from all this, we can observe that the relation between performance (both written and spoken) and competence has not so far been the object of systematic study, so that we have to be very careful in drawing conclusions about the extent to which the historical texts reflect the grammars of the native speakers who produced them.

The nature of the surviving text material makes it often difficult to find data of the subtlety required for many kinds of analyses. For example, it has been shown in van Kemenade (1987) and Koopman (1990) that we can get some interesting insights into Old English word order if we analyse sequences of verbs in embedded clauses as verbal clusters, which would essentially be morphological units. Two examples are given in (23):

(23) a. þæt hie gemong him   mid sibbe *sittan mosten*
         that they among themselves in   peace settle must   (*Or* 2.8.52.33)
         'that they must settle in peace among themselves'
      b. ðæt he Saul ne *dorste ofslean*
         that he Saul not dared murder
         'that he didn't dare murder Saul'   (*CP* 28.199.2)

This analysis is modelled on analyses for similar verbal clusters in modern German and Dutch, as exemplified in (24a) and (24b) respectively:

(24) a. dass der Johann das Büchlein *haben wollte*
         that John   the booklet have   wanted
      b. dat Jan   het boekje *wilde   hebben*
         that John the booklet wanted have
         'that John wanted to have the booklet'

If such an analysis in terms of verbal clusters is appropriate, we expect to find further parallelisms. For instance, German and Dutch have long verbal clusters as in (25a) and (25b) respectively.

(25) a. weil   er die Kinder *singen hören können hat*
         because he the children sing   hear can   has
      b. omdat   hij de kinderen *heeft kunnen horen zingen*
         because he the children has   can   hear sing
         'because he could have heard the children sing'

Such long verbal clusters do not appear in the Old English texts. There is a possibility that this is a coincidence: it would be interesting to see how frequent such clusters are in the written present-day languages. Or their absence might reflect their ungrammaticality in Old English, in which case it would be worthwhile to see if these constructions exist in Old High German or Old Saxon. But the simple fact is that we have no direct evidence as to the grammaticality of verb clusters in Old English.

On a more positive note, there is a lot of useful and interesting work to be done in interpreting the positive evidence we have from the texts to the best of our ability, even if we have to be aware of the limited evidential status of our data. Here we note again that a combination of quantitative and theoretical tools may be extremely useful in tracking down grammar change. A principled theory of the internal make-up of the grammar yields fruitful hypotheses on how changes may or may not be expected to coincide, as discussed above. This is of considerable help in working through the maze of historical language data and deciding in which cases we are looking at grammar change. Anthony Kroch's constant rate hypothesis, which was briefly touched upon above, predicts that such grammatically related properties will follow the same rate of change. This makes it a powerful tool in the quantitative investigation of grammar change, now applicable to increasingly large corpora of texts. These are important methodological points of support in tackling the evidential problems inherent in this approach to historical change. Let us briefly illustrate a case in point: the history of passivization of prepositional objects. A present-day example is *he was being looked at*, where the subject *he* corresponds to the object of the preposition *at* in the active sentence *someone was looking at him*. Such passive constructions are not attested in Old English; they start to occur with very limited frequency in early Middle English, and become firmly rooted in the late Middle English period. Some examples are given in (26):

(26)   a. þer   wes sorhe   te seon hire leoflich lich   faren so reowliche wiþ
          there was sorrow to see   her dear   body dealt so cruelly   with'
          'there was sorrow to see her dear body dealt with so cruelly'
                                                            (*St. Juliana* (Roy) 22.195)

        b. But nu   þan   am i efter send
          but now when am I after sent
          'But now when I am sent for'   (*Cursor Mundi* 14216)

From this evidence, we may safely conclude that the construction was ungrammatical in Old English, became grammatical in early Middle English, and fully productive by late Middle English. But this conclusion stands far more firmly on the basis of a theoretical analysis which relates the rise of such new passive constructions to other independently established cases of grammar change: changes in word order and the loss of inherent case marking (in this case by prepositions). For such an analysis, the reader is referred to van Kemenade (1987) and Lightfoot (1991).

When investigating any set of historical facts, it is useful and necessary to turn to the handbooks and other existing literature first. For the syntax, there are some important standard works. Visser's *An Historical Syntax of the English Language* (1963–73) gives an extensive data survey of the whole history, though it deals with verbal constructions only and must be used with some care. The chapters on syntax in the various volumes of *The Cambridge History of English* (Hogg 1999a; Blake 1992; Burchfield 1994; Romaine 1998; and Lass 1999) give a good overview of work done so far. For Old English, we have Mitchell's *Old English Syntax* (1985) and for Middle English, Mustanoja's *A Middle English Syntax* (1960). The picture emerging from the study of these standard works can be complemented with other secondary literature. A particularly useful source for summaries of the secondary literature on a variety of constructions is Denison's *English Historical Syntax* (1993). It will be found, however, that after these initial stages, the picture is still less than complete, and further textual work is needed. If one is interested in phenomena that are connected to particular classes of lexical elements, the various concordances will yield valuable information. If one's interest is in syntactic constructions, textual research, with or without the aid of corpora, is inevitable. For the data emerging from all these types of sources, any researcher is advised to check them carefully against the text editions for their reliability, context and date.

A recent development is computerized corpora. The *Helsinki corpus* (Kytö 1991) contains extracts of representative texts from all genres throughout the history of English until 1700. This can be searched for lexical strings. Grammatically tagged subcorpora, which are particularly valuable for syntactic research, of the Old English and Middle English parts of the Helsinki corpus are currently in production. The Old English prose part of the Helsinki corpus is being tagged morphologically at the Vrije Universiteit Amsterdam by several of the authors of this book and Frank Beths, and is being extended with larger files of prose. The morphologically tagged output of this corpus is tagged for constituent structure at Geneva and York by Eric Haeberli and Susan Pintzuk. The Old English poetry is being tagged in another ongoing project at the University of York by Susan Pintzuk and Leendert Plug. At the University of Pennsylvania in Philadelphia, the Middle English prose part of the Helsinki corpus is being tagged for constituent structure by Anthony Kroch and Ann Taylor, and is being further supplemented. These enriched corpora are available online, as far as they are ready. For Middle English, very substantial sources can be found in the *Middle English Compendium*, available online at the University of Michigan. This contains *The Middle English Dictionary* online, and a number of Middle English texts in full.

1.4.1   How to handle data

As observed above, we have to be aware of the restricted evidential status of our historical data. Nevertheless, the data can give us a good deal of information about the development of particular constructions.

There seems to be general agreement that data from prose sources reflect the language of speakers most closely. Given this, we are fortunate in having very long prose texts available in Old English, from various stages. Even there, however, we have to be careful in interpreting the evidence. The early Old English prose works from the time of King Alfred the Great are nearly all translations from Latin originals. Some of them are very literal (e.g. that of Bede's *Ecclesiastical History*), others rather freer (like that of Boethius' *De Consolatione Philosophiae*). However, they are all directly related to a Latin original, and as such have to be used with special caution. This is less directly the case with the tenth-century collections of homilies and saints' lives by Ælfric and Wulfstan. These contain passages that have been translated, but on the whole they are merely inspired by Latin texts. The dating of texts deserves special caution too. The collections by Ælfric and Wulfstan seem to represent a single state of the language of the authors. But Allen (1992) points out that the Pope edition of homilies of Ælfric contains a number of texts that were gathered from different manuscripts from different dates. This means that they contain a number of later copies of Ælfric's texts and this should be taken into account in interpreting the dating. The only substantial body of Old English prose that can be regarded as original Old English is the group of manuscripts known as the *Anglo-Saxon Chronicle*, whose writing was instigated by King Alfred and versions of which were kept up in various locations. This makes it a favourite for many scholars, though its annal style hardly represents a very sophisticated writing tradition. We see, then, that in the prose, there is a limited range of text types and there are various pitfalls to be considered. Given due care, this does not, however, detract from their evidential value.

Some people would say that prose sources yield the only reliable data. This is not necessarily true. In some cases, poetry, translations, and even word by word glosses, may provide evidence that comes closer to our modern grammaticality judgements than the evidence just discussed. We give two examples of this. The first is from the poetry.

Old English poetry is in the alliterative four-stress line: each verse line consists of two halflines and each halfline contains two stressed positions. At least two, but often three of these stressed positions alliterate, as in the following lines from *Beowulf* (stress is marked by an acute accent on the vowel of the relevant syllable, alliteration by italics):

(27)   þæt ge*s*yne wéarþ
                                 that evident became
        *w*idcuþ   *w*érum, / þætte *w*récend þa   gýt
        widely known to Men,   that   avenger then still
        *l*ífde æfter *l*áþum,/ *l*ánge þráge,
        lived after foe   long time,

æfter *gúðcéare* /
after   distress of war
'it became plain to everyone that an avenger had survived the fiend after the
struggle'   (*Beo* 1255–58)

This type of alliterative verse goes back to prehistoric Germanic times, and
finds its roots in a tradition of oral recitation. It is generally acknowledged
that the language of the poetry is very archaic. Nevertheless, it can be used as
an interesting source of data, given special consideration of its nature. Pintzuk
and Kroch (1989) base a word order argument on stress correspondences they
have found in *Beowulf.* They argue that the position of the main verb of the
sentence always corresponds with the last stressed position in a halfline, and
that this provides evidence for the basic OV (i.e. verb-last) character of Old
English word order. They could arrive at this conclusion because Old English
poetry is metrical, and this evidence is clearer than any evidence one could get
from prose.

The second example is from interlinear glosses. Interlinear glosses are
another source which is generally considered to be of dubious evidential value,
but which, with special consideration, can be turned into interesting evidence.
Koopman (1990) shows that a particular sequence of verbs in Old English
occurs sporadically in interlinear glosses, and nowhere else. He shows that the
interlinear glosses give a word-by-word translation of the Latin original, and
because the pattern does not occur elsewhere, concludes that it is ungrammatical in Old English. In another case, the glosses turn out to give particularly
interesting evidence for syntactic dialect features: Kroch and Taylor (1997)
consider the Old English tenth century Northumbrian glosses of the Latin
Vulgate Bible. They show that, where in the Latin original the subject pronoun
is omitted, the northern glosses in a number of cases translate this with a
subject pronoun that occurs in a position different from that in southern texts.
Such conscious deviations provide valuable evidence, and in this case establish
a syntactic dialect feature with some plausibility.

In the Middle English period, we are faced with a slightly different situa-
tion, which again needs to be considered with special care. The language of
Middle English texts is not nearly as uniform as that of the Old English texts.
Where the Old English texts, apart from a few exceptions, are in the West
Saxon dialect and literary tradition, there is no such uniformity in Middle
English. All the dialects are represented, though not at all stages and in all text
types. Diversity is what we find. Among the prose texts, we find quite a few
formal ones, and fewer informal ones. Middle English poetry is very different
from that composed in the Old English period. While Old English poetry in
the alliterative tradition is very archaic, Middle English poetry was written in

a variety of verse types, but dominantly metrical and rhyming, and is in many cases more colloquial than the prose. It is therefore generally considered to yield more useful evidence than Old English poetry.

1.4.2   Frequency

Of necessity, we have to rely solely on written data in historical language research. As a result, one of the prime diagnostics of change is the relative frequency of constructions undergoing change. There are some important methodological questions attached to this. First of all, it must be noted that frequency in no way corresponds with grammaticality in the generative approach. While there is every reason to assume that any construction that is frequent in the historical material at any stage is grammatical, there is no reason whatever to assume that an infrequent construction is less grammatical or marginally grammatical. However, as pointed out above, changes in relative frequency of constructions do seem to reflect change, and should, with caution, be regarded as shifts in grammaticality. Here again it should be noted that these shifts are to be interpreted against the background of a coherent analysis, and can, now that this is becoming possible, be backed up by quantitative evidence and analysed in terms of the constant rate hypothesis. A second methodological point attached to this is how we should go about the analysis and role of minor patterns. An illustration is in order here: Pintzuk (1991), looking at the position of the finite verb in Old English against the background of Kroch's competing grammars approach, analyses the various patterns in terms of shifts in (statistical) frequency. For grammatical significance, she assumes a threshold level of one per cent: patterns that occur with a frequency of one per cent or less, may be disregarded as ungrammatical. This is based on the general assumption that well-established generalizations are violated in naturally occurring language at that percentage. However, one per cent of the total of Old English sentences amounts to a substantial number, which many analysts would not feel comfortable at ignoring. There is no ready answer to such dilemmas, and in practice, individual historical linguists deal with them according to their own tastes.

1.4.3   The role of the theory in deciding data questions

Among generative syntacticians working on historical English material, it is an accepted strategy to make systematic comparisons with modern continental West Germanic languages such as Dutch and German. This is because Old English in many respects resembles these languages more closely than the present-day language. For instance, German and Dutch are typical OV languages, a characteristic shared to a considerable extent by Old English. Knowledge of Dutch and/or German, whether native or not, is therefore of help in constructing hypotheses about the nature of Old English syntax. This becomes even more important when we look at it from a theoretical point of view. In the Principles and Parameters models the aim is to discover more about UG, and a comparative appoach is an essential ingredient of the research strategy. Comparing Old and Middle English with its closely related sister languages is therefore of vital importance in discovering more about putative generalizations on Old English syntax. This has proved quite a productive strategy in investigating Old English and has led to interesting new discoveries about particular constructions. In part, it compensates for the absence of native speaker judgements, on the assumption that constructions shared by Old English and Dutch ought to be analysed in roughly the same way. It also gives further support in deciding whether particular syntactic features reflect grammar as understood here: for a contemporary language, this is easier to decide than for a dead language. If a comparative approach has established common features of the grammars of the continental West Germanic languages, and we come across the same or similar features in Old English, this strengthens the idea that we are dealing with a feature of grammar there. In sum, a comparative theoretical approach can teach us a good deal about the syntax of Old and Middle English, provided that it is exercised with due caution. The evidential problems of Old English are quite complex, and we should strike a balance between the potential of insight offered by a comparative theoretical approach, and due philological caution in resolving the evidential dilemmas.

The point discussed in the above paragraph is perhaps of more general relevance: it is sound methodology to formulate hypotheses with some precision before doing detailed data research, in order to narrow down the range of the investigation. But this always entails some risk of interpreting the data to suit one's theory, or of ignoring classes of counterexamples as irrelevant to one's established generalization.

Finally, we point out the position we take in this book with respect to the relation between theory and data. In subsequent chapters we will discuss wherever appropriate the issues that arise at points where we see friction between the theoretical approach and empirical matters. Our argument there will be driven by the aim of identifying grammar change. This chapter has given an overview of what the issues are that emerge from recent literature. The theoretical positions discussed and summarized do not always necessarily represent our own views. While we strongly feel that theory is of vital importance in interpreting our cases of language change as possible cases of grammar change, we will counterbalance this by presenting the theoretical considerations as interesting hypotheses, subject to empirical verification. Thus, each of the case studies we discuss in detail will provide an argument with respect to the syntactic construction under discussion. Because the case studies emerge from our own ongoing research, we are committed to a certain analysis of the case (our own!), but, we like to think, with sufficient distance to give an argued and balanced view of the literature.

1.5   Overview of the book

After this lengthy exposition, we give an overview of the chapters that follow. Chapters 2 and 3 give a descriptive survey of the core features of the syntax of Old and Middle English respectively. In these chapters, extra prominence is given to those features that are not discussed in detail in the remainder of the book. Chapters 4–9 present case studies on important syntactic changes in the history of English. The choice of topics is inspired by two combined considerations: the first is that they emerge from our own ongoing research, which is, of course, where we have the most to offer to the reader; the second is that they are connected with issues which are currently in the focus of interest in English historical linguistics.

Chapter 4 is on the development of the Verb-Second characteristics, such as they were, of Old English. Old English had some version of the Verb-Second constraint as we know it in the present-day Germanic languages. The chapter takes the reader through the development of ideas and arguments as they have emerged over the past decade or so.

Chapter 5 is on the development of OV/VO word orders in the course of the Old and Middle English periods. The topic is an evergreen, albeit one that has received increased attention with the advent of typological work from a variety of theoretical perspectives. The chapter considers recent Principles and Parameters work, and the arguments are examined for regarding Old English as basically OV, basically VO, or a mix of both OV and VO. The gradual shift to VO order plays an important role in these arguments.

Chapter 6 is about the historical development of phrasal verbs such as *call up, take off*. During the Old English period the particles that are nowadays part of the phrasal verbs, or preverbs as they are often called in the traditional literature, tended to signal the base position of the verb. Their position therefore correlated with that of the verb in the development from OV to VO order, as in chapter 5. After the establishment of VO order, this correlation broke down, and left the idiomatic combinations that the phrasal verbs are nowadays.

Chapter 7 is on the development of infinitive constructions, especially the origin and rise of Exceptional Case Marking constructions like *I expect him to win the race*, which were introduced sometime during the Middle English period, in part as a spin-off of the establishment of VO word order.

Chapter 8 is on the history of the 'easy to please' construction, so called because its core example in the literature is *John is easy to please*. This construction goes back to an Old English origin of adjective followed by a *to*-infinitive, which is argued to have been in essence a modal passive construction. Old English had another adjective + infinitive construction which was altogether different in structure, something like *this house is pleasant to live in*. These constructions existed side by side through the centuries, until as a result of surface similarities with new passives featuring preposition stranding, they were all reanalysed as cases of *wh*-movement.

Chapter 9 is on grammaticalization. Some of the basic tenets of grammaticalization theory are challenged, and it is shown how at least a number of aspects of these long-term changes can be analysed in an interesting way from a Principles and Parameters perspective. Two case studies are discussed to show this, the first relating to the development of the *have to* periphrasis expressing obligation, as in *I have to do this*; the second is an analysis of Jespersen's negative cycle in the history of English which focusses on the structural and morphosyntactic aspects of the change.

2

An outline of Old English syntax

2.1   Introduction

The aim of this chapter is to give a descriptive overview of a number of important features of the syntax of Old English, i.e. English from the earliest texts (c. 800) to about 1100. The material in this chapter is primarily based on the evidence from the two main bodies of prose text in Old English: the prose of King Alfred (ninth century) and that of Ælfric, abbot of Eynsham (tenth century). In the final section of the chapter, we will touch on some of the ways in which the syntax of the prose differs from that of the Old English poetry.

Old English is the language imported into the British isles by the immigrations from the continent in the fourth, fifth and sixth centuries. It therefore evolved from a number of continental West Germanic languages/dialects. The syntactic study of Old English can be reliably based only on one dialect: the West Saxon standard written language or *Schriftsprache*, in which the bulk of Old English writing has come down to us. There is little scope for work on dialect syntax in Old English; almost all the texts are in the West Saxon dialect, while those works of any length that were not written in West Saxon consist mostly of interlinear glosses on parts of the Vulgate bible, and are therefore of limited use for syntactic purposes. We will nevertheless be commenting upon those aspects where they do prove revealing, which is mostly in those cases where the gloss deviates from the original.

The view of Old English presented in this chapter should be seen as a digest of the consensus view in the literature. Where such consensus is non-existent, we will attempt to clarify what the issues are.

2.2   Morphology and case assignment

Old English had an inflectional system for both verbs and nouns that was a good deal more elaborate than the present-day one. It is not altogether clear that this was in every way a functional system in the sense that it was crucially needed to distinguish grammatical relations. For instance, the inflectional endings for the majority of noun classes were syncretized for nominative and accusative, and although it was possible to distinguish them by means of demonstrative pronouns, nominative and accusative were to a considerable extent distinguished by their position in the sentence. Thus, it is not obvious what the division of labour was between inflection and position. Even so, Old English was highly inflected compared with the present-day language. We will not go into morphological detail here; the reader is referred to Campbell (1959), and, for an illuminating discussion of the inflectional system as a system, Hogg (1992b). In this section we will discuss the inflectional system's effects on the syntax, which are mainly in the domain of case assignment.

2.2.1   Old English verbal and nominal inflections

In Old English, verbs were inflected for person (first, second, third), number (singular, plural), tense (present, past) and mood (indicative, subjunctive, imperative). It should be noted that the verbal endings too in Old English show a fair amount of syncretism: for instance, the form *fremmaþ* 'perform' could be indicative plural, without person distinctions, or imperative plural, and a form like *fremede* 'performed', while being unambiguously past tense, could be subjunctive singular (without person distinction), or indicative first or third singular. On the other hand, the singular present indicative always has three distinct person endings, as in: *ic fremme, þu fremest, he/heo/hit fremeþ* (the third singular -*s* was a Northern form, perhaps an innovation there, in Old English); the indicative second person singular is uniquely distinguished in the present and past tenses (at least in the weak verbs) by the -*(e)st* ending; the present/past distinction is unambiguous; and the singular/plural contrast, almost completely lost in the present-day language, is always systematically marked. The conclusion must therefore be that, in spite of some syncretism, the system is still largely intact.

There are several syntactic phenomena that are often associated with comparatively rich verbal morphology. The first of these is the phenomenon of *pro*-drop that is well-known in present-day languages like Spanish and Italian, where it is possible to omit an unstressed pronominal subject, presumably because its person and number can be read off from the verbal morphology, as in the Italian sentence in (1):

(1)   hanno parlato   troppo
       have   talked-3pl too much
       'they talked too much'

There are various forms of subject omission in early English too. The most frequently occurring one is what is often termed 'conjoined subject deletion'. This refers to instances where the subject is omitted in a conjoined sentence, as in the second clause of (2):

(2)   and him comon englas to, and him ðenodon
        and him came   angels to, and him served
        'and angels came to him, and served him'   (*ÆCHom* I, 11.174.17)

It should be noted that this phenomenon, though often interpreted as *pro*-drop, has nothing to do with verbal morphology. The identification of the omitted subject is not related to verbal morphology, but established under coreference with the higher subject *englas*. Discourse factors seem to be of prime importance here, although there is also a clear syntactic restriction in that coreference is always with the subject of the higher clause. More discussion of this phenomenon in Old English can be found in Allen (1995).

Old English has a very Germanic form of subject omission, which in the theoretical literature is often called 'expletive *pro*-drop'. This refers to a variety of impersonal contexts in which there is no nominative subject, and no insertion of a dummy subject *it*, as sometimes with weather verbs, as in (3), and regularly in impersonal passives, as in (4):

(3)   Ða cwom þær micel snaw &   swa miclum sniwde swelce micel
        then came there heavy snow and 0 so   heavily snowed as if   much
        flys   feolle
        fleece fell
        'and it snowed so heavily, as if a lot of fleece were falling'   (*Alex* 30.11)

(4)   . . . ðætte forðy   to ungemetlice ne sie geliðod ðæm scyldgan
              that therefore 0 too greatly   not be let-off to-the guilty
        '. . . that therefore it must not be let off too greatly to the guilty'
                                                                     (*CP* 20.149.24)

More discussion of the conditions that allowed such expletive *pro*-drop in Old English and other Germanic languages can be found in Hulk and van Kemenade (1993); van Kemenade (1997a). This type of *pro*-drop seems to have been largely lost by 1500.

Another syntactic phenomenon which in the theoretical literature is often associated with comparatively rich verbal morphology is that of the position of the finite verb. The putative generalization is that languages with comparatively rich morphology have a wider range of finite verb-fronting strategies than those without. This argument has been made in particular with respect to changes in late Middle English and early Modern English syntax (see chapter 3 and the detailed discussion in Roberts 1993, which also provides cross-linguistic evidence).

Old English had a wider range of verb fronting strategies than late Middle English. In those contexts in which the present-day language still has fronting of the auxiliary only, i.e. questions and negative-initial sentences, all finite verbs could be fronted in Old English. In (5), examples of the relevant contexts are given:

(5)   a. Hwæt sægest þu, yrþlingc?   Hu begæst þu weorc þin?
       what say   you, ploughman? How perform you work yours?
       'What do you say, ploughman? How do you go about your work?'
                                                              (*ÆColl* 22.23)
       b. ne sende se deofol ða   fyr of   heofenum, þeah ðe   hit
       not sent the devil then fire from heavens,   though that it
       ufan   come
       from-above came
       'the devil did not send fire from heaven, though it came from above'
                                                       (*ÆCHom* I, (Pref)6.13)

This option of fronting finite lexical verbs was lost in the course of the early Modern English period, as the modal auxiliaries achieved their modern status, and *do*-support became firmly entrenched. Whether the loss of this option results from the loss of verb morphology is a matter of considerable debate, for which the reader is referred to Roberts (1993), Lightfoot (1997) and Warner (1997).

There is clear evidence that Old and Middle English also had a second verb fronting strategy, particularly apparent in main clauses introduced by a topic. Let us consider the following examples (finite verbs and subjects italicized):

(6)   a. On twam þingum *hæfde God* þæs mannes sawle gegodod
       in   two   things   had   God the man's soul   endowed
       'With two things God had endowed man's soul'   (*ÆCHom* I, 1.20.1)
       b. Be ðæm *we magon* suiðe swutule oncnawan ðæt . . .
       by that we can   very clearly perceive that . . .
       'By that, we can perceive very clearly that . . .'   (*CP* 26.181.16)

While both clauses are introduced by a topicalized PP, and while in both clauses the finite verb is fronted with respect to the position of the non-finite verb, the nominal subject in (6a) follows the finite verb, whereas the pronominal subject in (6b) precedes it. We will discuss this construction in more detail in chapter 4, and present evidence that the position of the finite verb reflects a verb fronting option which was lost at the close of the Middle English period, with pronominal and nominal subjects occupying different positions. Here again there is cause for debate whether the loss of this strategy resulted from the loss of verbal inflections. Also, it is not clear in any detail how the loss of the two types of finite V-movement described here can be related to each other. They represent movement to different positions, but the dating of their respective losses, some way into the early Modern English period and the close of the Middle English period respectively, is just a bit too far apart to relate them both to the same loss of verb inflections. With respect to the former movement strategy, it has been argued that the loss of verb morphology was a necessary condition, but a further triggering factor was needed. We will leave this matter as one for which further research is needed.

We now turn to a discussion of the system of nominal cases and its effects upon the syntax. Old English NPs show a four-way case system with nominative, accusative, dative and genitive, although the noun itself never has more than three distinct forms; the nominative/accusative distinction is not marked on the noun except in the singular of the feminine -*o* nouns and the masculine and feminine weak nouns, but there, dative, genitive and accusative are not distinguished. Case contrasts within the NP are further marked by demonstrative pronouns, which in the masculine and feminine singular do distinguish nominative from accusative; and by adjectives, which have two main conjugations depending on whether the NP is definite or indefinite (see Spamer 1979). Demonstrative pronoun, adjective and noun always agree in case, number and gender.

There is good cause to assume that nominative case is associated with the syntactic subject. Accusative is associated most typically with the direct object, although, like dative and genitive case, it may be determined by the lexical properties of its governing verb or preposition. It is common in the literature to distinguish between structural and inherent case (see Chomsky 1981). Structural case is assigned to a NP according to its position in the syntactic structure: thus, nominative is assigned to the grammatical subject, accusative to the direct object. One criterion for deciding that it is structural is that accusative case is neutralized under passivization: the accusative object in an active sentence will be found as the nominative subject in a corresponding passive sentence:

(7)   a. Gregorius hine (A) afligde
          Gregory   him   put to flight
          'Gregory put him to flight'   (*ÆHom* 22.624)
       b. Ða wearð se god (N) afliged   of   þære fulan anlicnysse
          then was   the god   expelled from the   foul   idol
          'Then the god was expelled from the foul idol'   (*ÆHom* 22.593)

This is not true for other object cases: objects marked for dative or genitive case will retain their case under passivization. We call this inherent case, because the case is lexically associated with the governing verb or preposition. In (8), there is an example with the verb *helpan* taking a dative object, both in the active and in the passive.

(8)   a. Helpað earmum 7   hæfenleasum
       help   poor (D) and needy (D)
       'Help the poor and the needy'   (*WHom* 11.197)
       b. Ac ðæm   mæg beon suiðe hraðe geholpen from his lareowe
       but that (D) may be   very quickly helped by   his teacher
       'But that may be remedied very quickly by his teacher' (*CP* 33.225.22)

A second reason for saying that accusative is structural is that the correlation
between accusative case and the nature of the semantic relation between the
verb and its accusative object is less than straightforward. We can establish
such a correlation by contrasting accusative with other object cases, as discussed below, but it is a partial one at best, since there are also NPs marked
accusative which do not entertain a direct semantic relation with the verb. This
is particularly clear in AcI constructions with causative and perception verbs,
in which the subject of the non-finite complement clause is marked for
accusative case:

(9)   a. Se cing het   hi   feohtan agien Pihtas
       the king commanded them (A) fight   against Picts
       'The king commanded them to fight against the Picts'
                                          (*ChronA*(Plummer) 449.5)
       b. He hine   geseah sittan æt tolle
       he him (A) saw   sit   at toll
       'He saw him sitting at the toll'   (*ÆCHom* II, 37.273.24)

It is clear that the accusative NP receives its case under structural case marking
here, since it bears no direct semantic relation to the verb. Other object cases
do show such a correlation; this is another reason for calling dative and genitive inherent cases; they seem to be determined by a combination of association with semantic roles and selection by their governing verb or preposition.
While it seems impossible to establish a one-to-one correlation between case
and semantic role, some general correspondences can be drawn: dative is associated primarily with the experiencer role, with the animate goal (indirect
object) and with other NPs that signify a participant not directly involved in
the scene. The latter is best illustrated by contrasting dative with accusative
case in monotransitive complementation. Some verbs tend to show a distinction here (see Plank 1983). Consider the following two examples, both with the
verb *folgian*, which is a verb that can take a dative or an accusative object:

(10)   a. and ða   folgode feorhgeniðlan
       and then followed deadly foes (A)
       'and then he pursued his deadly foes'   (*Beo* 2928)
       b. him   folgiað fuglas scyne
       him (D) follow birds fair
       'Fair birds shall follow him'   (*Phoen* 591)

If the object of *folgian* 'follow' is accusative, as in (10a), this indicates that the NP, as the direct object, is engaged in direct interaction with the subject. This is less clearly the case if the object is dative, as in (10b). We can also tell this from the distinction in meaning: where the verb is followed by a dative, it means 'follow', where it is followed by an accusative, it means 'pursue'.

The genitive case corresponds with the role of Source and very often has partitive connotations. These readings may be illuminated by considering the most typical paraphrases of sentences with genitive objects in the present-day language, which show that they are predominantly part of a PP introduced by *from* or *of*, as in the following examples:

(11)   a. Ðæt ilce   eac Dryhten oðwat   Israhela folce, ða   hie
          The same also Lord   reproached Israel's people when they
          wæron gehergeode &   of hiera earde   alædde, &   swaðeah
          were   ravaged   and of their country led away and nevertheless
          noldon   *gesuican hiera yfelena weorca*,   ne hie noldon
          not-wanted *turn from their wicked deeds* (G) nor they not-wanted
          awendan of   hiera won   wegum;
          turn   from their perverse ways   (*CP* 37.267.13)
          'With the same also the Lord reproached the people of Israel, when their
          lands were ravaged, and they were led away from their country, and yet
          they would not cease their wicked deeds, nor turn from their perverse
          ways'

        b. Se scamfæsta hæfð genoh   on ðæm to his bettrunge ðæt his
          the modest   has enough in that for his reform   that his
          lareow hine suiðe lythwon *gemyndgige his undeawa* (G)
          teacher him very gently   *remind of   his faults*
          'It is enough to reform the modest man, if his teacher would remind him
          very gently of his faults'   (*CP* 31.207.3)

Beside such uses for the genitive object, genitive case is, of course, typically the case used to express possession.

In ditransitive complementation, the case marking for the two objects is usually a combination of accusative and dative, less commonly of accusative and genitive or dative and genitive, with semantic correlations as noted above.

(12)   a. Gif þu geoffrast Gode   ænige lac   æt his weofode
          if you offer   God (D) any   sacrifice (A) at his altar
          'If you offer any sacrifice to God on his altar'   (*ÆHom* 16.19)

        b. Ne mæg þara yflena   yfel þa goodan   beniman heora goodes
          not can of-the evil-ones evil the good (A) deprive their good (G)
          'The evil deed of the wicked cannot deprive the good of their goodness'
                                                                (*Bo* 37.113.4)

        c. and his magas   ðancodon mycclum ðæs   Gode
          and his kinsmen thanked   much   this (G) God (D)
          'and his kinsmen thanked God greatly for this'   (*ÆLS*(Swithun) 219)

Prepositions in Old English are typically associated with a selected case, mostly dative case, very often corresponding with a location or goal. Some prepositions select the accusative case, with connotations such as 'extent of time' (e.g. *oþ* 'until'), 'extent of space' (How far?, e.g. *geond* 'throughout', *ymb* 'around', *þurh* 'through'), and some the genitive case (e.g. *utan* 'outside of'). Quite a few can take more than one case, often dative and accusative. It is sometimes said that the choice of case marks a semantic distinction, with the dative indicating rest and the accusative indicating motion, but this is not consistently observed. The objects of prepositions could not be passivized in Old English, which is another indication that prepositions assign an inherent case. We come back to this below.

2.2.2   *Impersonal verbs*

The Old English impersonal construction and its historical fate have attracted a good deal of attention from historical linguists of various persuasions. The term 'impersonal' is a rather vague one in that different scholars subsume different things under it. Strictly speaking, it refers to constructions which have no nominative subject and have the verb in the default 'agreement' form: third person singular.

(13)   ðonne ofðyncð   him   ðæs ilcan   ðe   he ær   forbær
        then   displeases him (D) the same (G) that he before endured
        'then he regrets what he endured before'   (*CP* 33.225.18)

Verbs such as *ofþyncan* 'displease, regret' in (13), which have two arguments, denote a mental or cognitive experience in which one argument is expressed as the animate experiencer, the other as the cause/source of the experience. This is why such verbs are often called psych verbs. The class of such verbs in Old English includes: *hreowan* 'rue'; *(ge)sceamian* 'shame'; *eglian* 'ail'; *ofþyncan* 'displease'; *(ge)lician* 'like'; *(ge)lystan* 'desire'; *langian* 'long'; *(ge)lustfullian* 'please'. In syntactic treatments, the two arguments are often referred to as the EXPERIENCER argument and the THEME argument. They can be realized in the following core case configurations:

(14)   a. EXPERIENCER – dative   THEME – nominative
        b. EXPERIENCER – nominative   THEME – genitive
        c. EXPERIENCER – dative   THEME – genitive

(13) is an example of type (14c), which is attested with considerably less frequency than the two alternative types (see Fischer and van der Leek 1983, Anderson 1988, Allen 1986). (14a) and (14b) are exemplified by (15a) and (15b) respectively:

(15)   a. þæt we   þurh   þæt ealle Gode   lician
            that we (N) through that all   God (D) please
            'that we all please God with that'   (*HomU* 20(BlHom 10) 42)
        b. Hwæt þa   se   mæssepreost þæs mannes ofhreow
            lo   then the priest (N)   the man (G) pitied
            'Lo then the priest had pity on the man'   (*ÆLS*(Oswald) 262)

In (15a) the nominative THEME precedes the dative EXPERIENCER, perhaps because it is a pronoun. If both arguments are full NPs, the order dative–nominative is by far the most frequent. This phenomenon is widely attested in impersonal constructions in the Germanic languages and is often called nominative–dative inversion. An Old English example is (16):

(16)   Gif ðam gifran   ungemetlicu spræc   ne   eglde
         if the   greedy (D) eloquent   speech (N) not   afflicted
         'if the greedy were not afflicted by loquacity'   (*CP* 43.309.2)

While the EXPERIENCER is always an animate NP with nominative or dative case, the THEME may be alternatively realized as a clause, as in the following examples.

(17)   a. and me   ofhreow þæt hi   ne cuþon ne næfdon þa
            and me (D) regretted that they not knew nor not-had the
            godspellican lare   on   heora gewritum
            evangelical doctrines among   their writings
            'and I regretted that they knew not nor had not the evangelical doctrines among their writings'   (*ÆCHom* I, (Pref)2.7)
        b. Gif we   ðonne scomiað ðæt we to uncuðum monnum suelc
            if   we (N) then shame   that we to unknown men   so
            sprecen
            speak
            'If we are ashamed to speak to strangers like this'   (*CP* 10.63.5)
        c. Us   gelustfullað gyt furður to sprecenne be ðan halgan were
            us (D) delights   yet further to speak   of the holy   man
            Iohanne
            John
            'It delights us to speak yet further of the holy man John'
                                                        (*ÆCHom* I, 25.360.29)

There is in fact a group of verbs that is attested almost exclusively with a clausal THEME, consisting of the verbs *(ge)byrian, gerisan, gedafenian, behofian,* all meaning more or less 'behove', and *(ge)lympan, (ge)weorþan* 'happen'; *þyncan* 'seem'. Two examples are given in (18):

(18)   a. Ðe   gedafenað to lerenne and me to hlistenne
            you (D) behoves   to learn   and me to listen
            'It befits you to study and me to listen'   (*Solil* 1.33.4)

b. &   him   ðuhte,   ðæt . . .
   and him (D) seemed that
   'and it seemed to him that . . .'   (*Bede* 28.362.32)

2.3   Word order

It has often been said that Old English word order was rather free,
and that this was at least in part due to the relatively rich system of case
endings and other inflectional morphology. More recently, it has emerged that
the label 'free' would be an overstatement for the positional variety of Old
English. For a number of aspects of word order, there are strong preferences,
and these are often not that different from the norm today. This is as true at
the constituent level as it is at the clause level. Let us first consider word order
inside the nominal group.

2.3.1   Word order at the NP level

For NPs, the preferred situation is for all modifiers to precede the
head noun, and the most frequent order closely resembles that of the present-
day language: quantifier, demonstrative pronoun/possessive pronoun,
numeral, *oþer* 'other', adjective (one or more), genitive noun, head. NPs containing all these elements simultaneously are not attested, but the examples in
(19) illustrate the relative order (see also Mitchell 1985: § 143).

(19)   a. anum unwisum cyninges þegne
           to-an unwise   of-king   thane
           'to an unwise thane of the king'   (*ChronA*(Plummer) 874.5)
        b. ealle his woruldlican æðelborennysse
           'all his worldly nobility'   (*ÆCHom* II, 9.73.36)
        c. monige oþre   cyninges þegnas
           many   other of-king   thanes
           'many other thanes of the king'   (*ChronA*(Plummer) 894.85)

Exceptions to the preferred word order are not hard to find: *monig* 'many' can
follow a demonstrative pronoun, as in (20a); *oþer* can precede a quantifier, as
in (20b):

(20)   a. þara monegena gewinna
           'of the many battles'   (*Or* 5.2.115.29)
        b. oðre fela   bisceopas
           other many bishops
           'many other bishops'   (*ÆLS*(Basil) 629)

Postmodification is attested with quantifiers and with modifiers in -*weard*:

(21)   a. hlafordswican manige
           traitors   many
           'many traitors'   (*WHom* 20.1.64)
        b. þa scipo alle
           the ships all
           'all the ships'   (*ChronA*(Plummer) 885.7)
        c. alle Cent eastewearde
           all   Kent eastward
           'all eastern Kent'   (*ChronA*(Plummer) 865.1)

Other cases of following modifiers are infrequent and some of them only occur in poetry. Some examples are:

(22)   a. mægwine   mine
           kinsmen-dear mine
           'my dear kinsmen'   (*Beo* 2479)
        b. þa roda þreo
           the roods three
           'the three roods'   (*El* 867)
        c. tamra   deora   unbebohtra   syx hund
           tame (G) deer (G) unbought (G) six hundred
           'six hundred unsold tame animals'   (*Or* 1.15.8)

We also find cases with both the demonstrative and the modifying adjective in postposition. In these cases the demonstrative precedes the adjective:

(23)   cyle þone grimmestan
        cold the   grimmest
        'the grimmest cold'   (*HomS*17(BlHom5) 136)

Certain constituents always follow the rest of the NP: this is true for prepositional modifiers, as in (24), and also for relative clauses, as in (25):

(24)   . . . ane boc be cyrclicum ðeawum
        '. . . a book about ecclesiastical customs'   (*ÆCHom* II, 5.49.237)

(25)   to þam ylcan campdome   þe   heora fæderas on wæron
        to the   same military service which their fathers in were
        'to the same military service which their fathers were in' (*ÆLS*(Martin) 31)

The second of two conjoined premodifiers, with or without demonstrative, can also follow the head:

(26)   a. se   byrdesta   sceall gyldan . . . and berenne kyrtel   oððe
           the highest-born must pay   and bearskin garment or
           yterenne
           otterskin
           'the highest born must pay . . . and a garment of bearskin or otterskin'
                                                                (*Or* 1.15.17)

b. liflice onsægednysse and halige and Gode   andfenge
   living sacrifice   and holy   and to-God acceptable
   'living and holy sacrifice, and acceptable to God'
                                                  (*ÆCHom* I, 32.482.8)

Two nouns or NPs may stand in an appositive relation where one specifies or modifies the other. A frequently occurring type is that of an appellative in combination with a title:

(27)   Sidroc eorl se gioncga
          Sidroc earl the young
          'The young earl Sidroc'   (*ChronA*(Plummer) 871.14)

In Old English, the name usually precedes the title. Middle English has more variation in this respect. In Old English, there are examples with several appositions in one group:

(28)   heahfæderas, eawfæste and wuldorfulle weras on heora life, witegena
          patriarchs   religious and glorious   men in their   life of-prophets
          fæderas, þæra gemynd ne bið forgiten . . .
          fathers whose memory not is forgotten
          'patriarchs, religious and glorious men in their lives, the fathers of the
          prophets, whose memory shall not be forgotten'   (*ÆCHom* I, 36.540.17)

Pronouns can be modified by an appositive NP, as in (29):

(29)   a. He cwæð, se apostol Paulus
             'He said, the apostle Paul'   (*ÆCHom* I, 9.146.33)
          b. se heora cyning
             the their king
             'he, their king'   (*Or* 1.14.35.14)

NPs may also be discontinuous in Old English. Those elements that may occur as postmodifiers at the end of the NP can be separated from the rest of the NP:

(30)   Maran cyle ic geseah, and wyrsan
          greater cold I saw   and worse
          'I have seen a greater and worse cold'   (*ÆCHom* II, 23.202.107)

A similar example involving a relative clause is:

(31)   forðan þe manegum wæron his wundra cuþe   þe god worhte
          because that to-many were   his miracles known that God performed
          þurh   hine
          through him
          'because the miracles that God wrought through him were known to
          many'
                                                  (*ÆLS*(Martin) 1)

2.3.2   *Word order at the clause level*

Word order at the clause level in Old English is a puzzling combination of the familiar and the alien: while some word orders are rather like those of the present-day language, others are very different. Closer inspection indeed reveals that Old English word order differs in major respects from that of Modern English, and that some important changes must have taken place between the Old and Modern periods. The Old English situation and its subsequent upheaval are discussed in detail in chapters 4 and 5. We will therefore confine ourselves here to a broad outline.

It has often been said that Old English is of the SOV word order type. In reality, there is a good deal of variation, but we can see this clearly only when we distinguish the position of the finite verb from that of the non-finite verb. Let us first consider the position of the finite verb.

The word order of quite a few Old English main clauses with one finite verb is like that of the present-day language. An example is a subject-initial main clause with one verb:

(32)   We habbað hwæðere þa bysne on halgum bocum
        'We have, nevertheless, the examples in holy books' (*ÆCHom* I, 31.474.33)

In other sentence types, however, we see immediately that there are important differences: main clauses introduced by question words, negatives and topics have subject–verb inversion, which is illustrated for questions in (33):

(33)   a. Hwi wolde God swa lytles þinges him forwyrnan
           why would God so small thing him deny
           'Why should God deny him such a small thing?'   (*ÆCHom* I, 1.14.2)
        b. Hwæt scealt þu þinum hlaforde?
           what owe you your   lord
           'What do you owe your lord?'   (*ÆHom* 17.142)

An important difference between inversion contexts in Old English and their present-day counterparts is that the phenomenon is not restricted to auxiliaries in Old English; all finite main verbs may undergo inversion as well, as (33b) illustrates. Old English is like the present-day language in that inversion is restricted to main clauses.

Main clauses introduced by a constituent other than the subject show an interesting quirk: while inversion takes place with all types of finite verb in a large majority of cases when the subject is nominal, a personal pronoun subject remains in preverbal position. This is illustrated in (34) vs. (35) (see also (6a) and (6b)):

(34)   a. On ðam dæge worhte God leoht, and merigen, and æfen
           on that day   made   God light and morning and evening
           'On that day God made light, morning, and evening'(*ÆCHom* I, 6.100.5)
        b. Ðas ðreo ðing   forgifð God his gecorenum
           these three things gives   God his chosen
           'These three things God gives to his chosen'   (*ÆCHom* I, 18.250.12)

(35)   a. Forðon *we* sceolan mid ealle mod &   mægene to Gode gecyrran
           therefore we must   with all   mind and power to God turn
           'Therefore we must turn to God with all our mind and power'
                                                        (*HomU*19(BlHom8) 26)
        b. Be ðæm *we* magon suiðe swutule oncnawan ðæt . . .
           by that we may   very clearly perceive that
           'By that, we may perceive very clearly that . . .'   (*CP* 26.181.16)

While the facts concerning inversion in questions and main clauses with a
nominal subject introduced by a topic may tempt us to view Old English as a
Verb-Second language like Dutch, German and the continental Scandinavian
languages, the facts in (35) complicate this picture in an intriguing way. We will
discuss this in detail in chapter 4.

Word order in embedded clauses is different from that of the present-day
language as well. In general, inversion with front position of the finite verb
does not occur there. Nevertheless a number of cases suggest that a form of
finite verb fronting is operative in embedded clauses (see also Pintzuk 1991).
First consider the following examples:

(36)   a. þæt hi *mihton* swa bealdlice Godes geleafan *bodian*
           that they could so   boldly   God's faith preach
           'that they could preach God's faith so boldly' (*ÆCHom* I, 16.232.23)
        b. þæt we ealle *sculon* ænne geleafan *habban*
           that we all   must   one faith   have
           'that we all must have one faith'   (*Or* 5.14.131.13)

There are also a few examples with fronting of a finite verb from a verb–
particle combination, as in (37a), where the particle remains in clause-final
position, as can be seen when we compare it with (37b), where the auxiliary,
but not the non-finite verb, is fronted.

(37)   a. þæt he *wearp* þæt sweord *onweg*
           'that he threw the sword away'   (*Bede* 1.7.38.18)
        b. gif hio ne *bið* hrædlice *aweg* adrifen
           if she not is quickly away driven
           'if it is not quickly driven away'   (*CP* 13.79.23)

The behaviour of verb–particle constructions will be discussed in detail in
chapter 6. The kind of verb fronting illustrated in (36) and (37) differs in
several ways from that in main clauses. Specially fronted constituents such as

topics and question elements do not occur in subordinate clauses of this type. The constituent preceding the finite verb is always the subject (nominal or pronominal), except in special constructions such as passives. Moreover, verb fronting in main clauses is vastly more frequent than in subordinate clauses.

It has often been said that English changed from an OV language to a VO language. But this statement requires considerable qualification, since even in Old English, there is a good deal of variation between OV and VO word orders. We saw above that in main clauses, and to a more limited extent in embedded clauses, the finite verb can be fronted. It therefore comes as no surprise that VO word orders are most frequent in clauses with a single finite lexical verb, since fronting of the finite verb very often results in VO word order. This is illustrated by (32), repeated here as (38a), and by (38b):

(38)   a. We habbað hwæðere þa bysne on halgum bocum
         'We have, nevertheless, the examples in holy books'
         S V   (ÆCHom I, 31.474.33)
    b. þæt he forgeafe godne willan þam seocan hæðenan
       that he granted good will the sick heathen
       'that he granted good will to the sick heathen'   (ÆCHom II, 2.12.28)

Given the fact that the finite verb can be fronted, it is only to be expected that in subject-initial sentences, a single finite lexical verb follows the subject, resulting in an SVO order. This is much more frequent in main clauses, which is again unsurprising because verb fronting is more prominently established there. The position of the non-finite verb, unlike that of the finite verb, is independent of clause type. This is where we get a picture of variation between OV and VO word orders, and it becomes clear that objects and PPs can appear on the left or the right of the non-finite verb in main (39a–b) and embedded (39c–f) clauses alike (the nonfinite verbs are italicized):

(39)   a. þes mann nolde   *cyðan*   ðam syngigendum heora synna
       this man not-wanted make-known the sinning   their sins
       'this man would not make known to the sinning their sins'
                                   (ÆCHom II, 22.194.148)
    b. Se mæssepreost sceal mannum *bodian* þone soþan geleafan
       the masspriest must people preach the true faith
       'The masspriest must preach the true faith to the people'
                                   (Ælet2(Wulfstan1) 175)
    c. þe *geearnian* wile ece   myrhðe æt   ðam soðan Gode
       who earn   wants eternal joy   from the true   God
       'who wants to earn eternal joy from the true God'   (WHom 7.22)
    d. þæt hi   urum godum *geoffrian* magon ðancwurðe onsægednysse
       that they our   gods   offer   may   grateful   sacrifice
       'that they may offer a grateful sacrifice to our gods'
                                      (ÆCHom I, 38.592.31)

EDINBURGH UNIVERSITY LIBRARY
WITHDRAWN

    e. þæt hy   syððan   *faran* scoldon geond   ealne middaneard
       that they afterwards go   must   throughout all   world
       'that they must afterwards travel throughout the world'   (*WHom* 7.78)
    f. þæt hi   mihton swa bealdlice Godes geleafan *bodian*
       that they could   so   boldly   God's faith   preach
       'that they could preach God's faith so boldly'   (*ÆCHom* I, 16.232.23)

Nominal objects and PPs are the constituents whose position is variable with respect to the non-finite verb; the position of other elements is rather fixed. Personal pronouns almost always appear somewhere left of the non-finite verb (this is discussed in chapter 4). The same can be said for a variety of adverbs, including negation markers, and stranded prepositions and particles are usually immediately left of the non-finite verb. On the other hand, finite clauses and infinitives with *to* almost always appear in sentence-final position. The issues of OV and VO word order are addressed in chapter 5.

    Finally, we should touch briefly on a recalcitrant phenomenon in embedded clauses. In embedded clauses with two verbs, there are some intriguing variations in the relative positioning of finite and non-finite verb. If this variation were restricted to examples like (39f), where we could say that the finite verb is fronted by the rule of Verb-Second, and (39d), in which it is not fronted, we could straightforwardly say that we have optional verb fronting in embedded clauses. But this picture is complicated by examples like (40):

(40)   a. Se ðe   nan ðing *nele*   on ðissum life *ðrowian*
        he who no   thing not-wants in this   life suffer
        'He who will suffer nothing in this life'   (*ÆCHom* I, 10.164.22)
      b. Gif he ðonne ðæt wif   *wille forsacan*
        if   he then   the woman wish refuse
        'If he then wishes to refuse the woman'   (*CP* 5.43.15)

These are embedded clauses in which a nominal object (*nan ðing/ðæt wif*) appears left of the finite verb (*ðrowian/forsacan*). The finite verb is left of the non-finite verb, but next to the subject (as in (39f)), which is expected if fronting took place. The analysis of these word order patterns is rather problematic. One approach to the problem would be to say that they are variations on the types of verb clustering found in many of the present-day continental West Germanic languages and dialects. Detailed work still needs to be done here, but we think the problem may well continue to resist precise analysis.

2.3.3   Word order in coordinate clauses

    Having considered main and subordinate clauses, we should, following Mitchell (1985) and others, distinguish a third type of clause: the coordinate clause. Failure to recognize it as a separate category yields a very misleading picture of main clause word order. We saw above that main clauses generally have Verb-Second. By analogy, we would expect coordinate main clauses to exhibit Verb-Second phenomena, have topics, show inversion and have the word orders typical of main clauses. But very often they do not. Although a small number of main clauses have no Verb-Second (Koopman 1995), the number of coordinate main clauses lacking it is far greater (even ones starting with a topic) and they often have the verb-final word orders usually associated with sub-ordinate clauses. Consider (41):

(41)   7   þa   ongeat   se   cyning þæt 7   he on þa duru eode 7
        and then perceived the   king   that and he on the door went and
        þa   unheanlice hine   werede
        then nobly   himself defended
        'and then the king perceived this and he went to the door and then nobly
        defended himself'   (*ChronA*(Plummer) 755.13)

The first coordinate clause of (41) shows inversion after *þa*, which is character-istic of main clauses, but the second coordinate clause has no Verb-Second and the finite verb follows the PP *on þa duru*, while the third coordinate clause does not repeat the subject and again has the verb in clause-final position (see also Stockwell and Minkova 1990).

2.4   Some clause types

2.4.1   *Questions*

Question formation in Old English does not differ greatly from its counterpart in the present-day language. Most questions are of two main types: yes–no questions and wh-questions. The two types share the prominent syntactic feature of subject–verb inversion. In yes–no questions the truth value of the whole statement is questioned: they ask for an affirmative or neg-ative response and are typically verb-initial:

(42)   Truwast ðu   nu   þe   selfum and þinum geferum   bet   þonne
        trust   you now you self   and your   companions better than
        ðam apostolum . . . ?
        the   apostles
        'Do you trust yourself now and your companions better than the
        apostles . . . ?'   (*Solil* 2.61.24)

In wh-questions a constituent is questioned by fronting an interrogative pronoun or adverb, such as *hwelc* 'which', *hwær* 'where', *hwy* 'why', and *hwa* 'who'. An example is:

(43)   Eala, hwy is ðis gold adeorcad?
        'Oh, why is this gold tarnished?'   (*CP* 18.133.10)

The word order in both types of questions is the inverted order *finite verb–subject*, except when the question word is itself the subject. The main difference with the present-day language is that inversion is not restricted to auxiliaries; all lexical finite verbs take part in this, as noted above. When the question word is part of a PP, the preposition is fronted with its complement. There is no 'P-stranding' of the preposition equivalent to present-day '*Who* did you give the book *to?*':

(44)   To hwæm locige ic buton to ðæm eaðmodum . . . ?
        to whom look I except to the humble
        'To whom do I look except to the humble . . . ?'   (*CP* 41.299.18)

There are also (independent) questions introduced by *hwæþer*, which differ in important ways from the yes–no and wh-questions discussed above. The wh-word is always *hwæþer*, inversion does not occur as it does in other independent questions and the verb is in the subjunctive (almost always in the present tense):

(45)   Ða andsworede se Wisdom 7   cwæð: Hwæþer þu nu   fullice
        then answered the wisdom and said whether you now fully
        ongite   forhwy hit þonne swa sie?
        understand (subj) why it then so is (subj)?
        'Then Wisdom answered and said: Do you now understand why it is so?'
                                                              (*Bo* 33.74.25)

The subject–verb order, the use of the subjunctive and the frequency of OV word orders are all characteristics of subordinate clauses. This betrays the origin of this type of question as an indirect question, with *hwæþer* as a conjunction.

2.4.2   Negation

Old English is a negative concord language: any negative sentence can contain multiple negative elements, but this results in only one single logical negation. An example:

(46)   . . . þæt heora   nan ne mehte nanes wæpnes gewealdan
        that of-them none not could no   weapon wield
        '. . . that none of them could wield any weapon'   (*Or* 4.10.103.24)

A key element in Old English negation is the negative particle *ne*. This is used almost invariably in any negative clause and always occurs on the immediate left of the finite verb. In sentence negation, *ne* alone is used in the vast majority of cases:

(47)   ne sende se deofol ða fyr of   heofenum, þeah þe hit
        not sent the devil then fire from heavens   though that it
        ufan   come
        from above came
        'the devil did not send fire from heaven then, though it came from above'
                                                    (*ÆCHom* I, (Pref)6.13)

(48)   He ne andwyrde ðam wife   æt fruman
        he not answered the woman at first
        'He didn't answer the woman at first'   (*ÆCHom* II, 8.68.45)

There is a small minority pattern where two negation elements are employed
to express sentence negation. In that case, the element *na* or *no* is used as the
second element, although *noht* and *nawiht* are also attested. An example with
na is (49):

(49)   Ne bið na se leorningcniht furðor þonne his lareow
        not is not the apprentice   further than   his master
        'The apprentice is not ahead of his master'   (*ÆHom* 14.134)

Constituent negation is usually expressed by prefacing the relevant constituent with *na* or a phonological variant thereof. (46) is a case in point, *nan* being
a contraction of *na an*. Some other examples are given in (50). Observe further
in (50) the frequently attested contraction of the negative particle *ne* with the
finite verb: *næs* in (50a) is the contracted form of *ne wæs*; *nabbað* in (50b) the
contracted form of *ne habbað*.

(50)   a. þær næs   eac nan geðafung
           there not-was also no consent
           'there was also no consent'   (*ÆCHom* I, 11.176.7)
        b. Stanas sind gesceafta,   ac hi   nabbað   nan lif
           stones are   created things but they not-have no life
           'Stones are created, but they have no life'   (*ÆCHom* I, 21.302.13)

2.5   Subordinate clauses

Subordinate clauses are usually divided into adjective (= relative)
clauses, complement clauses and adverbial clauses, according to their function. We will look at them in turn in sections 2.5.1, 2.5.2 and 2.5.3. First, we
briefly address the issue of the origin and marking of subordinate clauses.
    It is a widely held view that subordination ('hypotaxis') arose through the
reinterpretation of a sequence of independent clauses ('parataxis'). Harris
and Campbell (1995: chapter 10) show that this is unlikely to be the origin of
all subordinate clauses, but given the properties of main and subordinate

clauses noted above, the features of some Old English subordinate clauses can reasonably be explained in this way. We discuss two examples.

The pronoun *se* 'the/that' as a demonstrative usually precedes the noun, but it can also be used independently, as in (51):

(51)   Ælc ðæra manna ðe hine   forhæfð from unalyfedlicere gesihðe ...
        each of-the of-men who himself abstains from unallowed   sight
        se hæfð mædenes naman for ðære anwalhnysse
        he has of-maiden name for that purity
        'Each of the men who abstains from . . . he has the name of virgin for that
        purity'   (*ÆCHom* II, 44.328.40)

Se can also function as relative, as we will see below in 2.5.1. The source for this may well have been two independent main clauses, the first with an NP (e.g. the object) in final position, the second beginning with independent *se* reinterpreted as relative. This would account for the fact that a comparatively large number of such *se*-relatives have Verb-Second word order. *Se* is in fact often ambiguous between demonstrative and relative, as illustrated by (52):

(52)   He cwæþ þæt he cuðe sumne man on Romabyrig . . . se læg bedryda fram
        cildhade
        'He said that he knew a man in Rome . . . he/who lay bedridden from
        childhood'   (*ÆCHom* II, 6.58.168)

Paratactic origin seems a likely source for certain object clauses as well. We saw above that Verb-Second and topics are really main clause phenomena, yet the complements of verbs of saying can show Verb-Second and have topics. Consider (53):

(53)   Ða cwæð se halga bisceop þæt on þam beame nære   nan
        then said the holy bishop that in that tree   not-were no
        synderlic halignyss
        special holiness
        'Then the holy bishop said that there was no special holiness in that tree'
                                        (*ÆLS*(Martin) 396)

It is as if a new main clause is introduced (with a topic and subject–verb inversion), in spite of the subordinator (*þæt*) and the fact that it is in the subjunctive mood. The reinterpretation plausibly came about by juxtaposing two main clauses ('The bishop said that. In that tree . . .'), with the demonstrative *þæt* reinterpreted as a subordinator. The fact that the second clause may be interpreted as a quoted main clause may have helped this along. Sentences such as (53) would then exemplify the initial stage of the process, later followed by word order changes bringing the clause into line with subordinate syntax.

Let us now look at subordinate marking in Old English. The word order in main and subordinate clauses today is identical (leaving aside questions and

inverted main clauses) and it is not surprising that unambiguous subordinating conjunctions are employed, in the almost complete absence of
further morphological or syntactic signals. Old English, beside unambiguous
subordinators, has other important clues such as word order and subjunctive
marking on the verb. Consider the examples in (54):

(54)   a. gif hit is hefigtyme on ðyssere worulde
           'if it is difficult in this   world'   (*ÆCHom* I, 3.56.3)
        b. siððan he papanhad   underfeng
           after   he papal-office received
           'after he received the papal office'   (*ÆCHom* II, 9.77.164)
        c. Secgað eowrum hlaforde þæt he unforht sy
           say   your   lord   that he fearless be (subj)
           'Say to your lord that he should be fearless'   (*ÆCHom* I, 37.568.30)

The word order in (54a) is SVO (frequent in main clauses), but *gif* clearly
marks it as a subordinate clause. In (54b) *siððan* could be an adverb or a
conjunction, but in this case the OV word order is decisive for interpreting it
as a conjunction. Finally, the subjunctive *sy* combines with OV word order in
marking (54c) as subordinate. Subordinate marking is achieved by the interplay of various signals then, and readers usually have little trouble recogniz-
ing subordinate clauses because of these signals, in conjunction with the wider
context.

In (54b) *siððan* is used as a conjunction, but it can also function as an
adverb. There are several more 'ambiguous adverbs/conjunctions', to borrow
Mitchell's phrase (1985: § 2536), the most prominent among them *þa*
'then/when', used at a goodly rate in practically all Old English texts. It
appears often in so-called correlative constructions, like (55):

(55)   Ða   se wisdom þa   ðis spell asæd hæfde, þa   ongan he eft
        when the wisdom then this story said had   then began he again
        singan
        sing
        'When Wisdom then had told this story, she began to sing again'
                                                                 (*Bo* 34.89.4)

The OV word order in the first clause of (55) suggests a subordinate clause,
while the VS word order in the second clause is typical of main clauses. We
saw above that inversion of pronominal subjects is regular only in questions,
negative clauses beginning with *ne* and this group of adverbs. These are precisely the ones that can also be used as conjunctions. Inversion therefore plays
an important disambiguating role. The lengthy discussion in Mitchell (1985: §
2536 ff.) makes it clear, however, that there are occasional cases where the
expected VS word order fails, and therefore interpretative problems sometimes
arise.

2.5.1   Relative clauses

Relative clauses are adjectival in the sense that they modify a noun. It is customary to make a distinction between restrictive relatives (which add essential information) and non-restrictive relatives (which give additional information), as in the present-day English *The car that was used in the robbery has now been found* vs. *The police found the car, which had run out of fuel.* The distinction between restrictive and non-restrictive is one of meaning, which in the present-day language is, however, reflected in important phonological and syntactic effects: non-restrictive relatives are often separated from their antecedent by an intonation break (in writing commas are used) and the relative pronoun/conjunction *that* or the 'zero' relative are employed in restrictive relatives alone. For Old English, we do not have many clear-cut criteria: the punctuation of the surviving manuscripts is different from what we use today, and it is not always easy to make a consistent distinction between restrictive and non-restrictive clauses.

We can make a formal distinction between three major types of relative clauses by the relative marker(s) used in them, and some minor types. The major types are:

1. *se* relatives, with a form of the demonstrative pronoun *se* as a relative pronoun:

(56)   he gefor mid firde ongean Aristonocuse þæm cyninge, se   wolde
        he went with army against Aristonocusus the   king   who wanted
        geagnian him   þa læssan Asiam
        usurp   to-himself the lesser Asia
        'then he went with an army against King Aristonocusus, who wanted to
        usurp Asia Minor'   (*Or* 5.4.118.1)

This is the type which was said above to illustrate plausible paratactic origin. This makes it likely that they were mostly non-restrictive relatives.

2. *se þe* relatives, combining a form of demonstrative *se* with the indeclinable relative *þe*:

(57)   þæt heo ne woldon heora Gode   hyran, þone þe heo gelyfdon
        that they not wanted their God (D) obey who (A) they believed
        'that they did not want to obey their God, in whom they believed'
                                                            (*Bede* 3.15.222.22)

3. *þe* relatives, introduced by the indeclinable relative *þe*:

(58)   Đa sende se biscop ðæm wife   ðe   þær untrum læg sumne dæl
        then sent the bishop the woman who there sick   lay a   part

þæs   haligwætres
of-the holy water
'Then the bishop sent the woman who lay sick there some of the holy
water'   (*Bede* 5.4.396.1)

The *þe* relatives are by far the most frequent (for some figures for Ælfric, see
Mitchell 1985: § 2165).

The case form of *se* in the *se þe* relative in (57) is the accusative (*þone*)
required by the relative clause, but it is not determined by its antecedent
Gode, which is in the dative. Case attraction, however, is possible, as illustrated
in (59):

(59)   fore generednisse heora freonda   þara   ðe   of weorulde
        for relief   of-their friends (G) whom (G) which of world
        geleordon
        departed
        'for the relief of their friends who had departed from the world'
                                                                    (*Bede* 4.23.330.16)

The case of the antecedent and the case of the relative required by the relative
clause can, of course, also be identical:

(60)   þæt se wære leoda   cyning   se þe   ær   wæs folce
        that he was of-people king (N) who (N) before was to-people
        þeow
        in-bondage
        'that he would be king who had been in bondage to the people'
                                                                    (*Or* 4.6.95.32)

When the relative pronoun corresponds with a prepositional object, the
preposition is fronted along with the relative pronoun. This is called pied
piping and is illustrated in (61a) and (61b). However, the preposition is
'stranded' in preverbal position when the relative pronoun is *þær* as the object
of a locative preposition (as in (61d)), in *þe* relatives (without a relative
pronoun) like (61c) and some minor types of relatives without a relative
pronoun. Such cases of preposition stranding are discussed further in 2.6.

(61)   a. þæt fyr getacnode ðone Halgan Gast, *ðurh ðone* we beoð gehalgode
           'The fire betokened the Holy Ghost, through whom we are hallowed'
                                                                    (*ÆCHom* II, 17.167.190)
        b. Hwæt sind þas   buton ðrymsetl heora Scyppendes, *on ðam ðe* he
           what   are   these but   thrones their of-Creator   on which he
           wunigende mannum demð
           dwelling   men   judges
           'What are these but thrones of their Creator, on which he, abiding, judges
           men'   (*ÆCHom* I, 24.346.11)

    c. On ðam munte   Synay, þe   se Ælmihtiga *on* becom, wearð
       on the mountain Sinai which the Almighty on came was
       micel ðunor   gehyred
       great thunder heard
       'On mount Sinai, on which the Almighty came, great thunder was heard'
                                      (*ÆCHom* II, 12.1.116.226)
    d. þa   for he to oðre byrg, *þær* Ambira se cyning *on* wunode
       then went he to other city where Ambira the king in lived
       'then he went to another city where King Ambira lived'
                                        (*Or* 3.9.73.28)

Minor types of relative clause include those introduced by adverbs such as *þanon/þonon (þe)* (62a), and *þider þe* (62b), and infinitival relatives (62c):

(62)   a. þa gelomp   for sumum intingan, þæt he semninga gewat in
         then happened for some   reason   that he suddenly left   for
         Hibernia Scotta ealond, *þonon*   he ær   cwom
         Ireland of-Scots island from-where he previously came
         'Then it happened for some reason that he departed to Ireland, the island
         of the Scots, from where he had come'   (*Bede* 4.26.352.2)
    b. gelæde us to ðam ecan   life *ðider ðe* he us gelaðode þurh
         lead   us to the everlasting life to-where he us invited   through
         hi   and ðurh   heora æftergengan
         them and through their successors
         'lead us to the everlasting life to which he has invited us through them
         and their successors'   (*ÆCHom* II, 41.309.139)
    c. Gif ðær   ðonne sie gierd mid to ðreageanne, sie ðær   eac   stæf
         if   there then be rod   with to beat   be there also staff
         mid to wreðianne
         with to support
         'If there is a rod to beat with, let there also be a staff to support with'
                                      (*CP* 17.127.1)

There are also relative clauses with an included antecedent. These are often taken to include examples like (63), in which it is not entirely clear whether it is the demonstrative pronoun that acts as antecedent for a *þe* relative (type 3; see (58)), or whether it is a *se þe* relative (type 2; see (57)) with an included antecedent. (64) represents another type which is often called a free relative:

(63)   þæt ælc preost scrife   and dædbote tæce þam þe him
        that each priest hear confession and penitence teach him who him
        andette
        confesses
        'that each priest should hear confession and teach penitence to the person
        who confesses to him'   (*WCan* 1.1.1(Fowler) 68)

(64)   Fæder and moder moton heora bearn to swa hwylcum cræfte
        father and mother must   their   child to so   which   occupation

```
gedon  swa  him  leofost        byð
put     as   him  most pleasing  is
```
'Father and mother must put their child to whatever occupation is most
pleasing to him'   (*ÆHom* 20.54)

Finally, relatives can be used without a relative pronoun. This happens primarily when the relative clause contains the verb *hatan* and the relative corresponds with the subject:

(65)   Him þa   andswarode his ealdorbisceop, Cefi wæs haten
        him then answered   his high priest   Cefi was called
        'The high-priest, who was called Cefi, then answered him'
                                                          (*Bede* 2.10.134.11)

The word order patterns in relative clauses are the patterns which occur in subordinate clauses in general, though they are more frequently OV than other
subordinate clauses.

   Relative clauses usually follow their antecedents immediately, as in most of
the examples given so far, but, as was pointed out in section 2.3.1, they can be
separated from them and then occur in clause-final position:

(66)   &   gesealde his suna þæt rice   Constantinuse þone he hæfde
        and gave   his son the kingdom Constantinus whom he had
        ær   be Elenan his ciefese
        before by Helen   his concubine
        'and gave the kingdom to his son Constantine whom he had by his
        concubine Helen'   (*Or* 6.30.148.8)
(67)   myccle swiðor we sceolan þam soðfæstan gode þas lac geoffrian þe
        much   rather we ought   the true   God this gift offer   who
        us alysde   fram deaðe
        us delivered from death
        'much rather we ought to offer this gift to the true God who delivered us
        from death'   (*ÆLS*(Basil) 279)

2.5.2   *Complement clauses*

Complement clauses are those clauses which function as complement
to a verb, adjective or noun. They can be finite or non-finite. A complement
clause which is a statement is usually a finite clause introduced by *þæt* 'that'.
The subordinating conjunction is sometimes omitted if the verb is one of
saying, such as *cweþan*, *secgan* 'say', where the clause reports what is being
said. The most important type of non-finite complementation in Old English
is the infinitival clause. As in the present-day language, there are infinitives
with and without *to*, but the system underlying the choice is different, as will
be sketched below. In Old English, the distribution of the various types of

complementation is quite different from that of the present-day language. While the *to*-infinitive is now the most extensively employed type, it was used less frequently and in fewer environments in Old English, where the *that*-clause was the most prominent form of complementation.

2.5.2.1 Finite clauses

Verbs of saying and declaring are obviously often found with a finite clause complement, as in (68), but many other verbs can take a finite clause complement as well, as in (69):

(68)   Ða behet   God þæt he nolde   næfre eft   eal mancynn mid
        then promised God that he not-would never again all mankind with
        wætere acwellan
        water   destroy
        'Then God promised that he would never again destroy all mankind with
        water'   (*ÆCHom* I, 1.22.8)

(69)   þeah   þe   nu   þince þæt ðu   deorwyrðe feoh forloren habbe
        though to-you now seems that you precious good lost   have
        'Though it may seem to you that you have lost precious goods'
                                                                  (*Bo* 20.48.17)

The finite clauses range from *þæt* 'that' clauses to dependent questions introduced by a range of question words. Finite object clauses always follow all other clause material. The conjunction *þæt* is sometimes left out (Mitchell 1985: § 1981 ff.), but not nearly as frequently as in Modern English.

2.5.2.2 Non-finite clauses

The most frequent and important type of non-finite complementation in Old English is by infinitives. There are two basic types of infinitive: the first is the 'bare' or 'zero' infinitive, ending in *-an* or *-ian*, e.g. *þincan* 'think', *lufian* 'love'; the second is the inflected infinitive or *to*-infinitive, which consists of *to*, followed by a verb stem and the ending *-enne*, e.g. *to þincenne* 'to think', *to lufienne* 'to love'. *To* in Old English infinitives is never separated from the verb form, as in present-day English *I intend to clearly show that* . . . The status of *to* as an infinitive marker is something of a puzzle. It is thought by some scholars to be a preposition governing the dative case on the infinitive form, which is nominal in origin. But the nominal character of Old English infinitives has been overestimated, and recent work (Los 1998) shows that *to*-infinitives behave more like clauses than like nominals.

Variation in the choice of infinitive is found only with monotransitive verbs. A prominent group forms the verbs of intention like *þencan* 'think, plan'. Two examples are given here; (70a) has a *to*-infinitive, while (70b) has a bare infinitive:

(70)   a. Hu   ðæt mod . . . ðonne hit ðencð fela   godra weorca *to* wyrcanne
        how the mind   when it thinks many good works to do
        'How the mind . . . when it intends to do many good works'

(CP 9.55.14)

        b. Ðonne ðæt mod ðenceð gegripan him to upahefenesse ða
        when   the mind thinks seize   itself to pride   the
        eaðmodnesse . . .
        humility
        'When the mind thinks of making humility a pretext for pride . . .'

(CP 8.55.12)

The system governing the selection of bare and *to*-infinitives has undergone some significant changes since the Old English period. The most conspicuous difference from today is that the bare infinitive, which in the present-day language is virtually restricted to the complementation of modals and verbs of direct perception and causation, occurs frequently in Old English as the object clause of a variety of verbs. In all other environments, adjuncts, complement to noun or adjective, the *to*-infinitive is the norm. It has therefore been held by many that after the Old English period, the *to*-infinitive encroached upon the territory of the bare infinitive. Los (1999), however, argues that this is not the case. One fact here is that Gothic had no complement *to*-infinitives. Another is that diachronically, *to*-infinitives tended to replace *that*-clauses, but not the other way around. Los (1999) believes we are dealing with free variation in (70). Fischer (1995; 1996a) thinks this is not the case for Middle English. This clearly needs to be explored further.

The non-finite complementation of adjectives and nouns is always formed with a *to*-infinitive. The history of the non-finite complementation of adjectives shows a number of interesting developments, which are the topic of chapter 8.

2.5.3   Adverbial clauses

A large number of subordinate clauses function as adverbials. They are usually subclassified on semantic grounds: clauses of time, place, purpose and so on (for an elaborate description see Mitchell 1985: §§ 2416–3721). The different types of clauses differ in the conjunctions that can be used to introduce them and in the extent to which the subjunctive is used. We will briefly discuss these issues in turn.

A wide range of subordinating conjunctions is available, depending on the type of clause. Clauses of time can be introduced by *þa* 'when', *þonne* 'when', *nu* 'now', *siþþan* 'after', *oþ þæt* 'until', and *þa hwile þe* 'while' to mention a few. Not every type of adverb clause has such a wide range of subordinators. Conditional clauses are commonly introduced by *gif* 'if', but a few others are occasionally used too such as *þær* 'if', *butan* 'except' and *nymþe* 'except'.

A particularly distinctive feature of Old English adverbial clauses is the use of 'compound' conjunctions, which disappear from English later on. They take the form of a preposition followed by the appropriate form of *se* (usually the dative or instrumental) and then the relative particle *þe* (occasionally *þæt*), which is however sometimes left out. Some combinations are: *for þæm/þon þe* (for that which = 'because'), *mid þæm þe* (with that which = 'when') and *ær þæm þe* (before that which = 'before').

The subjunctive mood in Old English was indicated by endings that were distinct in some respects at least from the indicative (see section 2.2.1). Clear subjunctive endings are found in the present tense except for the first person singular, in the past tense first and third person singular of strong verbs, in the second person singular of weak verbs and in the past tense plural of all verbs. Theoretically this plural subjunctive ending (*-en*) of all verbs is distinct from the indicative (*-on*), but later texts in particular do not always make a consistent distinction in the spelling.

Although the subjunctive is found in main clauses, it is more properly a subordinate clause phenomenon, but it is not found by any means in all types. Some adverbial clauses that regularly have the subjunctive are conditional clauses expressing hypothetical condition (71a), clauses of purpose (71b), and clauses of concession (71c):

(71)   a. Gif nu   eall þises   middaneardes wela   come to anum men
           if   now all   of-this of-earth   wealth came to one   man
           'If now all the wealth of this earth came to one man'   (*Bo* 13.28.8)
        b. and behyddon þæt heafod . . . þæt   hit bebyrged ne wurde
           and hid   the head   so that it   buried   not were
           'and hid the head so that it would not be buried'   (*ÆLS*(Edmund) 130)
        c. þeah se lichama geendige
           'though the body ends'   (*ÆCHom* I, 1.20.4)

Detailed information can be found in Mitchell's extensive discussion of subordinate clauses (1985, volume II).

2.6   Preposition stranding

In this section we draw together the observations made on prepositions through this chapter, and clarify the status of the phenomenon called preposition stranding. It is useful to consider the facts of preposition stranding in the present-day language first.

Preposition stranding refers to those constructions in which the object of a preposition is fronted, for instance by wh-movement (72) or by passivization (73):

(72)   a. Who did you talk to?
         b. Which garage did you put the car in?
         c. Which allegation did you take offence at?

(73)   a. The doctor reassured Harry that his mother was cared for
         b. John was taken advantage of
         c. Fred was kept tabs on

The effect of moving the object of the preposition is to leave the preposition stranded. The restrictions on such stranding are quite a bit more rigorous in passives than in sentences involving wh-movement. A general restriction is that the stranded preposition is part of a complement PP, i.e. a PP that is an argument of the verb. This is true for all the examples in (72)–(73); (74) illustrates the impossibility of stranding in a prepositional time adjunct:

(74)   a. *Which dinner did you arrive after?
         b. *The dinner was served an excellent Sauternes after

In wh-movement constructions, the stranded preposition is therefore always somewhere in the VP. The restrictions in passivization are even stricter: prepositional passives are really restricted to those cases where the preposition is adjacent to the verb, as in (73a), and to fixed lexical combinations of the sort exemplified in (73b–c). Thus, it is not the case that all prepositional objects in a complement PP can be passivized, as the ungrammaticality of the following examples shows:

(75)   a. *The garage was put the car in
         b. *The allegation was taken offence at
         c. *Syntax was written a book about

Preposition stranding in Old English had a very different distribution. We can be brief on prepositional passives: passivization of a prepositional object was impossible in Old English, presumably because prepositions governed an inherent case in Old English. We saw in section 2.2.1 (see (7a–b)) that only objects marked for structural case can be passivized, and there are no obvious further restrictions in Old English that would block passivization.

   We turn then to preposition stranding in wh-movement constructions. Wh-movement constructions comprise questions, relative clauses (including infinitival relatives), and some types of adjective + infinitive constructions which will be discussed in chapter 8. What these constructions share is movement of some constituent, a question word or relative pronoun (which may be phonetically empty), to the specifier of CP. This is called *wh*-movement. Our discussion is facilitated if we first discuss the status of pronominal objects of prepositions. The order of a preposition and its object when the object is a full NP is always: P–NP. When the object is a personal pronoun, or the locative pronoun *þær*, this order may be inverted, and the pronoun can also appear further to the left. We illustrate this here for *þær*:

(76)   a. and com ... to ðam treowe, sohte   wæstm *ðæron* ...
           and came   to the   tree   sought fruit therein
           'he got to the tree, sought fruit in it ...'   (*ÆCHom* II, 30.237.72)
        b. ðæt þu *þær*   nane myrhþe *on* næfdest
           that you there no   joy   in not-had
           'that you did not take joy in that'   (*Bo* 7.15.11)
        c. he *ðær*   wearð from þæm burgwarum *in* abroden
           he there was   by   the   citizens   in dragged
           'he was dragged in there by the citizens'   (*Or* 3.9.73.8)

Since *þær* is also used as a locative relative pronoun, this is where we find preposition stranding in relative clauses:

(77)   oð   þæt he gestod bufon ðam gesthuse, þær   þæt cild   on wunode
       until that he stood above the inn   where the child in stayed
       'until it (the star) stood above the inn where the child was staying'
                                                              (*ÆCHom* I, 5.78.21)

Apart from this type of relative clause, there is a simple generalization to be made about PPs in wh-movement constructions: when there is no overt pronoun, as in *þe*-relatives and infinitival relatives, we find preposition stranding, as in (78):

(78)   a. On þam munte   Synay, *þe*   se   Ælmihtiga *on* becom, wearð
           on the mountain Sinai   which the Almighty   on came, was
           micel ðunor   gehyred
           great thunder heard
           'On mount Sinai, on which the Almighty came, great thunder was heard'
                                                          (*ÆCHom* II, 12.1.116.226)
        b. Gif ðær ðonne sie gierd mid to ðreageanne, sie ðær   eac stæf
           if   there then be rod with to beat   be there also staff
           mid   to wreðianne
           with to support
           'If there is a rod to beat with, let there also be a staff to support with'
                                                                 (*CP* 17.127.1)

When an overt NP, wh-constituent or relative pronoun, moves to Spec,CP, the preposition moves along, as discussed in the various sections on questions and relatives above, and briefly illustrated again here in (79). This is called pied piping.

(79)   a. *To hwæm* locige ic buton to ðæm eaðmodum . . . ?
       to whom look I except to the humble
       'To whom do I look except to the humble . . . ?'   (*CP* 41.299.18)
    b. Ðæt fyr getacnode ðone Halgan Gast, *ðurh ðone* we beoð gehalgode
     'The fire betokened the Holy Ghost, through whom we are hallowed'
                            (*ÆCHom* II, 17.167.190)

These facts are discussed in meticulous detail in Allen (1977, 1980) and in van Kemenade (1987). Allen argues that they motivate the postulation of two strategies of relativization in Old English, one by wh-movement, as in (79), the other by controlled unbounded deletion of a relative pronoun, as in (78). We can then say that it was impossible in Old English to move a relative pronoun out of a PP, hence we get pied piping when a PP or prepositional object is relativized. Unbounded deletion of a prepositional object was possible, hence we get preposition stranding there. As far as we can ascertain, however, the two strategies, preposition stranding and pied piping, have exactly the same properties with respect to conditions on movement, and on the relation between a Spec,CP element and its trace(s). This, van Kemenade (1987) argues, supports the idea that they are both wh-movement constructions; and she goes on to analyse preposition stranding constructions in terms of wh-movement of the phonetically empty counterpart of a personal pronoun or *þær* (which we know can be moved out of a PP). We will not discuss the finer points of the analysis here. For our purposes, it is important to bear in mind the distinction between passives and wh-movement constructions here: preposition stranding in passives is not attested at all in Old English.

3

An outline of Middle English syntax

3.1   Introductory remarks

This chapter presents a broad outline of the syntax of Middle English, i.e. English in the period 1100–1500. Many of the syntactic phenomena found in Old English, as described in chapter 2, continue in this period, but there is also a great deal of change. In fact, it has often been said that, while Old English is to all intents and purposes a foreign language to present-day speakers of English, (late) Middle English writings, such as those of Chaucer, Gower and Malory, do not confront modern readers with any major syntactic obstacles to comprehension. As the editors of a widely used anthology of Middle English literature put it: 'There are many subtle differences in syntax between Middle English and Modern English, but few will present any difficulty to the reader' (Dunn and Byrnes 1973: 13). The main reason for this difference is no doubt the occurrence of change in many areas of grammar between the Old and Middle English periods.

In chapters 4 to 9, we shall trace some of the individual changes in detail. It is with the aim of providing a framework against which to interpret these changes that this chapter sketches the basics of Middle English syntax, corresponding to the sketch of Old English in chapter 2. In section 3.2 we consider inflections in Middle English, and look at two constructions (impersonals and passives) characterized by special inflectional marking of grammatical roles. Section 3.3 deals with word order, both within the NP and within the clause. Interrogative and negative clauses form the topic of section 3.4, and section 3.5 deals with various aspects of subordinate clauses, i.e. relative clauses, complement clauses and adverbial clauses.

As the descriptions in the following sections and chapters will make clear, Middle English syntax is characterized by greater variability than Old English syntax. This is due not only to the diachronic developments referred to above, but also to the lesser degree of standardization of written language in Middle English, and to the sheer bulk of the material that has survived, which exhibits more regional, stylistic and/or social variation than is found in the surviving Old English texts. However, partly due to difficulties in locating the manuscripts of the canonical Middle English texts socially and stylistically, the methods employed to study such variation have so far not been very sophisticated: they have mostly taken the form of a comparison between the language of prose and that of poetry. Overall, the situation seems to be that poetry makes use of a wider range of grammatical options, including more informal ones, than prose, but a great deal of more fine-grained work remains to be done in this area. A beginning has also been made on the study of regional syntactic variation, but – at least with respect to the type of phenomena focussed on in this book – this type of study is still in its infancy. Nevertheless, whenever specific information is available, we will remark on differences of this type in this and the following chapters.

3.2   Morphology and case assignment

While (classical) Old English had a rather elaborate inflectional system for both verbs and nouns, much of this had withered away by early Middle English, and further reductions took place in the course of the Middle English period. In this section we will discuss the main lines of this morphological development, in as far as it affects the syntax of the language, which is principally in matters having to do with case assignment.

3.2.1   Middle English verbal and nominal inflections

The categories expressed inflectionally on the verb in Old English were person (first, second, third), number (singular, plural), tense (present, past) and mood (indicative, subjunctive, and imperative). As we saw in chapter 2, even in Old English there was a great deal of syncretism, so that a form such as *lufode* (from *lufian* 'to love'), for example, could be any of the following: past tense singular indicative first person or third person, past tense singular subjunctive first, second or third person, and in some texts even an inflected participle. Tense distinctions continued to be formally marked on all verbs during the Middle English period, but the marking of other categories underwent further reductions, due to phonological erosion which resulted in the survival of just a handful of surface inflections by the end of the period: *-(e)st*, *-(e)th*, *-s* and *-(e)n*.

The ending *-(e)st* consistently and unambiguously marked second person singular indicative (as in Chaucer's *Thow comest hoom as dronken as a mous* (Chaucer *Wife of Bath* 246); it survived into the sixteenth century and beyond (as in Shakespeare's *Why, thou knowest I am as valiant as Hercules*; *1HIV* II.iv.266). The ending *-(e)th* marked the third person singular indicative present tense of all main verbs (as in Chaucer's *This Frere bosteth that he knoweth helle*; Chaucer *Summoner* 1672); in southern dialects, this ending was also used for the plural indicative present. Later, *-(e)th* was replaced by the modern ending *-(e)s*, originally only found in northern dialects (where it marked both third person singular and all persons plural). The ending *-(e)n* was used for the plural (as in *The grettest clerkes been noght wisest men*; Chaucer *Reeve* 4054) and also for the infinitive (as in *now, lat hem goon hir weye!*; Chaucer *Reeve* 4097); but in many texts this ending alternated with *-e* and zero, and it was on its way out for infinitive marking by 1480 and somewhat later for plural marking (see the figures given by Lass 1992: 97 f.).

As pointed out in 2.2.1, modern theoretical work has posited a relation between the richness of surface verbal morphology and the syntactic phenomenon of *pro*-drop (see Jaeggli and Safir 1989 for various views on this relation). We give another (Spanish) example in (1).

(1)   La compré   ayer
       it buy-PAST-1sg yesterday
       'I bought it yesterday'

Since Spanish has rich agreement morphology, a subject pronoun such as *yo* 'I' in (1) can be (and usually is) omitted. In late Middle English, verbs generally showed overt agreement with the subject only in the indicative in the second person singular and in the third person singular present tense, and it is therefore not surprising to find that late Middle English usually featured an overt pronoun in examples comparable to (1). Nevertheless, like other languages without rich verbal agreement, late Middle English sometimes allowed a subject pronoun to remain unexpressed. This is found in coordinate *and*-clauses even when the subjects are not identical, as in (2), and it also occurred in clauses with a marked topic in initial position, as in (3), and some other cases (see Burrow and Turville-Petre 1992: 41).

(2)   That made his face often reed and hoot/
       that made his face often red and hot
       For verray shame, and blamed   hymself for he/
       for very   shame and he-blamed himself for he
       Had toold to me so greet a pryvetee
       had told to me so great a private-matter
       'That often made his face turn hot and red with shame, and he blamed himself for having told me such a private matter.'
                                                    (Chaucer *Wife of Bath* 540)

(3)   as for Thomas Myller wyll   do nothyng in thys mater
       as for Thomas Miller he-will do nothing in this matter
       'As for Thomas Miller, he will do nothing in this matter'
                                                    (*Cely Letters* 8.6)

Elliott (1974: 186) characterizes example (2) as a 'sudden conversational transition from one subject to another', i.e. from *that* in the first clause to the unexpressed *he* in the second clause. It indeed appears that subject omission was associated with informal styles, as it still is in present-day English (consider for example: *Sorry, (I) can't help it*).

Early Middle English and Old English did not have very rich agreement either, since no person distinctions were visible on any plural or subjunctive verb, and presumably for this reason sentences with *pro*-drop were the exception rather than the rule in those periods too. However, there is one construction-type that commonly featured a null subject in Middle English (as it did in Old English; see 2.2.1). It consisted of sentences with a null expletive subject, as in example (4) and the first clause of example (5).

(4)   to us surgiens aperteneth that we do to every wight   the beste that
       to us surgeons befits   that we do to every person the best   that
       we kan
       we can
       'it is our duty as surgeons to treat every person as well as we can'
                                                              (Chaucer *Melibee* 1011)

(5)   hard is to knowe in al poyntis to holde the meene, lyght is hit to
       hard is to know in all points to hold the society easy is it   to
       faille
       fail
       'it is hard to know exactly how to rule society; it is easy to fail'
                                                              (*SSecr* 130/26)

In Modern English, this type of sentence has obligatory use of so-called dummy or expletive *it*, but in Old and Middle English it was also possible to leave the subject position empty. In the course of the fifteenth century, this option is used less and less frequently and by 1500 the use of expletive *it* has become the rule.

The Middle English reduction in verbal morphology is paralleled in nominal morphology. Theoretically, Old English nouns still showed a four-way distinction involving nominative, accusative, genitive and dative. However, as pointed out in chapter 2, in many nouns the opposition between nominative and accusative was not formally marked in the singular, and it was not marked in the plural of any noun. In late Old English and early Middle English it was levelled in all singular nouns as well, as a result of phonological attrition of word endings. It was retained in the personal pronouns, most of which indeed had a much more pronounced surface differentiation to begin with (compare Old English nominative *guma* 'man' and *he* 'he' with accusative *guman* and *hine*). The Old English demonstrative/definite article also had clear surface differentiation (compare masculine singular nominative *se* with accusative *þone*); this case difference continued into the fourteenth century in some southern dialects, but was eventually levelled out, with the case-invariant forms *the* (definite article) and *that* (demonstrative) being adopted throughout.[1]

The Old English dative endings also underwent attrition and levelling, coalescing with the already merged nominative/accusative form in all nouns and the definite article, and with the accusative forms in the pronouns (except for *hit*, which already had the same form), compare Old English dative *þæm hlaforde* 'the lord' and *him* 'him' with Middle English nominative/accusative/dative *the lauerd/lord* and dative/accusative *him*). The genitive, however, proved to be more resistant, and survived as an inflectional category throughout the Middle English period. Its formal marking showed quite some variety in Old English, depending on inflectional class; this variety survived for a while, but by the end of the Middle English period the present-day marker *'s* (in various spellings) had become the norm for nouns.

If these developments are considered in more detail for the various inflectional classes, they can be seen to consist of an intricate interplay between phonological weakening and analogical levelling, which proceeded along a number of intermediate (and dialect-specific) stages that we shall not consider here. The overall result was a morphological system in which singular nouns had two forms, one for genitive functions and one for all other functions. The terms genitive case and common case have been used to describe these forms. Pronouns, however, retained three forms, for which we can use the terms nominative case (*I, he,* etc.), genitive case (*my, his,* etc.) and objective case (*me, him,* etc.). These terms can also be used for nouns, as long as it is kept in mind that all nouns have syncretism of the nominative and the objective. By the fifteenth century, plural nouns regularly took the ending *-s*, a result of whole-sale simplification of the original Old English system, which had a wide variety of plural markers.

One of the syntactic effects of these changes was the breakdown of the system based on selection of dative versus accusative. This selection played a role in complementation patterns of Old English monotransitive verbs (with most verbs selecting an accusative internal argument, some verbs selecting a dative or genitive, and other verbs showing variation, apparently depending to some extent on the meaning intended), in complementation of ditransitives (most of which selected both a dative and an accusative, though the genitive was also found), in prepositional complementation (with variability similar to that for monotransitive verbs) and in voice alternations (only accusative

---

[1] The form *the* was also number-invariant, but singular *that* came to be paired with plural *those* (from the original plural form *þo*, through addition of the plural marker *-s*; the Old English plural demonstrative *þas* 'these' may also have played a role here).

objects of active clauses being eligible for promotion to subject in the passive).
Not surprisingly in view of the development of formal identity across the
board of (earlier) datives and accusatives, all these areas underwent change in
Middle English.

In the case of monotransitive complementation, the development was
simple: all internal arguments came to be marked by the objective case form,
and any semantic distinctions that existed earlier were lost or relocated to
different lexical items. In the case of the verbs *see* and *help*, for example, the
internal arguments were marked accusative and dative respectively in Old
English, as in (6a–b), but in Middle English both verbs took an objective internal argument, as in (7a–b).

(6) a. Sona   swa hio geseah þone   fordrifenan   cyning . . .
        as-soon as she saw   the-ACC driven-off-ACC king-ACC
        'As soon as she saw the king, who had been driven out of course . . .'
                                                                  (*Bo* 38.116.6)

     b. for ðan ðe he wolde gehelpan . . . þearfum   and
        because he would help   poor-people-DAT and
        wannhalum
        sick-people-DAT
        'because he wanted to help the poor and the sick.'   (*ÆLS*(Oswald) 272)

(7) a. Allas . . . / þat ich here þis sorwe see!
        alas   that I here this sorrow-OBJ see
        'Alas, that I should see this sorrow here.'   (*Havelok* 1878)

     b. Loke nou, hu   God helpen kan/
        look now how God help   can
        O mani wise wif   and man
        in many ways woman-OBJ and man-OBJ
        'Now look how God can help men and women in many ways.'
                                                                  (*Havelok* 1712)

As explained in 2.2.1, there were verbs in Old English that could take either a
dative or an accusative object, with in some cases a possible difference in
meaning (see Plank 1983). The difference involved the degree of affectedness
of the object, the dative signalling a lesser degree of affectedness than the
accusative. In Middle English, the distinction between dative and accusative
was lost, and with it the possibility of signalling a difference in meaning in this
way. In some cases, part of the semantic difference may have come to be
expressed by other lexical items (including verb + preposition combinations)
that were pressed into service for this.

In the case of ditransitive verbs, the two internal arguments, usually marked
accusative and dative in Old English as in (8), both received objective marking
in Middle English, as in (9).

(8)   Æfter ðisum sealde se ealdorman hine   sumum   frysan
       after this   sold the aldorman him-ACC some-DAT Frisian-DAT
       of lundene
       of London
       'Afterwards the aldorman sold him to a Frisian of London'
                                                        (*ÆCHom* II, 24.204.167)

(9)   Wolle we sullen Iosep   þis   chapmen   þat here come?
       will we sell Joseph-OBJ these merchants-OBJ that here came
       'Shall we sell Joseph to these merchants that have come here?'
                                                        (*Jacob&J.* 118)

In addition, the recipient argument could be marked by means of the preposition *to*, as in (10). In Old English, this pattern is found with only a few verbs, but it becomes a very productive one in Middle English.

(10)   Betir is that Y ȝyue hir to thee than to another man
       better is that I give her to you than to another man
       'It is better if I give her to you than to another man'
                                                        (*WBible* Gen 29.19; Denison 1993: 107)

As far as prepositions are concerned, the situation in Old English was that individual prepositions selected either the dative or accusative (and some the genitive). The underlying basis for selection, including the variability shown by some prepositions, is not entirely clear. In Middle English, the system was much simplified, since all prepositions were now followed by the objective case form.

The changes in marking of internal arguments in ditransitive constructions and in prepositional phrases were accompanied by changes in the possibilities for passivization, which we shall discuss in section 3.2.3. But first we present in section 3.2.2 a description of what happened to the Old English impersonal verbs. We saw in section 2.2.2 that these verbs showed rather special case marking in Old English. The overall simplification of the case system led to simplification of impersonal constructions as well, but we shall see that they nevertheless retained some of their special properties.

3.2.2   *Impersonal verbs*

It was shown in section 2.2.2 that Old English impersonal verbs with two NP arguments occurred in three distinct configurations, repeated here in (11).

(11)   a. EXPERIENCER – dative   THEME – nominative
       b. EXPERIENCER – nominative THEME – genitive
       c. EXPERIENCER – dative   THEME – genitive

The THEME could also have the form of a clause; for some verbs, this was in fact the most frequent pattern.

In present-day English, only the following two patterns are found:

(12)   a. EXPERIENCER – objective   THEME – nominative
           (they surprised me)
        b. EXPERIENCER – nominative   THEME – objective
           (I don't like them)

If the THEME is a clause in present-day English, it can function as the subject, with or without dummy *it* (*that you should say so surprises me*; *it surprises me that you should say so*).

Early in the Middle English period, the option of marking the THEME as genitive, as in (11b) and (11c), disappeared. Instead, the THEME argument came to be expressed by the objective form, as in (13a), or by a prepositional phrase, as in (13b), a possibility that in fact occurred (alongside the genitive) in Old English as well.

(13)   a. Ic hit   ȝierne
           I   it-OBJ yearn
           'I yearn for it'   (*Vices&V* 59.27; Allen 1995: 128)
        b. . . . yonge men . . . yurnes to gaumes
               young men   yearn to games
           '. . . young men like games'   (*Destr. Troy* 2937)

This change can be seen as part of a larger development, whereby the genitive ceased to be used to mark verbal arguments, also of non-impersonal verbs. This development is somewhat unexpected, since we have seen that the genitive survived as a formal category. However, after the Old English period, the status of this formal category changed: it became restricted to functions within a NP (most typically, possessive function).

Another early Middle English change is the general syncretism of dative and accusative, which coalesced into one objective case. The effect for impersonal verbs is that the Old English marking of EXPERIENCER as dative, as in (11a) and (11c), changed into marking as objective, as in (14).

(14)   sche him   pleseth/ of suche wordes as sche spekth
        she him-OBJ pleases by such words as she   speaks
        'she pleases him by the words that she speaks'
                              (Gower *Confessio Amantis* 1.1698; Denison 1993: 72)

The two changes affecting genitive and dative resulted in the Old English patterns (11a, b) being converted into the present-day (12a, b). Pattern (11c), which is often called a 'true' impersonal construction since it has no nominative (and therefore, under some interpretations, no subject), remained a true impersonal, as shown in (15) and (16).

(15)   swetest   him   ðuncheð ham
     sweetest him-OBJ seems   them-OBJ
     'they seem sweetest to him'   (*Ancr* 52a.15; Denison 1993: 70)

(16)   ne of al þet eauer wa is ne schal ham   neauer wontin
     nor of all that ever woe is not will   them-OBJ never   lack
     'nor will they ever be lacking in anything that is miserable'
                   (*SWard* 152; Denison 1993: 70)

This configuration with two objective NPs or one objective NP and a PP survived until 1500, but then disappeared, like all other constructions with a null
expletive subject (see 3.2.1 above).

   Impersonals were also used until the end of the Middle English period in the
pattern with an objective EXPERIENCER and a clausal THEME, as in (17).

(17)   me   marvaylyyth mychil why God ȝeuyth wyckyd men swych
     me-OBJ marvels   much why God gives   wicked men such
     power
     power
     'I wonder a lot why God gives wicked people such power'
                   (*Dives&Pauper* I.1.336.2)

Here the distinction between (12a) and (15–16) is in a way neutralized, since
the clause can be seen as parallel to either a nominative or an objective NP. In
either case, the sentence would lack a preverbal nominative subject. In example
(18), the same verb occurs with a nominative EXPERIENCER subject.

(18)   I   merveyll that I here no tidyngges from yow
     I-NOM marvel   that I hear no news   from you
     'I wonder why I don't hear any news from you'   (*Paston Letters* 76.38)

The specific verb used in (17) and (18), *marvel*, is a loan from French that is
first attested in English in the fourteenth century (see *OED*, s.v. *marvel*, vb.).
Its use in (17) and (18) clearly shows that impersonals formed a productive category also in Middle English. Another sign of this is the fact that some native
verbs that did not show impersonal syntax in Old English began to do so in
Middle English. The verb *must*, for example, is often found in true impersonal
constructions such as (19).

(19)   us   must worschepyn hym
     us-OBJ must worship   him
     'we must worship him'   (*Dives&Pauper* I.1.206.34)

The very brief presentation of the impersonal facts given in 2.2.2 and in this
section hides various controversial issues, brought out well in Denison (1990).
For one thing, we have not said anything about impersonal verbs with one argument (such as *rain* and *happen*); their behaviour is of course different, but also

needs to be taken into account in a full history of the impersonals. Secondly, among the category of two-place impersonal verbs that we have described, there appears to be lexical variation (synchronic as well as diachronic) as to which verbs occur in which configurations; since the available data are incomplete and only give us a partial view, scholars inevitably disagree about what the complete view would be like. Thirdly, cross-linguistically the relevant verbs (sometimes called psych verbs, since they tend to indicate various psychological states) also often show rather special patterns of case marking and grammatical relations, and so far there has been little consensus on their proper analysis. Some theories, for example, entertain the possibility that a fronted dative EXPERIENCER argument in some cases can function as subject of the clause; this of course will have consequences for the kind of empirical distinctions we will want to make (e.g. between fronted and non-fronted EXPERIENCERS) and for the way the diachronic development of these constructions is viewed (see Allen 1995 for a detailed analysis of Old and Middle English impersonals along these lines, with full references to earlier work).

3.2.3   Passives

In section 2.2.1, we saw that the prototypical Old English passive had a nominative subject corresponding to an accusative object in the active sentence, as in the passive (20) corresponding to the active in (6a).

(20)   þonne he   bið west   gesewen, þonne tacnað   he æfen
        when   it-NOM is   westward seen   then   signifies it evening
        'when it [the evening star] is seen in the west, it signifies evening'
                                                                    (*Bo* 39.135.32)

Passives of this type continue throughout the Middle English period (though, to be precise, the changes in the case system meant that the active sentence would no longer have an object marked accusative, since the accusative and dative had coalesced in the new category of objective case). The Middle English pair in (21)–(22) illustrates the simple active–passive alternation.

(21)   Sei þou ever þemperour?
        saw you ever the-emperor-OBJ
        'Did you ever see the emperor?'   (*WPal.* 276)

(22)   Nass   he   næfre seʒhenn her þurrh erþliʒ flæshess eʒhe
        not-was he-NOM never seen   here through earthly flesh-GEN eye
        'He was never seen here by the eyes of mortals'   (*Orm.* 19425)

But in addition to this simple type, two new types of passives began to appear in the Middle English period: the prepositional passive and the recipient passive, as illustrated in (23) and (24) respectively (see 3.5.2 and chapter 8 for a third new type, the passive infinitive preceded by *to*).

(23)   þis maiden . . . feld also bi her þi/   þat sche was yleyen bi
        this maiden   felt also by her thigh that she was lain   by
        'this girl felt by her thigh that she had been lain with.'
                                              (*Arth. & M.* 849; Denison 1993: 125)

(24)   whan he was gyvyn the gre   be my lorde kynge Arthure
        when he was given the prize by my lord king Arthur
        'when he was given the prize by my lord King Arthur'
                                        (Malory *Works* 699.19; Denison 1993: 111)

In (23), the subject corresponds to the object of a preposition in the active sentence (*lie by someone*), while in (24) the subject corresponds to the indirect object of an active sentence (*give someone the prize*). In the surviving Old English material, such passives do not occur.

Nor were these passives frequent in early Middle English. Denison (1985) examines all presumed early examples of the prepositional passive and observes that its spread appears to have followed a pattern of lexical diffusion, with a few sporadic examples dating from the thirteenth century but a greater number (of tokens and of verb–preposition types) appearing only after 1300. Moreover, the early examples tend to be of combinations of verb and preposition that semantically form a close unit, such as *lie by* 'sleep with' and *set of/let of/tell of* 'regard'. In such cases, it could be said that the following NP is in a way the direct object of the unit verb + preposition, and hence eligible for passivization, very much as in the pair in (21)–(22).

The rise of the prepositional passive is therefore not to be regarded as an automatic structural consequence of the changes in the case system, which resulted in prepositions always being followed by objective case, instead of either dative or accusative as in Old English. The development of objective case seems to have been a necessary condition for prepositional passives to develop, but not a sufficient one (compare also Modern Dutch, which has a case system like that of Middle English, but no prepositional passive).

The recipient passive, as in (24), appears on the scene somewhat later than the prepositional passive. Although there are some examples from the thirteenth and fourteenth centuries that could be interpreted as recipient passives, the first unambiguous examples are from about 1375, and they are not frequent even in the fifteenth century. This means that the disappearance of case distinctions cannot have been the direct cause of the rise of the recipient passive either, since there is a time lag of some 200 years. In a comprehensive study of this topic, Allen (1995) suggests that the recipient passive became structurally available around 1375 as a result of the fixing of word order in active ditransitives. Before that time, both [V–THEME–RECIPIENT], as in (9), and [V–RECIPIENT–THEME], as in (25), had been possible.

(25)   There the kyng graunted syr Ector   grete rewardys
        there the king granted sir Hector-OBJ great rewards-OBJ
        'There the king granted Hector great rewards'   (Malory *Works* 11.9)

When only the order of (25) remained, Allen suggests, the immediately post-verbal RECIPIENT NP came to be analysed as the direct object, and could therefore become the nominative subject of a corresponding passive. Another possibility might be that this change is related to the loss of Verb-Second as discussed in chapter 4. With the loss of this operation, a fronted dative could be reinterpreted as nominative, since the default first constituent position now became the nominative subject position, as suggested by van Kemenade (1998).

   In addition to its prototypical passive, Old English also had a passive construction in which there was no nominative subject, since the corresponding active sentence lacked an accusative object. Examples were given in section 2.2.1; we repeat one of them in (26).

(26)   Ac ðæm   mæg beon suiðe hraðe geholpen from his lareowe
        but him-DAT can be   very quickly helped by   his teacher
        'But he can be helped very quickly by his teacher'
                                            (*CP* 33.225.22; Denison 1993: 104)

As shown in example (6b), the verb *helpan* took a dative object in Old English, and this dative was retained under passivization. However, as shown in (7b), the object came to be marked with objective case in Middle English, and could therefore participate in the prototypical passive, as it does in (27).

(27)   Ne hadde he ben holpen by the steede of bras
        not had   he been helped by the horse of brass
        'If he had not been helped by the brass horse'
                                            (Chaucer *Squire* 666; Denison 1993: 105)

3.3   Word order

3.3.1   *Word order within the NP*

   The order of elements within the NP in Middle English does not differ greatly from that of Old English, nor indeed from that of present-day English. With regard to the determiner system, there are only some minor differences in terms of combinability, in the sense that some forms could precede the determiner that could not do so in Old English (e.g. *many* in (28)), or cannot do so any more in present-day English (e.g. *each* in (29)).

(28)   Ich aue hy go mani amyle
         I   have gone many a-mile
         'I have travelled many a mile'   (*King Horn* (Ld) 66.1215)

(29)   þurh out   vch   a toune
         throughout each a town
         'throughout every town'   (*King Horn* (Hrl) 12.218)

These small differences have not so far inspired any interesting theoretical work, perhaps because of their smallness, but perhaps also because there has long been no theoretical framework making very precise claims about NP-internal positions. It is possible that the so-called 'DP-hypothesis', which takes the determiner to be the head of what we are calling NP, will lead to fruitful work in this area.

Attributive adjectives in Middle English were usually in prenominal position, though – as in present-day English (see Ferris (1993)) – they sometimes followed the noun. The latter option was not unusual (especially in poetry) with single adjectives borrowed from French, as in (30), and with adjectives forming a longer phrase, for example when there were two coordinated adjectives, as in (31).

(30)   schame eternal schulde be my mede
         shame eternal should be my reward
         'eternal shame would be my reward'   (Lydgate *Troy Book* 1.2476)

(31)   þise byeþ gaueleres kueade and uoule
         these are usurers   evil   and foul
         'These are foul and evil usurers'   (*Ayenb*. 35.14)

It was also possible for one adjective to precede and one to follow the head noun, as in (32).

(32)   King Pandyones fayre doughter dere
         king Pandion's fair daughter dear
         'King Pandion's beautiful beloved daughter'   (Chaucer *Legend* 2247)

From the thirteenth century on, the second adjective was sometimes preceded by *and*. It could then be preceded by a determiner, as in example (33).

(33)   A trewe swynkere and a good was he
         a true labourer and a good was he
         'He was a good and faithful labourer'   (Chaucer *Gen. Prol.* 531)

In present-day English, the prop-word *one* would be needed in this construction, since only generic and/or abstract adjectives like *the poor* and *the oriental* can now occur without a nominal head. In early Middle English, there was still more freedom in this respect, but towards the end of the period such 'nominalizations' became lexically and syntactically restricted.

NPs containing a title of the form X (of) Y in the genitive often showed splitting, with X's preceding the head noun and (of) Y following it, as in (34) and (35).

(34)   þuruh   Iulianes heste   ðe amperur
        through Julian's command the emperor
        'by the command of Julian the Emperor'   (*Ancr.* (Nero) 109.11)

(35)   Philippes sone of Macidoyne he was
        Philip's son of Macedon   he was
        'He was Philip of Macedon's son'   (Chaucer *Monk* 2656)

The disappearance of this splitting option is probably due to the development of the group genitive (*Julian the emperor's, Philip of Macedon's*), which is first attested in the late fourteenth century. (36) is an example from Chaucer.

(36)   The grete god of Loves name
        'The great god of love's name'   (Chaucer *House of Fame* 1489)

Another Middle English genitive construction, first attested in the thirteenth century, has not the affix -*s* but the form *(h)is* written as a separate word. An example is (37).

(37)   Of seth, ðe was adam is sune
        'Of Seth, who was Adam's son'   (*Gen&Ex* 493)

Allen (1997) provides data and discussion of these two innovations. She links the origin of the group genitive with the generalization of the genitive -*s* ending to all nouns (see 3.2.1 above), and presents several arguments for interpreting the construction in (37) as a merely orthographical variant of the ordinary genitive.

3.3.2   Within the clause

Unlike the order of NP constituents, the order of clausal constituents has undergone major changes in the history of English, and their effects are particularly noticeable in the Middle English period. Since several of the changes are discussed in detail in later chapters, we present only a brief outline of this important topic here.

One aspect of word order that changed in Middle English was the relative positioning of direct object and verb. Whereas in Old English, the order object–verb was very frequent, in particular in subordinate clauses and when the object was a pronoun (see section 2.3.2), in Middle English this order became gradually less common, and ceased to show a correlation with clause type. In Chaucer's language, it was still reasonably well represented, but by 1450, object–verb order was found in no more than 1 per cent (in prose) to 6 per cent (in verse) of all possible cases. (38) contains an instance of object–verb order from a prose text written around 1430.

(38)   &   many tymes of þe mete sche seyd many good wordys as God
        and many times of the food she said many good words as God
        wold hem   puttyn in hir mende
        would them put   in her mind
        'and many times she said many good words about the food, as God would
        put them in her mind'   (MKempe 26.1)

There is a voluminous literature on the shift from object–verb to verb–object in English, which has focussed in particular on the causes of this development. However, some of this literature is based on the assumption that the shift was completed by 1200. The data show that the change was more gradual and took the whole of the Middle English period to come to completion; in chapter 5, we examine the change in detail.

Another, probably related, Middle English change affected the position of particles relative to the verb. We saw in section 2.3.2 that such elements were also often preverbal in Old English. In the course of the Middle English period they gradually came to be restricted to postverbal position, as in (39). In this case too, however, the older order continued to be used every now and then until the end of the Middle English period, as shown by (40). The development of phrasal verbs is considered in detail in chapter 6.

(39)   Trystrames sterte   up, and kylde that mon
        Tristram   started up and killed that man
        'Tristram suddenly came up and killed that man'   (Malory Works 413.2)

(40)   sir Raynold gan   up sterte with his hede all blody
        Sir Raynold began up start with his head all bloody
        'With his head all bloody, Sir Raynold suddenly moved up'
                                                               (Malory Works 276.25)

A further Middle English change involving verb position is the decline of the so-called 'Verb-Second' rule. As discussed in section 2.3.2, many Old English main clauses had the finite verb in second position, following a first element which could have a variety of functions (subject, direct object, adverbial adjunct, etc.). In this respect, Old English shows similarities with most of the modern Germanic languages. However, in those languages, the Verb-Second rule applies virtually without exception in every main clause. The discussion in chapter 2 shows that the situation in Old English was rather more complex. This will be treated in detail in chapter 4.

Verb-Second rapidly declined in the course of the last part of the fourteenth and in the fifteenth century, and saw a revival in the literary language in the sixteenth century. An example from Caxton's writings is given in (41).

(41)   Thenne sayd they to the x   men of armes
           then   said they to the ten men of arms
           'Then they said to the ten men of arms'   (Caxton *Paris&Vienne* 5.1)

It is worth emphasizing that the phenomenon of Verb-Second is in principle independent of the order of object and verb. This can be seen very clearly by comparing Modern Dutch with Modern Swedish. Both languages regularly have Verb-Second in main clauses, but Modern Dutch has object–verb order, while Modern Swedish has verb–object order. Therefore, a Dutch object will precede any verb which is not in second position, while a Swedish object follows it; examples are given in (42) and (43).

(42)   Vanavond wil ik kreeft eten. (Dutch)
           tonight   will I lobster eat
           'Tonight I want to eat lobster.'

(43)   I kväll vill jag äta hummer. (Swedish)
           tonight will I   eat lobster

In English, object–verb order declined earlier than Verb-Second: in late Middle English, examples like (38) are much rarer than (41).

Each of the changes in word order briefly described here is dealt with in greater detail in a later chapter. The development of Verb-Second is the topic of chapter 4, the changes in the order of object and verb are discussed in chapter 5, and particle position is dealt with in chapter 6.

3.4   Clause types

3.4.1   Question formation

This section can be brief because not much changed in this area compared with the Old English period. Concerning the two main types of question (yes–no questions and wh-questions), inversion of subject and finite verb was still the rule in main clauses in both, as shown in (44) and (45).

(44)   Woot ye nat where ther   stant   a litel toun . . .?
           know you not where there stands a little town
           'Don't you know where this little town is . . .'   (Chaucer *Manciple* 1)

(45)   Why make ye   youreself for to be lyk a fool?
        why make you yourself for to be like a fool
        'Why do you allow yourself to behave like a fool?'   (Chaucer *Melibee* 980)

As in present-day English, inversion was absent if the wh-word was itself the
subject. Although *do* is found (albeit rarely) in questions in Middle English,
such constructions should probably not be interpreted as containing the
empty operator *do* (cf. Ellegård 1953: 161–2, who shows that interrogative *do*
did not occur before 1400); rather, they were the questioned counterpart of a
clause already containing *do*. The first attested example is from Chaucer:

(46)   Fader, why do ye wepe?
        'Father, why do you weep?'   (Chaucer *Monk* 2432)

Only in the early Modern English period was there a sharp rise in the occurrence of *do* in interrogative (and negative) sentences.

    In Old English, as we have seen, *hwæþer* could be used in simple interroga-
tive clauses followed by normal, i.e. non-inverted, word order. Examples of
this seem to be extremely rare in Middle English; one instance is (47), found
in Chaucer's *Troilus and Criseyde* in a highly rhetorical passage. The verb was
usually in the subjunctive, as in Old English, because the construction was
mostly used as an expression of doubt.

(47)   'O Troilus, what dostow now?' she seyde./ 'Lord! wheyther thow yet
        o Troilus what do you now   she said   lord   whether you yet
        thenke [subjunct.] upon Criseyde?'
        think   on   Criseyde?
        '"O Troilus, what will you do now?" she said. "Will you still be thinking of
        Criseyde?"'   (Chaucer *Troilus* V 734–35)

Far more frequent was a construction with *whether* followed by inverted word
order and the indicative mood in so-called alternative questions like (48).

(48)   Wheither seistow this in ernest   or in pley?
        whether   say you this in earnest or in play
        'Are you saying this in earnest or in jest?'   (Chaucer *Knight* 1125)

In Old English, when a prepositional object was wh-moved, it was the rule for
the preposition to move along with the object (so-called 'pied-piping'). This
began to change in early Middle English. In the thirteenth century *Brut*, we
see the first sporadic instances of preposition stranding in wh-questions:

(49)   nuste   nan kempe, whæm he sculde slæn on
        not-knew no soldier whom he should hit on
        'No soldier knew whom he should strike at' (Layamon *Brut*(Clg) 13718–19)

Around the same time, preposition stranding also began to occur in wh-
relatives, topicalized constructions and passives (see section 3.2.3). It is quite

possible that preposition stranding in questions spread via the new relative constructions with wh-forms (see below), which most likely developed from Old English free relatives (OE (*swa*)*hwa*(*swa*), used in the sense of 'whoever', 'he who', as in *Who once steals is always a thief*). Preposition stranding with free relatives was already possible in Old English under certain conditions. Note that the subordinate clause in (49) could still, at a pinch, be interpreted as a free relative.

Subordinate interrogative clauses are found in the same functions that complement clauses can occur in, i.e. as a complement to a noun phrase, as object of a verbal or adjectival predicate and as subject. The usual subordinator in yes–no and alternative questions is *whe(the)r*, as in (50), but *(ȝ)if* is also found, as in (51).

(50)   I noot   wher   she be womman or goddesse
        I not-know whether she be woman   or goddess
        'I am not sure whether she is a woman or a goddess' (Chaucer *Knight* 1101)

(51)   She frayneth and she preyeth pitously . . . / To telle hir if hir child
        she asks   and she prays   pitifully   to tell her if her child
        wente oght   forby.
        went   ought past
        'She was asking and beseeching pitifully . . . to tell her whether her child
        possibly passed by.'   (Chaucer *Prioress* 600)

As a rule the subjunctive – or an appropriate auxiliary – is employed in such clauses when there is an element of doubt or uncertainty.

Dependent wh-questions were introduced by a wh-element just as in simple clauses; this element could be an adverb (*where*, *how*, *why*, etc.) or an interrogative pronoun (independent or used attributively), as in (52).

(52)   But sikerly   she nyste   who was who
        but certainly she not-knew who was who
        'But indeed she didn't know who was who'   (Chaucer *Reeve* 4300)

The mood in these clauses was as a rule the indicative.

3.4.2   *Negation*

Between the Old and the Middle English periods some important changes took place in the system of sentence negation. In Old English the negative adverb was *ne*, which could be combined, as we have seen, with other negative elements such as *nan*, *naþing*, *næfre* 'none', 'nothing', 'never'. It was possible to combine *ne* with *na* 'never' or *naht* (from *nawiht* 'nothing'). The combination with *naht* often had the effect of an emphatic negation ('by no means, not at all'). *Na* and *naht* could immediately precede *ne* in clauses in which the verb was not fronted (mostly subordinate) or the combination *ne +* verb could be fronted to the left of *na, naht.*

In early Middle English the emphatic negative *ne . . . naht* (*na* disappeared here quite quickly) began to be used more and more frequently and can no longer be considered to be truly emphatic. Jack (1978a: 300) shows that in the earliest preserved Middle English text, the *Peterborough Chronicle*, the percentage of *ne . . . naht* is still small (about seventeen per cent) but that in the *Ancrene Wisse* the number has risen steeply to about forty per cent. In early Middle English *naht* had also acquired a fixed position; it now, practically without exception, followed *ne* and was placed after the finite verb. In the course of the Middle English period, *ne . . . naht* (also *. . . nat, nought, not*, etc.) became the regular negator. When *ne* was not supported by *naht*, it was usually supported by another negative element such as *noon* or *never*. In other words, unsupported *ne* became the exception rather than the rule. Because *ne* was now normally supported by another negative, it could be dropped (cf. the similar dropping of *ne* in the combination *ne . . . pas* in present-day colloquial French). This indeed was the situation in late Middle English: *nat/not* had become the common negator (placed after the finite verb, unlike *ne*), while *ne* and *ne . . . not* had become infrequent (cf. Jack 1978b).

However, there are some texts of the South-Eastern region (notably Chaucer's prose and contemporary London documents; cf. Jack 1978b) where *ne . . . not* and unsupported *ne* were still regularly used. At first sight it looks as if *ne* and *ne . . . not* were on the whole simply alternatives except that *ne . . . not* was more frequently found when *ne* could be cliticized to an auxiliary, especially *is*, in cases like (53), while *not* alone was used after the conjunction *ne* 'nor', presumably in order to avoid the rather awkward *ne ne*.

(53)   Ther nys   nat oon kan war   by other be.
        there not-is not one can aware by other be
        'There is not a single person who learns from the mistakes of others.'
                                                    (Chaucer *Troilus* I 203)

The distribution of both *ne* and *ne . . . not*, however, is significant and usage of *ne* correlated with its use in early Middle English. *Ne* was the rule with other negatives such as *non* and *never* (we could call this 'supported *ne*' or negative concord). Unsupported *ne* is found with the (negative) adverb *but* and in complement clauses following a negative or interrogative clause, as in (54).

(54)   For ther nys   no creature so good that hym ne   wanteth somwhat
        for there not-is no creature so good that him not lacks   somewhat
        of the perfeccioun of God.
        of the perfection   of God
        'No one is so good that he doesn't lack something compared to the
        perfection of God'   (Chaucer *Melibee* 1080)

The use of unsupported *ne* here could be seen as a case of negative concord due to the negative character of the main clause.

Other types of clauses in which unsupported *ne* occurred are rather similar: it was found in inherently negative situations, i.e. contexts which are semantically negative and therefore may dispense with an explicit negator (for a list of these see Klima 1964). Examples are comparative clauses as in (55), conditional clauses as in (56), after verbs like *douten, denyen, forsaken*, etc., and after *lest*, as in (57).

(55)   And thanne al the derknesse of his mysknowynge shall [schewen]
        and then   all the darkness   of his mis-knowing   shall show
        more evydently to the sighte of his undirstondynge *then* the sonne
        more evidently to the sight   of his understanding   than   the sun
        ne semeth to the sighte withoute-forth.
        not   seems   to the sight   on-the-outside
        'And then all the darkness of his wrong thoughts shall show up more
        clearly to his mental sight than the clarity of the sun does to his outward
        sight.'   (Chaucer *Boece* III m.11, 24)

(56)   *If* God *ne* kepe the citee, in ydel waketh he that it kepeth
        if God not keep the city, in idelness watches he that it keeps
        'If God may not guard the city, he who does guard it, keeps watch in vain'
                                                   (Chaucer *Melibee* 1304)

(57)   . . . ther bihoveth greet corage   agains Accidie, *lest* that it *ne*
               there behoves   great courage against Sloth   lest   that it not
        swolwe the soule by the synne of sorwe, or destroye it by wanhope.
        swallow the soul   by the sin   of sorrow or destroy   it by despair
        'great strength is needed against Sloth lest it swallows up the soul through
        the sin of sorrow or destroys it through despair.'   (Chaucer *Parson* 731)

In all these instances, then, the presence of unsupported *ne* can be explained as a case of negative concord, i.e. *ne* is induced by the (implicit) negative already present. The situation was thus similar to the use of supported *ne* in Old English and in Middle English in combination with another negative element in the clause.

The disappearance of *ne* precipitates the erosion of multiple negation. The next step in this process was not taken until the Modern English period, i.e. it was still normal in Middle English, when two or more indefinite pronouns or adverbs were present, for all of these to be negative rather than for the negative element to be attached only to the first indefinite in the clause (or expressed by *not* when present). Thus, Chaucer still wrote,

(58)   But *nevere* gronte he at *no* strook but oon
        'But never groaned he at no blow but one'   (Chaucer *Monk* 2709)

where present-day English would prefer 'but he *never* groaned at *any* of the blows except one'. In Middle English the use of *any*, etc. was still confined to implicit negative contexts (as defined above); it did not as a rule occur in explicit negative clauses. Therefore, where present-day English has *not . . . any-thing*, *not . . . ever*, etc., Middle English normally (and this usage persisted into the seventeenth and eighteenth centuries) had *nothing*, *never*, etc., as in (59).

(59)   He was despeyred; no thyng dorste he seye
        'He was in despair; nothing dared he say'   (Chaucer *Franklin* 943)

3.5   Subordinate clauses

Traditionally a distinction is made between main and subordinate clauses. As shown in chapter 2, Old English had several elements (e.g. *þa*, *þonne*, *swa*) that could function either as an adverb or as a subordinating conjunction, so that often it was only the word order (but sometimes also the use of the unambiguously subordinating particle *þe*) that would signal whether a specific clause was main or subordinate. In early Middle English some of the Old English correlative constructions like *þa . . . þa*, *þonne . . . þonne*, 'then . . . when' and *swa . . . swa*, 'so . . . so' survived, but this was rapidly replaced by a system in which conjunctions were formally distinct from adverbs and word order no longer played an important role in signalling whether a clause was main or subordinate. Thus in early texts, we can still come across examples like (60) and (61).

(60)   & Ðat oþer dei *þa*   he lai an slep in scip, *þa*   þestrede þe
        and the other day when he lay in sleep in ship then darkened the
        dæi ouer al landes
        day over all lands
        'and the next day, when he lay asleep in the boat, (then) it became dark
        everywhere in the country'   (*ChronE*(Plummer) 1135.2)

(61)   *þanne* he com *þenne* he   were bliþe
        when   he came then   they were glad
        'When he came, they were glad'   (*Havelok* 778)

In (60), word order still plays a role, since there is inversion of subject and verb in the main clause but not in the subordinate clause. In (61), there is no such difference, although the conjunction and correlative adverb have the same form. In later texts, however, the correlative adverb was often dropped or one of the two conjunctives was replaced by one different in form. In Chaucer, for example, *tho* (from Old English *þa*) no longer functioned as a conjunction, but only as an adverb; the same is true, with one exception, for *þonne*/*þenne*. Normally, Chaucer used *whan (that)* (from Old English *hwænne*, an interrogative adverb) as the conjunction, with or without a correlative in the main clause. (62) exemplifies the former possibility.

(62)   Thanne rekke I noght, whan I have lost my lyf
         then   care I not   when I have lost my life
         'Then I don't mind if I lose my life'   (Chaucer *Knight* 2257)

Likewise, *though/þeih/þah* could still function as either an adverb or a conjunction in early texts. An example of the former is given in (63).

(63)   Ich wat   þah   to soþe þ[et] ich schal bituhen ham neomen
         I   know though to truth that I   shall between them take
         deaðes wunde.
         death's wound
         'Yet I know for certain that amongst them I shall receive death's wound.'
                                                           (*Ancr.*(Corp-C) 105b.11)

But in Chaucer *though* had become almost exclusively a conjunction.

The development concerning the marking of subordinate clauses seems fairly clear then: in Old English subordination was strongly syntactically marked (by differences in word order and also by the use of the subjunctive), whereas their marking in Middle English, where the word order of all types of clauses developed towards strict SVO order and the subjunctive form fell out of use, is mainly lexical. The conjunctive phrases used in Old English (*for þæm þe, æfter þæm þe, ær þæm þe*, etc.) became fossilized, their form was often reduced and their applicability was narrowed down (*for (that), after (that), ere (that)*) (see further also section 3.5.3).

As was said above, formally it is usually not difficult in Middle English to distinguish main from subordinate clauses. We also find coordinate clauses in Middle English which are conceptually subordinate, where modern English could only use the subordinate clause form. This also applies to Old English. In the medieval period, the written language often presented ideas paratactically where written present-day English would use subordination (hypotaxis). In Old and Middle English the written language appears to have been closer to the spoken language, which has always made heavier use of parataxis than of hypotaxis (cf. Phillipps 1966; Leith 1983: 112). It is only at the end of the Middle English period, with the development of a written standard, that the written language began to make more extensive use of complex structures, under the influence of both French and Latin prose styles (cf. Fisher 1977). Here follow some instances of such paratactic structures, where today we would prefer hypotactic ones:

(64)   and ek   wondit   so,/ *And* in his syd ware brokyne Ribys two.
         and also wounded so   and in his side were broken ribs   two
         'and also so wounded *that* two ribs were broken in his side.'
                                                           (*Lanc. of the Laik* 2729)

(65)   Now, or   I fynde a man thus trewe and stable,/ *And* wol for love
        now   before I find   a man thus true   and stable   and will for love
        his deth so frely take,/ I preye God let oure hedes nevere ake!
        his death so freely take   I pray God let our   heads never   ache
        'Now, before I find a man so true and loyal, *who* will so nobly accept death
        out of love!'   (Chaucer *Legend* 703)

Another consequence of the proximity of written and spoken language was
the high frequency of so-called anacolutha, i.e. sentences like (66) which are
'illogically' constructed from a purely formal point of view.

(66)   The reule of Seint Maure   or of Seint Beneit – / By cause that it was
        the rule of St   Maurus or of St   Benedict because   it was
        old and somdel   streit/ This ilke Monk leet olde thynges pace . . .
        old and somewhat strict this same monk let old   things pass
                                                     (Chaucer *Gen. Prol.* 173)

In this example the first line seems intended to function as the syntactic object
of *leet pace*, but it has been left dangling since a new object, *olde thynges*, is
introduced later.

    Likewise, we often come across constructions that contain elements which
look pleonastic in modern written English, such as (67).

(67)   Thanne dame Prudence, whan that she saugh how that hir
        then   Lady Prudence when that she saw   how that her
        housbonde shoop   hym   for to wreken hym   on his foes and to
        husband   prepared himself for to avenge himself on his foes and to
        bigynne werre, *she* in ful humble wise,   whan she saugh hir tyme,
        begin   war   she in ful humbe manner when she saw   her time
        seide . . .
        said
        'Then lady Prudence, when she saw how her husband prepared himself to
        take revenge on his foes and to start a fight, (she) very humbly, when she
        saw an opportunity, said . . .'   (Chaucer *Melibee* 1050)

We have referred several times now to the use of the subordinator *þe* in Old
English, which was a marker of relative clauses and of adverbial clauses (the
latter usually in combinations like *for þæm þe* 'because' and *mid þy þe* 'when').
In Middle English, *þe* came to be replaced by *þat*, which was already in use to
mark complement clauses in Old English. It is not entirely clear how this
development took place. Any explanation depends heavily on the syntactic
status one assigns to *þe* in Old English. According to some linguists (e.g.
Geoghegan 1975), *þe* must be interpreted as a marker of subordination, and
not as a relative particle, as for instance Allen (1977) has suggested, following
most traditional accounts (for a more detailed consideration of the various
arguments involved see Fischer 1992a: 293 ff.). The possible development may

have been as follows: (i) due to the loss of case forms and grammatical gender, the neuter relative pronoun *þæt* came to be the most frequently used form;[2] (ii) *þæt* came to be used as an invariant form, replacing all other case forms, i.e. like the particle *þe* in Old English; (iii) *þæt* replaced *þe* because (a) *þe* was phonologically rather weak, (b) *þe* also functioned as the new generalized definite article, (c) *þæt* was already used as a complementizer in other subordinate clauses. The replacement of *þe* by *þæt* may also explain why preposition stranding, which in Old English was only usual with *þe* relatives, spread to *þat* relatives in Middle English. Let us now turn to the relative clauses themselves and the changes that have occurred in them.

3.5.1   *Relative clauses*

In Middle English, the Old English relative system collapsed, due to the gradual loss of the particle *þe* and the replacement of the paradigm *se, seo, þæt* by indeclinable *that* (in the earliest period in the South, also by *þe*). In some early Middle English texts, remnants of the *se, seo, þæt* system are still found, often with analogical *þ*- rather than *s*-, but these are regular only in rewritings of Old English texts (cf. Allen 1977: 197 ff.), and are mainly Southern. In the Northern *Ormulum*, for instance, *þat* was the usual form. From the North, *þat* rapidly spread to the other dialects, and in the thirteenth century *þat* (also *þet*) was the rule everywhere. The only exceptions were South-Western and especially West Midlands texts, where Old English forms were preserved much longer due to the fact that the influence of the West Saxon 'Schriftsprache' was still strong in some of the scriptoria.

All this means that in the thirteenth century *that* stood practically alone as a relativizer. It was used in restrictive as well as non-restrictive clauses, with animate as well as inanimate antecedents. *That* was also used in Old English and early Middle English when the antecedent was a clause (cf. Mustanoja 1960: 190; this usage can still be found in early Modern English) but in this usage it was gradually replaced in early Middle English by *what* and in late Middle English by *which*. This was presumably part of the development in which *that* became confined to restrictive clauses. The beginnings of this latter development can be seen in Middle English, but it took place mainly in later periods (cf. Mustanoja 1960: 196–7).

---

[2] There are probably various reasons why the neuter *þæt* form became used most frequently. All non-human antecedents could take *þæt*, whereas human antecedents still had a choice between the masculine and feminine forms. Also *þæt* was phonologically more distinctive than the masculine and feminine forms and the alternative *þe* (see iii).

The use of wh-relatives (*whom, whose, what, (the) which (that)*) dates, it is true, from the beginning of the Middle English period, but they were very rare everywhere in the twelfth century, and rare enough in the thirteenth. *Which* was at first highly infrequent; *whom* and *whose* less so. They were more often found in non-restrictive clauses. *Whom* and *which* were generally preceded by a preposition (for this restriction in their use see also below). *Which* was found with both animate and inanimate antecedents, *whom* and *whose* mainly with animate ones. *Which* began to supplant *that* only in the fifteenth century. In the fourteenth century *that* remained the usual relative, especially in poetry; in the more formal prose *which* was somewhat more current. Chaucer, for instance, still used *that* in seventy-five per cent of all cases; in Caxton the use of *that* had been reduced to fifty per cent (see Mustanoja 1960: 197 ff.).

In Old English the wh-pronouns (*hwa* (neuter *hwæt*), *hwilc*) were not used as relative pronouns. The development of an interrogative pronoun into a relative pronoun is not an unusual process; it is well attested in a number of other Germanic and Romance languages. A point of contact is the use of interrogative pronouns in indirect questions such as *She asked who had kissed him*. Here the nature of *who* is still clearly interrogative because of the verb *ask*. But in sentences such as *He knew who did it* or *He wanted to know who did it*, the function of *who* comes very close to a so-called free relative (also called independent or headless relative), meaning 'the one who', or to a generalizing relative, meaning 'whoever'. In Old English the interrogative pronouns *hwa, hwæt* and *hwilc* – often accompanied by *swa*, which was lost in Middle English – were indeed used as free relatives next to the more usual *se þe*.

Another pattern which may have influenced the eventual development of wh-pronouns into relatives is the one in which the interrogative pronoun occurs in a reduced clause. (68) shows an example in Old English.

(68)   Ne meahte hire Iudas . . . / sweotole gecyþan   be   ðam
        nor could her Judas   clearly make-known about the
        sigebeame,/ on hwylcne se hælend ahafen   wære
        victory-tree on which   the saviour up-raised were
        'Nor could Judas tell her clearly about the victorious tree, [tell her] on
        which [tree] the Saviour was raised up'   (*El* 859)

Here the clause starting with *on hwylcne* appears to be the complement of the verb *gecyþan*, but this verb is not repeated. This makes another interpretation possible: the preceding NP, *sigebeame*, could be interpreted as an antecedent of *hwylcne*.

For the wh-word to develop from an independent or generalizing relative into a strict relative also requires the presence of an antecedent. The following example from Middle English shows how this could have come about:

(69)   hwam mai he luue treweliche hwa ne luues his broðer.
        'whom can he love truly, who(ever) does not love his brother.'

(Wooing Lord 275.18)

Here he can be interpreted as the antecedent of who, since it precedes this generalising or free relative.

The wh-form did not become frequent until the fourteenth century. The earliest instances are found mainly in non-restrictive clauses (which may point to the important influence of ambiguities such as presented in (68)–(69) above, which all concern non-restrictive cases), and preceded by a preposition. It seems clear that the inability of the relative particle that to take a preposition in front of it (just like its sister-particle þe in Old English) contributed to the rise of the new wh-pronoun, which did allow a preposition. This may be one of the reasons why the non-prepositional, nominative form who lagged behind in its development into a strict relative pronoun. Another possible reason may be the fact that the generalizing relative was used far more often in subject position than in any other function, so that who was still too strongly generalizing in sense to become a mere relativizer. For more information on this lag of who, see Meier (1967) and Rydén (1983).

Changes also occurred in the two minor types of relative clauses discussed in section 2.5.1. As in Old English, the adverbial relative ther(e) (from þær) was used after an antecedent with locative meaning:

(70)   But I cam   in þere   &   in othere places þere   I wolde . . .
        but I came in there and in other   places there I would
        'But I came in there and in other places where I wanted . . .'

(Mandev. 53.28)

But with the replacement of the demonstrative relative pronoun by the interrogative one, there was gradually also ousted by where. There was still the common form in early Middle English, while in late Middle English both there and where were common. The last instances of there date from the sixteenth century.

Zero relatives, as in (71) and (72), were most common in subject position in Middle English, as was the case in Old English.

(71)   Adam ben king and eue quuen/ Of alle ðe   ðinge [Ø] in werlde ben.
        Adam are king and Eve queen of all   the things   in world   are
        'Adam and Eve are king and queen of all the things that are in the world.'

(Gen.& Ex. 296–7)

(72)   . . . I know no knyght in this contrey [Ø] is able to macche hym.
        '. . . I know no knight in this country [who] is able to match him.'

(Malory Works 377.35–6)

As in Old English, omission is heavily constrained. The finite verb of the relative clause is almost always a stative verb, usually the verb *to be* or a verb expressing existence in time or place. These zero-subject relative constructions therefore closely resemble the zero-type still acceptable in colloquial present-day English, which is introduced by *there is* or *it is*, as in *There is a woman wants to see you.*

In addition to zero-subject relative constructions we also begin to find in Middle English constructions in which the object relative pronoun has been left out, but these were not at all as frequent as in present-day English. The Middle English instances are interesting in that they were basically of two types. They often involved the verbs *clepen* 'call' or *callen* (cf. the use of *hatan/haten* in the zero-subject relative in Old English), as in (73).

(73)   Of Northfolk was this Reve of which I telle,/ Beside a toun [Ø] men clepen Baldeswelle.
        'From Norfolk was this Reeve I am telling you about, close to a town people call Baldeswelle'   (Chaucer *Gen. Prol.* 619)

Other examples usually contained possessive *have* or an equivalent verb, often in the idiom *by the faith I owe to God*, and were rather similar to zero-subject relatives with stative verbs; (74) is an example.

(74)   Sir, be þe faith [Ø] i haue to yow . . .   (*Cursor Mundi* 5145)

So it looks as if the earliest zero-object constructions were an extension of the (older) zero-subject constructions. It is only after the Middle English period that the object construction gained ground and began to appear with all kinds of verbs in the subordinate clause. It is possible that the rise of the zero-object relative is connected with the word order change, as e.g. Phillipps (1965) has suggested; perceptual mechanisms (cf. Bever and Langendoen 1972) may also have played a role.

A construction new in Middle English is the infinitival relative clause with a wh-form, as in (75).

(75)   She has no wight   to whom to make hir mone.
        she has no creature to whom to make her moan
        'She has no one to whom she can complain.'   (Chaucer *Man of Law* 656)

It appeared late in the period; no examples have been attested before the fourteenth century. In Old English a relative pronoun was not possible here: the *to*-infinitive by itself was used. The new construction presumably developed out of questioned infinitives, which also first appeared in Middle English but quite a bit earlier. Examples with bare infinitives, such as (76), are found in early Middle English.

(76)   ant nuste   hwet seggen.
          and not-knew what say
          'and did not know what to say.'   (*St.Kath.(1)*) (Bod) 563

Again we see here how a construction with a relative wh-pronoun could develop out of a similar use of wh-forms in indirect questions.

3.5.2   Complement clauses

Complement clauses are nominal in function. They occur as complements to a noun, an adjective or a verb, and can be both finite and non-finite. Their functions are the same as those of the NP in the higher clause, i.e. object of a verbal or adjectival predicate, in apposition to another NP, as in (77), and as a subject complement, (78).

(77)   And aske hym counseill how thou may/ Do ony thyng that may hir
          and ask   him advice   how you   may do any thing that may her
          plese
          please
          'And ask him advice how you may do one thing that may please her'
                                                                      (*RRose* 2868)

(78)   In Cipre   is the manere of lordes &   all oþere men all to eten on
          in Cyprus is the manner of lords and all other men all to eat   on
          the erthe,   for þei   make dyches in the erthe . . . And the skyll
          the ground for they make ditches in the earth   and the reason
          is *for þei   may be the more fressch* for þat lond   is meche more
          is for they may be the more fresh   for that country is much more
          hottere þan it is here.
          hotter   than it is here
          'In Cyprus it is usual for the lords and all other men to eat everything on
          the ground, for they make ditches in the earth . . . And the reason is that
          they [the food] may be the more fresh for [in] that country [it] is much
          hotter than it is here.'   (*Mandev.* 17.29)

In present-day English a clause can appear as subject NP. There were some constructions in Middle English that could also be interpreted as having subject clauses, but their occurrence was rather restricted. The relevant cases feature impersonal verbs, as in (17), or comparable adjectival expressions, as in (79).

(79)   But bet is that a wyghtes tonge reste
          'But better is that a creature's tongue rests/remains silent'
                                                    (Chaucer *Parliament* 514)

Moreover, such 'subject-clauses' in Middle English only rarely occurred in initial position and it may therefore be preferable to interpret them as complements to an adjective, as in (79), or to a noun or verb, as in (17).

A complement clause was normally introduced by *that* if it was a statement, but, as in present-day English, it was possible for *that* to be omitted. This phenomenon, however, seems to have been somewhat restricted in Middle English (but cf. Warner 1982: 169–70), as it also was in Old English. It is mainly found after *seyn*, *thinken*, *witen* and verbs with similar meanings, and performative verbs like *sweren*, etc., when the clause reports more or less directly the actual words spoken or thought.

The most frequent type of non-finite complement in Middle English was the infinitival construction. There had been many new developments within this group since the Old English period. First, there was a difference in infinitive marker: this could be zero (bare infinitive) or *to*, as in Old English, but the innovative form *for to* also appeared, and the use of *to* increased vastly. Other Middle English innovations concern the much wider use of the passive infinitive (also preceded by *to*, which is never found in Old English), the extension of constructions with a lexical subject, the introduction of the perfect infinitive, and the so-called split infinitive.

In Old English the bare infinitive was by far the most frequent of the infinitives. This situation was completely reversed in Middle English, where the *to*-infinitive became the most common form and the bare infinitive came to be restricted to an increasingly smaller number of verbs. There are several causes for this development. One may be the progressive phonological weakening of the infinitive marker *to*, which made it less meaningful, i.e. it started to grammaticalize to a 'mere' infinitive marker.[3] Secondly, it is very likely that *to* increased its territory because it became a useful sign of the infinitive form, to distinguish it from other forms of the verb. Due to the reduction and loss of inflections, the infinitival endings (*-(i)an* and *-enne* for the bare and inflected infinitive respectively) could no longer serve that purpose. The main reason, however, why the *to*-infinitive increased so drastically is that infinitival constructions began to replace finite *that*-clauses (see Manabe 1989 and especially Los

---

[3] The exact status of *to* before the infinitive in Old English is not quite clear. Although the origin of *to* is probably that of a preposition, the *to*-infinitive in Old English clearly has verbal properties (cf. e.g. Fischer 1996b, Los 1999). It seems likely that in early Middle English *to* first weakened (grammaticalized) in its purpose meaning, which among other things occasioned the rise of *for to*. On the other hand there is evidence that full grammaticalization did not take place (as it did in Dutch and German), and that *to* as it were became semantically replenished. Evidence for this can be found in the fact that *for to* disappeared again at the end of our period, that split infinitives developed from early Middle English onward, and that *to* begins to function as a marker of indirectness in the new lexical subject constructions (more about this below). For a comparison of the development of *to* in English with that of *te* and *zu* in Dutch and German respectively, see Fischer (1997a).

1998). *To*-infinitives have more in common with *that*-clauses than bare infinitives because they share with *that*-clauses a time reference independent of that of the matrix verb predicate (see also below). In other words, *to*-infinitives did not *replace* bare infinitives; rather, they became more frequent proportionally. On the whole, the bare infinitive kept the position it had in Old English, except that in cases where verbs could select both bare and *to*-infinitives, the bare infinitives were often replaced by -*ing* forms (e.g. *to begin eat* becomes *to begin eating*), while the *to*-infinitive simply remained (*to begin to eat*).

The use of *to* and zero infinitive markers in verbal complementation was syntactically not entirely free in the Middle English period, though some linguists (e.g. Ohlander 1941, Kaartinen and Mustanoja 1958) have suggested so. For the form of the infinitive, a number of parameters are of importance. First, a general one. The presence or absence of an infinitive marker depended on the grammatical function the infinitive had within the clause, as has often been pointed out (cf. Kaartinen and Mustanoja 1958, Quirk and Svartvik 1970). Thus, variation might occur when the infinitive functioned as subject or object complement, but the (*for*) *to* infinitive was the rule after nouns and adjectives (as in Old English) and in adverbial function. When there was variation, which was especially the case in the complementation of monotransitive verbs, further factors played a role, such as the '(in)directness' of the relation between matrix verb and infinitival predicates (cf. Fischer 1995, 1996b). Thus, when the matrix verb and the infinitive shared the same tense domain (i.e. the activities expressed by the two predicates took place at the same time), the bare infinitive was the rule. This is especially clear after modals and verbs of direct perception; (80) is an example.

(80)   Ther saugh I pleye jugelours
        there saw   I play jugglers
        'There I saw jugglers performing'   (Chaucer *House of Fame* 1259)

When the relation is 'indirect', i.e. when the infinitival predicate has independent time reference, the *to*-infinitive occurs. In an example like (81), the *to*-infinitive clearly refers to some possible future event which is not part of the tense domain of the matrix verb (in present-day English this difference is more commonly expressed by the -*ing* form versus the *to*-infinitive).

(81)   How that the pope . . . / Bad   hym to wedde another if hym leste
        how that the pope   asked him to marry another if him pleased
        'How the Pope asked him to marry someone else if he wanted to'
                                                          (Chaucer *Clerk* 741)

Other differences that may be signalled by the use of the *to*-infinitive vs. the bare infinitive are indirect vs. direct perception, indirect vs. direct causation and factuality vs. non-factuality (for more details and examples see Fischer 1995, 1996b, 1997b).

Finally, the physical distance between a matrix verb and its infinitive may also function as a factor in the choice between bare and *to*-infinitive; that is, infinitive marking by *to* seems to be preferred when the infinitive is separated from the matrix verb. This is particularly noticeable with infinitives used in coordination. In that case even modals may be followed by a second, coordinated *to*-infinitive, as shown in (82).

(82)   Graitli   taght   he him þe gin/   How he suld   at   þe wif
promptly taught he him the scheme how he should with the woman
be-gin,/ And thorw   þe wijf   to wyn þe man
begin   and through the woman to win the husband
'Promptly he [the devil] taught him [the adder] the scheme, how he should
begin with the woman and through the woman [to] win over the husband'
(*Cursor Mundi*(Vsp) 741)

It is likely, however, (cf. Fischer 1992a: 323 f.) that even here the use of *to* is functional and meaningful. Finally, Warner (1982: 131–3) suggests that the fronting of some element within the infinitival construction may lead to increased infinitive marking (i.e. the use of *to*) for perceptual reasons.

A most interesting development in Middle English is the extension of infinitival constructions with a lexical subject (the so-called AcI, accusative with infinitive constructions), rather than the more usual PRO subject. We will look at this in more detail in chapter 7; at this point we will only give a brief sketch of the situation. In Old English, the only verbs that could take an infinitive with a lexically filled subject were causatives and verbs of physical perception. In Middle English, we see this possibility widening to certain object-control verbs (like *command, require, warn*, as shown in (83)) and later also to the so-called *verba declarandi et cogitandi* (e.g. *expect, believe*, etc., as in (84)). Thus the following clause types were new in Middle English:

(83)   And whan he had used hit he ded of hys crowne and commaunded the
crowne to be sett on the awter
'And when he had used it he took off his crown and commanded the crown
to be placed upon the altar'   (Malory *Works* 908.11)

(84)   . . . that namyth hym-self Paston and affermith hym vntrewely to be my
cousyn
'. . . who names himself Paston and affirms himself wrongfully to be my
cousin'   (*Paston Letters* 3.4)

Another new development is the reanalysis of a benefactive dative as an infinitival subject (later followed by the reanalysis of a benefactive *for* NP, whereby the preposition *for* became a complementizer), as in (85).

(85)   for hyt ys the custom of my contrey a knyght allweyes to kepe hys
            for it is the custom of my country a knight always   to keep his
            wepyn with hym
            weapon with him
            'for it is the custom in my country that a knight always keeps his weapon
            with him'   (Malory *Works* 83.25)

In (85) the NP *a knyght* functions more as the subject of the infinitive than as
an NP dependent on *custom*. It is likely that the developments shown in
(83)–(85) were connected, and that the spread of the passive infinitive also
played a role here, in that it enabled the AcI to spread from direct perception
verbs and causatives, to 'persuade' type verbs, as in (83), and later also to
'expect' verbs, as in (84). For more details we refer the reader to chapter 7.

  The spread of the passive infinitive may, in turn, be related to the change in
word order whereby objects ceased to occur in preverbal position. It is noteworthy, for instance, that a common Old English construction, the type *hit is
to donne*, as in (86),

(86)   Eac is ðeos bisen   to geðencenne
            also is this example to be-think
            'Also this example can/may/must be thought of'   (*Bo* 23.52.2)

began to be replaced by a passive infinitive in Middle English, so that we get
it is to be done, as in (87).

(87)   þey beþ to be blamed eft þarfore
            'they are to be blamed later for-that'   (Manning *HS* (Hr 1) 1546)

At the same time, a construction which was not found in native Old English,
viz. *he is to come*, began to become current in Middle English. The difference
between the two constructions is that the first has a transitive verb (*do*), while
the verb in the second, *come*, is intransitive. The first may have been transpar-
ent to speakers of Old English, a language with frequent preverbal objects,
because the NP preceding the (verbal) infinitive in sentences like (86) functions
not only as the subject of the matrix verb but also as the object of the infinitive,
from which it also receives its thematic role. In other words, the relation
between infinitive and NP is of both a semantic and a syntactic nature,
whereas the relation of the NP to the existential verb *is*, is only weakly syntactic. However, this construction may have become opaque to speakers of
Middle English: as preverbal objects became increasingly uncommon, speakers may have tended to interpret the NP–infinitive sequence as subject–verb.
Passivisation of the infinitive solved this particular problem, since it would
turn the original object NP *hit* into a subject NP. The change in object position and the passivization of *hit is to donne* also paved the way for the new *he*

is to come type, because confusion with the superficially similar *hit is to do* construction was now no longer possible (for more details see Klöpzig 1922 and Fischer 1992a: 336 ff.).

Similar (passive) developments took place in the *easy to please* construction. In late Middle English we occasionally come across examples like (88), with a passive infinitive; they become more frequent in early Modern English.

(88)   nothinge is more easye to be founde
        nothing is more easy   to be found
        'nothing can be found more easily'
                        (Visser §1921; Ralph Robinson *Utopia* 33)

However, in this construction the passive infinitive never became the rule, presumably because, unlike in the construction in (87), the subject NP in (88) has a strong thematic subject-relation with the adjectival predicate.

Finally, a word on the perfect infinitive. Although Mustanoja (1960: 517) gives an example of the perfect infinitive in Old English from Alfred's translation of *Boethius*, the construction was extremely rare then and remained so in early Middle English (cf. Sanders 1915: 4; Miyabe 1956). Only from the fourteenth century onwards do we come across it with any frequency (cf. Mustanoja 1960: 518). In present-day English the perfect infinitive usually refers to an action that has taken place before the moment of speaking or before some other point of reference given in the clause. However, most of the Middle English examples do not concern an action in the past; most often the perfect infinitive expresses the non-realization of an action, i.e. it signals what is often called an 'irrealis'. Examples are (89) and (90).

(89)   Than if I nadde   spoken . . . / Ye wolde han slayn youreself
        then if I not-had spoken   you would have slain yourself
        anon?
        at-once
        'Then if I had not spoken, would you have killed yourself at once?'
                          (Chaucer *Troilus* IV 1233)

(90)   The worste kynde of infortune   is this,/ A man to han ben in
        the worst   kind of misfortune is this a man to have been in
        prosperitee,/ And it remembren whan it passed is.
        prosperity   and it remember   when it passed is
        'The worst kind of misfortune is this, for a man to have prospered and to
        remember it when the time of prosperity has passed.'
                        (Chaucer *Troilus* III 1626)

This association of unreality and the perfect infinitive led to what Mustanoja (1960: 517) has called the 'peculiar' Middle English use of the perfect infinitive in sentences like (91).

(91)   And on hir   bare knees adoun they falle/ And wolde have kist
        and on their bare knees down they fell   and would have kissed
        his feet . . .
        his feet
        'They fell down on their bare knees and wanted to kiss his feet . . .'

(Chaucer Knight 1758)

Here the action expressed in the infinitive is simultaneous with that of the
matrix verb, and present-day English would employ a present infinitive. The
perfect infinitive is used in Middle English examples of this type in order to
indicate that the action of 'kissing' did in the end not take place, as the further
context of (91) indeed makes clear.

3.5.3   Adverbial clauses

In this section, we will highlight some new developments taking place
in the area of adverbial clauses. A fuller description of the types of adverbial
clauses, the various subordinators used, the order of the clauses and the mood
typical for each type of subordinate clause can be found in Fischer (1992a:
343–64).

As noted above, the distinction between subordinate and main clauses was
not always as clear in Old and Middle English as it is in the present-day language. One reason for this is the fact that the written language was still closer
to the spoken language. Subordination or hypotaxis is not a prominent
characteristic of spoken language, which is more heavily paratactic. This was
still visible in Old English. A good number of the subordinating conjunctions
were of the same form as adverbs (so that the clause introduced by them
resembled a main clause). Thus we have the typical correlative constructions
þa . . . þa, nu . . . nu, where the distinction between main and subordinate clause
only became clear (and this not always) by differences in word order. The only
clearly demarcated subordinate clause types in Old English were relative
clauses introduced by *þe*, and conditional clauses introduced by *gif*. Most
other subordinate clauses in Old English can actually be analysed as being a
type of relative clause, since they are introduced by phrases such as *for þæm
þe, æfter þæm þe*, etc., which consist of a preposition, a demonstrative
pronoun and the relative particle.

In Middle English, the language began to develop more specific markers for
each type of subordinate clause, and separate lexical items for subordinate and
main clauses. Three general developments may be observed:

(i)   The Old English correlative pairs disappear; the conjunctions are dis-
        tinguished from the adverbs. Thus, *þa . . . þa* becomes *when . . . then*,

and *nu . . . nu* becomes *now that . . . now.* At the same time inversion begins to disappear as a marker of the relation between main and subordinate clause.

(ii)   The old phrasal conjunctions are replaced by more explicit subordinators. We regularly see a process of grammaticalization here, whereby a preposition and a noun slowly develop into a conjunction. Thus, Old English *þe hwile þe* becomes *whilst* (with *whiles that* as an intermediate stage), and *by the cause that* develops into *because*.

(iii)   *That* begins to be used as a general indicator of subordination, used after original prepositions (*after that, for that, till that*), and adverbs (*so that, now that, siþ that*). After nouns it is frequent too, but there it still functions as a relative pronoun (cf. the use of *þe* in Old English): *to the entente that, to that forward that. That* even occurs with *(3)if*, a conjunction that was already a distinctive subordinator in Old English.

Even though the subordinators began to be more recognizable, this development was not as far advanced yet in Middle English as it is today. It is not always immediately clear what type of subordinate clause we are dealing with. This is because the general subordinator *that* served as a conjunction in quite a number of clauses where today we would use more precisely delineated ones. Thus, *that* could be used to indicate a temporal or causal connection, as in (92) and (93) respectively, in addition to being used in final and consecutive clauses, as is still the case today.

(92)   þat Toilus [sic] in þe toile þis torfer beheld . . . / He lyght   doun
        that Troilus   in the battle this harm beheld   he alighted down
        full   lyuely   leuyt his horse,/ And dressit to   Dyamede . . .
        very quickly left   his horse   and set   upon Diomede
        'When Troilus saw this harm afflicted in the battle, . . . he alighted very
        quickly of his horse and set upon Diomede . . .'   (*Destr. Troy* 7435)

(93)   But that science is so fer us biforn,/ We mowen nat . . . / It overtake,
        but that science is so far us before   we can   not   it overtake
        it slit   awey so faste.
        it slips   away so fast
        'But because science [i.e. alchemy] is so far beyond us, we cannot catch up
        with it, it slips away so fast'   (Chaucer *Canon's Yeoman* 680)

Similarly, there were quite a few conjunctions that could be used in more than one type of clause, and often indeed they served for two types at the same time. Thus *for* is ambiguous between purpose and cause in (94); *till that* may combine final (or consecutive) and temporal aspects in (95); and *so (that)* can be both conditional and consecutive in (96).

(94)   And for his tale sholde seme the bettre,/ Accordant to his wordes was his
        cheere . . .
        'And for his tale should seem the better, in accordance with his words were
        his manners'   (Chaucer *Squire* 102)

(95)   And þanne þei schullen dyggen & mynen so strongly, till þat þei fynden the
        ʒates þat kyng Alisandre leet make . . .
        'And then they must dig and excavate so strongly, till that they find the gates
        that King Alexander had made'   (*Mandev.* 178.19)

(96)   So he may fynde Goddes foyson there,/ Of the remenant nedeth
        so he may find   God's   plenty there of the rest   needs
        nat enquere.
        not enquire
        'So he may find Gods's plenty there, after the rest [he] need not enquire'
                                                                (Chaucer *Miller* 3165)

A more complicated case is presented by examples such as (97a–c).

(97)   a. þer   passes non bi þat place so proude in his armes/ þat he
           there passes none by that place so glorious in his arms   that he
           ne   dyngez hym to deþe with dynt of his honde . . .
           not beats   him to death with blow of his hand
           'none however glorious in arms will pass by that place without being
           beaten to death by one blow of his hand . . .'   (*Gawain* 2104)

        b. Was non of hem þat he ne gret . . .
           was none of them that he not wept
           'There was not one of them [such] that he did not weep . . .'
                                                                (*Havelok* 2160)

        c. . . . wente neuere wye in þis world þoruʒ   þat wildernesse/ That
               went never man in this world through that wilderness   that
           he ne   was robbed . . .
           he not was robbed
           'never did any man in this world go through that wilderness without
           being robbed . . .'   (*Piers Plowman* B.(Trin-C) xvii.101)

These examples seem to waver between a consecutive and a relative clause (a
relative with a resumptive pronoun). There are good reasons to assume,
however, that these clauses are in fact consecutive (cf. Diekstra 1984). Firstly,
there are restrictions on resumptive pronouns in relative clauses which are not
obeyed here (cf. Fischer 1992a: 345). Secondly, the main clause is formally distinct in other ways: it is always negative, the predicate is usually an existential
verb, and it often contains (explicitly as in (97a), or implicitly as in (97b) and
(97c)) a correlative element that strongly links it to the *that* clause.

4

The Verb-Second constraint and its loss

4.1 Introduction

A comparison of the position of the finite verb in Modern English with its precursors in Old English shows up some striking contrasts. As is well known, Modern English has regular SVO word orders in declarative clauses, regardless of whether the verb is finite or not. In questions and negative-initial clauses, we see the phenomenon of 'subject–aux inversion':

(1)   a. Who did you talk to at the party yesterday?
        b. Never have I talked to such a strange character.

Subject–aux inversion – as the name says – is restricted to auxiliaries. Main verbs do not invert in questions, even when they are finite. Rather, a 'dummy' auxiliary *do* is employed as a finite verb when the first verb in a sentence is not an auxiliary. Old English is different in most of these respects, although some of the patterns look rather familiar.

As we saw in chapter 2, Old English had many SVO word orders like those in Modern English, but at least as many SOV word orders, or orders that seem to be a mix of SOV and SVO. The position of the finite verb plays a special role in this: especially in main clauses, it is very often found following one initial constituent, regardless of whether that first constituent is the subject or not, and regardless of the rest of the word order of the clause. Thus, in Old English, we find word orders like those in (2):

(2)   a. King Alfred *will* at the battle of Ashdown the Vikings defeat
        b. King Alfred *will* at the battle of Ashdown defeat the Vikings
        c. The Vikings (object) *will* King Alfred (subject) at the battle of Ashdown
           defeat

In other words, the patterns with inversion occur in Old English in ordinary declarative clauses as well. And these patterns are not restricted to auxiliaries: all finite verbs take part in them. This affects questions and negative-initial sentences alike. Although in the latter the patterns resemble those of Modern English more closely, they are also found with lexical finite verbs:

(3)   a. Whom *defeated* King Alfred at the battle of Ashdown?
        b. Not *defeated* King Alfred at the battle of Ashdown the Vikings

These facts have led scholars to believe that with respect to the position of
the finite verb, Old English resembled closely its Germanic sister languages in
having a variant of what has come to be known as the 'Verb-Second' constraint. The term 'Verb-Second' refers to the characteristic that in main
clauses, the *finite* verb follows one initial constituent, regardless of the precise
position of the non-finite verb. The hypothetical present-day English examples (2) and (3) are an illustration of this; ample original illustration will follow
below. Some version of this characteristic is shared by all the present-day
Germanic languages, as well as Old English.

In the course of the Middle and early Modern periods, an interesting chain
of changes resulted in the positioning as we know it in Modern English: inversion in declarative clauses was largely lost during the late Middle English
period, petering out in the early Modern period, when inversion in questions
and negative-initial clauses became restricted to auxiliaries and *do* came to be
employed as a dummy auxiliary. We will be mainly concerned with the changes
in the Middle English period here, since they are the crucial ones setting the
scene for further developments.[1]

In this chapter, the Old English situation and subsequent changes will be
treated in some detail. We first present some of the basic facts in section 4.2,
and go on to discuss possible analyses of these facts as advanced in the literature in section 4.3. We will present some new facts which provide arguments
for refining the analysis. Finally, section 4.4 will consider the nature of the
changes that took place, mainly in Middle English.

4.2   The facts

In chapter 2, the general observation was made that the position of
the finite verb in Old English differs substantially between main and embedded clauses. We will now refine this observation, beginning with main clauses.
When the subject is the first constituent in the main clause, which happens very
often in Old English, we usually find the finite verb following it, regardless of
the word order of the rest of the clause. Consider (4) and (5):

---

[1] After this period, further developments took place, including a change often referred
to as loss of V-to-I movement, correlating with the rise of *do*-support. We will not
discuss this much further here. The reader is referred to Roberts (1985), Kroch
(1989), Warner (1997) and Lightfoot (1997).

(4)   We habbað hwæðere þa bysne on halgum bocum
       'We have, nevertheless, the examples in holy books' (*ÆCHom* I, 33.474.33)

(5)   Se Hælend wearð þa   gelomlice ætiwed his leornung-cnihtum
       the Lord   was   then frequently shown   his disciples (D)
       'The Lord then frequently appeared to his disciples' (*ÆCHom* I, 15.220.21)

While (4) is a VO sentence and (5) a Vfin–Adv–Adv–Vnonfin–O sentence, there is no difference between them with respect to the position of subject and finite verb.

When the first constituent in a main clause is not the subject, the finite verb very often follows it. This is what is traditionally called subject–verb inversion, and is exceptionless when the first constituent is a question element as in (6), or the negative adverbial *ne* as in (7). It is also extremely dominant after the short adverbial *þa* as in (8).

(6)   a. Hwi wolde God swa lytles þinges him forwyrnan?
          why would God so   small   thing   him deny
          'Why should God deny him such a small thing?'   (*ÆCHom* I, 1.14.2)
       b. for hwam noldest   þu   ðe sylfe me gecyðan   þæt . . .
          for what not-wanted you yourself me make-known that
          'wherefore would you not want to make known to me yourself that . . .'
                                                             (*LS* 7(Euphr) 305)

(7)   Ne sceal he naht   unaliefedes don
       not shall he nothing unlawful   do
       'He shall not do anything unlawful'   (*CP* 10.61.14)

(8)   þa wæs þæt folc   þæs micclan welan   ungemetlice
       then was the people the great   prosperity (G) excessively
       brucende . . .
       partaking
       'Then the people were partaking excessively of the great prosperity.'
                                                             (*Or* 1.23.3)

With the types of first constituents as in (6)–(8), it does not matter whether the subject is nominal or pronominal; it is always inverted. This is also true for those contexts where, in the absence of a first constituent, the finite verb is in first position. This happens in yes–no questions and in so-called *narrative inversion*, which is found in lively narrative:

(9)   Hæfst þu ænigne geferan?
       'Have you any   companions?'   (*ÆColl* 28)

(10)   Wæs Hæsten þa   þær cumen mid his herge
       was Hæsten then there come with his host
       'Hæsten then had come there with his host'   (*ChronA* (Plummer) 894.43)

Another verb-first context that we mention here for the sake of completeness is imperatives.

In an analysis that draws on a comparison with the present-day Germanic languages, these facts are typically seen as instances of movement of the finite verb to some presentential position, which is assumed to be in the CP domain. In this analysis, the first constituent is in Spec,CP, the finite verb in C, as illustrated here for (6a):

(11)   Hwi wolde God swa lytles þinges him forwyrnan
         [$_{CP}$ [$_C$ Vf [$_{IP}$ ⋯ ⋯⋯⋯⋯⋯⋯⋯.V]]]

This analysis captures the empirical generalization that Verb-Second takes place regardless of the word order of the rest of the clause. This is further supported by a variety of arguments, which will be discussed in 4.3.

In (6)–(8) above, we saw illustrations of Verb-Second when the sentence is introduced by an interrogative or negative constituent, or by þa. Apart from these contexts, when the first constituent is a non subject, verb–subject order is dominant only when the subject is a full noun, as in (12);[2] pronominal subjects precede the verb, as in (13)–(14). Note that the verb has clearly been moved, since, as in (12), its position is distinct from that of the non-finite verb:

(12)   On twam þingum hæfde God þæs mannes sawle gegodod
         in two   things had God the man's   soul endowed
         'With two things God had endowed man's soul'   (*ÆCHom* I, 1.20.1)

(13)   Forðon *we* sceolan mid ealle mod &   mægene to Gode gecyrran
         therefore we must   with all   mind and power to God turn
         'Therefore we must turn to God with all our mind and power'
                                                     (*HomU*19 (BlHom 8) 26)

(14)   Be ðæm *we* magon suiðe swutule oncnawan ðæt ...
         by that we may   very clearly perceive that ...
         'By that, we may perceive very clearly that ...'   (*CP* 26.181.16)

Part of the empirical motivation for assuming that there has been V-movement here is that in verb and particle combinations, particles are 'stranded' by movement. In embedded clauses, particles nearly always precede the (non-fronted) verb, but in main clauses, they often follow the finite verb in a position that correlates with what is assumed to be the position of the verb before movement. This is illustrated in (15)–(16); we come back to this in detail in chapter 6.

---

[2] Unlike the contexts of (6)–(8), where we always see verb–subject order, declaratives with a topic, like (12)–(14), have inversion dominantly but not invariably; cf. Koopman (1998).

(15)   þa *astah* se Hælend *up* on ane dune
        then rose the Lord   up on a   mountain
        'then the Lord went up on a mountain'   (*ÆCHom* I, 12.182.1)

(16)   þa *eodon* hie *ut*
        then went they out
        'then they went out'   (*ChronA* (Plummer) 894.83)

The above are fairly firm rules for main clauses, but certain exceptions should be noted. With some first constituents, inversion of subject pronouns is variable. An example of this is the word *nu* 'now' when used as a temporal adverb:

(17)   Nu *we* sculon eft,   cwæð Orosius, hwierfan near   Roma
        now we shall   again said   Orosius turn   nearer Rome
        'Now we should turn again nearer Rome, said Orosius'   (*Or* 2.5.49.10)

(18)   Nu hæbbe *we* gereaht   be   welan 7   be   anwalde
        now have   we discussed about wealth and about power
        'Now we have discussed wealth and power'   (*Bo* 33.77.14)

Occasionally the nominal subject is not inverted, as in (19).

(19)   Nu ealle ðas   ðing   synd mid anum naman genemnode, gesceaft.
        now all   these things are   with one   name   named   creature
        'Now all these things are called with one name: creature.'
        (*ÆCHom* I, 20.276.10)

In a limited set of cases, the finite verb is not moved in the main clause. The frequency of this varies from one text to another; Koopman (1995) found figures for various texts ranging between 0.5 and 6 per cent. The phenomenon is most clearly illustrated when the finite verb follows the non-finite verb:

(20)   þa folc   him   betweonum ful x   winter þa gewin wraciende
        the peoples them between   full ten winters the fight   carrying-on
        wæron
        were
        'The peoples kept up the fight between them for a full ten years'
        (*Or* 1.1.32.6)

(21)   Baloham ðonne fulgeorne   feran wolde ðær   hine mon bæd
        Balaam then   very-willingly go   wanted there him one bade
        'Balaam would very willingly have proceeded whither he was told'
        (*CP* 36.255.22)

We now turn to embedded clauses, where movement of the finite verb is much more restricted. Consider the following examples, which illustrate S–Vfin–XP–V word order:

(22)   þæt hi   mihton swa bealdlice Godes geleafan bodian
        that they could so boldly God's faith   preach
        'that they could preach God's faith so boldly'   (*ÆCHom* I, 16.232.23)

(23)   þæt he mehte his feorh generian
        that he could his life   save
        'so that he could save his life'   (*Or* 2.5.48.18)

There are also a few examples of movement of a verb from a verb–particle combination:

(24)   gif Crist *scute* ða *adun*
        if Christ casts then down
        'if Christ then casts himself down'   (*ÆCHom* I, 11.170.21)

The kind of V-movement illustrated in (22)–(23) differs in several ways from that in main clauses. Preposed constituents such as topics and question elements followed by the finite verb, are a main-clause phenomenon, as will be discussed further below. The nominative subject in embedded clauses (whether nominal or pronominal) always precedes the finite verb (as illustrated by (22)–(24)), except in special constructions such as passives. Regular topics followed by the finite verb as in main clauses do not appear in this position; very occasionally an object pronoun appears before the finite verb, but this merely shows that pronouns are special in their behaviour. Moreover, verb fronting in main clauses is vastly more frequent than in embedded clauses (about 95 per cent against 35 per cent). Thus, we can say that while there is undeniably V-movement in embedded clauses, the phenomenon appears to be rather different from that in main clauses. What seems to be the case is that there is a more restricted form of V-movement in embedded clauses, one that bears no relation to topicalization. Let us say, pending further discussion below, that this V-movement is to a position following the subject, and therefore lower than that in Verb-Second main clauses, as illustrated here with (25):

(25) $[_{CP} [_C$ þæt $[_{IP}$ hi $[_I$ mihton$_i$ swa bealdlice Godes geleafan bodian V_i]]]]

There are also some cases where the finite verb appears on the left of the non-finite verb, but with objects preceding it:

(26)   a. ðæt he wisdom mæge wið ofermetta æfre gemengan
           that he wisdom may with pride   ever mingle
           'that he may always combine wisdom with pride'   (*Met* 7.6)
        b. ðæt he Saul ne dorste ofslean
           that he Saul not dared murder
           'that he didn't dare to murder Saul'   (*CP* 28.199.2)

Such examples cannot be treated on a par with V-movement in main clauses, since both subject and object precede the finite verb.

4.3   The position of the finite verb: Verb-Second?

As we have seen, the positioning of the finite verb in Old English main clauses suggests strongly that Old English word order is subject to some variant of what has come to be called the Verb-Second constraint. As observed above, this is a phenomenon that is found in some form in most of the present-day Germanic languages; it is therefore useful at this point to consider how it is analysed for these languages. After all, since Old English is a dead language for which we have access only to textual evidence, it is important to know as much as possible about the scope of variation with respect to Verb-Second in the present-day languages, for which we also have access to native speaker intuitions. This is the task of the next subsection. After these general considerations, we will turn to analyses of Old English 'Verb-Second' as presented in the literature, introducing further detailed data where they are relevant for the argument.

4.3.1   Verb-Second in present-day Germanic

Verb-Second in the present-day Germanic languages is a process that takes place regardless of the basic sentence structure (OV or VO). It fronts Vfin to presentential position in all types of root clause, whether declarative, interrogative or imperative. One of the core characteristics of Verb-Second in this sense is the fact that it is largely restricted to main clauses, as we see in the following examples from German:

(27)   a Er *hat* ihn gestern   gesehen
           he has him yesterday seen
        b. Gestern   *hat* er ihn *gesehen*
           yesterday has he him seen
        c. ... dass er ihn gestern   *gesehen hat*
           that he him yesterday seen   has
        d. *... dass gestern   *hat* er ihn *gesehen*
           that yesterday has he him seen
        e. *... dass *hat* er ihn gestern   *gesehen*
           that has he ihn yesterday seen
        '. . . He saw him yesterday'

The usual analysis of these facts is as follows: in (27a–b) the finite verb is fronted with respect to the position of the non-finite verb, which in German follows objects and adverbs in surface word order. We assume that the base position of the finite verb corresponds to that of the non-finite verb, and that the finite verb moves to the CP domain. In (27c–e), we see that this movement does not occur in embedded clauses. Following the pioneering work of den Besten (1983), it is usually assumed that it is the complementizer *dass* that is responsible for blocking V-movement: its presence in (27d–e) is incompatible with a fronted finite verb. In formal terms, the derivation of a Verb-Second sentence (disregarding the relative order of I and VP, and word order within VP) would be:

(28)

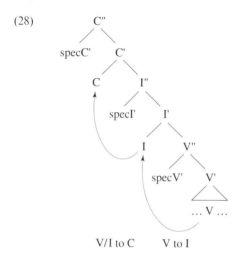

The finite verb, generated as the head of the VP, moves to I, undergoing head-to-head movement to pick up its inflectional features Tense and Agreement. Subsequently, V/I moves to C if C is empty. The canonical position of the subject is Spec,IP. An important consequence of this analysis must be noted: the first constituent, whether a subject (27a) or a topic (27b), is a constituent that has been moved to the Spec,CP position. Movement is blocked when C is filled by a lexical complementizer like *that*. This accounts for the incompatibility of a lexical complementizer with a fronted finite verb, as in (27d–e). While there is substantial consensus in the literature that the core property of Verb-Second languages like German is that V/I moves to C, the motivation for this movement has been the subject of much speculation. We remain neutral on this issue, and simply assume that in this type of Verb-Second language, C must be lexical, whatever the precise motivation.

In the modern languages, the Verb-Second phenomenon is not entirely restricted to main clauses. Verb-Second in embedded clauses is essentially of two types. The first type is attested in Frisian and Danish. These two languages allow embedded Verb-Second in the sentential complements of 'bridge verbs'. These are verbs which can be understood to quote a statement and allow a double CP complement, in the sense that there is a new Verb-Second structure following a *that*-complementizer (see e.g. Vikner (1995)). This is illustrated with (29) from Danish:

(29)   a. Vi ved   at   Bo har ikke læst denne bog
           we know that Bo has not read this   book
        b. Vi ved   at   denne bog   har Bo ikke læst
           we know that this   book has Bo not read
        c. *Vi beklag at   denne bog   har Bo ikke læst
           we regret that the   book has Bo not read

We follow current work in analysing this type of embedded Verb-Second as CP-recursion, which captures the intuition that these embedded clauses are actually quoted main clauses. German also allows this type of embedded Verb-Second, though only with a subset of bridge verbs and not with the overt complementizer *dass* 'that'.

Since cases like this are embedded clauses with V-movement, the term 'main clause' does not quite seem a felicitous one; Verb-Second clauses of this type are therefore often referred to as *root clauses* (clauses that are main clauses from an illocutionary point of view, and do not have a filled complementizer position at D-structure). Non-Verb-Second clauses are called *non-root clauses*. Verb-Second languages of the type discussed above are variously referred to as *C-Verb-Second languages* or *asymmetric Verb-Second languages*. Crucial for this notion is that Verb-Second is restricted to root clauses: there is a *root/non-root asymmetry* for Verb-Second. In this language type, Spec,IP is the canonical position for the nominative subject.

The second type of embedded Verb-Second is represented by languages like Yiddish and Icelandic. In these languages, embedded Verb-Second occurs more or less freely and is compatible with a base-generated complementizer. This is illustrated in (30) with some Icelandic examples from Rögnvaldson and Thráinsson (1990):

(30)   a. Jón efast   um að á morgun fari María snemma á fætur
           John doubts that   tomorrow get Mary early   up
           'John doubts that Mary will get up early tomorrow'
        b. Jón harmar að   þessa bók   skuli ég hafa lesið
           John regrets that this   book shall I   have read
           'John regrets that I have read this book'

There does not seem to be an asymmetry between root and non-root clauses with respect to V-movement in Icelandic and Yiddish, and it seems that V-movement is not related to the presence of a complementizer. According to

Rögnvaldson and Thráinsson (1990), this supports the idea that V-movement is to the I-position, (which could not be blocked by a complementizer) and that the Spec,IP position is not reserved exclusively for the nominative subject: in (30a–b) it is occupied respectively by an adverb *á morgun*, and an object topic *þessa bók*. This type of language is often called an *I-Verb-Second language* or *symmetric Verb-Second language*. In such languages, XP–Vfin–subject sequences occur more or less freely in both root and non-root contexts, and are to be analysed as instances of V to I. This view of Verb-Second in Icelandic and Yiddish is, however, not uncontroversial. Vikner (1995) for instance, argues that *all* Verb-Second is movement to C, and hence analyses embedded Verb-Second in Icelandic and Yiddish as a generalized form of CP-recursion.

Let us note the constructions in present-day English which still show Verb-Second: constituent questions, yes–no questions and negative-initial constructions, as in (31):

(31)   a. Why would Banquo make an appearance at the banquet?
        b. Did Banquo make an appearance at the banquet?
        c. Not a word did Banquo speak at the banquet.

It appears that this type of partial Verb-Second, when it does occur, observes the C-Verb-Second characteristics: it is restricted to root clauses and is incompatible with a complementizer unless the matrix verb is a bridge verb:

(32)   a. Macbeth wondered *why would* Banquo have made an appearance at the
           banquet
        b. *Macbeth wondered *if would* Banquo make an appearance at the
           banquet
        c. Macbeth said *that not a word did* Banquo speak at the banquet
        d. *Macbeth whispered *that not a word did* Banquo speak at the banquet

(32a) can be interpreted as Verb-Second in the absence of a complementizer (*why* is a *wh*-word moved to Spec,CP rather than a complementizer generated in C). This is confirmed by the ungrammaticality of (32b) with the complementizer *if* blocking V-movement. (32c–d) show the contrast between a negative-initial clause embedded (grammatically) in the *that*-complement of the bridge verb *say* and (ungrammatically) in the *that*-complement of the non-bridge verb *whisper*. (32c) can therefore be analysed as a case of CP-recursion, which is not possible after non-bridge verbs as in (32d).

There has been considerable debate on the question of whether Old English Verb-Second is symmetric or asymmetric. Before we go into this in the next section, it may be useful to see what predictions the two analyses would make with respect to the distribution of subject, finite verb and first constituent.

C-Verb-Second or asymmetric Verb-Second language:

- first constituent in root clauses is in Spec,CP
- no topicalization in non-root clauses, except in the complement of bridge verbs
- finite verb in root clauses in C; in non-root clauses in I

I-Verb-Second or symmetric Verb-Second language:

- first constituent is in Spec,IP
- topicalization more or less free in non-root clauses (Spec,IP is a topic position)
- finite verb in I in both root and non-root clauses

Let us now consider the analysis of Old English in more detail.

4.3.2   Verb-Second in Old English

The core facts of Old English word order were discussed in section 4.2. Let us see how they fit with analyses of Verb-Second as in section 4.3.1. There is ample evidence for movement of the finite verb in all types of root clause in Old English. We repeat some of the examples here:

(33)   Se Hælend wearð þa   gelomlice ætiwed his leornung-cnihtum
        the Lord   was   then frequently shown his disciples (D)
        'The Lord then frequently appeared to his disciples' (*ÆCHom* I, 15.220.21)

(34)   On twam þingum hæfde God þæs mannes sawle gegodod
        in two things had God the man's soul endowed
        'With two things God had endowed man's soul'   (*ÆCHom* I, 1.20.1)

(35)   hwi wolde God swa lytles þinges him forwyrnan?
        why would God so small thing him deny
        'why should God deny him such a small thing?'   (*ÆCHom* I, 1.14.2)

(33) is a subject-initial sentence; (34) a topic-initial sentence; (35) a constituent question. (34) and (35) have subject–verb inversion. Clauses like (33), with a subject followed by the finite verb, are also found in non-root contexts, as observed above:

(36)   Ac hie   næron   to ðan swiðe onbryrde. þæt hi   mihton swa
        but they not-were to that very excited   that they could so
        bealdlice Godes geleafan bodian
        boldly   God's faith   preach
        '. . . that they could preach God's faith so boldly'   (*ÆCHom* I, 16.232.23)

Although these are clearly cases of V-movement, they are equally clearly not cases of Verb-Second in the sense we are discussing. A moved finite verb in non-root clauses is never preceded by a topic, except in contexts we discuss below. Another argument is that beside the subject, objects or adverbs can precede the finite verb:

(37)   ðæt he wisdom mæge wið ofermetta æfre gemengan
        that he wisdom may   with pride   ever mingle
        'that he may always combine wisdom with pride'   (*Met* 7.6)

(38)   þæt hi   ofer þæt ne dorston nohte   gretan þa halgan stowe
        that they after that not dared   not-at-all attack the holy   place
        'that they didn't dare at all attack the holy place after that' (*GD* 1(C)4.43.4)

This makes it unlikely that (36) is a case of Verb-Second.

Let us now turn to the word order of embedded questions. In general, it can be said that embedded questions do not have verb–subject order. (39) and (40) illustrate some of the regular word orders in embedded constituent questions:

(39)   þa   com god and axode hwi he his bebod   tobræce
        then came God and asked why he his commandment broke
        'then God came and asked why he had broken his commandment'
                                                        (*ÆCHom* I, 1.18.12)

(40)   . . . þa ða his leorningcnihtas hine axodon for hwæs synnum se man
              when his disciples   him asked for whose sins   the man
        wurde   swa blind acenned
        became thus blind born
        '. . . when his disciples asked him for whose sin the man was thus born
        blind'   (*ÆCHom* I, 31.474.1)

Verb–subject order in this context is rare in the original prose, and the examples found are often in direct speech; the following example is from the Bible translation:

(41)   And þa   axodon hine Pharisei &   þa boceras   hwi ne gað
        and then asked   him Pharisees and the learned men why not go
        þine leorningcnihtas æfter ure yldrena   gesetnysse. ac besmitenum
        your disciples   after our forefathers' law   but with defiled
        handum hyra hlaf þicgað?
        hands   their bread eat?
        'Then the Pharisees and scribes asked him, Why walk not your disciples
        according to the tradition of their elders, but eat bread with unwashed
        hands?'   (*Mk* (WSCp) 7.5)

Since this seems to be a quoted root clause, it can be analysed as a case of Verb-Second in the absence of a complementizer, as discussed above for Modern English and illustrated with (32a).

Let us now consider topic-initial sentences. Examples of Verb-Second in the complement of a bridge verb, in direct or indirect speech, can be readily found:

(42)   þa   cwæþ se   halga wer,   of þam heofonlican leohte ne   beo ge
        then said   the holy   man, of the   heavenly   light   not be   you
        afyrhte.
        afraid
        'then the holy man said: do not be afraid of the heavenly light.'
                                                                (*ÆLS*(Vincent) 196)

(43)   a. Gregorius se   trahtnere   cwæð þæt forði   wolde   drihten
           Gregory   the interpreter said   that therefore wanted God
           getrahtnian þurh   hine sylfne þæt bigspel ðe
           interpret   through himself   the parable that
           'Gregory the interpreter said that therefore God wanted to interpret
           himself the parable that . . .'   (*ÆCHom* II, 6.53.33)
        b. Eala þu   min leofa man   ic þe   mid lufe secge ic hæbbe
           oh   you my   dear husband I   you with love say   I   have
           Godes encgel . . .
           God's angel
           'Oh you, my dear husband, I say to you with love, I have God's angel . . .'
                                                                (*ÆLS*(Cecilia) 31)

(42) and (43) bring out the contrast: when there is no complementizer, as in
(42), the embedded clause looks like a root clause, in direct speech. Indirect
speech emerges when there is CP-recursion as in (43a), or an embedded Verb-
Second clause in the subjunctive mood (43b).

Apart from this type of embedded topicalization, which we saw above is a
typical C-Verb-Second phenomenon, there is what looks like embedded topicalization, but this is restricted in a quite different way. To see this, consider
the following example:

(44)   for þan þe   on me is   afunden ætforan Gode rihtwisnyss
        because that in me is (3sg) found   before   God   justice (N, sg)
        'because justice before God is found in me'   (*ÆHom* 21.326)

This is a non-root clause with the complementizer followed by a PP and the
finite verb, which could be interpreted as a case of embedded topicalization.
However, upon closer inspection, it turns out that this kind of embedded topicalization is restricted to those contexts which are 'unaccusative', where the
cover term 'unaccusative' refers to those constructions in which the syntactic
subject receives its thematic role in a VP-internal position. This includes
constructions such as passives of various sorts, impersonal constructions as
discussed in chapters 1 and 2 and ergative verbs like *come, go, burst*, etc. These
are constructions which have no agent subject. The relevant context in (44) is
passive. Here are some more examples: (45) is an impersonal passive, (46) a
regular passive and (47) features an ergative verb:

(45)   þæt eallum folcum   sy gedemed beforan ðe
        that all   peoples (D) be judged   before   thee
        'that all the peoples be judged before you'   (*PPs*(prose) 9.18)

(46)   þonne ælce dæge beoð manega   acennede   þurh   hys mihte on
        when each day are   many (N, pl) given birth through his power on
        worulde
        world
        'when every day many are given birth through his power on earth'
                                                            (*ÆHom* 6.116)

(47)   forðam þe him burston ut   butu his eagan
        because that him burst out both his eyes (N, pl)
        'because both his eyes burst out'   (*ÆLS*(Alban) 116)

In van Kemenade (1997a), an argument is presented that such constructions
are in several ways special. The fact that Spec,IP here seems to host a non-
subject is argued to be a construction-specific feature that cannot serve as evidence that Spec,IP is the general topic position, and hence does not provide
evidence that Old English is a symmetric Verb-Second language. Another
feature of these constructions is that while the subject can immediately follow
the finite verb, it frequently occurs in clause-final position, as in (44)
(*rihtwisnyss*) and (47) (*butu his eagan*). Finally, this type of embedded topicalization often occurs without V-movement, as illustrated by the following
impersonal sentences:

(48)   ða   ðæm hearpere ða   ðuhte ðæt hine þa nanes ðinges ne
        when to the harpist then seemed that him then no   thing not
        lyste   on ðisse worulde
        pleased in this world
        'when it seemed to the harpist that nothing in this world would please him
        anymore'   (*Bo* 35.102.9)

(49)   gif ðam gifran ungemetlicu spræc ne eglde
        if the greedy eloquent   speech not afflicted
        'if the greedy are not afflicted by loquacity'   (*CP* 43.309.2)

The above provides evidence that topicalization in conjunction with Verb-
Second is asymmetric, suggesting that the topic position (and, by analogy, the
subject position in root clauses) is Spec,CP rather than Spec,IP. We come back
to more empirical evidence for this below.

There is a further source of complexity in topic-initial constructions. The
reader will recall that in topic-initial sentences, subject–verb inversion is the
norm only when the subject is nominal. Personal pronoun subjects appear left
of a preposed finite verb. Two examples illustrating the contrast are repeated
here:

(50)   On twam þingum hæfde God þæs mannes sawle gegodod
        in two   things had   God the man's soul   endowed
        'With two things God had endowed man's soul'   (*ÆCHom* I, 1.20.1)

(51)   Forðon *we* sceolan mid ealle mod &   mægene to Gode gecyrran
        therefore we must   with all   mind and power   to God turn
        'Therefore we must turn to God with all our mind and power'
                                                    (*HomU*19(BlHom 8) 26)

This contrast is found only in topic-initial sentences, and not in questions, negative-initial sentences, or sentences introduced by the adverb *þa*, as was discussed above. The grammatical status and the position of personal pronouns
have played a key role in the debate on Verb-Second in Old English. Let us
therefore consider that role in more detail.

4.3.2.1 The role of personal pronouns

In the previous sections, the position of subject pronouns in topic-
initial sentences was noted. From the perspective of the V-movement analysis,
the positional contrast between topic-initial sentences on the one hand, and
interrogative, negative-initial and *þa*-initial sentences on the other, is especially
intriguing; recall that in the latter, the pronominal subject always follows the
finite verb:

(52)   for hwam noldest   þu ðe sylfe me gecyðan   þæt . . .
        for what not-wanted you you self me make known that
        'wherefore would you not want to make known to me yourself that . . .'
                                                    (*LS*7 (Euphr) 305)

(53)   þa foron hie mid þrim scipum ut
        then sailed they with three ships out
        'Then they sailed out with three ships'   (*ChronA* (Plummer) 897.30)

(54)   Ne sceal he naht   unaliefedes don
        not shall he nothing unlawful   do
        'He shall not do anything unlawful'   (*CP* 10.61.14)

Several analyses of this contrast have been presented in the literature. Van
Kemenade (1987), who attempts to derive the full variety of Old English
clause structure from a single underlying OV order with Verb-Second in root
clauses, takes the position that, as far as V-movement is concerned, topic-
initial sentences as in (50)–(51) should be treated on a par with sentences introduced by a *wh*-element, negative element or *þa*, as in (52)–(54). The primary
motivation for this is that topicalization with Verb-Second is restricted to root
clauses, as we have seen above. This suggests that Verb-Second contexts occur
only in root clauses, and that V-movement is to the C-position, since it is
blocked by the presence of a complementizer such as *þæt* or *gif*. But then we

need a special account for the fact that in topic-initial sentences like (50)–(51), the pronominal subject precedes the finite verb, whereas the nominal subject follows it. Van Kemenade (see also Koopman 1997) places the special behaviour of pronominal subjects in topic-initial sentences in a wider context: personal pronouns in general observe positional restrictions in Old English, and the positions occupied by pronominal subjects are available to object pronouns as well. This is illustrated in (55); (55a) is a subject-initial root clause with an object pronoun on the left of the fronted finite verb (recall that subjects in subject-initial root clauses occupy the same position as topics, wh-elements etc.); and (55b–d) show that a pronominal object can also occur in the position following the finite verb in clauses with initial wh-, negative and *þa* (analogous to (52)–(54)):

(55)   a. God him   worhte   þa   reaf   of fellum
           God them wrought then   garments of skins
           'Then God made garments of skin for them'   (*ÆCHom* I, 1.18.18)
        b. Hwæt tacnað   us ðonne Saul buton yfle hlafurdas?
           what betokens us then   Saul except evil lords
           'What is signified to us by Saul but bad masters?'   (*CP* 28.197.22)
        c. þa   sticode him mon   þa eagan ut
           then stuck   him someone the eyes out
           'then his eyes were gouged out'   (*Or* 4.5.90.13)
        d. Ne geseah hine nan man nateshwon yrre
           not saw   him no man so little   angry
           'No-one ever saw him so little angry'   (*ÆLS*(Martin) 306)

Van Kemenade argues that the special behaviour of pronouns reflects a form of syntactic cliticization, whereby personal pronouns cliticize onto the finite verb. However, since the position of the finite verb is putatively the same in the various types of root clause, this still does not account for the positional discrepancy of pronouns between topic-initial root clauses and questions, etc. Van Kemenade argues that in the unmarked case, cliticization is on the left of the fronted finite verb, which is the position in topic-initial contexts:

(56)   [$_{\text{Spec,CP}}$ topic [$_{\text{C}}$ pron–Vfin [$_{\text{IP}}$ . . .]]]

In contexts with initial wh-, negative and *þa*, this procliticization is blocked, and pronouns are enclitic on the finite verb:

(57)   [$_{\text{Spec,CP}}$ wh/neg/þa [$_{\text{C}}$ Vfin–pron [$_{\text{IP}}$ . . .]]]

This approach relates the choice for procliticization/encliticization to the nature of the first constituent. The idea is that in interrogative and negative contexts (and, by distributional similarity, *þa*), there is a logical operator in Spec,CP which changes the character of the sentence (to interrogative, negative), whereas this is not the case in topic-initial contexts (topic sentences are, after all, declarative sentences). The presence of such an operator blocks cliticization on the left of the finite verb: nothing may intervene between the operator and C. Cliticization is then on the right of the finite verb. From a theoretical point of view, this analysis is not satisfactory; in particular, it is hard to see a principled rationale for the different directions for cliticization.[3] It should be observed, however, that the account does allow us to do justice to the root character of Old English Verb-Second and topicalization.

Susan Pintzuk (1991, 1993) presents an alternative to the analysis by van Kemenade that is inspired by the idea of phrase structure variation. Like van Kemenade, she takes Old English basic word order in the VP to be OV, but her starting point is the similarity between the position of the finite verb between root and non-root clauses. She proposes that IP comes in two variations: there are I-medial IPs and also I-final IPs. Based on the structure (28), this yields the following variation:

(58)   a.   b.

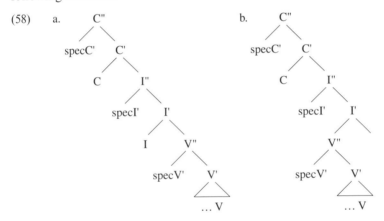

In both configurations, V moves to I, resulting in the following surface word orders:

(59)   þæt hi   mihton swa bealdlice Godes geleafan bodian
        that they could   so   boldly   God's faith   preach
        'that they could preach God's faith so boldly'   (ÆCHom I, 16.232.23)

(60)   þæt hie   gemong him   mid sibbe sittan mosten
        that they among themselves in   peace settle must
        'that they must settle in peace among themselves'   (Or 2.8.52.31)

---

[3] Tomaselli (1995) recasts this account in a way compatible with recent theoretical developments.

(58a) then yields a sentence with verb fronting as in (59); (58b) yields a verb-final word order as in (60). Observe that this analysis entails a form of V-movement in non-root clauses, for which Pintzuk provides independent evidence. Recall that verb fronting strands the particle in a verb–particle construction:

(61)   þæt he wearp þæt sweord onweg
        'so that he threw the sword away'   (*Bede* 1.7.38.18)

Particle stranding is found almost exclusively in root clauses, as is discussed in more detail in chapter 6, and this provides one more argument for the asymmetric character of Verb-Second. But Pintzuk (1991) argues that the few instances of particles following the finite verb in non-root clauses in fact give evidence of a process of V-movement to the left. This is supported by the fact that it is found considerably more frequently when the verbal part of the verb–particle combination is the finite verb, hence would be fronted, as in (61), than when the finite verb is modal, in which case the verbal part of the verb–particle combination is non-finite and hence not fronted. The details are discussed in chapter 6. This clearly suggests that the finite verb is moved, rather than the particle postposed, providing evidence for V-movement in non-root clauses. Pintzuk therefore analyses this as V-movement to I, and goes on to conclude that Verb-Second in Old English is asymmetric. However, the fact that we have V-movement in embedded clauses does not lead straight to the conclusion that Verb-Second is symmetric. The evidence for V-movement is clear, but Pintzuk skips over a step that is necessary to her argument, and that is to show that V-movement in embedded clauses goes together with topicalization. We have already seen ample evidence above that, unaccusative constructions aside, there is no embedded topicalization in Old English; preposed finite verbs in embedded clauses follow the subject, not a topic.

A further step in Pintzuk's account involves the position of pronouns, which she employs as a diagnostic for the position of the finite verb. Consider once more the contrast between topic-initial sentences and wh-initial sentences with respect to the relative position of pronoun and finite verb. This contrast reflects, according to Pintzuk, a genuine contrast with respect to the position of the finite verb. Her hypothesis is that only in those contexts where the pronoun is postverbal, i.e. in wh-questions, negative-initials and sentences introduced by þa, movement is to C. In topic-initial constructions, as the reader will recall, the pronoun is preverbal. This signals to Pintzuk that V-movement is to a position lower than C, namely I.

The convergence of the above two lines of argument, i.e. evidence for V-movement in non-root clauses, and the hypothesis that V-movement is to I in topic-initial sentences, leads Pintzuk to conclude that V-movement in non-root clauses and topic-initial root clauses is essentially the same, and that to that extent Old English Verb-Second involves V-movement to I, with the topic in Spec,IP. Verb-Second in questions, negative-initial and *þa*-initial contexts is truly asymmetric and involves V-movement to C, with the first constituent in Spec,CP. Observe that this account predicts that Verb-Second with topicalization occurs in non-root clauses as well as in root clauses.

Let us now consider some advantages and drawbacks of Pintzuk's account. The dual phrase structure proposed in conjunction with the hypothesis that V-movement is symmetric between topic-initial root clauses and non-root clauses, yields a clear rationale for some of the core word order patterns in Old English. It was observed above that there is a minority pattern where the finite verb is not fronted in root clauses. An example is repeated here for convenience:

(62)   þa folc   him   betweonum ful x   winter þa gewin wraciende
        the peoples them between   full ten winters the fight carrying-on
        wæron
        were
        'The peoples kept up the fight between them for a full ten years'
                                                                (*Or* 1.11.32.6)

This can be accounted for straightforwardly by assuming that here the I-final option of (58b) is at work, with movement of the finite verb to sentence-final I. Similarly, the patterns with V-fronting in non-root clauses can be viewed as instances of the I-medial option (58a), as was discussed above. Some critical remarks are also in order, however. The first is that, even though these patterns are attested in root as well as non-root clauses, there are massive differences in frequency between the two types of clause, which are left unaccounted for.[4] The V-final pattern is a very minor one in root clauses; the work of Koopman (1995) shows that it ranges from 0.5 to 6 per cent. Conversely, V-fronting is very much less frequent in non-root clauses than in root clauses. Secondly, there is also a set of patterns for which the hypothesis that V-fronting can occur in non-root

---

[4] Pintzuk's are the only precise figures available in the literature. She states that 84.7 per cent of main clauses are I-medial (with V-movement to I), and 48.9 per cent of embedded clauses. This is on the basis of a corpus of about 3,800 examples, from 19 texts/text fragments. Pintzuk's percentages, however, are biassed by counting all coordinate clauses as main clauses. In chapter 2.2.3, we discussed briefly the word order of coordinate clauses, noting that with respect to word order, coordinate clauses often behave as subordinate clauses. This means that, if we were to discount coordinate clauses, the percentages for main clauses would be higher, while for subordinate clauses they would be lower, perhaps considerably. More work needs to be done here.

clauses does not suffice. Recall that in non-root clauses, objects sometimes precede the fronted finite verb. The examples are repeated here for convenience:

(63)   . . . ðæt he wisdom mæge wið ofermetta æfre gemengan
               that he wisdom may   with pride   ever mingle
         '. . . that he may always combine wisdom with pride'   (*Met* 7.6)

(64)   ðæt he Saul ne dorste ofslean
               that he Saul not dared murder
               'that he didn't dare to murder Saul'   (*CP* 28.199.2)

The analysis will have to add a proviso to accommodate facts of this sort, which do not fit into either an I-medial or an I-final pattern. This is not necessarily a problem; in fact, an analysis for these facts is proposed in van Kemenade (1987), in which such constructions are viewed as variations on the V-clustering patterns attested in the present-day West Germanic languages. But it is clear that the phrase structure variation proposed by Pintzuk does not obviate the need to maintain an analysis for these special cases, leading to a degree of indeterminacy that is quite substantial. Third and most seriously, we noted above that Pintzuk's analysis predicts Verb-Second with topicalization to occur in non-root clauses as well, contrary to fact. After this brief review of problems and perspectives, let us repeat two gains of Pintzuk's approach, which we should want to maintain in any account: the first is that there is evidence for V-movement in non-root clauses, although it does not go together with topicalization; the second is the insight that V-movement in wh/negative/*þa*-initial contexts is to a higher position than in topic-initial clauses, with the position of pronouns as a diagnostic. Let us now turn to a new set of facts that gives further insight into the precise representation of Old English clause structure, the position of the verb, and the position of pronouns. These facts come from the area of double sentential negation.

4.3.2.2 Sentential negation and its implications for Verb-Second

Old English is a negative concord language, as discussed in chapter 2. In the case of constituent negation, the negative particle *ne*, procliticized to the finite verb, marks the sentential scope of what is morphologically the constituent negation, which is usually expressed by *na/no*. This distinguishes it from sentential negation, in which no constituent negation interpretation is available. (65)–(66) are cases of negative concord (*ne* is procliticized to the finite verb and one or more constituents are also negated):[5]

---

[5] For general discussion concerning the facts of OE negation, the reader is referred to Mourek (1903); Einenkel (1912); Mitchell (1985).

(65)   ... þæt he *na*   siþþan   geboren *ne* wurde
        that he never afterward born   not would-be
        '. . . that he would not be born afterward'   (*Or* 6.9.139.10)

(66)   ... þæt *heora*   *nan*   *ne* mehte *nanes wæpnes* gewealdan
        that of-them none not could no   weapon wield
        '. . . that none of them could wield any weapon'   (*Or* 4.10.103.24)

Sentential negation is nearly always marked by *ne* procliticized to the finite
verb. By sentential negation, we mean those cases where the only interpretation available is that the whole statement is negated:

(67)   Ne sende se deofol ða   fyr of   heofenum, þeah   þe   hit
        not sent   the devil   then fire from heaven   though that it
        ufan   come
        from-above came
        'The devil did not send fire from heaven, though it came from above'
                                                        (*ÆCHom* I(Pref)6.13)

(68)   He ne andwyrde ðam wife   æt fruman
        he not answered   the   woman at first
        'He didn't answer the woman at first'   (*ÆCHom* II, 8.68.45)

There is also a (minority) negation pattern in which sentential negation is
expressed by *ne* + finite verb as well as *na* or some variant thereof.[6]

(69)   þonne ne miht þu na þæt mot   ut   ateon of ðæs mannes eagan
        then   not could you not the speck out draw of the   man's   eye
        'then you could not draw the speck out of the man's eye'
                                                        (*ÆHom* 14.153)

(70)   Ne bið na se   leorningcniht furðor þonne his lareow
        not is   not the apprentice   further than   his master
        'The apprentice is not ahead of his master'   (*ÆHom* 14.134)

These are examples of multiple sentential negation, and they show that the
phenomenon existed at a rather earlier period than is usually assumed, since
the – sometimes implicit – assumption in the literature is that multiple sentential negation is first attested in Middle English.[7] In both of (69) and (70),

---

[6] This is discussed in more detail in van Kemenade (1999). The pattern is a very minor
     one: an exhaustive study of all the major prose texts has thrown up some 330 exam-
     ples. It is hard to quantify this percentagewise, since the number of examples of sen-
     tential negation with *ne* alone is vast, but 330 examples is certain to be well below 5
     per cent of the potential. This pattern is also discussed in section 9.3.2.
[7] Detailed discussion of multiple sentential negation in Middle English can be found
     in Jack (1978a, b, c).

the element *na* cannot be interpreted as modifying the constituent it precedes; in (69), *na* does not modify *þæt mot* (the sentence does not mean: 'it is not the speck that you can draw . . .'); similarly in (70) it does not modify *se leorningcniht*. It is the whole sentence that is being negated by both negation elements. We will illustrate this with examples of *na/no*.

One very striking observation stands out when we consider the examples (69)–(70): when the subject is a pronoun, it appears on the left of *na*; when the subject is a noun, it appears on the right of *na*. Furthermore, object pronouns may occur on the left of *na*, as in (71a). This discrepancy is remarkably systematic in this minority pattern, which is found most prominently in negative-initial sentences. Here are some more examples:

(71)   a. Ne het   he us na leornian heofonas to wyrcenne
           not ordered he us not learn   heavens   to make
           'He did not bid us learn to make the heavens'
                                                    (*ÆLS*(Memory of the Saints) 127)
        b. Nis   na se halga gast wuniende on his gecynde swa swa he
           not is not the holy ghost existing in his nature   as   he
           gesewen wæs
           seen   was
           'The Holy Ghost is not existing in his nature as he was seen'
                                                    (*ÆCHom* I, 22.322.17)
        c. Ne wende   na Ezechias Israhela kyning ðæt he gesyngade . . .
           not thought not Ezechias Israel's king   that he sinned
           'Ezechias, king of Israel, did not think he was sinning . . .'   (*CP* 4.39.2)

These facts show very clearly that the position of the nominal subject is really different from that of the pronominal subject, as these two positions are separated by the reinforcing negation element: the position for the nominal subject is to the right of *na*, and the position on the left of *na* is a general position for pronouns, subject or object, rather than a subject position.

This observation provides a fresh perspective on the discussion of the status of personal pronouns in Old English, and on the nature of the position of pronouns in topic-initial constructions. Before we go on to discuss this, let us consider a more articulate sentential structure than we have assumed so far for Old English, one which is clearly suggested by the negation facts. This structure is in line with recent generative syntactic theorizing in that each morphological element, e.g. tense inflection, negation, agreement inflection, heads its own projection according to the general phrase structure format. Thus, the by now familiar CP/IP format, is further articulated into CP, FP (a projection hosting pronouns), NegP (for negation) and TP (where T stands for Tense). This results in the following structure:

(72)

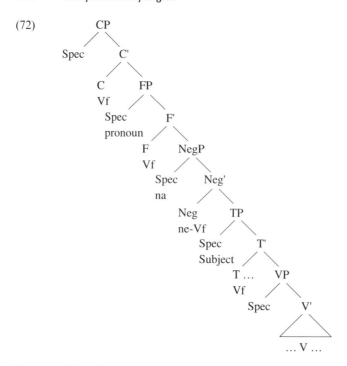

In general, such a structure, with NegP splitting TP from the projection hosting subject pronouns, is motivated by negation facts from languages as diverse as Old French (Hulk and van Kemenade 1997) and modern Hebrew (Shlonsky 1997); the reader is referred to van Kemenade (1999) for further discussion. Recall that the position for pronouns in Old English is not restricted to subject pronouns; object pronouns can occur here as well, as in (71a). Therefore, the projection dominating NegP is one that hosts pronouns, not a feature like, e.g. nominative case. We remain neutral on its precise properties and call it FP. Let us assume that pronominal subjects (and, optionally, objects) inhabit Spec,FP in the structure (72).[8] *Ne* is the head of NegP, and requires incorporation of the finite verb, since it is always proclitic on the finite verb. Let us suppose furthermore that *na* as a second sentential negation element is in Spec,NegP. This is suggested first of all by its fixed position; the

---

[8] This begs some questions concerning the nature of pronouns. The underlying assumption here is that Old English personal pronouns are Germanic-style weak pronouns rather than Romance-style phonologically reduced clitics, according to the typology of NP types in Cardinaletti and Starke (1996). This is in line with the findings of Koopman (1997), who shows that the criteria for clitic status formulated by Kayne (1975) (which are geared toward the properties of French clitics) give rather equivocal results for Old English.

position of specifier elements is fixed because it is determined by licensing requirements. The fact that this is a fixed position is supported further by the fact that *na*, even when it is morphologically a constituent negation, sometimes moves away from its constituent to the characteristic position for *na*, as observed above. (73) illustrates this:

(73) a. ne leofað se   mann *na* be hlafe anum, ac lyfað be eallum ðam
          not lives the man   not by bread alone but lives by all   the
          wordum þe gað of   godes muðe
          words   that go from God's mouth   (*ÆCHom* I, 11.166.15)
      b. Ne lifað *na* se   man be hlafe anum, ac lifað be ðam wordum
          not lives not the man by bread alone, but lives by the   words
          ðe gað of   godes muðe
          that go from God's mouth   (*ÆCHom* I, 11.168.26)
          'Man lives not by bread alone, but lives by the words that go from the
          mouth of God'

The contrast between (73a) and (73b) is interesting. (73a) shows the essential constituent negation of *na*: 'man lives *not by bread alone*'. But on the next page, we find the same sentence with the same constituent negation meaning, but with *na* in the position characteristically as in (71): on the left of the nominal subject. We can account for this fixed position of sentential *na* by assuming that the second sentential negator occupies Spec,NegP, and that sometimes, in a case of constituent negation with sentential scope like (73), the constituent negator *na* moves to Spec,NegP.

In the structure (72), we can account for the basic Verb-Second patterns as discussed above. Recall that the core patterns are as follows:

(74)   a. Wh-element (or *ne* or *þa*)–Vf–Subject . . .
          b. Topic–Vf–Subject NP . . .
          c. Topic–Spronoun–Vf . . .

If the first constituent is an interrogative constituent, as in (74a), that constituent is in Spec,CP and Vf moves to C (through intermediate head positions as indicated in (72)). If the subject is a noun, it is in Spec,TP in (72); if it is a pronoun, it is in Spec,FP. This difference in position is not visible on the surface in wh-questions. It emerges very clearly, however, in (74b–c). Topics move to Spec,CP like wh-constituents (recall that this is shown by the fact that they occur only in root clauses). But they do not draw Vf to C, as seems to be true for all historical stages of English, except in some Northern texts in Middle English, as will be discussed below. Rather, Vf moves to the head position of FP, where it is followed by the nominal subject (in Spec,TP) as in (74b), or preceded by the pronominal subject (in Spec,FP), as in (74c). The advantage of this analysis over previous ones is that there is a separate position for pronouns, and that this position is not contingent on proclisis to Vf or enclisis to the topic. Rather, pronouns have a position of their own, and their position relative to Vf is determined by the movement requirements on Vf, to C in interrogative and negative-initial contexts, to F in topic-initial contexts, and presumably also in subject-initial contexts. This appropriately captures Pintzuk's insight that the position of the finite verb in wh-initial clauses is higher than in topic-initial clauses, while at the same time maintaining that topic-initial 'Verb-Second' is restricted to root clauses: this is because the topic position is Spec,CP and hence restricted to root contexts. V-movement is to F, a position lower than C, but the facts show that a more articulate version of IP, consisting of at least three projections FP, NegP, and TP, is well supported.

This more articulated structure brings us back to the phrase structure variation proposed by Pintzuk, in which the contrast between topic-initial sentences with and without preposing of the verb is attributed to variation in the headedness of IP. We have now seen clear evidence that in topic-initial sentences, V-movement is to F, the head of the projection hosting pronouns, and we might ask ourselves whether it would be attractive to assume that FP has a similar variation in headedness. At this stage, it seems difficult to answer this question. If the possibility of phrase structure competition is countenanced and if variation in headedness is likewise countenanced – but these are questions on which there is by no means consensus in the literature – there is no reason why FP could not have variation in headedness. One may wonder why it is FP that gives evidence of this variation and not other functional projections. This is presumably an empirical problem and one which cannot be solved without very (perhaps impossibly) detailed data research. We leave this problem for now, noting, as discussed in chapter 1, that optionality is a persistent challenge for any theoretical approach that aims at generalization. The assumption of phrase structure competition is only one out of several approaches with which this problem can in principle be tackled.

4.3.2.3 Quantitative evidence

After these analytical issues, let us return to evidential issues and look at some figures for topic-initial constructions as we have now analysed them. Koopman (1998) presents some quantitative data on finite verb position in clauses introduced by object topics and PP topics: his article shows that the pattern discussed above with pronominal subjects in topic-initial clauses is absolutely predominant: V-movement to F, with 'non-inversion' of pronominal subjects is the norm (9 out of 624 examples have inversion, i.e. just over one per cent). For topic-initial constructions with nominal subjects, the facts are more variable: while inversion of the nominal subject is the norm in the works of *Ælfric* (the most substantial part of Koopman's corpus, with percentages ranging from ninety-one to ninety-four per cent), the figures are equivocal for the two early texts, *Cura Pastoralis* and *Orosius*. There may be several reasons for this, not the least of which may be that both are early texts translated from Latin, which was not a Verb-Second language. Another, more tentative, suggestion that must await further research is that Verb-Second in topic-initials may be an innovation in progress in early Old English, the time when both texts were written. This suggestion cannot, however, be correct for another text where inversion of nominal subjects is also variable (occurring in roughly fifty per cent of all cases): *The Homilies of Wulfstan*. Wulfstan was a contemporary of Ælfric and his thunderous homilies are from the late tenth and early eleventh centuries. Their different grammatical patterning may be due to their highly rhetorical character, which tends to take the form of spoken address. These suggestions must, of course, remain somewhat speculative, and a good deal of more fine-grained quantitative analysis needs to be done. But we can draw the following conclusions: first of all, Verb-Second in topic-initial constructions as analysed here is a robust grammatical option in Old English, indeed in our most substantial body of texts (the works of *Ælfric*), it is used in over ninety per cent of the cases. But other, perhaps competing, grammatical options, are also employed at varying rates: there is a minority pattern where the finite verb is not moved in root clauses, as noted above; and there are also topic-initial sentences where the finite verb is moved to a position below that of the nominal subject (hence the varying percentage of non-inversion of nominal subjects). The refinement of the analysis of clausal architecture gained from the facts concerning multiple sentential negation allows a very precise view of positions within the sentence and provides a good basis for further (future) quantitative research.

Summarizing this section, we observe that real asymmetric Verb-Second in Old English, involving V-movement to C, is found in wh-initial, negative-initial and *þa*-initial contexts (beside imperatives, etc., which we have not discussed here). Topic-initial Verb-Second is slightly different in nature: it is asymmetric because the topic position is Spec,CP; nevertheless it involves a type of V-movement that is also found in non-root clauses, albeit at a considerably lower frequency, and in which V moves to F in the structure (72). This movement does not always take place.

4.4   Developments after the Old English period

In the transition from Old to Middle English, the basic Verb-Second patterns that we have seen for Old English in the previous section were preserved. The following examples show that, in a variety of texts from various dates and dialects, topicalization in root clauses continues to go together with verb–subject order with nominal subjects (75), and subject–verb order with pronominal subjects (76).

(75)   a. On þis gær wolde   þe king Stephne tæcen Rodbert . . .
        in this year wanted the king Stephen seize   Robert
        'During this year king Stephen wanted to seize Robert . . .'
                                    (NE.Midl, C12; *ChronE* (Plummer) 1140.1)
        b. ȝewiss   hafð godd forworpen ðan ilche mann . . .
        certainly has   God rejected   that same man
        'certainly God has rejected that same man'
                                    (EMidl. C13; *Vices&V* 13.31)
        c. Nu loke euerich man toward himseluen
        now look every   man to   himself
        'Now it's for every man to look to himself'
                                    (South-East, C13; *Ken.Serm* 218.134)
(76)   a. Das þing we habbað be   him gewritene
        these things we have   about him written
        'These things we have written about him'
                                    (NE.Midl, C11; *ChronE*(Plummer) 1086.139)
        b. bi þis ȝe mahen seon ant witen . . .)
        'by this you may see and know . . .' (W.Midl, early C 13; *SWard.* 263.23
        c. alle ðese bebodes ic habbe ihealde fram childhade)
        'all these commandments I have kept from childhood'
                                    (EMidl. C13; *Vices&V* 67.32)

The main word order difference between Old and Middle English is that in the latter, considerably fewer OV orders are found. This change does not seem to bear a direct relation to the positioning of the finite verb; it is discussed in detail in chapter 5. Another difference from Old English is that in early Middle English, personal pronoun objects cease to occur in Spec,FP, to the left of a finite verb moved to F in the structure (72).

The positional discrepancy between nominal and pronominal subjects with respect to the finite verb attested to by (75) and (76) likewise continues to be attested in multiple negation patterns. In the Middle English period, *na* and its variants were replaced by *not* and variants thereof as the second negator, and by the end of the Middle English period, *ne* (procliticized to the finite verb) had almost disappeared and had been replaced by *not*. The different positions of nominal and pronominal subjects can be seen in early Middle English in what was then a minority set of environments: negative-initial and negative topic-initial sentences, as in (77) and (78).

(77)   þis ne   habbe ic nauht ofearned
        this not have I not   earned
        'this I have not earned'   (*Vices&V* 17.9)

(78)   Forþi   ne schal nouȝt þe wicked arise in iugement
        therefore not shall not   the wicked arise in judgement
        'Therefore, the wicked shall not rise in judgement'   (*EARLPS* 1.6)

Kroch and Taylor (1997) present some quantitative evidence from texts in the Southern and Midlands dialects which suggests that nominal subjects precede the finite verb in percentages varying from five to 20 per cent, depending in part on the precise nature of the first constituent. Compared to the figures for Old English from Koopman (1998) discussed above, this cannot clearly be interpreted as a significant development.

Kroch and Taylor (1997) offer a tempting argument in favour of dialect variation with respect to the position of the finite verb between the Northern Middle English dialect attested in the prose version of *The Rule of St. Benet*, from the early thirteenth century, and Southern dialects such as those illustrated in (75) and (76). In *The Rule of St. Benet*, no trace is found of the positional contrast between nominal and pronominal subjects with respect to the finite verb in topic-initial constructions; nominal and pronominal subjects are both inverted, which leads to the conclusion that finite V-movement is always to C in this dialect:

(79)   a. Allekin   mekenes   sal   man muster til þe gestis
           all manner of meekness shall man muster to the guests
           'All manner of humbleness shall be shown to the guests'
                                                    (*Ben. Rule(1)* (Lnsd) 35.11)
        b. Oþir labur   sal   þai do
           other labour shall they do
           'They must do other labour'   (*Ben. Rule(1)* (Lnsd) 33.20)
        c. In þa dais sal   we here sumþing   of godes seruise
           in the days shall we hear something of God's service
           'In those days (Lent) we will hear something about the service of God'
                                                    (*Ben. Rule(1)* (Lnsd) 33.35)

Kroch and Taylor present an argument that the dialect contrast should be attributed to Scandinavian influence in the Northern and Eastern dialects of English. The Scandinavian invasions in England in the eighth and ninth centuries presumably led to a large-scale situation of language contact in everyday communication, which is evident from the nature of the loanwords that entered English from the Scandinavian languages. These loanwords comprise such grammatical words as the pronoun *they*, the infinitive marker *at* and everyday words like *egg, sky, skin, skill*. The impact of this is not visible before the Middle English period, because the Old English text material was from areas outside Scandinavian influence.

The Northern syntax as it appears in *The Rule of St. Benet* has categorical subject–verb inversion in root contexts only and should, according to

Kroch and Taylor, be analysed as an asymmetric Verb-Second language in which the finite verb always moves to C in root clauses. This contrasts with the southern dialects of Middle English, in which, as we have seen from the above data, the Old English situation with respect to Verb-Second was continued. Kroch and Taylor analyse the position of the finite verb in the Southern dialect in the same way as Pintzuk analyses Old English. The dialect contrast is then one between a categorical C-Verb-Second dialect (the North) and I-Verb-Second dialects (the Southern dialects). We have seen in the previous sections that Pintzuk's analysis for Old English can be refined in interesting ways when we take into account the negation data as we have in section 4.3.2.2; and in the light of the positional contrast between nominal and pronominal subjects that we still see in Middle English, this revised analysis applies to Middle English as well. This detracts in no way from the interest of Kroch and Taylor's findings; the contrast is then one between a categorical C-Verb-Second dialect (the North) and a group of dialects in which in subject- and topic-initial clauses, the finite verb very often moves to a position F which is lower than C (the Southern dialects). It may be noted that in other texts from the Northern dialect, facts similar to those in *The Rule of St. Benet* are found, but not nearly as systematically. Conversely, there are texts like the Middle English part of the E manuscript of the *Anglo-Saxon Chronicle*, better known as *The Peterborough Chronicle*, which show strong Scandinavian influence in their vocabulary, but whose Verb-Second syntax patterns with that of the Southern dialects (in fact, examples (75a) and (76a) are from this text). Yet another slightly complicating fact is that in one prose translation (but not others) by Geoffrey Chaucer, the late fourteenth century *Treatise on the Astrolabe*, Verb-Second with inversion is categorical in all root contexts, and this is a text in which there is no clear Scandinavian influence. All this leaves a somewhat confusing picture – there is a lot left to investigate here, and even then, the precise picture may well remain hidden by the mists of time.

In the late fourteenth and early fifteenth century, the variant of the Verb-Second phenomenon in topic-initial constructions as discussed above shows a sharp decline. While in earlier stages a positional discrepancy between nominal and pronominal subjects with respect to the finite verb was found, verb–subject order with nominal subjects was lost. The first texts where we see this happening with considerable frequency are the prose writings of Richard Rolle, which were written in the mid-fourteenth century in Yorkshire. In (80), some examples are given of non-inversion with nominal subjects. The same situation obtains in the writings of Wycliffe (this is confirmed by the figures on a sample of Wycliffe in MacLeish (1969)), as illustrated in (81). The

writings of Wycliffe date from the last quarter of the fourteenth century and
were written in Oxfordshire.

(80)   a. Thare-fore Ihesu es noghte funden in reches
          'Therefore Jesus is not found in riches'   (*Rolle* 5.8)
       b. Sothely þe ryghtwyse sekys þe Ioye and . . .
          'Truly the righteous seeks the joy and . . .'   (*Rolle* 4.24)

(81)   a. And by þis same skyle hope and sorwe schulle iugen us
          'And by this same skill hope and sorrow shall judge us'
                                 (*Wycl.Serm.* 372.97)
       b. bi song the fend lettiþ men to studie
          'by song the devil prevents men from studying'
                              (Wycl *Feigned Cont. Life* 112)

In the fifteenth century, inversion of nominal subjects, i.e. V-movement to F,
declines further. The quantitative results in various studies are rather variable:
what makes them of limited use is that none of these studies make a distinction between nominal and pronominal subjects, which was seen to be of crucial
importance in Old and Middle English. Some conclusions can still be drawn,
however, since the presence of inversion implies that the older pattern remains,
presumably mainly with nominal subjects. Jacobsson (1951), in a general
survey of inversion in sentences introduced by *then, now, there, here, so, yet* and
therefore, records percentages between eighty-five and ninety per cent for the
late fourteenth century; twenty-eight to thirty-nine per cent for the mid-
fifteenth century; and ten per cent and lower for the end of the fifteenth century.
This is confirmed by the findings of Schmidt (1980). On the other hand, in
Jacobsson's figures, individual texts from the sixteenth century have inversion
percentages ranging between three per cent and eighty-five per cent and anything in between, to an average of thirty-four per cent. This bewildering variation between texts would seem to suggest that inversion comes to reflect
stylistic rather than grammatical preferences, and it is at this stage difficult to
say whether we are dealing with a grammatical phenomenon or not. In the
seventeenth century, inversion is really disappearing: in most texts in
Jacobsson's figures, the percentage is well below ten per cent, although there
are two with percentages between forty and fifty per cent. The sum of these
figures suggests that there is a grammatical decline of V to F in the fifteenth
century, a revival, perhaps as a stylistic feature, in the sixteenth century, and a
final decline in the seventeenth century and later. But Jacobsson's figures do not
fit with those of Nevalainen (1997), based on *the Helsinki Corpus*: Nevalainen's
figures show that in her corpus, inversion after adverbs steadily declines
between 1420 and 1710 from about thirty-seven per cent to well below ten per
cent, although this may be due to the fact that her figures are averaged over

rather long periods. In Nevalainen's *Corpus of Early English Correspondences*, the inversion figures are even lower.

Another general problem with the figures available in the literature is that no distinction is made between finite lexical verbs and (pre)modals. Nevertheless, this distinction may well be vitally important in view of the changes in the (pre)modals taking place around this time, as discussed in chapter 1. For instance, in chapter 5 we will see that in the fifteenth century, some word order phenomena are restricted to environments with an 'auxiliary'. Clearly, this remains to be sorted out further, on the basis of quantitative analysis of a substantial corpus, with special attention to a distinction between lexical finite verbs and modals and other auxiliaries in the making in the fifteenth century and perhaps to possible differences between texts that reflect colloquial speech more closely, and others. Pending such further research, we cannot but draw the conclusion that inversion, i.e. V-movement to F, although possibly subject to widely varying individual or stylistic differences, was not lost before the eighteenth century. This date raises the question of how the loss of V to F is related to what is in the literature called the loss of V to I, as in Roberts (1985), Kroch (1989), Lightfoot (1997) and Warner (1997). On the analysis of Old English Verb-Second of Pintzuk (1991) and Kroch and Taylor (1997), where Verb-Second is analysed as V to I, one would expect the change we identify here as the loss of V to F, and that of the loss of V to I, to be identical. There is evidence against this: the loss of V to I is generally assumed to be correlated with the rise of *do*-support; this correlation is made particularly forcefully by Kroch (1989). If the loss of V to F and the loss of V to I are the same thing, Kroch's constant rate account breaks down, since V to F saw a sharp decline in the fifteenth century, some time before the rise of *do*-support started taking off seriously by the close of the fifteenth century. Moreover, there is some independent evidence for a separate V-movement strategy, V-to-T movement as in Roberts (1995), the loss of which set in later, and whose dating seems to tally more closely with the loss of V to I as discussed in the literature. While fine-grained quantitative research remains to be done, it seems safest to say that the loss of V to F and the loss of V to T (in the literature V to I) are separate developments, each with their own rate of change.

Whatever the details, it is of some interest to consider the nature of this change. Van Kemenade (1987) attributes it to the changing character of subject pronouns: whereas previously they behaved like weak pronouns (in terms of the analysis in the present chapter, they occupied FP), this special behaviour was lost, and as a result nominal and pronominal subjects began to behave alike, which triggered the loss of V-movement to C, or, in our analysis here, V to F. The negation facts discussed above show that this view cannot be correct. We saw above that nominal and pronominal subjects occupy different positions with respect to the negation element (77)–(78). And at the time when inversion of nominal subjects in topic-initial constructions is being lost, and hence the evidence for Verb-Second was lost, this positional discrepancy continues to be found. In fact, Rissanen (1994, 1999) shows that this positional discrepancy is found until well into the seventeenth century. We can see this clearly in negative questions: as observed above, negative-initial sentences and questions continued to have movement of the finite verb to the C-position, as they still do nowadays. If we then consider negative questions like those in (82), in which the finite verb has moved to C, the position of *not* continues to have the diagnostic value for the position of the nominal and pronominal subject.

(82)   a. why shulde hee not . . .
        'why should he not . . .'
                        (*Trial of Throckmorton*.70.C2; Rissanen 1994: 339)
        b. Dyd not christ lykewyse ascend vnto his father . . . ?
        'Did not Christ likewise ascend to his Father . . .?'
                                    (Fischer 317; Rissanen 1994: 340)
        c. why ordeyned not God such   ordre
        why ordained not God such an order
        'why did not God ordain such an order'
                                    (Wycl. *Sermons* 32.358; Rissanen 1994: 341)
        c. why is there not a schole for the wardes . . .
        'why is there not a school for the wards . . .'
                                    (Latimer 28; Rissanen 1994: 342)

This gives us clear evidence that the loss of inversion with nominal subjects (the loss of movement of the finite verb to the position F in the structure (72)) is not related to the putative change in the character of pronouns, since the behaviour of pronouns remains the same. Rather, we are forced to the conclusion that the change is simply that the finite verb ceases to move to the position F. What could be the trigger for such a change? We will make a tentative suggestion. The reader will recall that functional projections such as FP, NegP, TP, often encode information about inflectional morphology. Suppose that FP represents the morphology for subject–verb agreement. This seems attractive, because it is the landing site for the finite verb, which is where agreement is expressed. From this perspective, it is interesting to note that around the same time as V-movement to F was lost, a number of verb-agreement inflections were lost as well, in particular a number of singular–plural contrasts. We might therefore hypothesize that movement of the finite verb to the position F in (72) was lost because in many cases the relevant specifications for agreement inflection on the finite verb were lost. This ties in with current literature in which V-movement strategies are keyed to the presence of inflectional morphology, e.g. Roberts (1993) and Rohrbacher (1994).

There are some drawbacks to the postulation of loss of morphology as a trigger for loss of V-movement: the most important reservation may certainly be that such an analysis of the change has important implications for how language change works, for it implies that language learners draw conclusions about word order, not on the basis of word order patterns themselves, but on the basis of inflectional morphology. This recalls our discussion in section 1.2 on the question to what extent grammar change can reasonably be supposed to be UG-driven. Let us consider this in some more detail for the case in point: suppose there was some stage at which the word order patterns still give clear evidence for V-movement to F (i.e. we still have robust inversion of nominal subjects in topic-initial constructions), but agreement morphology lacks the relevant specifications. This scenario allows for the possibility that the language learner concludes that the relevant agreement specifications are missing and that the finite verb must hence not be moved to F, even though the word order patterns give clear evidence for this. This means that the language learner ignores positive word order evidence and constructs a grammar that systematically deviates from his language environment. While there are some case studies in the literature which suggest that this can happen (in particular, Henry (1997); a similar approach is allowed for by the theory presented in Clark and Roberts (1993), both discussed in 1.2), many others believe that this is not how word order change can work. They would prefer an approach in which changes in word order patterns are analysed in their own terms, and would favour an analysis in which we could see that the evidence for certain patterns becomes too infrequent. For instance, Lightfoot (1999), working on the cue-based model of grammar acquisition, follows up on the grammar competition approach in Kroch and Taylor (1997), and suggests that, as a result of dialect contact between the Northern and Southern dialects, the cue feeding into the parameter setting for Verb-Second, verb–subject order after a topic, fell below the required threshold of robustness. It is unclear, however, whether this hypothesis will stand the test of detailed quantitative investigation, which has yet to be done. We will leave the matter for further exploration.

Summarizing, we have considered in this chapter a detailed argument towards the proper analysis of Old English word order where it concerns the position of the finite verb. There is good reason to analyse negative-initial sentences and questions as involving movement of the finite verb to the C-position in the structure (72) throughout the history of English. Subject-initial sentences and topic-initial sentences are a different matter: in Old English, subjects and topics occur in the Spec,CP position in root clauses, whereas the finite verb moves to F. In topic-initial clauses, pronouns appear on the left of the finite verb in F (and to the left of the second negation element), whereas nominal subjects appear on the right of finite verb and second negation element. During the late Middle English and early Modern periods, movement of the finite verb to F was lost, for which we have tentatively suggested a motivation.

5

The loss of object–verb word order

5.1 Introduction

One of the most prominent syntactic differences between present-day English and earlier English involves the order of object and verb. Consider, for example, the sentences in (1)–(3), which are from the Old English, Early Middle English, and Late Middle English periods, respectively. We have italicized the relevant object(s).

(1)   ond he *his feorh* generede, ond þeah he wæs oft   gewundad
         and he his life   saved   and yet   he was often wounded
         'and he saved his life, although he was often wounded'
                                            (*ChronA* (Plummer) 755.38)

(2)   Hi   hadden him *manred* maked and *athes* sworen,
         they had   him homage done   and oaths sworn
         ac   hi   *nan treuthe* ne   holden
         but they no   truth   not kept
         'They had done him homage and sworn oaths of allegiance to him, but they
         did not keep their word'   (*ChronE* (Plummer) 1137.11)

(3)   If so be that thou ne   mayst nat *thyn owene conseil* hyde,
         if so be that you   not can   not your own   counsel hide
         how darstou   preyen any oother wight *thy*   *conseil* secrely to kepe?
         how dare-you ask   any other   person your counsel secret   to keep
         'If it is the case that you cannot hide your own counsel, how could you dare
         to ask anyone else to keep your counsel secret?'   (Chaucer *Melibee* 1147)

Each of these sentences has one or more objects preceding the lexical verb(s). In Modern English, of course, the object has to follow the verb, as the translations of (1)–(3) show.

It has often been observed on the basis of facts like these that English changed from an OV language to a VO language, and over the years, many researchers have addressed the question why this should have happened. In this chapter, we shall discuss this change, and the analyses and arguments that have been advanced in the generative literature dealing with it. However, before we come to the theoretical considerations that may play a role in accounting for this change, we shall need to establish precisely when and how it took place. This is an aspect of the change that has not received much attention. Indeed, one might get the impression from some of the literature that OV order disappeared completely after the Old English period. But examples such as (2) and (3) (and we shall give many more in what follows) show that OV remained possible throughout the Middle English period. In fact, it did not disappear from prose writings until the sixteenth century, while in verse it continued being used as a productive option well into the nineteenth century.

And not only did OV order continue after the end of the Old English period; the modern order, VO, is also found before the start of the Middle English period. This means that, as far as surface order is concerned, the development was more gradual than has often been suggested. It is true that there is a rapid increase in surface VO order between the Old and Middle English periods, but as we shall show in detail below, this largely takes the form of a shift in frequency among patterns already in existence.

Section 5.2 contains a descriptive overview of the word order patterns found in Old English. As shown in chapter 4, there is an operation of V-movement that affects many clauses containing only one (finite) verb in Old English, obscuring the basic positional patterns of the object vis-à-vis the verb. In the second section of this chapter, we shall therefore concentrate on clauses with a non-finite verb, or with a finite verb that has not been fronted. In section 5.3, we will discuss how these Old English clauses are to be analysed. The development during the Middle English period is the topic of sections 5.4 and 5.5. In section 5.4, the emphasis is on the empirical details of the changes affecting verb-object order. After these have been established, we will consider in section 5.5 how the Middle English data can be analysed. Section 5.6, finally, will deal with the question how a theoretical perspective might illuminate the nature of the changes involving the order of the object and the verb in the Old and Middle English periods.

5.2   Old English: the basic facts

In chapter 2, we saw that the order of object and verb was considerably freer in Old English than it is in present-day English. Let us consider this picture in more detail now. As pointed out above, we will focus the discussion on the position of the non-finite verb and that of the finite verb when it is not fronted. The non-finite verb forms in Old English are the infinitive, and the present and past participles.

While the position of the finite verb is in part dependent on the type of clause (main, embedded or coordinate), the position of non-finite forms does not appear to be determined by clause type. (4) and (5) illustrate the core variation that we address in this chapter: in (4) the object precedes its lexical verb; in (5), the object and other elements follow it.

(4)   ðæt he *hwelc gerisenlic wundor* wyrcean mæge
       that he some suitable   miracle perform can
       'that he is able to perform some suitable miracle'   (*CP* 17.119.9)

(5)   þæt he nolde   niman *mancyn*   neadunga of   ðam deofle
       that he not-would take mankind forcibly from the   devil
       'that he would not have taken mankind forcibly from the devil'
                                                        (*ÆCHom* I, 14.1.216.4)

Not all elements can freely appear to the right or left of the verb. Let us first consider those that appear to the left predominantly or exclusively. This class of elements comprises negative adverbs, verb particles, stranded prepositions, pronominal objects, and – probably – adverbs.

The negative adverb *ne* is always on the immediate left of the finite verb, whatever the position of the latter, which is a strong argument for the assumption that *ne* is proclitic on the finite verb, as we also saw in chapter 4. Some examples are given in (6) and (7).

(6)   þæt he na   siþþan   geboren *ne* wurde
       that he never afterward born   not would-be
       'that he would not be born afterward'   (*Or* 9.139.10)

(7)   *Ne* sende se   deofol ða   fyr of   heofenum,
       not sent   the devil then fire from heaven
       þeah þe hit ufan   come
       though that it from-above came
       'The devil did not send fire from heaven, though it came from above'
                                                        (*ÆCHom* I(Pref) 6.13)

More generally, sentential negation markers are on the left of the verb, as in (8):

(8)   þas þing gedafenode soðlice to donne,
       these things was-fitting truly   to do
       and eac þa oðre   *na* to forlætene.
       and also the others not to neglect
       'it is indeed fitting to do these things, and also not to neglect the others.'
                                                        (*ÆHom* 3.104)

Verb particles are commonly found in a position to the immediate left of the lexical verb, as in (9) and (10).

(9)   gif hio ne   bið hrædlice aweg adrifen
         if she not is   quickly   away driven
         'if it is not quickly driven away'   (*CP* 13.79.23)

(10)   þæt hie mid þæm þæt folc   ut   aloccoden
         that they with that the people out enticed
         that they with that the people out enticed
         'that with it they might entice the people to come outside'   (*Or* 5.3.117.5)

Particles sometimes appear in a higher position in the clause, as in (11), but in such cases the particle usually precedes a PP and is likely to be a modifier of the PP.

(11)   ðeah   ðu sie up ofer ðine mæð   ahæfen
         though you are up over your condition raised
         'although you are raised above your condition'   (*CP* 65.467.1)

Particles are occasionally found to the right of a non-fronted verb. An example is given in (12).

(12)   þa   wolde   seo Sexburh æfter syxtyne gearum
         then wanted the Sexburh after sixteen years
         don hire swustor ban   of   ðære byrgene   up
         take her sister's bones from the   burial-place up
         'After sixteen years Sexburh wanted to take up her sister's bones from their
         burial-place'   (*ÆLS*(Æthelthryth) 73)

These are the main patterns involving particles that are relevant in this chapter; see chapter 6 for a more detailed treatment.

The position of stranded prepositions is similar to that of particles, but it is even more restricted: stranded prepositions are nearly always left-adjacent to the verb, as in (13). Instances where the preposition is on the right are even rarer than those with particles, but again the occasional example is found with the preposition right-adjacent to a non-fronted verb, as in (14).

(13)   þa   wæs hiora   an   se Apollinus þe we ær   ymb   spræcon
         then was of-them one the Apollinus that we before about spoke
         'Then one of them was the Apollinus that we spoke about before'
                                              (*Bo* 38.116.1)

(14)   þæt is þæt uplice   rice,   þe he sylf wunaþ
         that is the heavenly kingdom that he self lives
         on mid eallum his halgum a   butan   ende.
         in with all   his saints forever without end
         'that is the heavenly kingdom, which he himself forever dwells in with all
         his saints.'   (*HomU* 46(Nap 57) 245)

Personal pronoun objects often occupy a position immediately after the subject and finite verb, as in (15), and sometimes on the immediate left of a non-finite verb, as in (16). A rare example of a different position is given in (17).

(15)   nu   wille we *eow* hwæt lytles   be   him gereccan
        now want   we you   what of-little about him tell
        'now we want to relate to you a little thing concerning him'
        (*ÆCHom* II, 35.260.1)

(16)   þonne wolde þæt Iudeisce folc,   æfter Godes
        then   would the Jewish   people   after God's
        æ,   mid stanum *hi* oftorfian
        law   with stones her   stone
        'then the Jewish people would have stoned her to death with stones after
        God's law'   (*ÆCHom* I, 13.196.10)

(17)   nu   wylle we sum ðing scortlice *eow* be   him gereccan
        now want   we some thing briefly   you   about him tell
        'now we want to tell you briefly something about him' (*ÆCHom* II, 9.72.9)

Pronominal objects very occasionally occur on the right of a non-fronted verb; (18) and (19) are two examples. Note that in (18) there are two objects, one of which is pronominal.

(18)   We wyllað secgan *eow* sum bigspell
        We want   tell   you   a   parable
        'We want to tell you a parable'   (*ÆCHom* I, 14.1.212.6)

(19)   He nolde   geniman *us* neadunge of deofles anwealde
        he not-wanted take   us   forcibly of devil's power
        'He would not forcibly take us from the devil's power' (*ÆCHom* I, 1.26.29)

Koopman (1994) notes that pronominal objects following the non-finite verb are very infrequent and are found only in texts later than 950. This must therefore be considered an innovative pattern.

Adverbs of any kind usually appear in some position to the left of any non-fronted verb, which suggests that they are restricted to preverbal position. This is illustrated by (20) and (21). (22) is an exceptional example where the adverb follows the infinitive:

(20)   Simon ... getigde ænne ormætne ryððan innan ðam geate ...
        Simon   tied   a   huge   mastiff inside the gate
        þæt   he færlice   hine abitan sceolde
        so-that he suddenly   him   bite   might
        'Simon . . . tied a huge mastiff inside the gate . . . so that he might suddenly
        bite him'   (*ÆCHom* I, 26.372.33)

(21)   Hwa wolde me æfre gelyfan ...?
        who would me ever believe
        'Who would ever believe me . . . ?'   (*ÆCHom* II, 6.53.37)

(22)   Ac we sceolon biddan soðlice þa halgan . . .
        but we must   pray   truly   the saints
        'But we must truly pray to the saints . . .'   (*ÆLS*(Swithun) 284)

It must be said, however, that the positioning of adverbs in Old English is an
under-studied topic. There are no comprehensive investigations of all their
word order possibilities. The examples quoted in Swan (1988) suggest that sentence adverbs do not really have a fixed position, but it may be that other
adverbs (such as e.g. *þa* 'then') do.

Let us now consider the elements that have greater distributional freedom
with respect to the verb. Nominal objects, PPs and infinitives without *to*
belong to this class. On the face of it, the first two types of elements may occur
anywhere between subject and non-finite verb, as in (23) and (24), and very
often appear left-adjacent to it, as in (25).

(23)   He mæg *ða synfullan sawle þurh*   *his gife geliffæstan*
        he can the sinful   soul through his gift endow-with-life
        'He can endow the sinful soul with life through his grace'
                                                         (*ÆCHom* I, 33.496.30)

(24)   þæt he *ure sawle fram synna fagnyssum gehælan mæge*
        that he our soul from of-sins ulcers   heal   can
        'that he can heal our soul from the ulcers of sin'   (*ÆCHom* I, 8.122.24)

(25)   Ða se Wisdom þa   *þis fitte* asungen hæfde,
        when the Wisdom then this poem sung   had
        þa ongon he eft   seggan spell
        then began he again tell   story
        'When Wisdom had sung this poem, he again began to tell a story'
                                                                      (*Bo* 30.68.6)

(24) also illustrates the position of the bare (i.e. without *to*) infinitival complement when it is preverbal. The infinitival complement *ure sawle fram synna
fagnyssum gehælan* precedes the finite verb. When a non-finite verb form precedes the finite verb, nothing can intervene between them. There are examples
where an object of the infinitive follows the finite verb, as in (26), but these are
not very frequent.

(26)   þæt gehwær   on Godes gelaðunge   se sacerd
        that everywhere in God's congregation the priest
        bletsian sceole *palmtwigu* on ðisum dæge
        bless   should palmtwigs on this   day
        'that everywhere in God's congregation the priest should bless palm-twigs
        on this day'   (*ÆCHom* I, 14.1.218.1)

The NP *palmtwigu* is the object of the infinitive *bletsian*, and it follows the
finite verb.

All of these elements are also readily found to the right of a non-fronted verb: examples can be seen of a nominal indirect object in (27), a nominal direct object in (28), a PP in (29), a PP and a subject complement in (30) and a bare infinitival complement in (31).

(27)   þæt he hæfde his ðing   and hine sylfne betæht   *þam halgan were*
        that he had   his things and him self   committed the   holy   man
        Benedicte
        Benedict
        'that he has committed his property and himself to the holy man Benedict'
                                                            (*ÆCHom* II, 11.105.449)

(28)   þæt hi   urum godum geoffrian magon *ðancwurðe onsægednysse*
        that they our   gods   offer   may   grateful   sacrifice
        'that they may offer a grateful sacrifice to our gods' (*ÆCHom* I, 38.592.31)

(29)   þæt hy   syððan   faran scoldon *geond   ealne middaneard*
        that they afterwards go   must   throughout all   world
        'that they must afterwards travel throughout the world'   (*WHom* 7.78)

(30)   ðe   is genemned *on Læden Pastoralis*, &   *on Englisc*
        which is called   in Latin   Pastoralis and in English
        Hierdeboc
        shepherd's-book
        'which in Latin is called Pastoralis and in English Shepherds' Book'
                                                            (*CP*LetWærf 58)

(31)   þæt hi   mihton swa bealdlice Godes geleafan bodian
        that they could   so   boldly   God's faith   preach
        'that they could preach God's faith so boldly'   (*ÆCHom* I, 16.232.23)

As noted in chapter 4, subjects occupy a high position in the clause, but in passive and unaccusative constructions they can also be found lower, and even to the right of a non-fronted verb, though this is not very frequent. (32) and (33) illustrate this possibility.

(32)   ðonne ne   magon ðider fullice becuman
        then   not can   there fully   arrive
        ða stæpas ðæs   weorces ðieder ðe   he wilnað
        the steps   of-the work   where that he wants
        'then the steps of the work cannot arrive at the desired point' (*CP* 11.65.16)

(33)   þurh   ða wifunge   sind getacnode þæs   lichaman lustas
        through the wife-taking are   signified   of-the body   lusts
        'The taking to wife stands for the lusts of the body' (*ÆCHom* II, 26.215.72)

Finally, clausal objects (*that*-clauses and infinitives with *to*) always occur on the right of the verb. This is a characteristic which all the Germanic languages share, and which is often attributed to psycholinguistic factors, in that 'centre embedding' is believed to cause severe processing problems.

We can summarize this section as follows: the negative adverb *ne* always precedes the finite verb immediately, since it is proclitic on it but we have seen that there is an asymmetry between the positions certain other clause elements can have in relation to the non-finite verb. Some are virtually restricted to preverbal position; they include verb particles, stranded prepositions, pronominal objects and (probably) adverbs. There are very few cases indeed where these are in postverbal position. When they are, the finite verb almost always precedes the non-finite verb; examples occur primarily in late texts. The positioning of nominal objects, complements and PPs with respect to a non-fronted verb is rather free: they are found in both preverbal and postverbal positions. Preverbal objects are not very frequent in the pattern $[O \, v_{fin} \, V_{nonfin}]$, and postverbal objects in the pattern $[V_{nonfin} \, v_{fin} \, O]$, but examples do occur, as shown by (26), (28) and (50).

During the transition from Old English to Middle English, there is a clear increase in the frequency of postverbal orders, as we shall see in 5.4. However, first we shall turn to the question of how the Old English patterns described in this section can be analysed. In this, we should bear in mind that any analysis of Old English word order should allow a plausible perspective on the changes that take place in Middle English.

5.3   Old English word order: OV or VO?

In this section, we will discuss arguments for the analysis of Old English word order. This will lead us to look more selectively at some word order patterns that speak in favour of or against particular analyses. We will focus on the structural treatment of word order. For a survey of the descriptive literature, the reader is referred to Denison (1993: 27–58). Traugott (1992) presents an approach to Old English word order in terms of typologies of surface word order.

In a variety of theoretical approaches to word order and word order change, scholars consider that there is something like a basic word order on which other word orders are variations. Some take the most frequent word order to be the basic one, while others consider that there is something like an unmarked word order and take discourse factors to be the prime motivating force behind word order variation. In this book, we adopt the position that the grammar of the speaker defines the word order options; within the bounds of these options, variations may be motivated by considerations that lie outside the domain of grammar in a strict sense (markedness, social factors, pragmatics, discourse, etc.). In the generative approach to grammar, it is customary to

regard one word order as basic in the sense that this is regarded as the underlying order. Variations on that order should then be plausibly derivable by
transformational rule, such as we have proposed in chapter 4 for the position
of the finite verb in terms of V-movement. We saw in the previous section,
however, that nominal objects and PPs can appear on the left or the right of
the non-finite verb, arbitrarily, as far as we can tell. Given this positional
freedom, it is an interesting question whether the uniform underlying order in
Old English, if there is one, is OV, as in (34a) or VO, as in (34b):

(34)   a.

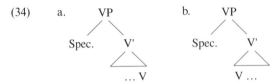

If we postulate an OV base order as in (34a), variations should be derivable
by rightward movement; if we postulate VO as in (34b), we have to motivate
leftward movement rules. The choice between the two is to some extent dictated by theoretical considerations. If both phrase structures in (34) are in
principle allowed by the phrase structure component of the grammar (a question to which we return below), the choice for (34a) or (34b) will depend on
the theoretical justification for the rules that we formulate for the variant
word orders. In the following subsections, we will consider the empirical and
theoretical arguments for regarding OV or VO word order as basic. First,
some initial discussion is given of the OV approach and the VO approach.
Furthermore, we will discuss a variationist approach, in which synchronic
variation between OV and VO orders is viewed from the perspective of
competition between grammars, one with OV and another with VO phrase
structures, following the work of Anthony Kroch discussed in chapter 1.
Then we will draw the argument to a more theoretical plane, and explore an
analysis inspired by recent theoretical innovations, in which VO is taken as
the only possible underlying order, leaving open some provoking questions
for further research.

5.3.1   *One uniform clause structure?*

We will first discuss some of the consequences of the various
approaches to Old English word order from the perspective of one uniform
underlying order. We will do this by discussing analyses presented in the literature, as far as they are available. After this, we discuss an approach which
posits variation in underlying order in Old English.

5.3.1.1 The OV approach

In the OV approach to Old English word order, the assumption would be that the constituents of the VP are base-generated in preverbal position, in conformity with (34a). Those surface patterns where VP constituents follow the non-finite verb should be derivable by motivating rightward movement rules that apply optionally to those constituents that *may* occur postverbally (object NPs, PPs), obligatorily to those constituents that *must* occur post-verbally (clauses), and cannot apply to those constituents which must occur preverbally (personal pronouns, stranded prepositions, particles, at least some types of adverb, negative *ne*). Perhaps the strongest evidence in favour of an OV approach is the fact that there is a variety of constituents that is always preverbal. If OV is regarded as the underlying order, one is absolved, so to speak, from coming up with a rationale for preposing a variety of constituents which are not uniform in type. On the other hand, given the fact that NPs and PPs can be optionally postposed, we must be able to see why the obligatorily preverbal elements are prevented from being postposed, and this may well be equally difficult.

There are no analyses available that are explicit about all the different types of constituent. Let us first discuss some analyses in the literature that give a partial analysis from the OV perspective.

Pintzuk and Kroch (1989) analyse the language of *Beowulf*. This long specimen of heroic poetry is, like all Old English poems, written in four-stress lines. Each line consists of two half-lines, which in turn consist of two syllables with prominent stress (plus a number of weakly stressed syllables). In each line, two or three of the four stressed positions alliterate. An example of this is given in (35):

(35)		bealocwealm hafað	
		baleful-death has	
	*f*ela	*f*eorhcynna	*f*orð onsended
	many	of-race-of-men	forth sent
		'baleful death has sent forth many of the race of men'	(*Beo* 2265–6)

Pintzuk and Kroch argue for uniform OV underlying order in Old English on the basis of metrical evidence. Poetic half-lines form prosodic units and the VP-final verb, they argue, appears in the last stressed position of a half-line. In those instances where complements and adjuncts follow the verb, they occur in the initial syllables of the next half-line. An example of this is (36).

(36)	*S*ceotend *S*cyldinga	to *s*cypon *f*eredon
	warriors of-Scyldings	to ships brought
	eal ingesteald	eorðcyninges
	all house-property	of-king-of-the-land

'The Scylding warriors brought to the ships all of the king's household
goods'   (*Beo* 1154–5)'

The verb *feredon* occurs in the last stressed position of its half-line, and the
complement NP *eal ingesteald eorðcyninges* follows it in the next half-line. The
fact that the position of the verb coincides with the last stressed position of a
half-line indicates that it precedes an intonation break: the end of the (underlying) VP. This in turn suggests that any material following it has in fact been
postposed. Pintzuk and Kroch argue that the postposed material in *Beowulf*
is always 'heavy'. This reasonably applies to the NP *eal ingesteald eorðcyninges*
in (36), and they extend this to all instances of postposed material. The
motivation for this postposing is then plausibly analysed as stylistic or perceptual: heavy constituents can be postposed, as in present-day English (37b).

(37)   a. I met a man from Paris yesterday
        b. I met yesterday # a man from Paris

Typically, such postposing involves a comma intonation, indicated by # in
(37b), which makes an attractive parallel with the half-line break in Old
English. If heaviness of the constituent is the motivating force for postposing,
a good rationale is provided for the obligatory postposing of clauses as discussed above.

The conclusions reached by Pintzuk and Kroch, although interesting and
suggestive for early poetry like *Beowulf*, do not readily carry over to the bulk
of the Old English text material, i.e. the prose, early as well as late. The prime
reason for this is, of course, that there is no metrical evidence available for the
prose. But this is not the only problem. If we consider the relevant word order
patterns in classical Old English prose, it turns out that there are many
instances where complements and adjuncts follow the verb while they do not
plausibly qualify as 'heavy', as the following two examples show.

(38)   þu hafast gecoren þone wer
        'You have chosen the man'   (*ApT* 34.23)

(39)   ða ongunnon hi   wepan mid him
        then began   they weep   with him
        'then they began to weep with him'   (*Bo* 35.102.25)

Although we do not have access to direct evidence for the intonation of such
examples (which are very numerous), it is hard to read them with anything like
a comma intonation. This suggests that, if we are to treat all such phenomena
as postposing, which is essentially the position taken in van Kemenade (1987),
the postposing rule must be very liberal indeed. This conclusion is further reinforced by the existence of many sentences like (5), repeated here as (40), where
several constituents must be assumed to be postposed.

(40)   þæt he nolde   niman *mancyn*   neadunga of   ðam deofle
        that he not-would take   mankind forcibly   from the   devil
        'that he would not have taken mankind forcibly from the devil'

(ÆCHom I, 14.1.216.4)

The postposing rules must include object NPs, complement and adjunct PPs, *that*-clauses and *to*-infinitives, and allow for the possibility that more than one such constituent is postposed. Further, we need to account for the fact that the odd personal pronoun, adverb or particle may occur on the right.

The excessive power of such postposing rules must surely require considerable motivation. Moreover, we must assume that they are not obligatory, which from our theoretical perspective may be a problem, as discussed in chapter 1. In addition to this, we should again consider why some classes of elements are never or almost never postposed: personal pronouns, stranded prepositions, verb particles, negative *ne* and some adverbs. The motivation for this need not be the same for all these elements: as we saw in the previous chapter, personal pronouns must appear in certain positions and the same may apply to adverbs, while we assume negative *ne* to be a clitic that incorporates with the finite verb. This leaves stranded prepositions and particles. Their behaviour actually seems the least problematic in an OV approach: if adjacency between verb and stranded preposition/particle is required for grammatical reasons, as has often been suggested, it follows from an OV approach that this type of element should appear canonically on the left; see chapter 6 for detailed discussion of the particle facts from this viewpoint.

Let us now briefly consider how the transition to Middle English can be analysed from the perspective of underlying OV order in Old English. The reader will recall that there is an increase of VO orders in the transition from Old English to Middle English. If Old English is analysed as OV, we are bound to regard the transition to Middle English as a change in underlying order from OV, as in (34a), to VO, as in (34b), perhaps because during late Old English, the frequency of surface VO word orders had increased to such an extent that they led to a reinterpretation of VO order as representing underlying order. This is in itself not too problematic, but the result is that the remnant OV orders in Middle English will then have to be analysed as the result of leftward movement of objects. It remains a question how these rules are to be formulated.

5.3.1.2   The VO approach

In the VO approach to Old English word order, the assumption is that the constituents of the VP are base-generated postverbally, as in (34b). Those surface patterns where VP constituents precede the non-finite verb should be derivable by motivating leftward movement rules that apply optionally to those constituents that *may* occur preverbally (object NPs, PPs, bare infinitives), obligatorily to those constituents that *must* occur preverbally (personal pronouns, stranded prepositions, particles, some types of adverb, negative *ne*), and cannot apply to those constituents which must occur postverbally (finite clauses and *to*-infinitives).

There are no complete analyses of Old English word order that take the VO perspective. In 5.3.2, we will explore the possibility of analysing Old English as having underlying VO structure, pointing out the potential gains of and problems for such an approach.

5.3.1.3   Variation between OV and VO order

In recent work, Susan Pintzuk (1991, 1996) analyses Old English word order from the perspective of variation between two different phrase structures. This is inspired by Kroch's (1989) approach to synchronic variation in terms of grammar competition, which was discussed in 1.2.4. We will briefly recall the essence of this approach here. In the course of any syntactic change, which typically follows an S-curve, there is a transitional stage in which the older and newer patterns are attested side by side at shifting frequencies. From the perspective of a restrictive theory of grammar, we have to assume, according to Kroch, that these patterns represent grammars in competition, grammars which differ in the value for one parameter, in this case the one determining the word order inside the VP.

Pintzuk takes the earliest Old English, as represented by the language of *Beowulf*, to reflect an OV grammar, following Pintzuk and Kroch (1989), and traces the earliest evidence for VO orders in the Old English prose. The exceptional cases of postverbal particles, as in (12), and personal pronouns, as in (18) and (19), are taken as diagnostics for VO basic word order. She then goes on to analyse the transition from Old English to Middle English in terms of competition between an OV grammar and a VO grammar. During the Old English period, VO is a relatively small minority pattern. In the transition to Middle English, it gains ground rapidly and OV order becomes a minority pattern. The change follows the type of S-shaped curve discussed in chapter 1.

Pintzuk's analysis provides a good way of modelling the time course of the change. Nevertheless, some critical observations seem in order. In Pintzuk's analysis of Old English, the crucial evidence for a VO grammar comes from very small minority patterns. This means that a vast majority of the attested patterns, which comprise many OV *as well as* VO orders, are derivable from OV base structure. Hence, the analysis may share the gains of both approaches but, to accommodate only a few patterns, it also needs the full range of rules (including their problems) required by both of them. Moreover, the VO orders among the attested patterns are also derivable from a VO base structure, which means that there is a great deal of indeterminacy. It is also noteworthy that Pintzuk does not say much about what triggered the introduction of VO order in (early) Old English, or what led to the loss of OV order in the Middle English period.

It therefore remains to be seen whether an analysis in terms of phrase structure competition offers a profitable research strategy. With these critical comments, we in no way wish to detract from the value of the observations concerning variation made by Pintzuk. But it might well be the case that the locus of the variation, i.e. its place within the grammatical system, is different, and we will explore a possible alternative in the next section.

5.3.2   *Towards a VO analysis*

In this section we will work towards an analysis of Old English word order in terms of a VO underlying structure. It was observed above that there are no complete analyses of Old English object position available from a generative perspective. Some approaches to Old English word order observe that SVO seems the most likely underlying order (e.g. Malsh 1976, Allen 1980, Reddick 1982), but these works do not offer a fully fleshed-out proposal as to how the patterns deviating from this order are to be analysed. This is what we will attempt here. The analysis is theoretically inspired by innovations proposed by Chomsky (1993) and Kayne (1994).

In chapters 1 and 4, we introduced the idea that sentences may have a rather elaborate functional structure in the sense that certain elements of morphology – subordination marking, tense, agreement, mood, negation and so on – project their own phrasal category according to the standard format of X' theory. Lexical heads and phrases may subsequently move to the head position or specifier position of these functional phrases to be associated with the relevant morphology. This type of morphologically driven movement has become an important element in the typology of word order. One of the central ideas introduced by Chomsky (1991) and further constrained in Chomsky (1993) is that movement can only take place to satisfy a morphological feature. When such a feature is 'strong', movement takes place in the overt syntax; when a feature is 'weak', movement is not visible but does take place at the semantic interface level LF. In Kayne (1994), a further constraint on sentence structure is proposed which is of prime importance from the perspective of word order variation: he proposes that the relation of c-command is fundamentally asymmetric, and that (by virtue of a principle that he calls the Linear Correspondence Axiom, for which we refer to his work) this translates into phrase structures in which specifiers can only be generated on the left, and complements must always follow the head. Moreover, adjunction to a phrase can only take place on the left. This leaves no room for variation in the underlying order of head and complement: in effect, from this perspective, SVO is the only possible underlying word order.

To illustrate this, we can consider a simple present-day English clause such as (41).

(41)   The students bought the book.

At the point in the derivation at which the lexical elements have all been introduced, the structure is as in (42). Note that the subject is base-generated as the specifier of VP, and that the object is postverbal; these are assumed to be universal properties, holding at the initial structure level of all sentences in all languages.

(42)

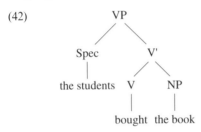

In (42), the subject *the students* has a nominative Case feature, while the object *the book* has an objective Case feature; the verb has an objective Case feature (in earlier terms: it assigns objective Case), an Agreement feature (in earlier terms: it agrees with the subject) and also a Tense feature (past tense). Case and Agreement features are called N-features; Tense features are among the V-features. Concentrating on the verb and object, the basic idea is that at some point in the derivation these two elements have to move to the functional projection AgrOP ('object agreement phrase') which dominates VP, for their features to be checked, yielding (43).

(43)

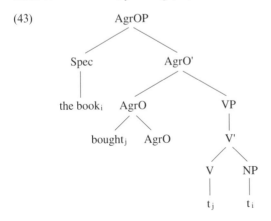

The verb *bought* adjoins to AgrO and gets its V-features checked there against the V-features of AgrO. The object *the book* also moves into AgrOP for checking purposes – in (43), it is shown as being in the specifier position; another possibility would be for it to adjoin to AgrOP, as shown in (44) (in technical terms, the adjoined position is also part of AgrO's checking domain; see Chomsky 1993: 12). In either case, the object will check its N-features against those of AgrO.

(44)

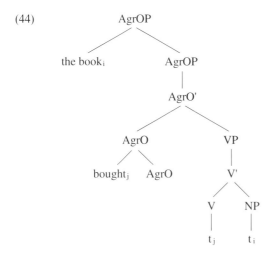

We should also note that the two applications of movement in (43) and (44) are linked, in that (for technical reasons that we will not go into here) movement of V to AgrO is seen as a precondition for movement of the object to the specifier position of AgrOP.

Although we have used an English sentence as an example, it is assumed in Chomsky (1993) and much later work that any sentence with a NP object in any language will have a derivation of this type: the object starts out post-verbally in VP, but at the semantic interface level LF it must have moved into AgrOP for checking purposes. Where languages differ is in the point of the derivation at which the rules of the phonological component operate. In some languages, they do so at a point before object movement into AgrOP, i.e. at a stage when the order of object and verb is still as in the initial structure (42); this possibility is instantiated by present-day English, which has surface VO order. In surface OV languages, however, the phonological rules yielding the actual pronunciation take as their input a structure in which the object has already moved into AgrOP, i.e. a structure as in (43) or (44). Using the technical term Spell-Out for the point at which the phonological rules operate, we can represent the two possibilities as in (45).

(45)   initial   intermediate   LF
        structure   structure

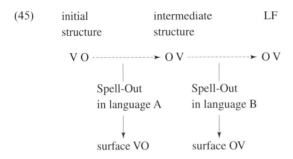

In language A, Spell-Out occurs relatively early in the derivation, with the result that the underlying VO order is reflected in the pronunciation of sentences. At some point before LF, both object and verb move into AgrOP, yielding OV order, but in language A, this movement is covert or invisible: it takes place after Spell-Out and therefore has no effect on the actual pronunciation. In language B, Spell-Out applies later in the derivation, i.e. after verb and object have moved into AgrOP. This movement is therefore reflected in the pronunciation of sentences in language B, and is called overt. As for the reason for this difference between language A and language B, within the framework of Chomsky (1993) this is generally held to be due to a difference in strength of the features of AgrO. In language A, these features are weak, which means that they can be checked after Spell-Out (i.e. covertly); in language B, they are strong, and therefore need to be checked before Spell-Out (since unchecked strong features are not permissible in the phonological component). We note that, in the absence of clear surface correlates of richness or weakness of features, this element of the model introduces a certain degree of circularity into the enterprise. More precisely, the model as it stands does not provide independent criteria for arguing about the question of whether a language has Spell-Out before or after object movement; we return to this issue below.

This, in essence, is the way in which the model of Chomsky (1993) captures the difference between surface OV and VO languages. The remainder of this section is an exercise in how Old English word order can be analysed from this perspective, to see what kinds of leftward movement rules would be needed to derive the OV word orders, and to discuss some of the problems that such an analysis faces. The analysis is similar in spirit, though not in execution, to Roberts (1997). We start off by recapitulating the descriptive requirements which a VO account must satisfy. Those surface patterns where VP constituents precede the non-finite verb should be derivable by motivating leftward movement rules that apply optionally to those constituents that *may* occur preverbally (object NPs, PPs, bare infinitives), obligatorily to those constituents that *must* occur preverbally (personal pronouns, stranded prepositions, particles, some types of adverb, negative *ne*), and cannot apply to those constituents which must occur postverbally (finite clauses and *to*-infinitives).

Let us first go into the possibility of optional leftward movement rules for NPs, PPs, and bare infinitives. Recent theoretical developments as mentioned above suggest a clear motivation for such leftward movement rules for object NPs and perhaps bare infinitives, but less clearly for PPs. For object NPs, we can say that they have to move to the specifier of AgrOP in order to check their case features. Let us consider an illustration of this, involving example (24), which is repeated here for convenience as (46); the discussion of this example illustrates how the position of both object and bare infinitive can be derived.

(46)   þæt he ure sawle fram synna fagnyssum gehælan mæge
        that he our soul from of-sins ulcers   heal   can
        'that he can heal our soul from the ulcers of sin'   (*ÆCHom* I, 8.122.24)

Assuming as in chapter 4 that there is a functional projection FP into which the clausal subject will move, the underlying structure for this sentence would be as in (47).[1]

(47)

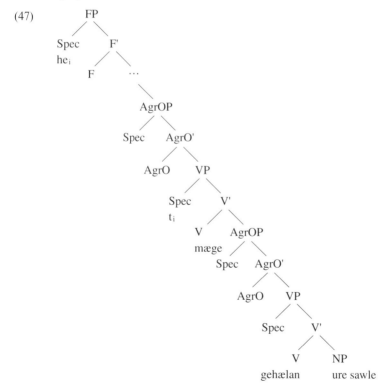

---

[1] The representation in the tree diagram presupposes several notions that are supported
     in the literature. First, it is assumed that the modal verb is a main verb with some type

The surface word order would be derived as follows: the object NP *ure sawle* starts out inside the VP, but moves to the specifier of the lower AgrOP, to check for case. For technical reasons, this movement has to be preceded by movement of the verb *gehælan* to the head AgrO, as pointed out above. The lower AgrOP as a whole then moves to the specifier of the higher AgrOP, which – on the assumption that AgrOP is a noun-like constituent – can also be viewed as being motivated by the need for case checking. This gives the OVv order of this sentence. Several other possible word orders can be readily derived by assuming that the two instances of movement are both optional. This is illustrated by the following two sentences.

(48)   þæt hi   mihton swa bealdlice Godes geleafan bodian
        that they could so boldly   God's faith   preach
        'that they could preach God's faith so boldly'   (*ÆCHom* I, 16.232.23)

(49)   þæt hie ofer þæt ne dorston nohte   gretan þa halgan stowe
        that they after that not dared   not-at-all attack the holy   place
        'that they did not at all dare to attack the holy place after that'
                                                              (*GD* 1(C)4.43.4)

In (48) the word order can be derived by assuming that the object *Godes geleafan* has moved to the AgrOP directly dominating the VP headed by *bodian*, but that there has been no movement of the infinitival complement as a whole to the specifier position of the higher AgrOP. The order in (49) can be derived by saying that neither the object *þa halgan stowe* nor the lower AgrOP as a whole has undergone movement.

The variation in word order seen in examples such as (46), (48) and (49) is thus attributed to the optionality of movement. It must be said, however, that optionality itself is problematic for a theory which assumes that movement is only allowed when triggered by the need to check a morphological feature. One solution would be to say that the trigger itself is optional, i.e. that the relevant feature is variably strong; this is the approach taken by Collins and Thráinsson (1996: 393) to explain comparable word order facts in Modern Icelandic. While this may not seem to be a principled solution, it should be observed that the essence of this kind of optionality might lie in the presence of overt case inflections. Potentially, this might offer a way of approach to the

Footnote 1 (*cont.*)
    of sentential complement. For a recent detailed treatment of modal verbs, see Warner (1993). Second, it is assumed that the sentential complement is an AgrOP. This reflects the nominal character of OE bare infinitives. The most recent discussion of this can be found in Beths (1999). Note that strictly speaking, the various functional projections in (47) would appear in the derivation only at the point that elements move into them, and not before; for ease of exposition, we ignore this here.

traditionally observed correlation between rich inflection and freedom of word order, though this remains to be worked out.

Another solution would be to apply to Old English the analysis of the Modern Icelandic facts proposed by Kitahara (1995: 67–74). He argues that, if a feature is strong, movement indeed has to take place overtly, but that in other cases, the choice between derivations with overt or covert movement depends on the number of steps that either derivation will contain. Generally, the shortest derivation will be selected, but if two derivations contain an equal number of steps, both will be allowed. This of course raises the question what exactly will count as a 'step' in the derivation; the answer to this question is rather technical, and we refer to Kitahara (1995) for a full exposition. The result of applying his counting procedure to Icelandic, and equally to Old English, is that both overt and covert movement of the object are allowed, since the number of steps in the two derivations is the same. One of the further ingredients of Kitahara's theory of movement too is that, for object move- ment to the specifier of AgrOP to be overt, there must first be overt V-move- ment to AgrO. As we shall see in 5.6, this point may have a bearing on the disappearance of OV order.

It thus appears that the problem of optionality might receive a satisfactory solution within this model of word order, although there are various issues that still need to be worked out. There are, however, some further empirical problems with the analysis that we are developing here. We stated in 5.2 that there are cases where the infinitival verb is to the right of the finite verb, whereas the object of the infinitive appears on the left. We give an example in (50).

(50)   ðæt he Saul ne dorste ofslean
        that he Saul not dared murder
        'that he didn't dare to murder Saul'   (*CP* 28.199.2)

From the perspective of the analysis pursued here, there may be a problem with these sentences. It seems as if the infinitival complement remains in its base position, while the object has moved to the specifier position of the higher AgrOP. The object of the infinitive can apparently 'choose' to move to either the higher or the lower AgrOP. Since double checking of case is not allowed by the theory (i.e. we cannot say that the object checks case in the lower AgrOP and then again in the higher one), the best solution is probably to say that AgrOP may freely contain features or lack them. In the case of (50), the lower AgrOP lacks N-features, so the object cannot check its case features there; however, the higher AgrOP does have N-features, and the object can move on to it for case checking.

Let us turn now to the position of PPs. This position can presumably not be derived by checking movement, since it is hard to provide a motivation for the checking of PPs. We could say that PPs can be adjoined to VP or to AgrOP. This would allow them to occur in the following positions, shown in (51): on the right of the verb (no movement, PP1 and PP2, the first a complement, the second an adjunct), on the immediate left of the verb (adjunction to VP, PP3) or preceding objects (adjunction to AgrOP, PP4):

(51)

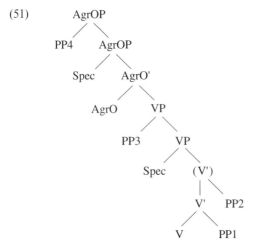

Such free adjunction may not seem like a theoretically principled solution. In a feature checking approach, we might want to formulate separate functional projections to derive the position of PPs, but these are issues that have not yet been addressed in detail in the theoretical literature, and we must therefore leave them open here.

We now turn to a further complexity: the position of stranded prepositions. Let us recapitulate the basic facts concerning preposition stranding in Old English, summarized in 2.6: preposition stranding occurs in PPs with a pro- nominal or locative object, and also in those wh-movement constructions in which there is no overt wh-element; the stranded preposition is always part of a complement PP, and it nearly always immediately precedes the verb. In those cases where it is not on the immediate left, it is right-adjacent to the verb. We repeat the preposition–verb example (13) here for convenience:

(13)   þa   wæs hiora   an   se   Apollinus þe   we   ær   ymb   spræcon
        then was of-them one the Apollinus that we   before about spoke
        'Then one of them was the Apollinus that we spoke about before'
                                                              (*Bo* 38.116.1)

If the position of PPs is variable, it may seem surprising that stranded preposi- tions have a fixed position. The theoretical literature on preposition stranding in Old English, which is all formulated from the perspective of underlying OV order for Old English, argues that, since Old English has OV order, the preposition must be on the left for a well-formed movement chain to be formed between the moved prepositional object and its trace (we leave technical details aside). On the assumption of VO underlying order, such an account is not open to us. However, given that stranded prepositions in Old English are always adjacent to the verb, we could say that they form a lexical combination with the verb, in the spirit of the rule of V–P reanalysis formulated by Hornstein and Weinberg (1981) for preposition stranding in present-day English. This amounts to saying that stranded prepositions in Old English were somewhat like (possibly valency-changing) prefixes. While we realize that this cuts a number of corners, we will leave it at that, pending further research into the precise status of stranded prepositions.

Let us now turn to particles, whose position is predominantly like that of stranded prepositions: they usually occur on the immediate left of a non-moved verb, as illustrated in examples such as (10), which we repeat here.

(10)   þæt hie mid þæm þæt folc   ut   aloccoden
        that they with that the people out enticed
        'that with it they might entice the people to come outside'   (*Or* 2.5.3.117.5)

Having said this, we should also note that the position of particles is not as narrowly defined as that of stranded prepositions, in a way which suggests that, although they most often occur in immediate preverbal position, they differ from stranded prepositions in not being positionally dependent on V. This implies that they have independent syntactic status. Zwart (1993), in a minimalist VO-based analysis of Modern Dutch syntax, analyses particles as secondary predicates. On such an analysis, the sequence *þæt folc ut* in (10) is base-generated in postverbal position as a small clause, with *ut* as the predicate; it then moves for feature checking, much like the movement of infinitives discussed above. This will be discussed in more detail in chapter 6.

Let us now turn to *that*-clauses and *to*-infinitives, the former of which are always in final position, as are the latter with very few exceptions. On a VO analysis, this means that, unlike other types of objects, *that*-clauses and *to*-infinitives do not move to a higher functional projection such as AgrOP. Since the model of clause structure adopted above only allows movement which is triggered by the need for feature-checking, the obvious conclusion is that Old English *that*-clauses and *to*-infinitives do not have a feature that needs to be checked, and hence do not move. Again, this conclusion raises wider issues that are still awaiting adequate treatment in the literature, but for our purposes at this point, it suffices to note that the behaviour of these elements does not endanger the account of word order that we are exploring in this section.

The preverbal elements that we have not discussed so far are personal pronouns, negative *ne* and certain adverbs. For the first two, an account was already suggested in chapter 4: personal pronouns check a feature in a relatively high position preceding NegP and negative *ne* is a NegP head which incorporates with the finite verb.

We may conclude this section with the observation that a Kayne-style VO account of Old English word order faces some empirical problems, for which we have tried to sketch possible theoretical solutions in this section. The success of this account depends on the feasibility of these solutions, and on the potential for finding more of them. We now turn to an investigation of how this same account fares when it is applied to the word order data and the changes that they show in the Middle English period, on the assumption that, if the account succeeds in throwing light on these changes without assuming drastic discontinuities, some support is provided for the overall approach. But before we turn in 5.5 and 5.6 to such theoretical issues raised by the Middle English data, we first present in 5.4 a brief descriptive account of these data themselves.

5.4   Middle English: the basic facts

We have seen that, in the Old English period, the object sometimes follows the finite verb even when it has not been moved and that it sometimes also follows the non-finite verb. In both cases, the result is VO order. Sentences with this order become more frequent during the Middle English period, and it is the empirical details of that development that we shall trace in this section.

The change in question has of course not escaped the attention of earlier investigators of word order in Old and Middle English, but there have been surprisingly few attempts at a comprehensive quantitative study of it. In this section, we shall therefore be drawing on a number of separate small-scale studies focussing on individual subperiods. Moreover, some of the existing descriptions of Middle English word order do not take into account the possible effects of V-movement; as will be clear from chapter 4, however, failure to do so will result in an inadequate picture of the patterns involved. In a study that recognizes this potential problem, Kroch and Taylor (1994) consider the position of the object in embedded clauses containing a finite auxiliary and a non-finite lexical verb in several prose texts from the early thirteenth century (the *Katherine* group and *Ancrene Riwle*, from the West Midlands; *Vices and Virtues*, Trinity Homilies and the Kentish Sermons, all from the South-East). Kroch and Taylor distinguish three positions for objects: following the non-finite verb, as in (52), in between finite and non-finite verb, as in (53), and preceding the finite verb, as in (54).

(52)   þet ʒe   mahen ane   pine   me here
        that you may   alone torture me here
        'that only you can torture me here'   (*St. Juliana* 182)

(53)   ðat we moten mid ʒeure helpe and mid
        that we may   with your help and with
        his hale grace swa ðis scorte lif her laden
        his holy grace thus this short life here lead
        'that we may thus lead this short life here with your help and his holy grace'
                                                            (*Vices&V* 21.23)

(54)   þat he deaþ scolde þoliʒen
        that he death should suffer
        'that he should suffer death'   (*Vices&V.* 113.21)

Kroch and Taylor report that in the West Midlands texts, about half of all pronominal objects follow the non-finite verb; an example can be seen in (52). In the South-Eastern texts, pronouns disfavour this position: only five per cent of them occur there. In this respect, the South-Eastern texts resemble Old English, which, as we saw in 5.2, also has very few examples like (18) and (19), with a pronominal object following a non-finite verb. The West Midlands texts, however, clearly represent a stage of the language which has undergone a major increase in the frequency of this VO pattern.

The two groups of early Middle English texts show a similar kind of difference, though at a higher level of frequency, for objects that consist of full NPs (at least if heavy NPs, consisting of four or more words, are excluded, since these overwhelmingly follow the non-finite verb in both groups of texts). In the West Midlands texts, circa seventy per cent of the clauses with a full NP object show VO order, while this percentage is only thirty per cent in the South-Eastern texts. As Kroch and Taylor point out, the overall result is that the South-Eastern texts appear to be relatively conservative in this aspect of their word order, while the West Midlands texts seem to be relatively modern. However, it is far from being the case that OV order has disappeared from these 'modern' texts, since they still feature OV order in one third to half of all cases, not only with pronouns, but also with full NPs.

By concentrating on the type of environment (embedded clauses with an auxiliary) that best reveals the position of the object, Kroch and Taylor (1994) contribute valuable data to the study of OV/VO order in Early Middle English. The conclusion that can be drawn from their findings is that earlier studies are right in suggesting that there was a shift from OV to VO order during the twelfth century (see Canale 1978 and a great deal of subsequent work). However, the change does not entail an abrupt break between Old and Middle English: we saw in 5.2 that surface VO order is not at all unusual in Old English, especially with nominal objects, and the data in Kroch and Taylor (1994) show that OV order continues as a productive pattern in early Middle English texts.

It is only after about 1300 that clauses with VO order begin to vastly out-number those with OV order, also with pronominal objects. As a result, it becomes somewhat difficult to make a meaningful comparison of the frequencies of OV and VO order in particular linguistic environments. As the review in Fischer (1992a: 372 f.) makes clear, studies of Late Middle English word order have therefore tended to concentrate on the distribution of OV tokens over various syntactic contexts, taking for granted the fact that VO is much more frequent in each context. Several studies of individual works and authors have found that OV in Late Middle English indeed seems to favour certain contexts over others. However, these studies are few and different in methodology, and they do not add up to a systematic sampling of texts written in the course of the Late Middle English period.

In an attempt to remedy this, Foster and van der Wurff (1995) looked at the survival of OV order in all types of verb groups and clauses in a range of texts from the early fourteenth century to the late fifteenth century. Their results first of all show a considerable difference between prose and verse texts, with OV order being found in verse much more often, and in more syntactic con-texts, than in prose, no doubt due to the the stronger tendency in verse to exploit linguistic resources for the sake of rhyme, metre and emphasis. However, more immediately relevant to our present concerns is the behaviour of OV order in late Middle English prose texts. There, its frequency drops from about twenty per cent of all transitive clauses in the middle of the fourteenth century to only one per cent in the middle of the fifteenth century. Clearly then, VO order had become the norm by the mid-fifteenth century (perhaps somewhat earlier in Northern texts).

When we consider the syntactic contexts in which OV order is still found in late Middle English, we also see a difference between texts from the fourteenth and the fifteenth centuries. In the fourteenth century, OV order can still be found with pronominal as well as nominal objects, and in VPs containing only a finite verb as well as ones containing an auxiliary and a non-finite verb. We give examples in (55)–(59).

(55)   I n'am but a lewd compilator of the labour of olde astrologiens, and have it
         translatid in myn Englissh oonly for thy doctrine
         'I am only an ignorant compiler of the work of old astronomers, and have
         translated it into my Enlish only for your instruction.'
                                                                      (Chaucer *Melibee* 61)

(56)   alle that him feith berith and obeieth
         'all that have faith in him and obey him'   (Chaucer *Astrolabe* 58)

(57)   me ssel hine loky   and ureþie zo holyliche
         one must it   observe and honour so religiously
         'one must observe and honour it so religiously'   (*Ayenb.* 7.22)

(58)   I may my persone and myn hous so kepen and deffenden.
        'I can keep and defend myself and my house in such a way.'
                                                    (Chaucer *Melibee* 1334)

(59)   Ne he ne   may habbe skele: þet he him moȝe excusi
        nor he not may have   reason that he him may   excuse
        'Nor may he have a reason to excuse himself'   (*Ayenb.* 7.1)

In examples (55) and (56) the object is in front of a finite lexical verb, in (57) and
(58) the object comes in between the auxiliary and the non-finite verb, and in (59)
the object precedes the auxiliary. We can therefore say that fourteenth-century
English basically allows the same word order options as early thirteenth-century
English: the patterns in (55)–(59) correspond exactly to those in (52)–(54).

This rather full distribution of OV order across syntactic environments
comes to an end in the fifteenth century. By that time, OV order is quite infrequent, but in a study of a large amount of fifteenth-century prose (van der
Wurff 1997b) it was found that OV shows not only a quantitative but also a
qualitative decline. Apart from its use in fixed expressions such as *so God me
help*, OV order becomes restricted to just two syntactic contexts. One of these
is constructions which have an empty subject, such as coordinate and relative
clauses, of which we give one example each in (60) and (61).

(60)   summe he exiled, summe he put out here rite eyne, and namely þe worthi
        man, Athanasius, whech mad *Quicuncque vult*, pursewed so feruently þat he
        durst not appere openly vii ȝere
        'some he exiled, of some he put out their right eye, and especially the
        honourable man Athanasius, who composed the *Quicumque vult*, he
        pursued so intensely that he did not dare to show himself in public for
        seven years'   (Capgrave *Cronicles* 62.23)

(61)   alle þat þis writinge reden or heere
        'all that will read or hear this writing'   (*Sermon* 2250)

The other surviving productive OV context in the fifteenth century is clauses
featuring an auxiliary and an object that contains a negative or quantified
element, as in (62)–(65).

(62)   þei schuld no meyhir haue
        'they were not allowed to have a mayor'   (Capgrave *Cronicles* 199.6)

(63)   I haue non schepyde as yete
        'I have shipped none yet'   (*Cely Letters* 87.11)

(64)   he haþ on vs mercy, for he may al þynge do
        'he has mercy on us, for he can do everything'   (*Barlam* 2740)

(65)   Item, whethyr ye haue eny thyng spokyn of my going to Caleys.
        'Another point: have you said anything about my going to Calais'
                                                    (*Paston Letters* 355.28)

In terms of frequency, this pattern is predominant: it accounts for half or more of all OV tokens in most fifteenth-century texts.

The final demise of productive use of OV order in prose texts takes place in the first half of the sixteenth century. The last examples are like those found in the fifteenth century, in that they occur in clauses with an invisible subject or with an auxiliary and a negative or quantified object. We give two examples in (66) and (67).

(66)   Some are there also that such tales tell them for consideration of another fear
        'There are also some that tell them such tales because they consider some other fear'   (More *Dialogue of Comfort* 181.25)

(67)   Mine own good cousin, I cannot much say
        'My good cousin, I cannot say much'   (More *Dialogue of Comfort* 144.9)

We have seen in this section how the occurrence of OV order became progressively limited in the course of the Middle English period. It underwent a steady decrease in frequency throughout the period and around 1400 a noticeable narrowing of its syntactic scope of occurrence set in. In the following section, we shall provide a theoretical analysis of these Middle English word order patterns. The approach we shall pursue is that of 5.3.2, where we explored how the Old English facts could be made to follow from underlying VO order; we shall also comment on the feasibility of the alternative analysis of Pintzuk (1996), which posits variation between underlying OV and VO order also in Middle English.

5.5   Analysing the Middle English word order patterns

In 5.3.2, it was pointed out that Kayne (1994) argues that the VP always has VO as its underlying order, a consequence that he derives from the fundamental asymmetry of the relation of c-command. This idea has also been incorporated in the Minimalist framework of Chomsky (1995), in which surface order is regarded as being determined by movement of constituents to higher functional projections, in particular AgrOP in the case of object movement. Such movement is motivated by the need for feature-checking, and it can take place either overtly or 'invisibly', i.e. at LF, as shown in (45).

The relation between these two options and the issue of feature strength is potentially a problem for this type of approach, but we noted that solutions can and have been devised. We then showed in some detail that the approach works well enough when applied to Old English objects, which occur in nearly all the word order patterns generated by a system with, essentially, optional object movement as well as V-movement. However, we also showed that the analysis faces various problems in Old English, especially when the field is broadened somewhat and made to include the position of other VP elements, such as PPs, stranded prepositions and particles, which show regularities not easily captured within the feature-checking approach. In this section, we will explore the merits of the approach for Middle English, contrasting it with the alternative OV/VO approach of Pintzuk (1996). Since there are relatively few quantitative studies of the syntax of Middle English, it is not yet possible to determine the implications of the checking approach for all VP elements. In what follows, we shall therefore largely restrict ourselves to the position of objects *per se*, drawing on the empirical material presented in 5.4 and the analysis of it developed in van der Wurff (1997a, 1999).

We may begin by noting that for the material from the thirteenth and four-teenth centuries, a movement approach has some *prima facie* plausibility in view of the fact that OV tokens can feature other elements intervening between the lexical verb and its object. Thus, in examples (53) and (58), there is an intervening adverbial (*her*, *so*), while (54) and (59) have an intervening auxiliary (*scolde*, *mo3e*). If these patterns are derived through movement, as seems plausible, movement can also be invoked to derive OV tokens with the object adjacent to the verb. Instances with surface VO order would then reflect covert application of object movement (or, in cases with a finite lexical verb, overt object movement followed by further overt movement of the verb to a higher functional projection, as discussed in chapter 4).

If such a movement analysis of the OV data can be maintained, there may be no need to postulate OV as a possible underlying order in Middle English in addition to (and in competition with) VO order, the way Pintzuk (1991, 1996) proposes. In 5.3.1.3, we discussed Pintzuk's idea of competing VO and OV grammars as applied to Old English; for Middle English, a problem for the analysis might be the lack of clear motivation for OV base order, since it appears that all instances of OV order can be derived by the leftward movement operation that seems to be needed anyway for examples like (53), (54), (58) and (59). Nevertheless, Pintzuk (1996) maintains the competing OV/VO hypothesis for Middle English, arguing that it is needed to account for the occurrence of preverbal particles, which are found, though with decreasing frequency, throughout the Middle English period (see Hiltunen 1983). If particles cannot be moved leftward, Pintzuk argues, their occur-rence in preverbal position provides evidence for underlying OV order in Middle English.

However, this argument is not watertight, since particles do seem to undergo leftward movement in some cases. In Modern Icelandic, for example, the fol-lowing type of sentence can be found:

(68)   Fundurinn sem fram hafði farið í Ósló   var skemmtilegur.
         the-meeting that on   had gone in Oslo was fun
         'The meeting that took place in Oslo was fun.'

Sentences like (68) are usually analysed as featuring particle movement, an instance of the more general operation of Stylistic Fronting (see Maling 1990: 82), which occurs in clauses with a subject gap. It has in fact been suggested (see Roberts 1993: 252–4) that Middle English also has the process of Stylistic Fronting; an example in which a particle has been fronted might be (69) (note that (69) is a relative with the passive subject relativized, i.e. it has a subject gap):

(69)   An hevenyssh perfit creature, That down were sent in scornynge of nature.
         'A perfect, heavenly creature, which was sent down to mock nature.'
                                                              (Chaucer *Troilus* I 104)

It therefore seems possible that preverbal particles in this type of sentence could undergo movement from a postverbal base position, making these sentences irrelevant for deciding whether Middle English had underlying OV order in addition to VO order, and to that extent weakening Pintzuk's case. It is true that the competing-grammars analysis of Pintzuk (1996) has the potential virtue of unifying the phenomena of preverbal particles and preverbal objects, while a movement analysis of preverbal objects requires additional mechanisms to account for preverbal particles (such as Stylistic Fronting and/or the movement processes referred to in 5.3.2 for Old English particles). Still, the difficulty of finding unambiguous evidence favouring the competing-grammars approach to OV/VO variation in Middle English would make us hesitant to adopt it.

Let us try to determine, then, how the idea that all objects are underlyingly postverbal could be applied to the thirteenth- and fourteenth-century cases of surface OV order described in 5.4. The first and simplest type to consider has the object adjacent to the lexical verb, as in (56), which we repeat here.

(56)   alle that him feith berith and obeieth
         'all that have faith in him and obey him'   (Chaucer *Astrolabe* 58)

Adopting the ideas on feature-checking set out in 5.3.2., we can posit the following relevant stages in the derivation of this sentence:

(70)   a. [$_{VP}$ berith feith]
         b. [$_{AgrO'}$ berith$_i$-AgrO [$_{VP}$ t$_i$ feith]]
         c. [$_{AgrOP}$ feith$_j$ berith$_i$-AgrO [$_{VP}$ t$_i$ t$_j$]]

In (70a), the VP has been formed, with the head *berith* being followed by its complement *feith*. In (70b), AgrO has been inserted in front of the VP, and together they form AgrO'; simultaneously, the head of VP, *berith*, has adjoined to AgrO. In (70c), finally, the object *feith* has moved out of VP into the specifier position of AgrOP, for reasons of case checking. A tree diagram for that stage would look as in (71).

(71)

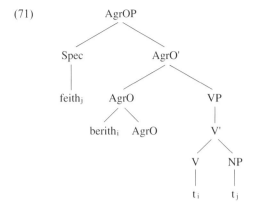

In (71), the object has moved to SpecAgrO and has its features checked there. But, as pointed out in 5.3.2, the features of the object can in principle also be checked in a position adjoined to AgrOP, as shown in (44) there. This means that an alternative to (70c) might be (70d), in which AgrOP has an empty specifier and *feith* is adjoined to it.

(70)   d. [$_\text{AgrOP}$ feith$_j$ [$_\text{AgrOP}$ berith$_i$-AgrO [$_\text{VP}$ t$_i$ t$_j$]

While (70d) may seem superfluous for the derivation of sentences like (56), it provides a plausible structure for sentences in which the object is separated from the lexical verb by an adverb, such as (58).

(58)   I may my persone and myn hous so kepen and deffenden.
         'I can keep and defend myself and my house in such a way.'
                                                    (Chaucer *Melibee* 1334)

The structure of this sentence after movement of verb and object could be as in (72).

(72)

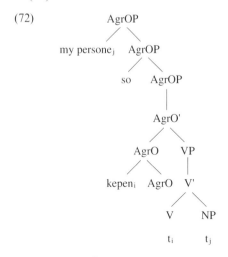

We assume that AgrOP in (72) has two elements adjoined to it: the adjunct *so*, base-generated in left-adjoined position, as all adjuncts are, and the object *my persone*, which has moved to an adjoined position for case checking. The net result is that the object ends up being separated from the lexical verb.

Another type of sentence with non-adjacency between lexical verb and object has an intervening auxiliary, as in (59), the relevant part of which we repeat in (73).

(73)   þet he him moʒe excusi
        'that he may excuse him'

In dealing with the comparable Old English pattern of (50), we suggested that in such cases movement of the object is still motivated by the need for feature checking, but that the checking takes place not in the AgrOP directly dominating the VP headed by the lexical verb but in the AgrOP associated with the auxiliary verb. This idea readily carries over to Middle English examples like (73), resulting in a structure as in (74).

(74)

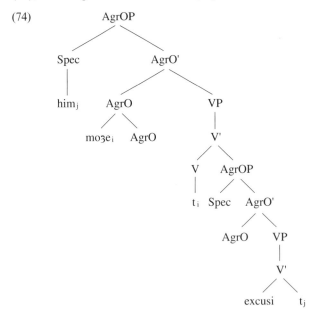

These then would be the structures associated with examples like (52)–(59), which are all from the thirteenth and fourteenth centuries. Under a feature-checking analysis like this, OV order would not be expected to be restricted to certain types of clauses or certain types of object only, since the mechanisms involved would make OV order available quite generally. The textual record indeed suggests that, in this period, all kinds of object, whether nominal or pronominal, could occur in preverbal position in all kinds of clauses.[2] However, as we saw in 5.4, OV order became grammatically restricted in the fifteenth century, when it ceased to be productive except where the clause featured an empty subject, or an auxiliary and a negative or quantified object. This implies that the status of OV order in the fifteenth century cannot be the same as in the two preceding centuries, and a different analysis is therefore needed.

For fifteenth-century OV tokens in clauses with an invisible subject, a plausible analysis would be one involving topicalization of the object. The relevant parts of sentences (60) and (61) would then have the structures shown in (75), where *e* stands for the empty subject of the clause IP.

(75)   a. summe he exiled, summe he put out here rite eyne, and [þe worthi man]$_i$
           [$_{IP}$ e pursewed t$_i$]
        b. alle þat [þis writinge]$_i$ [$_{IP}$ e reden t$_i$]

In other words, we would suggest that these are actually instances of preclausal rather than preverbal objects. Support for this idea can be found in the presence of topicalization in the initial clauses in (75a), where the element *summe* is clearly in preclausal position; this parallel is also found in several other coordinate sentences with OV order in the final clause. Further support for the analysis in (75) can be found in sentences of this type which contain an auxiliary: as would be expected on the basis of (75), they have the object linearly preceding the auxiliary. Examples are given in (76) and (77).

(76)   diuers of the seid mysdoers . . . greuously vexe and trobill hem . . . and
        summe haue bete and left for ded
        'several of the aforesaid miscreants vex and trouble them grievously . . . and
        some they have beaten and left for dead'   (*Paston Letters* 36.46)

(77)   He slewe his broder Amon that suche desloyaltee and vntrouth had done to
        his suster
        'He killed his brother Amon, who had done such dishonour and outrage to
        his sister'   (Caxton *Knight of Tower* 87.15)

As for the motivation for the movement process represented in (75), it has often been suggested that there is a Topic position at the left boundary of the clause. In Rizzi (1997), this idea takes the form of a proposal for a functional projection TopP (topic phrase) in this position, which would make it possible to say that topics move to the specifier of TopP for the purpose of feature-checking. This analysis would then apply to (75).

The second type of OV sentence found in the fifteenth century has a negative or quantified object and an auxiliary. Making use of the by now well-established

---

[2] Again, we note that the structural trigger of overt movement (i.e. the nature of the strong features) remains less than clear.

idea that negation projects a functional category of its own, as we also did in
4.3.2.2, we would suggest that the structure of a sentence such as (62) is as in
(78). Here the negative object *no meyhir* has overtly moved from its base position in VP into the specifier of NegP in order to check its negative feature against
the head Neg. We adopt in (78) the clausal architecture argued for in chapter 4.
If the object is licensed in SpecNegP, the auxiliary *schuld* presumably moves to
the head position F left of Neg, and the pronominal subject *þei* is in Spec,FP.

(78)

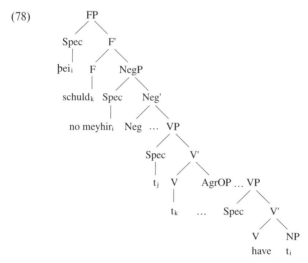

This analysis would mean effectively that we regard Aux–negative object–V
orders as persistent occurrences of V to F as discussed in chapter 4. The attraction of this account is that it enables us to see a rationale for the fact that these
OV orders only occur in clauses with a high auxiliary. On the plausible assumption that at this time, modals could still be main verbs, we can see that movement of the object to Spec,NegP is contingent on V-movement to F, as discussed
above. On this view, the loss of this subcase of OV order is related to the reanalysis of modals from main verbs to auxiliaries. A reasonable perspective on this
reanalysis is that modals were reanalysed as base-generated functional heads.
Because modals ceased to undergo movement, the grammar no longer allowed
the overt checking of a negative object in Spec,NegP contingent on it.

For sentences with a quantified preverbal object, like (64) and (65), an
analysis making use of NegP does not seem natural, but for these sentences
the rule of quantifier raising of May (1985) could be invoked. For the sentence
in (65), a possible (condensed IP) structure might then be (79), where the
quantifier has adjoined to VP for reasons of scope.

(79)

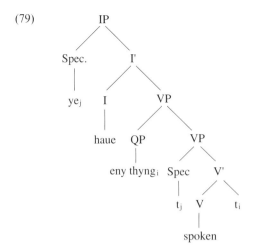

This analysis commits us to the view that quantifier raising may take place overtly, which is not a standard assumption. However, there are some facts in Modern French which are similar to our fifteenth-century English data and for these, Belletti (1990) and Cinque (1995: 276–86) have also invoked an overt process of quantifier movement. An example is given in (80).

(80)   Je ne   peux pas   tout   faire.
        I   NEG can   NEG everything do
        'I can't do everything.'

To conclude this section, let us evaluate what we have done. Our attempt to analyse the Middle English data from the perspective of a Kayne-style approach to word order has brought to light a certain degree of continuity in the order of object and verb and the mechanisms responsible for it during the Old and Middle English periods until about 1400. Before that time, OV order appears to be a productive process, found in a range of syntactic contexts, all of which can be made to follow from a feature-checking account without raising insuperable difficulties. However, as we noted for Old English in 5.3.2, the position of other elements, such as PPs and particles, may be more difficult to account for, and it is not surprising to see that these still stand out as problem areas when it comes to deciding between the feature-checking approach and the alternative competing-grammars approach of Pintzuk (1996).

For the post-1400 data, an approach incorporating the idea of feature checking also offers a reasonable analysis, although the data are sharply differ-ent from the pre-1400 data in showing OV order in only two or three very specific syntactic contexts. As we suggested above, the fifteenth-century OV data in fact instantiate overt checking of a topic feature and a negative feature. A further question raised by the data is why, around 1400, OV order ceased to be productive in most contexts and survived in the few contexts that it did. This brings us to issues of diachrony, which is the topic of the next section.

5.6   The diachrony of OV and VO order

It may be good to begin this section by emphasizing once again a particular aspect of the history of OV/VO order in English that has been neglected in earlier research, which commonly states that the shift took place in the twelfth century and then quickly moves on to the question of what factors brought it about. On the basis of the empirical material presented in 5.2 and 5.4, it is clear that the change-over from surface OV to VO is slower and more gradual than such an account implies; it is true that surface VO order gained a lot of ground during the eleventh and twelfth centuries, but it already had a firm foothold before that time, and it took several more centuries before surface OV order as a productive option disappeared from prose writings. The data presented in 5.4 show that it is not until 1400 that there is a discontinuity in terms of the types of syntactic contexts allowing OV order, with most contexts losing this option but two or three contexts retaining it until 1650. It is discontinuities like these that are the clearest signs of grammatical change, and below we try to interpret them from the perspective of the Kayne-style approach to word order variation developed in 5.3 and 5.5.

Before we consider the situation in Middle English, let us first look at the Old English facts from a diachronic point of view. As we saw in 5.3.1.1, Pintzuk and Kroch (1989) argue that the language of *Beowulf* has consistent surface OV in cases where the verb has not been fronted, with only heavy objects occurring postverbally. From the perspective of the analysis developed in 5.3.2, it might therefore be possible to say that the case features of AgrO were uniformly strong at this stage of the language, forcing overt movement of the object to the specifier of AgrOP, and hence consistent surface OV order (though we note that this leaves the position of heavy objects unexplained). In the stage of the language represented by the prose texts, objects are still frequently preverbal, but light postverbal objects are also common. We have argued in 5.3.2 that this could be interpreted as a sign that the case features were not uniformly strong, making both overt and non-overt object movement possible (an idea that in itself raises some thorny questions for the approach as a whole, as we noted).

To the extent that *Beowulf* indeed represents an earlier stage of Old English, we can therefore identify a historical change, taking place at some point in the period 600–900. Viewed within the analysis developed in 5.3.2, the change would consist in the loss of uniformly strong case features. Next, of course, we would like to know what caused this grammatical change. Within the model of change described in chapter 1, we want to know what changes there may have been in E-language to bring about the change in I-language, i.e. what was different in the language environment of English children acquiring a grammar around 900 compared with children acquiring it around 600? In the absence of sufficient textual records from this period, it is somewhat difficult to establish this with any great precision. However, the literature on the change from OV to VO contains several proposals for the cause of the increase in surface VO order (see Denison 1993: 27–58 for a useful summary and critical evaluation) and some of these may be relevant for the explanation of the loss of uniformly strong features.

Stockwell (1977), for example, attributes the rise of VO order to the prevalence of, amongst other things, postverbal afterthought-like elements, such as relative clauses, second conjuncts of coordinated phrases, appositions and adverbs (to these, we can add heavy objects). The accumulated evidence of all these sentence types, Stockwell (1977) argues, would at some point lead language learners to conclude that surface VO was possible quite generally. Another idea is that postverbal position was generalized from heavy objects to progressively lighter objects, with this position perhaps initally having some expressive value that became bleached due to common use (see Lightfoot 1979: 393 ff.; 1981b: 231 f.) and/or to diffusion across dialects (see van der Wurff 1990b: 42–4). Yet another factor that has been invoked for the shift from OV to VO is processing problems that might be caused by the consistent use of OV order for internally complex objects (for a detailed demonstration, see Colman 1988). What may also have played a role is the scantiness of evidence for OV order in main clauses, which is the prime environment guiding language learners (see Lightfoot 1991); in particular the position of finite verb and particles may have been significant in this respect (see chapters 4 and 6). Finally, it has been proposed that the change to VO order may have been due the loss of overt case marking of NPs, either directly or mediated through a system of identification or licensing (see Weerman 1989: 157–78, and Kiparsky 1997).

On the basis of suggestions like these, we can imagine a child acquiring a grammar of English around 900 which would be exposed to a language environment which was different from that of earlier generations in the following respects: it contained more elements such as relative clauses, adverbs, appositions and heavy objects in postverbal position; it also contained postverbal objects that were only marginally heavy or pragmatically marked; it had fewer preverbal objects that were internally complex or unambiguously accusative, more main clauses with a fronted verb, and fewer clause-final particles. This evidence from E-language would trigger a grammar or I-language allowing post-verbal constituents, and in particular the object, to move to their associated functional projection covertly. At the same time, the language environment that learners around 900 were exposed to contained very robust evidence for overt object movement, in the form of many clauses with an object preceding a non-fronted verb. The result would be that children acquired a grammar allowing both options, as sketched in 5.3.2.

The textual record suggests that in the late Old English period, sentences derived from the option of covert object movement, i.e. with VO order, remained relatively infrequent, but within the analysis that we are exploring here, this may – indeed, *must* – be taken to be an E-language phenomenon. This is also true of the rise in frequency of VO order in the eleventh and twelfth centuries, and the differences that there may have been in this respect between main and embedded clauses (see Lightfoot 1991: 42–77 for a different view). The figures of Kroch and Taylor (1994), discussed in 5.4, show that OV order still occurred in thirty per cent or more of all early thirteenth-century (embedded) clauses that they examined, a clear sign that the grammar still made both options available at this time.

The grammatical system in which AgrO was not uniformly strong persisted until the beginning of the fifteenth century. Throughout this period, object movement could take place either overtly (resulting in surface OV order, unless the verb moved to a functional projection higher than AgrOP) or non-overtly (resulting in surface VO order). Which option was chosen in any specific situation, and how many instances were produced of either type, is an E-language phenomenon, and not a strictly grammatical one. Of course, in this case as in others, the possibilities made available by the grammar (I-language) were not distributed randomly in actual language use (E-language); rather, speakers and writers would tend to use a particular syntactic variant in particular contexts or situations, for various kinds of reasons.

Interestingly, the choice between OV and VO order in Middle English seems to have depended on the same kinds of factors as have typically been found to determine linguistic variation in studies of contemporary material. Thus, there appears to have been stylistic differentiation (as between poetic style, in which high proportions of OV were used, versus prose style; see MacLeish 1969 and Foster and van der Wurff 1995), discourse factors (involving the distinction between given and new information, the latter disfavouring OV; see Foster and van der Wurff 1997), and perhaps ease of processing of specific clauses (leading to somewhat greater use of OV in clauses lacking an overt subject; compare Bauer 1995 on a similar constraint in French). In addition, there was social or dialectal differentiation, in particular correlating with English versus Scandinavian ethnicity, the latter showing greater use of surface VO (see Danchev 1991, Weerman 1993 and, more tentatively though with better empirical support, Kroch and Taylor 1994).

But around 1400, a qualitative change can be observed in the textual record, from which we can deduce a change in the underlying grammar. The occurrence of OV order becomes limited to just a few syntactic patterns, specifically clauses with an invisible subject and clauses containing an auxiliary and a negative or quantified object. This means that children born around 1400 acquired a grammar that no longer made sentences with surface OV order available, except in the contexts just specified, while children born one generation earlier had still acquired a grammar yielding OV order in all kinds of syntactic contexts. Within the feature-checking approach to OV/VO order, the relevant change can be interpreted as the loss of the option of overt object movement to the functional projection AgrOP. Note that this interpretation of the change as a unified phenomenon receives support from the fact that, apart from the exceptions mentioned above, all other OV contexts seem to be lost simultaneously around 1400: the change affects not only cases of OV with the object adjacent to the lexical verb, but also cases where the object precedes an adverbial or an auxiliary. In 5.4, we argued that the existing variety of OV patterns in the thirteenth and fourteenth century could receive a unified analysis within a feature-checking approach, while this might be difficult in Pintzuk's (1991) competing-grammars approach. The fact that all variants seem to disappear at the same time is a further argument supporting our position.

We now have to ask the question: what difference in the language environment around 1400 was responsible for children no longer acquiring the option of overt object movement? We shall indicate here the general directions in which we think an answer may be sought. One factor that comes to mind is the dwindling frequency of surface OV tokens discussed in 5.4. If children around 1400 were exposed to so few data necessitating the assumption of overt object movement, they may not have acquired it through lack of robust evidence for it in the primary data. While this scenario is certainly possible, it amounts to saying that OV order disappeared because it became infrequent. Clearly, we then still have to explain why the evidence for OV order (i.e. the data triggering overt object movement) fell below a threshold of robustness. Since we argued above that the frequency of OV and VO order in the period 900–1400 is an E-language phenomenon, the eventual explanation will have to address matters of language use, in particular the factors determining the choice between the two possible word orders in the fourteenth century.

Another direction to take would be to try and link the change involving object movement to some other grammatical property that was undergoing change at this time. As we saw in 4.4, in the literature on verb positions a connection has sometimes been proposed between the richness of verbal inflections and the possibility of overt V-movement. Phonetic weakening of verbal inflections, in particular the loss of plural marking on the verb, has been claimed to correlate with the loss of V-movement in the Scandinavian languages (see Platzack and Holmberg 1989). Building on this work, Roberts (1993: 246–73) suggests that both developments also took place in English. From the perspective of the checking approach to OV/VO order, it is interesting to explore the idea that the loss of V-movement also meant that the verb could no longer move overtly to AgrO. This would enable us to posit the following chain of events: at some point, erosion of verbal agreement led to the V-features of AgrO losing their strength, making overt V-movement impossible, which in turn meant that overt object movement became impossible as well (since, as pointed out in 5.3.2, movement of V to AgrO is seen as a precondition for movement of the object to AgrOP, as shown in derivations such as (43)). For language learners, there would be a clear trigger in the primary data, in the form of uninflected plural verb forms.

This explanation for the loss of surface OV order in English would have the attractive property of tying up this change with other, independently established changes (perhaps involving not only verbal endings and verb positions, but also some further phenomena, for which see Bobaljik and Thráinsson 1998). Such a unification of a whole set of changes would certainly be quite elegant. However, in historical syntax as in life in general, things are seldom so neat and clean. In 4.4 we commented on the possible undesirability of making the existence of word order patterns directly dependent on the nature of verbal inflections. In addition, this explanation for the loss of overt object movement around 1400 faces problems of timing. Firstly, the loss of verbal plural marking is not really complete in texts even from the late fifteenth century (see the data in Lass 1992: 97 f.). It may be possible to attribute this to the slow spread in written texts of endingless forms that were already in general use in spoken language, but such a move will not help for the second problem: *do*-less negative and interrogative clauses are found until the eighteenth century (see especially the data given by Tieken-Boon van Ostade 1987). Such sentences seem to necessitate the assumption of overt V-movement, with the verb leaving VP and moving to the head I of IP (or the head of some other functional projection, called FP in chapter 4), and from there to C in the case of questions. A seventeenth-century example is given in (81), and the relevant part of its structure in (82).

(81)   For to write unnatural things, is the most probable way of pleasing them,
         who understand not Nature. (Dryden 'Preface to *An Evening's Love*', 1671)

(82)   who understand$_i$ not [$_{VP}$ t$_i$ nature]

As Warner (1997) and Lightfoot (1999: 163) point out, it therefore appears
that V-to-I movement remained possible until some time in the eighteenth
century. It will be clear that this causes problems for the explanation of loss of
overt object movement given above; we must leave the solution open here.

   Another question needing to be answered is why, as the general possibility
of OV order disappeared after 1400, two or three surface OV patterns
remained possible. Recall that OV order is still found in the fifteenth century
in cases where the clause contains an auxiliary and a negative or quantified
object, or a non-overt subject. We repeat two of the relevant examples here.

(61)   alle þat þis writinge reden or heere
         'all that will read or hear this writing'   (*Sermon* 2250)

(62)   þei schuld no meyhir haue
         'they were not allowed to have a mayor'   (Capgrave *Cronicles* 199.6)

What made children acquire a grammar making available OV order in such
cases? The answer, we think, lies in late fourteenth-century children's drive to
assign structures to utterances they were exposed to. These utterances might
include sentences like the following, produced by speakers of the older generation:

(83)   if he do no vengeance of hem that it han disserved
         'if he gives no punishment to those that have deserved it'
                                                          (Chaucer *Melibee* 1435)

(84)   they ne kan no conseil hyde
         'they can hide no counsel'   (Chaucer *Melibee* 1193)

What did little Lowys make of such sentences when he heard his father utter
them? Since, for some reason, late fourteenth-century children were acquiring a grammar disallowing overt movement of the object to Spec,AgrOP, a
structure for (83) and (84) with the object (*it, no conseil*) being located in
Spec,AgrOP was not possible. However, sentences of these specific types
could have a different structure: as proposed in 5.5, sentences like (83) can
have the object in the specifier of the TopP, as is shown in (75), and sentences like (83) can have the object in the specifier of the functional projection NegP, as shown in (78). On the basis of utterances like (83) and (84),
children would construct a grammar incorporating these options, which
would mean that they could produce a very restricted number of surface OV
patterns.

It is difficult to say what structure the grammar of the older generation assigned to sentences like (83) and (84). For them, they may have been instantiations of overt object movement to Spec,AgrOP, much as shown in (72) and (74), in which case the change which took place around 1400 would amount to a structural reanalysis, with instances of overt movement to AgrOP being reinterpreted as instances of overt movement to NegP and movement to TopP. But perhaps the sentences had these structures before 1400 too, in which case they did not undergo any change, and all that happened was the loss of the general option of overt object movement to AgrOP. Deciding between these two possibilities is no simple matter and can only be done on the basis of a full description of the facts of negation and topicalization in fourteenth- and fifteenth-century English.

What, finally, is our overall assessment of the approach to the changes in English word order based on VO as a uniform underlying order, with movement to preverbal position being due to the need for feature checking? The approach has some possible weaknesses, which have to do partly with theory-internal issues and partly with empirical matters. Thus, the apparent optionality of overt object movement in (Late) Old English and Middle English may be problematic. It can be captured within this framework, but only by either a mechanical application of the notions 'weak' and 'strong' or a fairly drastic revision of key concepts of the framework. There is, moreover, as yet no convincing way of linking feature strength to the presence or absence of overt case morphology. The vital role played by feature checking of the object also means that the analysis cannot be straightforwardly used to explain the order of other elements vis-à-vis the verb. Furthermore, the analysis has nothing to say about the rapid increase of surface VO order in the eleventh and twelfth centuries.

On the other hand, empirical work by Pintzuk (1991, 1996) and Kroch and Taylor (1994) has made clear that the crucial case of VO order with a light object in an embedded clause was neither new nor categorical in early thirteenth-century texts: it first arose in Late Old English and did not become categorical until the late fourteenth century. In addition, the potential problems of the checking approach need to be weighed against some positive strengths. First of all, this approach has the advantage of being rooted in a relatively well-articulated structural theory of word order. Moreover, it can be applied to the Old and Middle English evidence on object positions with a fair degree of success: nearly all the empirical data can be accounted for by the application, overtly or covertly, of object movement into AgrOP. As we have seen, the analysis also receives support from the fact that the various OV patterns disappear around the same time, and it suggests possible (though still tentative) connections between this change and at least two other changes occurring in the same period. Lastly, the feature-checking framework also suggests plausible structures for the few OV patterns that survive for another 150 years: they can be viewed as instances of movement of the object to a functional projection other than AgrOP, thus accounting for their survival after other cases of OV order had ceased to be productive.

6

Verb–particles in Old and Middle English

6.1   Introduction

Verb–particle combinations, such as *look up (the information), call up (somebody), cough up (the money)*, are a characteristic feature of present-day English. In fact, there are so many today that it has proved useful to devote separate dictionaries to them (see e.g. Cowie and Mackin 1975 and Courtney 1983). Their meaning often cannot be inferred from the meaning of the verb and the particle (adverb or preposition), which seems to suggest that we are dealing with semantic units. Syntactically, they form a fairly well-defined class, which is evident, for instance, from their word order properties. When the object is a full NP, two word orders are possible: V–NP–particle and V–particle–NP. A pronominal object, however, only has the former word order. The contrast between the verb–particle combination *look up* (= to search for), and a verb plus a preposition (*look up*) is illustrated in (1):

(1) a. They looked up the information   e. They looked up the chimney
      b. They looked the information up   f. *They looked the chimney up
      c. They looked it up   g. *They looked it (= the chimney) up
      d. *They looked quickly up the   h. They looked quickly up the
         information[1]   chimney

Verb–particles have been frequently discussed in the generative literature, and various analyses have been proposed; for an overview and extensive discussion, the reader is referred to den Dikken (1995).

The earliest English texts that have come down to us also seem to have verb–particle combinations, though there are not nearly as many of them as there are today. Some Old English examples are given in (2).

(2) a. þa   *feol* he *adune*
       then fell he down
       'then he fell down'   (*ÆCHom* I, 22.316.28)

---

[1] The particle in a phrasal verb is normally stressed. See Quirk et al. 1985, section 16.2 ff. for details and ways of distinguishing between phrasal verbs ('call up') and prepositional verbs ('call on').

b. þæt hie   mid   þæm   þæt folc   *ut*   *aloccoden*
that they with   that   the people out enticed
'that they might entice the people with it (to come) outside' (*Or* 5.3.117.5)

The Old English facts have attracted a good deal of attention and have played a crucial role in discussions about the underlying word order of Old English. Building on earlier work by Koster (1975) for Dutch, Koopman (1984) and van Kemenade (1987) have used the distribution of verb + particle to determine the underlying structure of Old English, while Pintzuk (1991) argues that the position of particles provides evidence for V-movement in subordinate clauses. The change in the position of the particle from Old English to Middle English has been interpreted as the result of a change in underlying word order from OV to VO. In this chapter we will mainly survey work that has been done within this approach, as there are some detailed proposals available. Similar detailed work has not been done within a universal VO base hypothesis, which is assumed in much recent work in generative theory, as discussed in detail in chapter 5. Interpreting the distribution in Old English and the change in the particle position from Old English to Middle English within a universal base hypothesis constitutes a considerable challenge and has so far not been undertaken. We can therefore only sketch how the facts could be accounted for within this new hypothesis and what sort of problems are encountered.

We will first define what we mean by 'verb–particle' (section 6.2), and indicate what syntactic means are available to distinguish particles from prefixes. In section 6.3 we will describe what the distribution is of verb and particle in Old English. Section 6.4 investigates whether Koster's (1975) idea that the particle marks the position of the verb in Dutch carries over to Old English and presents Pintzuk's evidence for V-movement in subordinate clauses. We will outline in section 6.5 how the Old English facts can be accounted for in a universal base hypothesis. Some problematic cases are focussed on in section 6.6. Section 6.7 will be devoted to the Middle English evidence, which is very close to the Modern English verb–particle combination. We will discuss how the change in particle position has been interpreted in the traditional framework and suggest how it could be accommodated within a universal base hypothesis.

6.2   Particles: some general considerations

6.2.1   *Problems of definition: what is a particle?*

Words such as *adune* and *ut* in (2) have been given various names. Harrison (1892) calls them 'separable prefixes', implying that they are similar to those found in German (e.g. *aufwachen* 'to wake up') and Dutch (e.g. *uit-lachen* 'to laugh at'). Hiltunen (1983) calls them 'phrasal adverbs', and Mitchell (1978, 1985: § 1060 ff.) is not certain which term to use for Old English. It is, he characteristically says, largely a matter of terminology. As it is not our intention to try to resolve this terminological puzzle, it seems best to use 'particle' as the most neutral term.

Hiltunen (1983: 20) defines particles (his 'phrasal adverbs') as follows: 'I will define phrasal adv(erbs)s as those that indicate location or direction (or both) and do not normally appear as prepositions.' Particles in Old English include *adun* 'down', *aweg* 'away', *forþ* 'forth', *up* 'up' and *ut* 'out'. Not all loca-tional/directional adverbs are included. Hiltunen (1983: 21) limits them to those 'that may function as such in M[iddle]E[nglish] and M[odern]E[nglish] phrasal verbs', a somewhat odd criterion. Adverbs such as *ham* 'home' and *norþryhte* 'due north', which are locational/directional in meaning are excluded, because they do not occur as part of a phrasal verb in present-day English.

If we can interpret the evidence in such a way that particle and verb are con-sistently in the same underlying position, it is reasonable to assume that they form a syntactic combination (e.g. something like $_V$[V particle] or $_V$[particle V]). It is uncontroversial that *look up* (in the sense of 'search for something') in present-day English forms a semantic unit, as the meaning of the combina-tion cannot easily be predicted from its parts. It is less easy to determine this for Old English, and consequently less easy to be confident that something is a particle. In particular, we need criteria by which we can distinguish between bound elements (prefixes) and those that can be separated from the verb (par-ticles). For example, is *ut* in (2b) a prefix or a particle? We will tackle this problem in the next section.

6.2.2   Differences between particles and prefixes

Word division in Old English manuscripts is inconsistent and a poor guide to morphological unit status, and does not help us decide whether we should interpret combinations like *ut aloccoden* in (2b) as two words or perhaps as a single one, made up of a verb with a prefix. Dictionaries of Old English list many combinations of verb + particle under the relevant particle, implying that they form a unit of some sort, but what exactly the unit is sup-posed to be is often not made explicit. We can illustrate this by looking at the way combinations with *aweg* 'away' are treated in Bosworth and Toller (1898) and Toller (1921), and the *Dictionary of Old English* (letter A, Healey et al. 1994). Bosworth and Toller (1898) list thirteen verbs with *aweg* 'away' as their first element, which look like prefixed verbs, but there is almost always a reference to the uncompounded verb. Thus for *awegberan* 'to carry away' it adds: v. *beran*. No combinations with *aweg* are illustrated under *beran* 'to carry', and *aweg* is not listed as one of the prefixes that *beran* combines with (s.v. *beran*), from which we must conclude that Bosworth and Toller do not consider *awegberan* to be a verb + prefix combination. Toller in his supplement (1921) clarifies this earlier position and states that *aweg* should be separated in those verbs listed with *aweg* as a first element, implying that he regards these verbs as combinations rather than as verbs with prefixes. The *Dictionary of Old English* (Healey et al., letter A, 1994) treats this material in similar fashion. It does not list any verbs with *aweg* as a first element, but gives lots of illustrative quotations of the way *aweg* combines with certain verbs (s.v. *aweg*). However, it also states that '[t]he collocations *aweg cuman, aweg fleon, aweg gan* and *aweg gewitan* have alternatively been taken as compounds' (s.v. *aweg*).

From all this, it is not clear what the status of *aweg* is. However, even though it is difficult to distinguish between particles and prefixes in a dead language such as Old English, there are some constructions in which particles show different behaviour from prefixes:

1. *Negation.* The negative *ne* 'not' always comes immediately before the finite verb. In the case of a particle the negative will come between the particle and the verb, as in (3a), but it will precede any prefixes there might be, as in (3b) where *ne* precedes the prefixed verb *ahyldan* (away-bend = 'to alter'):

(3) a. forðæm hio nanne swetne wæsðm *forð   ne*   bringð
        because she no   sweet fruit   forth not brings
        'because it does not produce any sweet fruit'   (*CP* 45.341.22)
     b. ne on naþre healfe he *ne a*hylde   his þeawas
        nor on neither side   he not away-bent his conduct
        'nor did he alter his conduct in any way'   (*ÆLS* Edmund) 16)

2. *To-infinitives. To* precedes an inflected infinitive immediately. A particle will come before *to*, illustrated for *ut* 'out' in (4a), but *to* will precede a prefixed verb as in (4b):

(4) a. þæt him wære alyfed   *ut   to* farenne
        that him was   allowed out to go
        'that he was allowed to leave'   (*GD2* (H) 25.155.26)
     b. 7   hio bið micle ðe ieðre *to o*ferfeohtanne
        and she is   much the easier to over-fight
        'and it (= the city of the mind) is much easier to conquer' (*CP* 38.277.21)

3. *Constructions with auxiliary or modal verbs.* Particles, unlike prefixes, can be separated from the verb by an auxiliary or modal verb:

(5)   a. ær   he *ut wolde   faran* to gefeohte
            before he out wanted go   to fight
            'before he wanted to go out to the fight'   (*Or* 3.8.122.11)
         b. þæt entas woldon *aræran* ane burh
            that giants would up-raise a   city
            'that giants would raise up a city'   (*ÆCHom* I, 22.318.14)

4. *Preposition stranding.* Particles, unlike prefixes, can precede a stranded preposition (*of* in (6a) and *on* in (6b)):

(6)   a. . . . ðæt ealond . . . ðæt we ær   *ut   of   gongende* wæron
                 the island   that we before out from going   were
            '. . . the island . . . from which we had previously put out'
                                                               (*Bede* 5.1.384.23)
         b. 7   het   forbærnan þæt gewrit þe   hit *on* awriten wæs
            and ordered burn   the letter which it on written was
            'and ordered to burn the letter in which it was written'   (*Or* 6.13.141.21)

This syntactic behaviour of Old English particles is comparable to that of Dutch and German separable prefixes. Although separable prefixes are often identical in form to prefixes of inseparable verbs, the difference shows up syntactically by the position of auxiliaries and modals, and the infinitive marker *te* 'to'. Auxiliaries and modals can (but need not) come between the particle and the verb, but must precede prefixed verbs. The infinitive marker *te* comes between particle and verb, but immediately before a prefixed verb. This is illustrated in (7) for *'doorlopen* 'walk on/press on', a separable verb (i.e. *door* is a particle), and in (8) for *door'lopen* 'complete/finish', an inseparable verb (i.e. *door* is a prefix):[2]

(7)   a. omdat je   moet *doorlopen*/*door* moet *lopen*
            because you must walk-on/on   must walk
            'because you must press on'
         b. Het heeft geen zin   *door* te *lopen*/*te doorlopen*
            it   has   no   point on   to walk/*to on-walk
            'There is no point in pressing on'

---

[2] The stress is on the prefix in separable verbs, on the verbal part in inseparable verbs (see Geerts et al. 1984: 498 ff. for further differences). Although it is in general difficult to find evidence for stress in a dead language like Old English, the poetry shows that adverbs such as *up* 'up' can be stressed because they can alliterate:
                 Siþþan meotodes sunu
                 when of-God son
            engla   eþel   up gestigan
            of-angels home   up ascend
            wolde
            wanted
            'When the son of God wanted to ascend into the home of angels'
                                                               (*ChristB* 629–31)

(8)   a. omdat   je   deze school eerst moet *doorlopen*/**door* moet *lopen*
            because you this   school first must complete
            'because you must complete this school first'
      b. Het heeft geen zin   deze school **door* te *lopen*/te *doorlopen*
            it   has   no   point this school   to complete
            'There is no point in completing this school'

Apart from intonation, the difference in Dutch between particle and prefix is shown by these syntactic tests. It may be that a similar distinction held in Old English, but it is much more difficult to establish, because there are no native speakers' intuitions to rely on. When there are no recorded examples with the negative *ne*, nor the infinitive marker *to*, nor an auxiliary or modal verb, and the particle is in front of the verb, we do not have absolute certainty about its status. We will return to this point in section 6.3.1.

6.3   Particles in Old English

In this section we will describe the syntax of particle verb in Old English, using quantitative data taken from Hiltunen (1983), a thorough study of the rise of the phrasal verb.[3] Theoretically there are four ways in which particle and verb can be ordered in the surface string, taking into account that other clause elements (X) could intervene:

(9)   a. part–X–V
      b. part–V
      c. V–part
      d. V–X–part

The frequency of these patterns depends on clause type. As stated in chapter 2, it has become common to distinguish three types of clauses: main clauses, coordinate clauses and subordinate clauses, and we will look at each in turn.

---

[3] Hiltunen studied twelve Old English and fifteen Middle English texts, with few exceptions *in toto*. The Old English texts include the major prose works (CP, Or, GD, Bede, Laws, BlHom, ChronA, ChronE, extracts from the WS Gospels, WHom, ÆCHom I&II, ÆLS and ApT). The Middle English texts are: ChronE (continuations), Trinity Homilies, Vices&Virtues, þe Wohunge of Ure Lauerd, Lambeth Homilies, Chad, St. Katherine, St. Marherete, St. Juliana, Hali Meiþhad, Sawles Warde, Ancrene Riwle, History of the Holy Rood Tree and the Vespasian A Homilies. The complete database is given in an appendix, and has been used by subsequent scholars (Koopman 1985, van Kemenade 1987, Pintzuk 1991).

6.3.1   Particles in main clauses

In his study, Hiltunen (1983: 114) gives the following figures for particles in main clauses:

Table 6.1

	part . . . V	part–V	V . . . part	V–part
main clauses	9 (3%)	103 (38%)	107 (39%)	54 (20%)

As discussed in chapter 4, the finite verb in Old English is usually moved to a position F high in the clause. This yields surface V . . . part patterns. The subject often comes between verb and particle, as in (10). The subject and a PP are between verb and particle in (10a), while in (10b) a pronominal object, the subject and a nominal object intervene:

(10)   a. Æfter þissere rædinge and oðrum tihtingum *gewendon* þa halgan
           after   this   reading and other   persuasions turned   the saints
           to þam hælende *upp*
           to the   saviour   up
           'After this reading and other persuasions the saints turned back to the
           Saviour'   (*ÆLS*(Julian&Basilissa) 73)
        b. þa   *sticode* him mon   þa eagan *ut*
           then stuck   him someone the eyes   out
           'then his eyes were gouged out'   (*Or* 4.5.90.13)

There are two constituents between verb and particle in (10a) and three in (10b), but Hiltunen (1983: 137) observes that '[t]he intervening elements, if there are any, rarely exceed three words'. He gives one quote in which there is a great deal of material between verb and particle, but most of it is a further specification of a short phrase (*mid lacum* 'with gifts'):

(11)   Eft   on ærne mergen *sende* se arwurða benedictus twægen his
        later in early morning sent   the venerable Benedict two   his
        muneca   to maure mid lacum   þæt is mid haligdome of þæs
        of-monks to Maurus with presents that is with relics   of of-the
        hælendes rode and of marian   reafe   and of michaheles pelle
        saviour's cross and of of-Mary garment and of Michael's   covering
        and of stephanes lichaman and of martinus reliquium and an
        and of Stephen's body   and of Martin's relics   and a
        ærendgewrit mid þysum wordum *forð*
        letter   with these words   forth
        'Afterwards in the early morning the venerable Benedict sent forth two of
        his monks to Maurus with gifts, that is, with relics of the Saviour's cross

and of Mary's garments and of a covering of Michael('s altar) and of
Stephen's body and of Martin's relics and a message with these words'

(*ÆLS*(Maur) 70)

Particles after the *non-finite* verb are rare. We will discuss this in section 6.4.3.

As can be seen from table 6.1, in forty-one per cent of the main clauses in
Hiltunen's corpus the particle precedes the verb. In a small number of these,
the particle does not immediately precede the verb; the intervening element is
almost always a PP, as in (12).

(12)   ða   ne   dorste he   nawuht   hrædlice *ut* of ðære ceastre *faran* ...
        then not   dared he   not-at-all quickly from the city   go
        'then he dared not go quickly from the city'   (*CP* 51.397.32)

We will return to this in section 6.3.3.

Many of the main clauses with particles have either a modal or an auxiliary
verb, as illustrated in (13), where the finite modal verb has been fronted and
the particle appears before the non-finite (lexical) verb:

(13)   þonne ne   *miht* þu   na   þæt mot   *ut*   *ateon* ...
        then   not can   you not the mote out   draw ...
        'then you cannot draw the mote out ...'   (*ÆHom* 14.153)

There are also main clauses such as (14) with a single verb and a preceding
particle:

(14)   Stephanus *upastah* þurh   his blod   gewuldorbeagod
        Stephen   up-rose through his blood crowned with glory
        'Stephen ascended, crowned with glory through his blood'

(*ÆCHom* I, 3.56.31)

Clauses like (14) call for some comment. This is a context in which we cannot
adequately distinguish between particles and prefixes. It is therefore possible
that *up* is a prefix, in which case we have the usual V-movement in a main
clause. Whether we actually interpret *up* as a prefix or not depends on the way
the combination is normally used, and whether it occurs in any of the syntactic constructions discussed in section 6.2.2, by which particles can be distinguished from prefixes (the position of *ne*, *to*, modals or auxiliaries, and
stranded prepositions). If a particle interpretation is likely, it would seem that
particle and verb have been moved together by verb fronting, but there is
another possible explanation. In Old English there are main clauses where
verb fronting fails to take place, as shown in (15), where the nominal object
ðone man is found between subject and verb (see also chapter 4):

(15)   Se   fullwuht *ðone mon* geclænsað from his synnum
        The baptism the   man   purifies   from his sins
        'Baptism purifies a man from his sins'   (*CP* 54.427.6)

Verb-final main clauses appear in all major texts (though at a low frequency; see Koopman 1995) and it is possible that (14) belongs in this category too.

6.3.2   Particles in coordinate clauses

Hiltunen (1983: 114) gives separate figures for coordinated main clauses:[4]

Table 6.2

	part . . . V	part–V	V . . . part	V–part
coordinated main clauses	18 (8%)	115 (52%)	51 (23%)	38 (17%)

As with main clauses, there are coordinated clauses with the particle before and separated from the verb:

(16)   7   mid his eagum *up* to heofenum *locade*
        and with his eyes   up to heaven   looked
        'and looked up to heaven with his eyes'   (*LS* 17.1(MartinMor) 288)

Most of these again have the particle before a PP. Sixty per cent of coordinated main clauses in Hiltunen's corpus have the particle preceding the verb, which is a higher percentage than was found for main clauses. The reason is that coordinate main clauses show OV as well as VO surface syntax (see Mitchell 1985): in some respects they are like main clauses, with verb fronting as in (17a), while in other respects they are like subordinate clauses, which frequently have OV patterns, as in (17b).

(17)   a. Ond þa *ahof* Drihten hie   *up*
           and then raised God   them up
           'And then God raised them up'   (*LS* 20(AssumptMor) 353)
        b. and hine   ðær *ut* *aspaw*
           and him (= the prophet Jonah) there out spat
           'and spat him out there'   (*ÆCHom* I, 18.246.12)

It has been suggested by Lightfoot (1991: 58) that Old English coordinated main clauses could be CPs or IPs. Verb fronting is possible in CPs (as in (17a)), but coordinated IPs lack the functional head for the final verb to move to. The problem of coordinated clauses is also discussed in Stockwell and Minkova (1990).

---

[4] It should be noted that Hiltunen (1983) includes coordinate subordinate clauses in his figures for subordinate clauses. Coordinate subordinate clauses are not nearly as frequent as coordinate main clauses, as the figures in Koopman (1990) for the double object construction show.

6.3.3   Particles in subordinate clauses

The distribution of particles in subordinate clauses differs somewhat from main and coordinated clauses, as the figures taken from Hiltunen (1983: 115) show:

Table 6.3

	part . . . V	part–V	V . . . part	V–part
subordinate clauses	41 (12%)	251 (72%)	18 (5%)	37 (11%)

Far fewer subordinate clauses have the particle after the verb (sixteen per cent as against forty per cent for coordinate clauses and fifty-nine per cent for main clauses). We will discuss this in more detail in section 6.4.3. In the great majority of subordinate clauses the particle comes immediately before the verb and this is clearly the norm, illustrated in (18a) (earlier given as (2b)) and (18b):

(18)   a. þæt hie mid þæm þæt folc   *ut*   *aloccoden*
              that they with that the people out enticed
              'that they might entice the people with it (to come) outside'
                                                                    (*Or* 5.3.117.5)
         b. swa þæt se scinenda lig   his locc *upateah*
              so   that the shining flame his locks up-drew
              'so that the shining flame drew his locks up'   (*ÆCHom* II, 39.1.295.241)

As with main and coordinate clauses, particles are sometimes found to the left of the verb and separated from it, as in (19):

(19)   ðeah   ðu sie *up* ofer ðine mæð   *ahæfen*
         though you are up over your condition raised
         'although you are raised above your condition'   (*CP* 65.467.1)

Again, in almost all of them the particle precedes a PP. If we interpret the particle in this position as an adverbial modifier of the PP, as van Kemenade (1987) and Pintzuk (1991) suggest, we have a way of treating these in a uniform manner. The Old English particles are directional or locative and their meaning usually goes well with the following PPs. Let us look at some further examples, two subordinate clauses in (20a) and (20b) and a coordinate clause in (20c):

(20)   a. he bæd   hine . . . þæt heo *ut* of þæm byrene *gan* sceolde
              he asked her   that she out of the stable go should
              'he asked her . . . to go out of the stable'   (*GD*1 (C) 9.69.1)
         b. þonne hi ðe *forð* mid him to ðam ecan   forwyrde *gelædon*
              than they you forth with them to the eternal damnation led
              'than that they led you with them to eternal damnation'
                                                              (*ÆCHom* I, 34.516.13)

c. and þærrihte   wearð þæt fæt   *upp* to heofonum *abroden*
   and straightaway was   the vessel up to heavens   pulled
   'and straightaway the vessel was pulled up to heaven'
   (*ÆLS*(Peter's Chair) 94)

Modification of a PP seems plausible in these examples. Interpreting elements
in this position as PP modifiers (and therefore not as particles at all) allows us
to make an important generalization about the position of particles: if they
precede the verb they do so immediately. There are only a few exceptions to
this general rule; we will deal with them separately in section 6.6.

6.4   Position of the particle marks the position of the verb before movement

We have seen that particles in main clauses come after the finite
(lexical) verb, but precede the non-finite (lexical) verb. A reasonable assumption therefore is that V-movement 'strands' the particle, and that the surface
position of the particle actually marks the underlying position of the verb.
Koster (1975) has investigated this idea for Dutch. We will consider how far
his arguments carry over to Old English and whether the evidence from coordinate clauses and subordinate clauses is compatible with this hypothesis too.

6.4.1   Koster's (1975) arguments for Dutch

Dutch does not have phrasal verbs, but it has separable verbs (see (7)
and (8) and the discussion preceding them), which resemble the combinations
we find in Old English. In Dutch the relevant verbs are compounded verbs
with a noun, adjective or adverb as first element (the 'particle') (see Geerts et
al. 1984: 488 ff), which can be separated from the verb in certain syntactic contexts. Separation is obligatory in main clauses when the verb is finite. This is
illustrated in (21a) for *lesgeven* 'to teach' (lit. lesson-give) with a noun as first
element, in (21b) for *losmaken* 'to untie' (lit. loose-make), with an adjectival
first element, and in (21c) for *opbellen* 'to phone' (lit. up-ring) with an adverb
as separable element:

(21)   a. Marie *geeft* al   jaren *les*
          Marie gives already years lesson
          'Mary has been teaching for years'
       b. Snel   *maakte* zij de knoop *los*
          quickly made   she the knot   loose
          'She quickly untied the knot'

c. Jan *belt* Piet vaak *op*
John rings Peter often up
'John often phones Peter'

We will concentrate on separable verbs with adverbs as first elements, as these are closest to particle + verb combinations in Old English. In Dutch main clauses the particle follows the object (as in (21c)), but the finite verb precedes it, due to the Verb-Second rule of Dutch discussed in chapter 4. In subordinate clauses the verb will always come after any object there may be (with the exception of a clausal object) and the particle characteristically precedes the verb, as in (22):

(22)   omdat Jan *Piet* vaak *opbelt*
because John Peter often up-rings
'because John often phones Peter'

Koster's (1975) essential insight is that sentence elements that can be found to the right of the verb in subordinate clauses, such as most PPs, clausal objects and adverbs after an intonation break, can also be found to the right of a particle in main clauses with a single finite verb. We can illustrate this for PPs as in (23):

(23)   a. Marie *gaf* het boek *terug aan Judith*
         'Mary gave the book back to Judith'
        b. omdat   Marie het boek *teruggaf aan*   Judith
         because Marie the book back   gave to Judith
         'because Mary gave the book back to Judith'

Similarly, clause elements that cannot follow the verb in subordinate clauses cannot follow the particle in main clauses either, as shown by the object *Jan* 'John' in (24):

(24)   a. *Piet *belt* vaak *op Jan*
          Peter rings often up John
        b. *omdat Piet vaak *opbelt*   Jan
          because Peter often up-rings John

This is not the place to discuss Koster's tests in detail (see Koopman 1984 and van Kemenade 1987 for an extensive discussion), but they all show that the distribution of particles in main clauses and verbs in subordinate clauses is very similar. Koster's findings for Dutch separable verbs can be summarized as follows:

(25)   a. separation is obligatory in main clauses with a finite separable verb
        b. separation is ungrammatical in subordinate clauses[5]
        c. verbs in subordinate clauses and particles in Verb-Second clauses are sentence-final, unless followed by a PP or an adverbial after an intonation break, or a clausal object

[5] Auxiliaries and modals can intervene; see (5).

It is therefore reasonable to assume that the particle in main clauses and the verb in subordinate clauses mark the same position. Because the verb follows the object in Dutch subordinate clauses, Koster draws the conclusion that Dutch is an SOV language and that the finite verb in main clauses is moved to C, in accordance with its Verb-Second character as discussed in chapter 4. The particle is not subject to this movement and remains in D-structure preverbal position. It therefore marks the position of the verb before movement. Schematically we can represent this in the following way:

(26)   Jan belt Piet vaak op
        $_{NP}$[Jan] $_C$[belt$_i$] $_{VP}$[Piet vaak op t$_i$]

Usually, it is assumed that verb and particle form a syntactic unit (as represented in (27a)), but Bennis (1992) argues that the particle in Dutch can move independently and that the structure in (27b) captures this:

(27)   a.   V

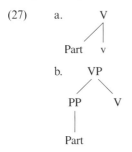

b.   VP

In (27b) the particle really is an intransitive preposition, and as a PP can be moved independently. Either way, the position of the particle in sentences like (21)–(24) is interpreted as marking the underlying position of the verb.

6.4.2   *Koster's test applied to Old English*

When we try to apply Koster's tests to Old English, we find that they do not give the same clearcut results. This is partly because it is difficult in some cases to establish whether a test applies because we lack native speakers' intuitions. We must necessarily depend on the texts that have come down to us, which are mostly formal in nature and in which certain constructions may be rare or completely absent. We do not have reliable information about stress and intonation patterns outside the poetry, and the punctuation of Old English manuscripts is not the same as we would use today and is therefore a poor guide (cf. chapter 1 and Mitchell 1980).

In spite of these limitations, some generalizations can nevertheless be made about particle position in Old English. As far as can be established, it appears that in Old English, as in Dutch, elements that can follow the particle in main clauses can also follow the finite verb in subordinate clauses. Thus we can find PPs and clausal objects behaving in this way, shown for PPs in (28):

(28)   a. þa   gecyrde he *ut   ymbe þæs   cuman þenunge*
           then turned   he out about of-the guest   service
           'Then he went out for the service of the guest'   (*ÆCHom* II, 10.83.65)
        b. forðam ðe he hine   *ætbræd   þam flæsclicum lustum*
           because he himself withdrew the fleshy   lusts
           'because he had withdrawn himself from fleshly lusts' (*ÆCHom* I, 4.58.16)

A major difference with Dutch is that Old English allows objects to appear to the right of the non-finite verb in main clauses and to the right of the verb in subordinate clauses (see also chapter 5). This is illustrated in (29a) for main clauses and in (29b) for subordinate clauses:

(29)   a. Se   mæssepreost sceal mannum *bodian þone soþan geleafan*
           the masspriest   must people preach the true faith
           'The masspriest must preach the true faith to the people'
                                                              (*Ælet*2 (Wulfstan1) 175)
        b. forðan ðe hi   *awriton   Cristes   wundra*
           because they down-wrote of-Christ miracles
           'because they wrote down the miracles of Christ' (*ÆCHom* I, 21.298.18)

If the particle marks the position of the verb, we would expect that the object can also follow the particle in main clauses and this is indeed the case:

(30)   þa   ahof Paulus up *his heafod*
        then raised Paul   up his head
        'Then Paul lifted up his head'   (*LS* 32(Peter&Paul) 303)

One of Koster's tests involves certain adverbs that can, after an intonation break, follow a particle in a main clause and a verb in a subordinate clause. It is hard to establish whether this applies or not, but the scanty evidence there is suggests that certain Old English adverbs can indeed follow the verb in subordinate clauses. No examples with a particle and such an adverb in main clauses have come to light (cf. van Kemenade 1987: 36).

Though the evidence provided by Koster's tests is limited in some respects, we can say that it supports an interpretation in which the particle marks the position of the verb before movement. It is less easy, however, to establish whether there are elements that cannot appear to the right of particles (as is the case for objects in Dutch), since this depends on negative evidence. Only when we have looked at all the available Old English will we be able to say positively that some pattern does not occur in the material that has come down to us. Nevertheless it is possible to say that some elements have restricted positions. There do not seem to be instances of a pronominal object after the particle in main clauses, while a pronominal object does occasionally follow the verb in subordinate clauses. Koster's generalization for Dutch was that elements that follow the particle in main clauses can also follow the finite verb in subordinate clauses. This generalization does not seem to hold for Old English in all respects. Particles themselves have restricted possibilities, as we have seen. Generally they precede the verb when the verb is not subject to movement (e.g. a non-finite verb in a main clause, as in (13)), but are 'stranded' when the verb moves. Therefore we would not expect cases of particles after the non-finite verb in main clauses, and indeed there are very few of them. Nevertheless particles can freely occur after the verb in subordinate clauses. If it is correct that the particle marks the underlying position of the verb, then we should conclude that there is V-movement in subordinate clauses. We will look at this in the next section.

6.4.3   Particles following the verb in subordinate clauses: evidence for V-movement

As the figures in table 6.3 show, sixteen per cent of the subordinate clauses in Hiltunen's corpus have the particle to the right of the verb, as in (31):

(31)   forðan þe stream *berð aweg* Placidum
'because the stream carries away Placidus'   (*ÆCHom* II, 11.95.97)

We have seen in (29) that objects can be found to the right of the finite verb in subordinate clauses. They can even occur to the right of the non-finite verb as in (32), where the finite verb follows the non-finite one:

(32)   þæt hi   urum godum *geoffrian magon ðancwurðe onsægednysse*
that they our   gods   offer   may   grateful   sacrifice
'that they may offer a grateful sacrifice to our gods' (*ÆCHom* I, 38.592.31)

Do particles, then, behave like objects in this respect? In the classic OV analysis of van Kemenade (1987) the finite verb in subordinate clauses remains in clause-final position. The C-position to which the finite verb can move in main clauses is already filled in subordinate clauses and movement is impossible. Anything to the right of the finite verb must therefore have been moved there by extraposition. Following this analysis, we are forced to conclude that particles can be extraposed in Old English too. Here is another example:

(33)   þæt Egypti *adrifen* Moyses *ut* mid hys leodum
'that the Egyptians drove Moses away with his people'   (*Or* 1.5.24.7)

As can be seen from Hiltunen's statistics quoted above, a good many subordinate clauses have a particle to the right of the finite verb.

As particles cannot be found to the right of the non-finite verb in modern Germanic languages such as German and Dutch, Pintzuk (1991) doubts whether there is indeed extraposition of the particle in Old English and considers whether

Table 6.4. *Distribution of particles in Old English subordinate clauses*

clause type	before lexical verb	after lexical verb	total
with auxiliary/modal			
INFL-final clauses	24 (100%)	—	24
INFL-medial clauses	60 (96.8%)	2 (3.2%)	62
with inflected lexical verb			
INFL-final clauses	69 (98.6%)	1 (1.4%)	70
INFL-medial clauses	98 (73.1%)	36 (26.9%)	134
total	251	39	290

a different explanation might not be possible. The distribution of particles in fact forms an important piece of evidence for Pintzuk's idea that there can be V-movement in subordinate clauses, as discussed in chapter 4. We will briefly repeat the main features of her analysis here. Pintzuk analyses (early) Old English as an OV language, but her hypothesis is that the position of INFL may vary. It may either precede the VP, so that the order is SIOV (with movement of the finite verb to I; this gives surface word order SVO) or follow it, so that the order is SOVI (with movement of the finite verb to I; this gives surface word order SOV). The two positions are called INFL-medial and INFL-final. Many SVO clauses are structurally ambiguous in this analysis (either there is simple INFL-medial or there is INFL-final with a postverbal object). On the other hand, when there are heavy elements (such as nominal objects) before the verb, the clause can only be interpreted as INFL-final. Pintzuk (1991) shows that the distribution of particles is different when we make a distinction between clauses with auxiliaries/ modals on the one hand and clauses with just a (lexical) verb on the other. We will start with the figures Pintzuk (1991: 88) gives for subordinate clauses.[6] The INFL-medial clauses include the structurally ambiguous ones.

As can be seen from table 6.4, a particle appears after the inflected lexical verb quite often, but, with a single exception, this always occurs in clauses which can be analysed as INFL-medial. When there is an auxiliary, it is extremely unusual for a particle to appear after the non-finite verb. The evidence provided by table 6.4 strongly suggests that there is V-movement in subordinate clauses, and that particles can be 'stranded' just as in main clauses. It should also be noted that the two cases with the particle after the non-finite verb occur in clauses which can be analysed as INFL-medial, and in fact have the present-day word order,

[6] Pintzuk (1991) included poetry and prose in her database. Some texts were sampled exhaustively, while from other texts the first fifty instances each were taken of main, coordinate and subordinate clauses with auxiliary/modal verbs. For a full description see Pintzuk (1991: 288 ff.).

Table 6.5. *Distribution of particles in Old English clauses with auxiliary/modal verbs*

clause type	before lexical verb	after lexical verb	total
main			
INFL-medial	63 (90%)	7 (10%)	70
INFL-final	11 (100%)	—	11
subordinate			
INFL-medial	60 (96.8%)	2 (3.2%)	62
INFL-final	24 (100%)	—	24
total	158	9	167

illustrated in (34). It is possible that these represent innovations with a new structure (i.e. SIVO), and represent the beginning of the change by which particles no longer mark the base position of the verb.

(34)   He *wolde   adræfan ut*   anne æþeling
        he   wanted drive   out   a   prince
        'He wanted to drive out a prince'   (*ChronB* 82.18–19 (755))[7]

The figures in table 6.4 are for subordinate clauses only. Further support for this pattern of particle distribution comes from main and subordinate clauses with an auxiliary or modal verbs and a non-finite verb, as shown in table 6.5.[8]

Slightly more main clauses than subordinate clauses have the particle after the non-finite verb, but they are not unambiguously INFL-final. For instance, there are no cases where a particle follows a verbal cluster in which the finite verb comes last, a word order which must necessarily be INFL-final. Apart from the nine clauses Pintzuk found in her corpus, another twenty-one instances have come to light in the major Old English prose texts and there could be more in other texts too. All of these are similarly not unambiguously INFL-final. Often the particle precedes a PP:

(35)   Hwæt synd ða lytlan   ðe   he wolde *habban up to his*
        what   are   the little (ones) which he wanted have   up to his
        rice?
        kingdom
        'Who are the little ones he wanted to raise up to his kingdom?'
                                                          (*ÆCHom* I, 9.138.6)

---

[7] MS B of the Anglo-Saxon Chronicle is not included in the electronic texts in the *Dictionary of Old English Corpus*. Other manuscripts of the Chronicle do not have a particle here.
[8] The figures are for Pintzuk's database. Texts not investigated by Pintzuk show a similar distribution.

In line with our earlier analysis we could maintain that the particle here is a modifier of the PP (see section 6.3.3). If this interpretation is correct, the clause does not involve a particle as such, but a modified PP, which can freely occur to the right of the non-finite verb. There are also some instances with an object NP, as in (34) given above, and (36):

(36) a. and man ne mihte swa ðeah *macian hi*   *healfe up*
          and one not could so   however make   them half   up
          'and not even so could half of them be put up'   (*ÆLS*(Swithun) 431)
      b. þa   wolde seo Sexburh æfter syxtyne gearum *don hire   swustor*
          then wanted seo Sexburh after sixteen years   do of-her sister
          ban of ðære byrgene   *up*
          bones from the   burial-place up
          'After sixteen years Sexburh wanted to take up her sister's bones from
          their burial-place'   (*ÆLS*(Æthelthryth) 73)

Both (36a) and (36b) have word orders that still retain an OV character, yet the particle follows the non-finite verb. We may be dealing here with an innovation, in which the position of the particle is no longer linked to the position of the verb before movement. Pintzuk's (1991) material is taken from the whole of the Old English period, and it may be significant that practically all the clauses such as (36) come from late Old English texts.

Evidence for V-movement in subordinate clauses also comes from the position of pronominal objects and one-syllable adverbs. These, like particles, are rare after the non-finite verb, but occur often after an inflected verb in a subordinate clause (Pintzuk 1991: 95). As with particles, this is mainly found in late Old English texts. There are apparently no cases in main clauses of a pronominal object after a particle.

We have seen in this section that the general distribution of particles supports an analysis in which the particle marks the base position of the verb in all types of clauses. Verb movement is then responsible for 'stranding' the particle. When the verb is non-finite, it is not subject to movement and the particle precedes it. In section 6.6 we will consider some puzzling cases which do not seem to fit in with this hypothesis.

6.5   The universal base hypothesis

So far we have described the distribution of particles, concentrating on the way this evidence has been used to support an OV base word order for Old English (section 6.4.2). We have also seen that within these assumptions there is evidence that the finite verb moves in subordinate clauses too (section 6.4.3). In recent theoretical developments, there is a prominent school of thought in which underlying VO order is thought to be universal (Kayne

1994), as was discussed in chapter 5. This requires an analysis in which particles must move leftwards and end up to the left of the verb. The verb fronting analysis for main and subordinate clauses alike is maintained, but the basic structure is assumed to be different.

We saw in section 6.4 that the particle is to a certain extent positionally dependent on the verb, though not as strictly as stranded prepositions. The constructions discussed in section 6.2.2 show that particles have some independent syntactic status. We have also seen that particles in Old English behave in much the same way as separable prefixes in Dutch. One approach then would be to see whether the analysis proposed for Dutch by Zwart (1993) carries over to Old English. In Zwart's analysis particles are base-generated as small clause predicates to the right of the verb and then move for feature checking. This reflects the insight that particles behave as secondary predicates, and that the combination of NP object + particle is a verbless clause, which in generative grammar is often represented as a small clause (see, for instance Stowell 1981 and Hoekstra 1988; for a dissenting view, see Neeleman 1994). The position to which these small clauses move must be such that it leaves room for stranded prepositions. A possible substructure of the relevant part of (18) is (37):

(18)   þæt hie mid þæm þæt folc   *ut   aloccoden*
        that they with that the people out enticed
        'that they might entice the people with it (to come) outside'   (*Or* 5.3.117.5)

(37)   ... AgrOP

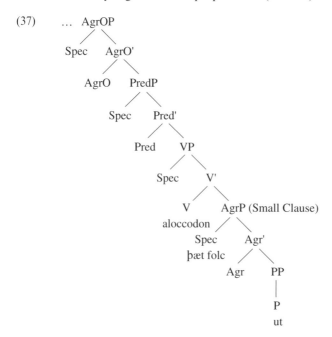

(37) represents the structure before movement. One approach would be to say that the whole small clause moves to check a predicate feature in Spec,PredP (so that the whole of AgrP moves to Spec,PredP). Alternatively, the particle *ut* might adjoin to the head of Pred, and the object might move to check a feature in Spec,AgrO, along the lines discussed in chapter 5. The issues in fact revolve around the same problems as those discussed in chapter 5 to derive the word order options of bare infinitival clauses, though we should realize that particles on this analysis are checked overtly with a considerably higher frequency than bare infinitivals. It may be observed that (37) also reflects the surface word order of postverbal NP + particle attestations like those exemplified in (36) above, so that this would allow us to say that those cases have the same structure with covert checking. For V . . . particle + NP orders like (30), we would indeed have to assume that the particle moves independently of the NP, presumably to the head Pred, while the verb has been moved to F. The details of an analysis along these lines remain to be worked out, but it should at least be clear that the above sketch allows an account of the variety of positions occupied by the Old English particles also within the universal base hypothesis.

6.6   Some remaining problems: particles separated from the verb (part . . . V)

Above we have discussed the distribution of particles showing that it provides strong support for the assumption that the particle marks the base position of the verb in Old English in an OV analysis and does not undergo movement of any kind. In a universal base hypothesis the particle is moved to a position left of the finite verb, which itself is moved there for checking purposes (see chapter 5). Essential in both approaches is that the particle is analysed as being immediately to the left of the finite verb. However, we have shown that what appears to be a particle can precede and be separated from the verb. This happens in some of the constructions discussed in section 6.2.2, but also when the particle precedes a PP. In some cases we can reasonably argue that we are not dealing with a particle but with an adverb modifying the PP. There are, however, a few cases that are not open to this analysis and we will look at them in this section.

Two subordinate clauses, given in (38a–b), and a coordinate main clause, given in (38c), have what looks like a particle left of the verb, which is separated from it by an object. The subordinate clauses come from texts that are not in Hiltunen's corpus:

(38)   a. Ic on neorxnawonge niwe   asette
        I in paradise   newly set
        treow mid telgum, þæt   ða tanas   *up*
        tree with boughs, so-that the branches up
        æpla   bæron . . .
        apples bore
        'I had newly established a tree in paradise with boughs whose branches
        bore aloft apples'[9]   (*Sat* 479)
        b. þæt heo eft   *up hyre leoman ætywe*
        that she again up her   light   shows
        'that it [the sun] shows its light again above'
                                        (*ByrM* 1(Baker/Lapidge) 2.3.13)
        c. &   eac *ut   hiora eðel   gerymdon*
        and also out their territory enlarged
        'and also enlarged their territory abroad'   (*CP*LetWærf 6)

It is difficult to maintain that in (38) the particle marks the underlying position of the verb, as this would commit us to assuming that the verb moves
rightwards, which would be an unorthodox and unfounded assumption in the
model of grammar we are using. Alternatively, we might want to claim that
we have a leftward particle movement rule, but there is little support for this
either. We should, therefore, consider other explanations. Notice that (38a)
comes from poetry and the poetic form may have something to do with the
position of *up*, which is at the end of the verse line. Krapp (1931) does not feel
it necessary to comment on the position of *up*, but it is clear that the more
regular position before the verb would result in a metrically deficient half-line.
We cannot explain (38b) in this way, since it comes from a prose text. The most
recent editors (Baker and Lapidge 1995) do not comment on the unusual position of the particle. The clause is part of a sentence explaining that it is in the
nature of a day to have twenty-four hours from sunrise until the sun shows its
light again above (the horizon). It is reasonable therefore to interpret *up* in
(38b) as an adverb and not as a particle. The coordinate clause in (38c), finally,
has a deleted subject. We can therefore not be certain about its exact structure,
but the context suggests that *ut* may be an adverb here too rather than a particle. The passage comes from King Alfred's preface to the *Pastoral Care*,
where he contrasts the situation 'at home' with that 'abroad', so that an interpretation of *ut* as meaning 'abroad' is plausible. Also note that Bosworth and
Toller (1898), Toller (1921) do not list the combinations *upætywan, *upberan*
or *utgeryman*; this in itself is not proof that they did not exist, but the evidence as a whole strongly suggests that what we have in (38a–c) are not particle + verb combinations.

[9] The translation is taken from Bradley (1982).

There are also a few cases where what appears to be a particle precedes an adverb rather than the verb. Examples are given in (39):

(39)   a. swa eac se ðe *ut wel lærð*   mid his wordum, he onfehð
          so   also he who out well teaches with his words   he receives
          innan ðæs   inngeðonces fæstnesse, ðæt is wisdom
          in   of-the of-mind   fastness   that is wisdom
          'so also, he who externally teaches well with his words, shall receive
          internally firmness of mind, that is, wisdom'   (*CP* 49.381.4)
       b. 7   geseoh þæt þu *ut þonon* ne *gonge*
          and see   that you out thence not go
          'and see that you do not go away from there'   (*Bede* 3.10.186.26)
       c. Ah in dagunge he eft   acuicode 7   semninga *up heh asæt*
          but at dawn   he again revived and suddenly up high sat
          'But at dawn he revived again and suddenly sat up straight'
                                                              (*Bede* 5.13.422.28)
       d. and ða maðm-fatu   þæs temples   ungerime... mid oðrum
          and the costly-vessels of-the of-temple innumerable with other
          goldhordum *forð samod*   *ferodon*
          treasures   forth at-the-same-time carried
          'and carried the innumerable costly vessels of the temple ... away at the
          same time'   (*ÆCHom* II, 4.36.218)

From the context of (39a) it is clear that we should interpret *ut* as a straightforward adverb and not as part of a verb + particle combination, as a contrast is made here between *ut* 'externally' and *innan* 'internally'. In (39b) *ut* can reasonably be interpreted as modifying *þonon* 'thence'; a similar combination is found in *Bede* 5.5.398.3. For the case in (39c), it is to be noted that three out of the four other manuscripts of Bede omit *heh* altogether from this sentence. Finally, one other manuscript has *samod mid him* in (39d).

We may conclude this section, then, by observing that the Old English data support the generalization that the position of the particle is to the left of the verb, where it is stranded when V-movement obtains; if we follow the universal VO base hypothesis, the particle can be said to be in its checking position Pred. Let us now look at the distribution of particles in Middle English.

6.7   Particles in Middle English

The surface word order patterns of Middle English are predominantly VO but, as we saw in chapter 5, OV survived as a minority pattern for a long time. Some early Middle English texts, such as the Vespasian Homilies, are assumed to be modernizations of Old English texts, and they still show O–particle–V patterns quite frequently. In them we can still find particles used in much the same way as they were in Old English:

(40)   &   eft   binnen seofen gearen his ban   *up genumen* wurðen
        and again within seven years his bones up taken   were
        'and again within seven years his bones were taken up'   (*VespHom* 132)

In (40) the finite verb follows the non-finite verb (a characteristic OV pattern) and the particle precedes the non-finite verb. Now texts like the Vespasian Homilies are not likely to be good indications of what Middle English syntax was like, but even early Middle English texts that do not seem to go back to earlier material still occasionally have particles before the verb:

(41)   a. þat nan godes word *upp* ne mai *springen*
           that none of-god word up not can spring
           'that no word of God can spring up'   (*Vices &V.*(1) 69.17)
        b. hie bieð *ut-iworpen* ðurh   dieueles lare
           they are out-cast   through devil's teaching
           'they are cast out through the teaching of the devil'   (*Vices &V.*(1) 73.19)

It may be observed that examples such as those in (41) are compatible with the analysis presented above for Old English on a universal VO base hypothesis. They would then reflect the same analysis with overt checking of the particle as was adduced for Old English above in (37).

We should not think, however, that cases like (41) are frequent in Middle English. The figures that Hiltunen (1983: 110) gives for fifteen early Middle English texts (see note 3) show that V (. . .) part is the dominant pattern by far:

Table 6.6. *Verb and particle order in early Middle English texts (figures from Hiltunen 1983)*

	part (. . .) V	V (. . .) part
main clause	7 (4%)	169 (96%)
coordinate clause	30 (14%)	197 (86%)
subordinate clause	23 (14%)	138 (86%)

These figures bring home the fundamental change that has occurred in particle position in Middle English. Compared to the figures for Old English quoted from Hiltunen in sections 6.3.1, 6.3.2 and 6.3.3, part (. . .) V has dropped from forty-one per cent to four per cent in main clauses, from sixty per cent to fourteen per cent in coordinate clauses, and from eighty-four per cent to fourteen per cent in subordinate clauses, and V (. . .) part has become the norm. Middle English particles freely follow the non-finite verb. Below are some representative examples taken from the work of Margery Kempe (a late Middle English writer), as well as from Hiltunen's early Middle English corpus:

(42) a. þe   þæt swuch fulðe *speteð ut*   in ani encre   eare
         who that such   filth   spews out in any anchoress's ear
         'who spews out such filth in the ear of any anchoress' (*Ancr* (Nero)35.29)

      b. þat he neure mare sculde *cuman ut*
         that he never more should come   out
         'that he should not come out anymore'   (*ChronE* (Plummer) 1140.48)

      c. He þonkede him & heo wes *icleopet forð*
         'He thanked him and she was called forth'   (*St Juliana* (Bod) 9.93)

      d. ah, whuch se ha euer beo, let *bringen* hire *forð*
         but, who so she ever be, let bring   her forth
         'but whoever she is, let her be brought forth'   (*St Kath.*(1) 30.5)

      e. þat þei wold *gan awey* . . .
         that they would go   away
         'that they would go away . . .'   (*MKempe* 19.31)

      f. Margery, yf her come a man wyth a swerd &   wold *smyte of*
         Margery, if here come a man with a sword and would smite off
         myn hed
         my head
         'Margery, if a man would come here with a sword and cut off my head'
                                                            (*MKempe* 23.14)

Hiltunen's corpus consists exclusively of prose texts, but his findings are also confirmed by the distribution of particles in the Ormulum, an early text from the North-East Midlands of mechanical metrical regularity (c. 1180). The figures are quoted from Denison (1981: 180).

Table 6.7. *Verb and particle position in Ormulum*

part (. . .) V	V (. . .) part
28 (5%)	184 (95%)

In this text too, the norm is V (. . .) part.

6.7.1   *Material between verb and particle (V . . . part)*

As we have seen in the previous section, V . . . part becomes the norm in Middle English. This is also one of the surface patterns found in Old English (see sections 6.3.1–6.3.3). The distribution of pronominal objects and nominal objects in this pattern show some important differences. Pronominal objects always precede the particle in main clauses in Old English, but nominal objects may precede the particle, as in (43a), or follow it, as in (43b):

(43)   a. . . . þa geleaffullan ælc hylt *his æftergengan up*
                 the faithful   each holds his aftercomer   up
            '. . . each faithful person holds up his follower'   (*ÆCHom* II, 45.339.126)
        b. þa   ahof   Paulus *up his heafod*
            then raised Paul   up his head
            'Then Paul raised his head'   (*LS* 32(Peter&Paul) 303)

And the particle is often stranded by V-movement, both in root and in non-root clauses:

(44)   þa   *awende* se encgel *aweg*
        then turned the angel away
        'Then the angel turned away'   (*ÆLS*(Agatha) 205)

(45)   buton ða lareowas *screadian* symle   ða leahtras þurh heora
        unless the teachers prune   constantly the sins   by   their
        lare   *aweg*
        teaching away
        'unless the teachers constantly prune away sins by their teaching'
                                                                 (*ÆCHom* II, 5.43.58)

The position of particles after the verb in Old English resembles in some respects the Modern English distribution (nominal objects before or after the particle, pronominal objects only before the particle), but it is not so restricted, because other sentence elements (such as adverbs and PPs) can come between verb and particle, as in (45).

From Hiltunen's evidence for Middle English it is clear that the surface word orders closely resemble those of present-day English, in that the particle must follow a pronominal object, but can precede or follow a nominal object. Hiltunen's data show that pronominal objects invariably precede the particle (as they did in Old English), as in (46a), and that nominal objects can precede or follow the particle, as in (46b) and (46c):

(46)   a. 7 heo holden *hire up*
            'and they held her up'   (*Ancr.*(Nero) 62.34)
        b. heo hef *up hire hond*
            'she raised up her hand'   (*St Marg.*(1) 19.22)
        c. & hef *hire honden up*
            'and raised her hands up'   (*St Marg.*(1) 22.9)

It must also be observed, however, that these options tally closely with the OV/VO word order distributions characteristic for the Middle English of the thirteenth and fourteenth centuries, as discussed in chapter 5, on the assumption that, as for Old English, the particle marks the position of the verb before V-movement.

There are in principle a number of ways in which the word orders of (46) can be derived. One straightforward way that is consistent with the universal base hypothesis is to say that particles are still base-generated according to the structure (37) above, as in Old English. Object and particle then together form a verb-less clause, a small clause, which is not an implausible analysis since they can easily be paraphrased as a resultative clause ('as a result of the raising, her hands are up'). (46a) then reflects that base word order, like (46c). Supposing that the learner constructing a grammar works on this assumption, she is faced with the problem of how to analyse (46b). As linguists, we can see that (46b) is a continuation of an Old English pattern in which the particle is checked to the left of the base position of the verb, in Pred. And it is standard in Old English and in Middle English for the finite verb to be checked overtly in F, as we saw in chapter 4. But we are then faced with the question of whether there is sufficient evidence for the learner in the language environment to postulate such an analysis. Since (46b) is the most frequent pattern, this may seem reasonable. Such an analysis still leaves open the possibility that the finite verb might have undergone overt checking in the functional position F in all three examples.

A second way to analyse (46) is to say that, since (46b) is the most frequent pattern, we should take this as primary, and say the verb and particle form one complex verbal head, with an object in a VO structure. On this assumption, it is very difficult to derive the alternative word orders in a principled way: since verb and particle form a unit, it is impossible to insert functional projections between them, hence no object can be checked in that position. Another objection is that it should probably still be possible to move the verbal part to check against a functional feature, leading to word orders like 'raised XP up her hand'. But such word orders are not attested, as far as we are aware. Clearly, if we aim for one uniform analysis, the first analysis seems the more attractive, and this once again provides some support for the universal base hypothesis of Kayne (1994).

There is, of course, a third option, which is to say that all V–part word orders are simply lexical units at this time, while for the V . . . part word orders, a Small Clause analysis still seems feasible. Effectively, this amounts to saying that V–part orders are defined in the lexicon as idiomatic combinations, and that there is a second lexical entry for V–NP–part word orders, in which the verb is subcategorized for a Small Clause predicate.

We do not yet have sufficient factual details of Middle English to be able to decide which of these possible analyses seems the most viable. While we know that V-movement continued to be an option until late Middle English and beyond, as we saw in chapters 4 and 5, it is a good deal more difficult to find out whether the learner had enough evidence available in the language environment to recognize that particles were stranded by V-movement. Some very, perhaps impossibly, detailed data research will need to be done before this question can be answered.

6.7.2   Analyses of the change in particle position

The surface syntax of Middle English is predominantly VO (see chapters 3 and 5). For those who analyse Old English as an underlying OV language this represents a change in the base word order: the verb now precedes its complement. In section 6.7.2.1 we will describe how particles are affected by this change and what effect this has on the generalization that particles mark the base position of the verb.

As we have said earlier, recent theoretical developments have led to the hypothesis that all languages have complements to the right of their heads, so that they have a base VO word order. In this view the change in Middle English syntax lies in the loss of overt movement of objects to the left of the verb, so that they are now found in their base position to the right of the verb. Particles, which in Old English must move too to appear on the left of the verb, no longer appear to be doing so. In section 6.7.2.2 we will consider some of the advantages of such an approach and also note some problems a minimalist analysis faces in accounting for this change.

6.7.2.1   OV→VO: particles no longer mark the position of the verb in Middle English

There is a clear increase in VO surface patterns when we compare late Old English texts with even the earliest Middle English texts (see chapter 5). The suddenness of the change may be more apparent than real because the late Old English texts were standardized and formal in nature, and perhaps not altogether representative of the language of the time when they were written. SVO predominates in Middle English texts, right from the beginning of the period. We have seen in section 6.3 that part . . . V order is often found in OV surface patterns and that V . . . part can be analysed as the result of V-movement to F as discussed in chapter 4. V to F does not disappear until later in Middle English and not everywhere at the same time, as discussed in chapter 4.

The change to VO conceals much of the evidence for V-movement to F in subordinate clauses. Particles and pronominal objects now naturally appear to the right not only of the finite verb, but also of the non-finite verb (if there is one). It was the virtual absence of particles/pronouns after the non-finite verb that was crucial in Pintzuk's analysis of V-movement in subordinate clauses.[10] There is no longer a discrepancy between the position of particles (and pronominal objects) in subordinate clauses with a single (inflected) verb and those with an auxiliary/modal and a non-finite verb, as noted for Old English by Pintzuk (1991) (see section 6.4.3). The statistical evidence for Old English quoted from Pintzuk (1991) shows that particles can follow the verb in subordinate clauses, but only rarely do so when the verb is non-finite. We have also seen in applying Koster's (1975) tests to Old English that what can follow the particle in main clauses can also follow the non-finite verb in subordinate clauses (PPs, certain adverbs, object clauses and even nominal objects). The data collected by Hiltunen (1983) show clearly that the situation is different in Middle English. Main as well as subordinate clauses characteristically have VO patterns, and particles now commonly follow the verb. This is the pattern, for instance, in the two continuations of the *Peterborough Chronicle* (ChronE), with one single exception,[11] even when the object precedes the verb, as in (47):

(47) þat he ealle his castles *sculde   iiuen   up*
       that he all   his castles should give   up
       'that he should give up all his castles'   (*ChronE* (Plummer) 1140.42)

We can conclude from (47), the figures quoted in table 6.6 and the examples given in (42) that the order of particle and verb has been reversed in Middle English. Although V-movement to F persists in main clauses in Middle English (see chapter 4), it is clear that for the very frequent pattern illustrated by (47) the particle no longer marks the position of the verb before movement. If it did, we would have to assume that the non-finite verb was moved in (47).

It would seem that it is possible to analyse particles in Middle English in much the same way as in present-day English,[12] but the Middle English distribution is not quite the same as that of the present-day language. A crucial difference is that not only an object but also an adverb or a PP can intervene between verb and particle, something that is not allowed in present-day English.

(48)   a. 7 *com* baldeliche *forð*
          'and came quickly forth'   (*St Marg.*(1) 40.28)

---

[10] If Lightfoot (1991, 1999) is correct in believing that embedded domains are not accessible to children and cannot play a role in syntactic change, it is problematic how children could have acquired V-movement in subordinate clauses in Old English. For the view that subordinate clauses played a crucial role in the change from OV to VO see Stockwell and Minkova (1991).

[11] 7 hi togædere comen (*ChronE* (Plummer) 135.23).

[12] Particles are analysed either as forming a lexical unit with the verb or as an independent syntactic head (see den Dikken (1995) who opts for the second approach).

b. 7   swa me   schal, amid   te   burh, *setten* hit on heh   *up*
     and so   people shall, in-the-middle the city,   set   it   on high up
     'and so people shall set it up very high in the middle of the city'

                                                 (*St Kath.*(1) 68)

This may indicate that at this stage, the particle could still be stranded by V-movement. We do not know when this pattern became obsolete. We already remarked above on the difficulty of deciding at what point particles were no longer analysed by the learner as part of a productive syntactic pattern. At some point they must have been reanalysed as idiomatic constructs, and perhaps that happened earlier for the V–part orders than for the V . . . part orders. At the latest, this must have happened when the various types of V-movement were no longer constructible from the language environment. This will depend, among other things, on how robustly examples like (48) were represented in the language environment.

If there was a strong tendency to change part–V into V–part because it fitted better with the prevailing VO patterns of the language, we must address the question of why part–V was not reanalysed into a prefixed verb. This may have been the other option open to language learners to remove the anomaly in the system. However, there is evidence that the prefixal system itself was in decline since many prefixes disappeared (see Hiltunen 1983). It seems unlikely, therefore, that the reanalysis of part–V into a prefixed verb can have been a very important factor, but it cannot be ruled out completely. The *OED* has this to say about *out* (s.v. out):

> . . . with verbs *ut* like other adverbs formed separable collocations or semi-compounds, in which the position of the adv. was shifted according to the construction of the sentence, as in the separable compound verbs of Modern German (although in OE the order was not yet so rigid . . .)
>
> As to the verbs themselves in M.E., usage became more lax. On the one hand the adv. began to be placed after or away from the vb. in the subordinate clause . . . on the other hand the older usage of the inf. in *ut gan*, and the like, was often extended to the indicative, so that we find *he out yede, the blood out barst*. This was partly due to a general levelling and loss of old syntactic distinctions, so that beside *he sprang out* and *then sprang he out* it became allowable also to say *he out sprang* and *out sprang he*, in both of which the adv. stands before the vb. These novelties in word order were especially employed by metrical writers as facilitating the exigencies of rhythm and rime.

The *OED* adds that true compounds are from a later date (a few from the end of the fifteenth century). Under *up* the *OED* (s.v. up III F4) says that the use of *up* as a prefix 'is thoroughly established . . . some as early as the 13thC and many more are found from about 1300 onwards'. There are therefore early compounds with *up* and later ones with *ut*. It seems possible that part–V was sometimes reanalysed as a prefixed verb, possibly earlier with *up*, as examples of this often involve transitive verbs. The presence of an object after the verb would be an important signal of VO word order.

It may be interesting to note that such reanalysed prefixed verbs could be used until very recently and some can apparently still be used today. The *OED* records instances of the verb 'to uprise' until late in the nineteenth century. Joseph Conrad, though a foreigner by birth, used such prefixed verbs regularly:

(49)   The spires of churches, numerous, scattered haphazard, *uprose* like beacons
         on a maze of shoals without a channel.   (Conrad *Lord Jim* 1949: 254)

6.7.2.2 Universal base hypothesis

So far no detailed minimalist analyses have been worked out for either the Old English or the Middle English particle facts. We have seen that particles in Old English behave syntactically much like Dutch separable prefixes, but it remains to be investigated whether the analyses proposed for Dutch work for Old English too. In this section we will sketch some of the problems a minimalist analysis for Middle English faces and outline what points may have to be considered in developing a coherent and insightful account.

Within the framework developed by Kayne (1994), the Middle English evidence shows that there has been a change in whatever it is that triggers the movement of the particle in Old English to a position left of the finite verb. If we assume that particles are secondary predicates in Old English, and that an account as proposed for Dutch by Zwart (1993) is feasible for Old English, in which overt movement is necessary for feature checking, we must conclude that overt movement is no longer necessary in Middle English. It is not immediately obvious what the motivation for the change could have been. One thing that may be noted though, is that we can derive the Middle English word orders on the same analyses as those independently needed to derive Middle English OV and VO word orders, as we saw in chapter 5, and this should certainly be considered as support for the universal base hypothesis.

An account for Middle English will have to consider that particles before the verb characteristically occur in OV structures and that V-movement to AgrO is not lost before the end of the Middle English period. Chomsky (1993: 18) states that overt movement of the verb to AgrO is a necessary step in deriving OV word order. Without it the object cannot move overtly (see chapter 5), nor, it seems, can the small clause containing the particle. If this dating is correct, and if the order V–NP–Part reflects stranding of the particle by V-movement, this may be taken to suggest that the V–NP–Part word orders froze into idioms before the point in time when overt checking in AgrO was lost.

There seems to be a link with preposition stranding, too. The particle in Old English is found left of the stranded preposition, before the verb; this is still the case in Middle English and later, but now it is found after the verb. As we have shown in (48), the distribution in Middle English differs in one important respect at least from the distribution today in that adverbs and/or PPs can come between the object and the particle. This must find its place in the analysis too.

One aspect of the history of particles has not really changed, and finds a more natural interpretation in a minimalist account. Pronominal objects come before the particle right from the Old English period onwards. In an OV analysis for Old English we can say that personal pronouns cannot be extraposed and therefore are not found to the right of a particle, which, we have argued, marks the (underlying) position of the clause-final verb. The particle no longer marks the verb position in Middle English and the traditional accounts have a particle movement rule, which is blocked by pronouns. A minimalist approach deals with this differently. There is good evidence that pronouns can be clitics in Old English and we can assume that the pronoun goes to a higher position than the particle. A clitic position has been proposed for Middle English by van der Wurff (1997a) and arguments that pronouns are different play a role in analyses for present-day English as well (Haegeman and Guéron 1999).

6.8   Conclusion

In this chapter we have investigated particle + verb combinations in Old and Middle English, and shown that in Old English the particle regularly precedes the verb and that, when it does not do so, it marks the position of the verb, with the verb moving through the rule of Verb-Second in main clauses and a V-movement rule in subordinate clauses. In Middle English the particle regularly follows the verb, and we can no longer show a relation between the position of the particle and the position of the verb. The change in particle position has been interpreted as a consequence of the change of OV to VO, an approach no longer possible in a minimalist framework. We have discussed some of the problems a minimalist analysis faces, which seem considerable, but we have also indicated where it possibly provides better insight.

7

Changes in infinitival constructions

7.1   Introduction

Constructions with infinitival verb forms are a prominent feature of present-day English syntax. The infinitive without *to* occurs routinely after modal auxiliaries (e.g. *I will/might/could* do *my homework now*) and after verbs of perception and causation (e.g. *I saw/heard/made him* do *his homework*), while the infinitive with *to* occurs after a range of verbs with widely varying properties (*I tried* to do *it*; *I promised Peter* to do *it*; *I ordered Peter* to do *it*; *I persuaded Peter* to do *it*; *I believe him* to be *innocent*). If we compare the distribution and properties of infinitives in the present-day language with their Old English counterparts, the conclusion must be that some pervasive changes have taken place. Some of these changes seem to be largely quantitative: Manabe (1989) has shown, on the basis of a large collection of data, that infinitival clauses replaced finite ones at a fast rate in Middle English. Thus, in Old English (as in present-day German and Dutch), the usual construction after verbs expressing purpose or intention was a *þæt*-clause, as in (1):

(1)   ... and bebead ðam cwellerum þæt hi   hine mid wiððum,
             and ordered the   torturers   that they him with cords
         handum and fotum on þære rode gebundon
         hands   and feet   on the   cross bound
         'and [he] ordered the torturers to fasten his hands and feet with cords to the
         cross'   (*ÆCHom* I, 38.594.29)

In Middle English the *to*-infinitive became more and more usual after these verbs, and in some cases it even replaced the *that*-clause altogether so that with a number of these verbs, *that*-clauses sound distinctly odd in present-day English,

(2)   a. *?He commanded them that they should tie him up
         b. ?We warned them that they should not go skating

whereas in German and Dutch the equivalent *dass/dat*-clause would be more usual or even obligatory here.

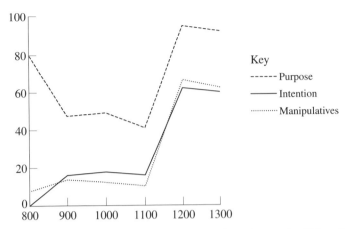

Figure 1 *Ratios of* to-*infinitives to* that-*clauses in OE and eME*
(Los 1998)

Many traditional scholars suggest that the increase in the use of the *to*-infinitive in Middle English took place at the expense of the bare infinitive (i.e. an infinitive without the marker *to*). In these accounts the bare infinitive was generally replaced by the *to*-infinitive when, due to the loss of verbal inflections, it became difficult to distinguish the infinitival form from other verbal forms. As a result, they suggest, *to* began to function as a mere marker of the infinitive, losing its original 'purposive' sense (see, for example, Mustanoja 1960: 514, 522, and, more recently, Jack 1991). However, Fischer (1995, 1996b, 1997b) and Los (1998) suggest that the change is of a different nature: the *to*-infinitive and the bare infinitive remained more or less distinct in function and meaning, and the increase of the *to*-infinitive takes place because the form is used to replace *þæt*-clauses. Figure 1, taken from Los (1998: 27), shows the rapid change in frequency of *þæt*-clauses versus *to*-infinitives after directive verbs (i.e. verbs like 'order') and verbs expressing purpose or intention ('seek, desire') in the early Middle English period.

Beside an enormous increase in number, infinitival constructions also show some interesting spin-offs of the changes discussed in the previous chapters, in particular the loss of the case system and the emergence and gradual fixing of surface VO word order. This is reflected in the rise of the following new constructions in the Middle English period:

(3)   i. *infinitivals with a lexical subject*:
          a. *for NP to V constructions*
             It is ridiculous for you to imagine that he would give you that amount.

b. *Accusative and infinitive (AcI) or ECM constructions*[1]
I expect you to be bright and cheerful.

ii. **passive infinitives, other than after modals**:
a. *after adjectives and nouns*
She is likely to be chosen as our next president.
b. *after semi-modal* 'to be'
This is to be understood as follows.
c. *after main verbs*
If my son dies, let him be buried beside me.

iii. **subject-raising constructions**:
Daniel seems to have full control of the matter.

iv. **infinitival relatives**:
He is a person to avoid.

Various causes for the rise of (3i–iv) have been suggested in the literature, both internal and external to the grammar. Since many of the constructions in (3) are grammatically related, it is tempting to try and interpret their appearance in Middle English as the result of one fundamental change, and attempts have indeed been made to do so. In this chapter, we will only be concerned with the new structures under (3i–ii), i.e. with the infinitives with a lexical subject and the new passive infinitives. We will argue that the rise of these new constructions can be related to the word order changes in Middle English, in particular to the change to uniform (S)VO order dealt with in chapter 5.

In the work of Lightfoot (1991: 82–94), the new structure given in (3iii) is also connected to the constructions in (3i–ii). Lightfoot argues that all three are due to a parameter change that *to* has undergone, which involves the coalescence of *to* with the governing verb, enabling *to* to transmit certain properties of government. Similarly, Kageyama (1992: 92, 125) assumes a link between (iv) and (i–ii), explaining their origin with reference to a change in the status of *to*, this time involving the loss of certain properties that *to* had in Old English due to its being in the AGR position. It is not clear, however, whether the change that *to* has undergone in their view, is the cause of the new constructions or the result; or whether, more likely perhaps, both are part of

---

[1] AcI constructions are new in English after the so-called *verba declarandi et cogitandi*. Infinitival constructions with a lexical subject do occur in Old English after causatives and perception verbs, but these can be shown to have a different structure, see also below and Fischer (1989).

an interrelated chain of causes.[2] The status of *to* will not be discussed in any detail here – we will deal with this in section 9.3.2 of chapter 9, and concentrate now on how the increasing fixation of surface VO word order in all types of clauses may have affected infinitival constructions.

What we will argue is that the new constructions can be viewed as a by-product, so to speak, of the fixation of VO word order: the increased frequency of SVO order led to surface adjacency of elements which in Old English could still be found in a variety of positions, depending on clause type. Furthermore, in the course of the Middle English period the primary data that language learners were exposed to came to contain various sentence types closely modelled on Latin. Children exposed to this different type of input would, as a result, acquire a different grammar, with the mechanisms of analogy and reanalysis playing an important role in the process of acquisition. In this chapter too, then, we will be interested in determining how the language environment changed in such a way that new grammatical structures were postulated by the language learner/speaker.

7.2   New infinitival constructions: constructions containing a lexical subject

7.2.1   *The rise of the (for) NP to V construction*

First, we will briefly look at the rise of construction (3i a), i.e. the *(for) NP to V* construction, because the word order changes play a somewhat clearer role here than in the other types of (3i–ii). The basic idea that we will

---

[2] There are problems with both Kageyama's and Lightfoot's reanalysis of *to*. The Old English data do not quite bear out Kageyama's claim that *to* was positioned in AGR in Old English. The change he proposes for *to* in Middle English (i.e. *to* 'lost the ability to absorb the external θ-role of an infinitive verb and instead began to serve as a transmitter of the θ-role and phi-features to the subject NP, [enabling] the SPEC of AGRP to function as the syntactic subject of the infinitive' (Kageyama 1992: 125)) depends on this, and would therefore also become invalid (for a more detailed critique of his arguments, see Fischer 1996a). Lightfoot's proposal for *to* as a 'transmitter' is similar, but it is not built on the assumption that Old English *to* was an agreement marker. In his view the underlying SOV > SVO change functioned as the instigator of the change (we will also argue here that word order is crucial), but for Lightfoot it is only a 'prolegomenon' to the 'crucial Middle English innovation' (Lightfoot 1991: 91), which is the shift in parameter setting involving *to*. At the end of section 7.2.4, we will briefly discuss Lightfoot's proposal. We will argue that the innovation concerning *to* does not *explain* the new developments in lexical subject constructions, but rather that *to* is reanalysed *as a result* of these new developments.

put forward is that a reanalysis took place in the *(for) NP to V* construction, in such a way that *for* came to be analysed as a complementizer rather than a preposition. The idea that word order changes must have played a crucial role in this was first sparked off by the awareness that Dutch and German, both of which have firmly retained the OV word order patterns also occurring in Old English, did not undergo any reanalysis of this type.

Thus, consider the following sentence type, which is acceptable in English and German/Dutch:

(4)   a. It is bad for you to smoke.
        b. Es ist ungesund für dich zu rauchen.
        c. Het is slecht voor je om te roken.

Here the phrase *for you/für dich/voor je* functions as a prepositional phrase which receives its thematic role from the adjectival matrix predicate *is bad/ist ungesund/is slecht*. In other words, the structure of (4a–c) would be as in (4′).

(4′)   [$_{AP}$ bad/ungesund/slecht [$_{PP}$ for you/für dich/voor je]] [$_{CP}$ PRO to smoke/zu rauchen/om te roken]

Sentences like (5), however, only occur in English.

(5)   a. It is intolerable for John to get away with this.
        b. *Es ist inakzeptabel für Johann ungeschoren davon zu kommen.
        c. *Het is onverdraaglijk voor Jan om hieronder uit te kunnen komen.

In (5a) *for* cannot be interpreted as a preposition because the lexical entry of *intolerable* does not allow for a benefactive role, i.e. *for John* cannot be accounted for in the same way as in (4). Rather, the NP *John* functions as the subject of the infinitival clause, and the structure of (5a) would be as given in (5′).

(5′)   [$_{AP}$ intolerable] [$_{CP}$ for [$_{IP}$ John to get away with this]]

In German and Dutch a *dass/dat*-clause as in (5″b,c) would be necessary to express the same meaning since, unlike *for*, the prepositions *für* and *voor* did not develop into complementizers.

(5″)   b. Es ist inakzeptabel, dass Johann ungeschoren davon kommt.
        c. Het is onverdraaglijk dat Jan hieronder uit zou kunnen komen.

Notice that *for* in English still allows both the benefactive reading and the complementizer reading. An example combining the two different readings is given in (6).

(6)   It is bad for the baby for you to smoke.

Here, the benefactive role is pre-empted by the prepositional phrase *for the baby*, so that the sequence *for you* can only be interpreted as consisting of a complementizer (*for*) followed by the subject (*you*) of the embedded clause.

Historically, what seems to have happened is that sentences like (4a) were at some point reanalysed from a benefactive construction as in (4′) into a *(for) NP to V* construction as in (5′). To see what made the reanalysis from (4′) into (5′) possible, we must first turn to Old English. Old English was like German and Dutch in that the construction in (5) was not possible, while the construction in (5″) was. In (7) there are several Old English instances of this type with an adjectival predicate and a *þæt*-clause; as the translations supplied show, the use of a *for* complementizer would be possible or even preferred in present-day English.

(7)   a. Hit is gecyndelic þæt ealle eorðlice lichaman beoð
        it is natural   that all   earthly bodies   are
        fulran on weaxendum monan þonne on wanigendum
        fuller on waxing   moon than on waning
        'It is natural for all earthly bodies to be fuller under a waxing moon than
        a waning moon'   (*ÆTemp* 8.13)
    b. forðæm hit is riht   þæt ða goodan hæbben good
        therefore it is right that the good   have   good
        edlean hiora godes, 7   þa yflan hæbban wite
        reward of-their good and the evil have   punishment
        hiora   yfles
        of-their evil
        'therefore it is good for the good to be rewarded for the good deeds that
        they do, and for the evil to be punished for their evil deeds' (*Bo* 39.135.15)

Old English also had the benefactive construction of (4), but with the benefactive role expressed by the dative case, and not yet by a *for*-phrase, as the examples in (8) show.

(8)   a. Hit is swiðe earfoðe ænigum [DAT] to ðeowienne twam hlafordum
        'It is very difficult for-anyone to serve two lords'   (*ÆAdmon* 1.2.46)
    b. nis   me [DAT] earfeðe to geþolianne þeodnes willan
        not-is me   difficult to suffer   lord's   will
        'it is not hard for me to endure the will of the Lord'   (*Guth*A, B 1065)
    c. þes traht is langsum eow [DAT] to gehyrenne
        this tract is long   for-you   to hear
        'this treatise is tedious for you to listen to'   (*ÆCHom* II, 41.308.138)

These constructions still occur in Middle English, but often with the preposition *for* instead of a dative inflection, due to the general loss of inflections that is taking place at this time. The construction without *for*, however, also still occurs in Middle English, and begins to be used very much like the Modern English *for NP to V* construction as in (5), i.e. with the original dative NP as the subject of the following infinitive. This is made possible of course by the fact that for nominal NPs, the dative ending is no longer distinguishable from other case forms. Unambiguous examples of this new use first begin to appear in late Middle English. In (9), we give some instances where it is clear that the NP has been reanalysed as the subject of the infinitival clause, with the COMP position being empty.

(9)   a. But a man to lyve pesibly with harde & overthwarte men . . . is a gret grace & a commendable and a manly dede.
      'But for a man to live peacefully with hard and hostile men . . . is an act of grace and a commendable and manly deed.'   (*Imit. Chr.* 2.3.14)
      b. *Me*, here to leue, & þe, hennys þus go, hit is *to me* gret care & endeles wo
      'For me to stay here and for you to go away from here like this, is immensely hard and painful for me'   (*Rel. Lyrics* 128.3)
      c. No thing . . . so bitter is . . . As mon for God & heuen blis to suffre deth with gode wille
      'Nothing is so bitter as when a man, for God and to attain the bliss of heaven, suffers death with good will'   (*Stanzaic Life of Chr.* 6078)
      d. What profite is it wallis to schyne wiþ preciose stonys and crist to die for hunger in þe pore man
      'What use is it for walls to glitter with precious stones and for Christ to die from hunger in the poor man [= while Christ dies . . .]'
      (Pecock, Visser 1963–73: § 912)

In (9a), front-placement of the whole infinitival clause (*a man to lyve pesibly* . . .) shows that the NP *a man* cannot have the benefactive role, just as front-placement is not possible in the German and Dutch clauses of (4):

(4″)   a. For you to smoke is bad.
       b. *Für dich zu rauchen ist ungesund.
       c. *Voor jou om te roken is slecht.

In (4″a), the sequence *for you*, rather than being a complement of the adjectival predicate *bad*, forms a constituent with the rest of the infinitive and *you* is interpreted as the subject of the infinitive. (9b) is similar to (6); it is not possible to have a double benefactive phrase. *Me* and *þe* must function as subjects of the infinitives (in spite of their dative form) since *to me* has already taken up the benefactive role. In (9c) *mon* cannot have a benefactive role since it is preceded by *as*; it can only be interpreted as subject of the infinitive. In (9d), finally, *wallis* is inanimate, and as a rule only animate NPs can function as benefactives.

It seems fairly clear that the examples in (9) are due to a reanalysis whereby the benefactive dative originally governed by the matrix verb, as in (10a), has come to be interpreted as the subject of the infinitival clause, as shown in (10b).

(10)   a. NP V NP [$_{CP}$ [$_{IP}$ PRO to V]]
       ('benefactive construction', traditionally called 'organic *for*')
       b. NP V [$_{CP}$ [$_{IP}$ NP to V]]
       ('subject construction', or 'inorganic *for*')

It is likely that this reanalysis took place initially in existing sentences of the type *It is bad (for) you to say things like that*, and that the new constructions in (9) are an effect of it. As usual, it is only through the emergence of what would earlier have been ungrammatical constructions that we can obtain evidence for reanalysis.

What has happened in the case of reanalysis shown in (10) is that the child on the basis of the grammatical rules available to her guesses at the structure (rule) of the grammar that has produced this particular construction. The child may deduce the rule that corresponds to the older structure, but she may also postulate an innovative structure (based on some other pattern) which produces the same surface structure but also some 'wrong' or certainly innovative results (the examples in (9)). This is what Andersen (1973) calls abduction, and – as we saw in chapter 1 – is important in language change because it is the only type of 'logical inference which can introduce and create novel ideas' (McMahon 1994: 94). The notion of abduction is closely related to that of reanalysis as many analysts see it.

The innovative structure will of course be based on certain features of the primary data that the language learner is exposed to. There must be a triggering experience, and it is here that the mechanism of analogy plays an important role. In fact, analogy can be regarded as an important factor not just in language learning but in learning of all kinds (see Itkonen 1994, Holyoak and Thagard 1995) because it is a way of patterning and interpreting the world. When applying it to cases of syntactic change during acquisition, as we are doing here, it is useful to distinguish two subtypes: analogy may either extend an existing construction or it may create a new construction on the basis of a grammatical pattern used elsewhere (for more discussion of how this kind of analogy works, see Hofstadter 1995: 200 ff.). It is this latter subtype that is very close to the concept of reanalysis used by many historical linguists. The 'input' pattern that forms the basis for creative analogy in the case at hand is the fixed SV word order pattern. It makes it possible for the child to reanalyse the pre-verbal NP in (10a) as a subject rather than an indirect object, even if the relevant NP clearly has an oblique case form.

It is likely that children often abduce through creative analogy during the acquisition process. Most abductions, however, do not stick, and get ironed out. New structures only get established if the same abduction process is carried out by many speakers (and perhaps not just children but also adults). This generally seems to happen in cases where surface strings have become ambiguous. In any case of syntactic innovation due to reanalysis of ambiguous surface strings, the causes for the emerging ambiguity therefore have to be explained for the account to be complete.

We have already indicated that the reanalysis shown in (10) became possible because the loss of case inflections made the interpretation of the relevant NP ambiguous. The fact that it was rendered possible does not, however, mean that the loss of inflections made the reanalysis in (10) necessary. The loss of dative case had no particular effect in other constructions, such as the double object construction (in which the indirect object NP may have been sufficiently identified by its position in the clause). We may expect, therefore, that there were further contributing factors. One of these is probably the fixing of VO word order as discussed in chapter 5. This can be shown by means of two typical examples from Old and Middle English:

(11)   leohtre is þam bearnum maga   swingcela to geþolianne
         lighter is for-children   of-kinsmen lashes   to suffer
         þonne Godes yrre on to beyrnanne
         than   God's ire   to run-into
         'it is less painful for children to suffer the lashes of their kinsmen than to
         incur God's anger'   (*ThCap*2(Sauer) 33.369.8)

(12)   if it be a foul thing a man to waste his catel on wommen
                                                   (Chaucer *Parson* 848)

In Old English, illustrated by (11), the infinitival object nearly always precedes the infinitive in surface word order (i.e. *swingcela* and *yrre* come before *geþolian* and *onbeyrnan* respectively). The matrix benefactive object is found both before and after the matrix verb, depending on the type of clause and also on stylistic factors (in (11), *bearnum* follows the predicate *leohtre is*). In Middle English, surface VO word order becomes the norm. As shown in chapter 5, sentences with overt movement of the object to AgrOP (yielding surface OV order) become ever rarer in the course of the thirteenth and fourteenth centuries, and by 1400 this option has virtually disappeared. This can indeed be seen also in (12), where both objects (the matrix benefactive object *man*, and the infinitival object *catel*) follow the verb. This means that in Middle English the (old) benefactive phrase comes to be positioned next to the infinitive. Through this fixed adjacent position and the loss of dative marking, an interpretation becomes available in which the older benefactive is the subject of the infinitive.

This reanalysis was unlikely to occur in Old English, because Old English still had a wider variety of surface word orders, resulting from the V-movement processes discussed in chapter 4 and from the overt checking of object cases discussed in chapter 5. This then may also explain why the reanalysis did not take place in either German or Dutch: since Dutch and German are firmly SOV in their surface word order, and have maintained word order asymmetries between main and subordinate clauses due to V-movement, the benefactive phrase and the infinitive are not in a fixed adjacent position. Thus in Modern Dutch, and also German, the order still varies between main and subordinate clauses due to the rule of Verb-Second:

(13)   a. Het is slecht voor je om te roken (main clause)
           'It is bad for you to smoke'
        b. (Je   weet) dat het slecht voor je   is om te roken (subordinate clause)
            you know that it   bad   for you is to smoke
           'You know that it is bad for you to smoke'

In the subordinate clause in (13b), the infinitive and the benefactive phrase are not adjacent but are separated by the matrix predicate. Thus, the grammars of Dutch and German, with overt checking of object cases, produce surface word orders that preclude a reanalysis as in (10), simply because the word orders required for the reanalysis do not arise.

The reanalysis first affected the 'bare' dative NP, but the later structure – with the dative replaced by the *for*-phrase – appears to have followed the same route, albeit quite a bit later, and also acquired the double interpretation of (10).[3] Indeed, in more recent times, the development has progressed further in that now we can even have a dummy NP following *for*:

(14)   It is essential for it to rain soon.

Examples like these show clearly that the idea of a benefactive role has disappeared altogether.

7.2.2   *Accusative and infinitive constructions (AcI)*

The development which took place within the group of AcI constructions ((3i b) above) is different from that which affected the *(for) NP to V* group in that there is no reanalysis in a construction like *I expect you to be bright and cheerful*; instead the whole construction is new. At the same time, there are some clear similarities in that both types are infinitives with lexical subjects. It is perhaps not surprising, therefore, to see in Lightfoot (1981a) the suggestion that the appearance of the new AcI was, among other things, furthered by the occurrence of reanalysed *(for) NP to V* constructions. We do not believe, however, that there was a kind of chain reaction here; rather, it appears that both changes are ultimately related to one and the same factor, i.e. the fixation of VO word order (see Fischer 1988 and also Lightfoot 1991: 84). We put this carefully, because again, as in the *(for) NP to V* change, there are a number of

---

[3] Most of the examples in Visser (1963–73) where *for* functions unambiguously as a complementizer do not pre-date the sixteenth century; cf. §§ 914, 937, 961, 972, 975, 986.

subsidiary factors at work without which these individual developments might not have taken place. Let us first have a look at the situation in Old English.

In Old English (as in present-day English and other Germanic languages), one would regularly come across constructions such as:

(15)   a. þa   geseah heo þæt cild   licgan on binne
          then saw   she the child lie   in manger
          'then she saw the child lying in the manger'   (*ÆCHom* I. 2.42.24)
       b. ic geseah hwilon ðe   tæcan ðam cildum
          I   saw   once   you teach the children
          'I once saw you teach(ing) the children'
          (uidi aliquando te docuisse pueros)   (*ÆGram* 150.13)

where, semantically, *þæt cild* and *ðe* 'you' are as much objects of *geseah*, as they are subjects of the infinitive, *licgan* and *tæcan*. However, we do not find constructions like (16) in Old English (or in German and Dutch):

(16)   She believed the event to be of minor importance

Here the NP *the event* has no direct syntactic or semantic relation with the verb *believe*. Both the perception verbs in (15) and the verbs of the *believe* type in (16) are essentially monotransitive verbs: they select one complement, expressed as a NP or some type of clause. But there are differences too between the two types of verbs. Whereas *ic geseah þe* is structurally a complete utterance with a meaning similar to (15b), in which the infinitive is predicated on the direct object, a sentence such as *she believed the event* is clearly defective in that it represents a different meaning compared to (16).[4] Thus, Ælfric in his *Grammar*, translates the Latin AcI in (15b) by an AcI in Old English, but he does not do so in (17):

(17)   uideo te docturum esse [INF]
          ic geseo þæt ðu wylt tæcan
          'I see that you will/are going to teach
          (*ÆGram* 150.16)'

Here, *ic geseo þe* would not be an equivalent utterance: the speaker cannot actually see the addressee in the activity of teaching because that activity will take place in the future.

---

[4] We are not implying that there is no relation at all between the matrix verb and the following NP, *event*. Bolinger (1967) has argued convincingly that some relation must exist, or we could not account for the fact that a verb like *believe* accepts e.g. *I believe John to be a man of integrity*, while *I believe you to think I am lying*, is distinctly odd, if not unacceptable (examples taken from Bolinger). But this distinction involves the nature of the predicate selected, rather than the choice of subject. In other words, the nature of the secondary predicate imposes constraints on the structure selected by the matrix verb (i.e. the choice between infinitival structures and *that*-clauses). Apart from that, it is most likely that discourse factors play a role here too, as Noël (1997) has shown convincingly.

For a full understanding of the developments that have taken place in AcI constructions, it is essential that a distinction be made between instances like (15), with a perception verb followed by a bare infinitive clause, and those in (16), with a 'believe' verb followed by a *to*-infinitive. One of the problems in the analysis of these constructions has indeed been that the differences between them have often been ignored both by philologists, who have studied the constructions from a diachronic perspective, and by modern theoreticians, who have taken a synchronic perspective. For instance, both Zeitlin (1908) in his monograph on the AcI in English and Visser (1963–73) do not distinguish the two types in (15) and (16), and therefore believe that the AcI was always part and parcel of the English language, which would leave nothing to explain. Likewise in some more recent theoretical work, no distinction is made between AcI constructions after verbs of physical perception and after *believe* type verbs; syntactically they are often treated alike (see Fischer 1989 for a more detailed discussion). We will find it useful to distinguish between the AcI construction proper, found after verbs of perception and causation, and the type in (16), which we will call the ECM construction.

The problem is further compounded by the fact that there are some instances of AcIs in Old English which look very much like the type given in (16). Consider the following examples:

(18)   a. quarum in Germania plurimas nouerat esse nationes
       þara   cynna monig he wiste in Germanie wesan
       of-the tribes many he knew in Germany be
       'many of the tribes he knew to be in Germany'
              (*Bede* 9.408.21, Plummer 1896: 296; Visser 1963–73: § 2079)
    b. Sed scimus te mansuetum esse
       Ac we witun þe   bilewitne wesan
       but we know you innocent be
       'But we know you to be innocent'   (*ÆColl* 9)
    c. . . . forþon ic wat   me   to beonne unscadwis on swa
        because I know myself to be   unskilful in such
       deorwurðra spræca
       worthy   languages
       '. . . because I know that I am not skilful in such worthy languages'
                                 (*LS*29 (Nicholas) 7)
    d. Funde ða   on bedde blacne licgan his goldgifan
       found then on bed   pale   lie   his goldgiver
       'Then found his lord lying pale on his bed'   (*Jud* 278)
    e. Ic wat   eardfæstne anne standan, deafne, dumban
       I know (see) firmly   one stand   deaf   dumb
       'I see someone standing firmly, deaf, dumb'   (*Rid* 49.1)
    f. . . . þær he glædmode   geonge wiste wic   weardian
         where he gentle-minded young knew dwelling-place inhabit
       '. . . where he knew that the gentle-minded young woman lived'   (*Jul* 89)

Examples (18a) and (18b) are direct translations from Latin. These types are only found in glosses and translations of texts heavily influenced by Latin, such as Bede's *Ecclesiastical History* and Gregory's *Dialogues* (for the influence of Latin on the syntax of these texts, see Scheler 1961). Normally the translator uses a *þæt*-clause, as we have seen in (17). It is noteworthy in this respect that the Old English 'literal' translator wavers between a bare infinitive and a *to*-infinitive, contrast (18a–b) with (18c). *To* versus zero is a distinction which becomes important in the later period, once the *believe* type ECM construction has become acceptable.

Examples (18d) and (18e) are different, because they occur in original Old English texts and must be looked upon as native constructions. Notice, however, that these instances closely resemble the perception verb constructions in (15). In both (15) and (18d–e), the infinitive conveys a concrete activity that can be directly perceived and located. Also, the infinitive does not have a separate tense domain (the state of affairs described by it is simultaneous with the event expressed by the matrix verb). And, finally, there is usually a locative adjunct present, which renders the scene concrete by turning the state of affairs into a physical experience. (18f) is slightly different again, but we would still argue that it resembles (15) and (18d–e): since the speaker has *seen* where the young woman lives, he now knows it *by experience*. In cases such as (18f), the infinitive always has a locative sense (verbs meaning 'dwell', 'live', 'lie', 'stand', etc. are found there), and again a locative adjunct is present. Another point of interest is that the matrix verb *witan* in (18e–f) was originally a perception verb, meaning 'to see'. Indeed, this type of construction occurs in Old English only with *witan* and never with *cunnan* or *gecnawan/oncnawan*, which also mean 'to know', but have a different etymology (cf. Ono 1975). This shows how a syntactic structure can become subject to various kinds of restrictions when, through semantic change, it ceases to instantiate the productive pattern that it formerly did.[5]

Having established that a distinction must be made between the two types of AcIs, and that Old English did not possess the ECM type with *to* illustrated

[5] Interestingly, the Dutch counterpart of (18f) is still possible with the cognate verb *weten*, as in:

    Ik weet hem te wonen
    I   know him to live
    'I know where he lives'

This construction is possible only in a locative sense, as in (18f). Dutch does not allow:

    *Ik weet hem onschuldig te zijn
    'I know him to be innocent'

which is, of course, the only type possible in Modern English. For an analysis of the Dutch AcI with *weten*, see den Dikken and Zwart (1996).

in (16), we now turn to the questions of why Old English did not have this ECM construction and why it developed later in the Middle English period. Some Middle English examples are given in (19).

(19)   a. Which that he knew in heigh sentence habounde
           'Whom he knew to abound in high moral sense'   (Chaucer *Monk* 2748)
        b. . . . the weche xx[ti] marke she hath delyuerd to me in golde for you to haue
           at your comyng home, for she dare not *aventure here money to be brought*
           vp to London for feere of robbyng for it is seide heere that there goothe
           many thefys be-twyx this and London . . .
           '. . . which 20 marks she has delivered to me in gold for you to have at
           your home-coming, for she dare not venture her money to be brought up
           to London for fear of robbing, for it is said here that many thieves go
           around between this place and London . . .'   (*Paston Letters* 156.7)

In the literature, various causal factors for the rise of the ECM construction have been proposed and discussed, the main ones being analogy with the AcI after perception verbs and borrowing from Latin (for details see Fischer 1989). Both of these factors seem to have been influential, but we will argue that the crucial factor was the rigidification of word order discussed above. As noted above, there are two types of evidence to show that the rise of the Latin-type AcI in English became possible only after the word order changes, and that borrowing and analogy are the mechanisms by which the change took place. The first type of evidence is comparative in nature, the second involves a detailed investigation of all the constructions that could be said to be near equivalents (semantically and/or syntactically) of the AcI construction.

Let us first look at the comparative evidence. If analogy and borrowing in themselves were the forces that turned the scale for the Latin-type AcI in English, it is hard to see why the AcI did not catch on in sister languages like Dutch and German, which were structurally very similar to Old English, and in which the cultural influence of Latin was as important as it was for English. In addition, borrowing does not explain why the AcI was not already used more frequently in the Old English period, when Latin had enormous influence and prestige via Christian writings. The same reasoning would apply to analogy or analogical extension. If indeed the AcI spread by a type of lexical diffusion from verbs of physical perception to verbs of mental perception, as Zeitlin (1908) among others suggested, why did this not happen already in Old English, and why did it not also happen in Dutch and German? It looks as if, on the level of syntax at least, both analogy and borrowing need to be fed by (changes in) internal structure. In terms of the process of language acquisition, the primary data that Old-English-speaking children were exposed to contained both the potential source for analogy (i.e. perception verbs followed by an AcI pattern) and the potential source for borrowing (i.e. the occasional calque of the Latin-type AcI pattern, as in (18a–b)). Yet children acquiring Old English did not construct a grammar yielding ECM constructions, and comparative evidence may make clear why they did not.

There are two studies that consider the rise of the Latin-type AcI in Germanic languages other than English. Krickau (1877) looks at its occurrence in German, and Fischer (1994b) looks at Dutch. Both confirm that the AcI did make some inroads in these two languages in the Renaissance period, when the influence of Latin was at its peak. But at the same time, they show that the influence remained confined to works that consciously tried to imitate a Latin style, and that the AcI did not catch on outside such works and was dropped again altogether later. In English too, the frequency of Latin-type AcIs is higher in works closely modelled on Latin, as Warner (1982: 134 ff.) has demonstrated in his comparison of the Early (more literal) and the Late (more idiomatic) Version of the Wycliffite Bible. Warner (1982) and Fischer (1994b) also show that in both Middle English and Renaissance Dutch the AcI, when it was first used, was more frequent in those contexts where its occurrence was less noticeable, for instance in clauses where the accusative NP had undergone movement, as in topicalization or passive constructions (see (20a)) or constructions with *wh*-movement (see (20b)).

(20)   a. but this pope or þese prelatis we shulden not bileve to be of Cristis
            Chirche
            'but this pope or these prelatis we should not believe to be belonging to
            the church of Christ'   (*Wycl. Serm.* (Arnold) ii.388.2; Warner 1982: 136)
        b. whom to be prince of the paleis and of myche power thei knewen
            'whom they knew to be prince of the palace and to have great power'
                                        (*WBible* Esther 9.4; Warner 1982: 142)

For more discussion of this point, see section 7.3 below, which also discusses similar examples from older Dutch.

What makes a comparison with German and Dutch so interesting in this case is the fact, already remarked upon in 7.2.1, that German and Dutch did not share the increasing fixation of one type of surface word order for all clauses; unlike English these languages still have surface SOV in subordinate clauses, and a Verb-Second rule in main clauses. This gives us a clue to the importance of word order in the change under discussion. We will therefore now look more closely at how exactly the Latin-type AcI came to be introduced into English.

Old English used the following types of infinitival complements:

(21)   i. *after verbs of physical perception*
       a. Ic wiht   geseah on wege feran
         I   someone saw   on way go
         'I saw someone travelling along'   (*Rid* 36.1)
       b. Ic seah turf tredan
         I   saw turf tread
         'I saw grass being trodden'   (*Rid* 13.1)

    ii. *after causatives*
       a. . . . yfele hyrdas ðe lætað godes scep losian ðurh gymeleaste
         '. . . evil shepherds who let God's sheep perish through negligence'
                                       (*ÆCHom* I 17(App)177.8)
       b. he sette   scole, 7   on þære he let cnihtas læran
         he set-up school, and in it   he let boys   teach
         'he set up a school in which he had boys taught'   (*Bede* 3(O)14.208.8)

    iii. *after object-control verbs*
       a. and his bebod   tobræc þe   he him   bebead   to
         and his command broke which he them commanded to
         healdenne
         hold
         'and broke the command which he had ordered them to observe'
                                        (*ÆHom* 11.103)
       b. Moyses forbead swyn to etenne
         Moses forbade pigs to eat
         'Moses forbade the eating of pigs'   (*ÆLS*(Maccabees) 85)

    iv. *after ECM verbs*
       infinitival complements are found here only in direct translation from
       Latin

Next to infinitival complements, we also find finite complements, usually *þæt*-clauses. *þæt*- clauses are very frequent after perception verbs as in (21i). They are highly infrequent after the core causatives *lætan* and *don*, but occur regularly after *hatan*, which is a verb that syntactically belongs both in (21ii) and (21iii) (cf. Fischer 1989). After object-control verbs, the *þæt*-clause is in fact far more usual than the infinitival complement. Infinitives, as noted in section 7.1, only become frequent here in Middle English. A finite complement is the *only* possibility after verbs of group (21iv). Other differences between these four groups of verbs may also be noted. Groups (21i) and (21ii) always take a bare infinitive, while (21iii) always has a *to*-infinitive. Groups (21i), (21ii) and (21iv) govern a direct object in the accusative, which may be animate as well as inanimate. Group (21iii) has both a direct (usually inanimate) and an indirect object (always animate); the former has accusative case, the latter is usually in the dative, but the accusative occurs too with some verbs (usually verbs that are semantically close to causatives).[6]

What is remarkable about the infinitival constructions that we find in Old English is that they are of two kinds, indicated in (21) by (a) and (b). The (a) examples all have a matrix verb object that controls a PRO subject in the infinitival clause (i.e. *wiht* in (21i), *scep* in (21ii), *him* in (21iii)).[7] We will refer to this type as the 'subject infinitival'. In the (b) examples, the object of the matrix verb (which controls the PRO subject of the infinitive) is left unexpressed, and the object NP that is present is the object of the infinitive (these constructions are often called passival infinitives in the literature; we shall use the term 'object-infinitival' for them). The difference is shown in the following structures:

(a) $NP_S\ V_{finite}\ NP_{Oi}\ [PRO_i\ V_{infinitive}]$
(b) $NP_S\ V_{finite}\ [PRO_{arb}\ NP_O\ V_{infinitive}]$

The infinitive in (b) has an implicit subject with generic interpretation (i.e. 'arbitrary PRO'). Note that the object in (b) regularly precedes the infinitive, as one would expect in subordinate clauses in Old English.

We will now consider in detail a corpus of Middle English texts in order to see what changes occur with respect to these four groups of verbs. The corpus investigated consists of around 850,000 words and contains a selection of early and late Middle English texts, poetry as well as prose: the Caligula Ms. of Layamon's *Brut* from the second half of the thirteenth century (verse; 75,500 words); John Gower's *Confessio Amantis* from the late fourteenth century (verse; 207,300 words); the *Paston Letters* from the last three quarters of the fifteenth century (prose; 235,300 words); and Malory's *Morte Darthur* from the third quarter of the fifteenth century (prose; 336,700 words).[8] The frequency of the different types of infinitival complements in these texts is given in table 7.1.

The following changes in Middle English are noticeable. The 'subject-infinitivals' (the (a) examples in (21)) occur with all three groups of verbs and throughout the whole period. With some verbs, there is an increase in infinitival

---

[6] When verbs of group (21iii) are semantically close to causative verbs, they are sometimes followed by the bare infinitive that is usual after true causatives,

and bead . . .   hi   up ahon bi þan fotum
and commanded them up hang by the feet
'and commanded them to be hanged by their feet'

(*LS* 14(Margaret Ass 15) 279)

[7] We are ignoring at this point whether the structure involved is mono- or ditransitive; in both the objects can be functionally subjects, and both constructions can appear in the passival (b) form.

[8] What follows is a summary of the main points of Fischer (1992b).

Table 7.1. *Complement types occurring after perception verbs, causatives and object-control verbs in four Middle English texts:*
Layamon's Brut: verse, 75,000 words (sec. half thirteenth century)
Confessio Amantis: verse, 207,300 words (late fourteenth century)
Paston Letters: prose, 235,300 words (1425–1500)
Morte Darthur: prose, 336,700 words (c. 1475)

Perception verbs	subj. infinitival	object infinitival	how/that- clause	passive infinitive
Lay. Brut	11	2	31	—
Conf. Amantis	107	3	105	5
Paston Letters	8	1	29	2
Morte Darthur	267	—	207	4
causative verbs				
Lay. Brut	63	6	66	1
Conf. Amantis	228	13	7 + 7?	4
Paston Letters	155	5	9	31
Morte Darthur	261	—	6 + 1?	31
causative *let*				
Lay. Brut	48	23	—	1
Conf. Amantis	61	7	—	6
Paston Letters	226	—	—	42
Morte Darthur	229	—	—	19
obj. control verbs				
Lay. Brut	—	—	2	—
Conf. Amantis	27	2	107	—
Paston Letters	221	—	240	13
Morte Darthur	244 + 1?	—	156	6

complements, which, as we said above, was a general phenomenon in the Middle English period. The 'object-infinitivals' are generally less frequent than the 'subject' ones (except after the verbs *let* and *hear*), but we can notice an overall, steady decrease in their use in Middle English. While the object-infinitival decreases, there is an increase in passive infinitives, a type that we have not discussed yet. Before we can continue this investigation, we must therefore consider the use of the passive infinitive in both Old and Middle English.

7.2.3 Passive infinitives

The use of the passive infinitive in Old English is generally speaking restricted to the position after modal verbs (*cunnan, motan,* etc). As the auxiliary of the passive voice, usually *beon* was used, but *wesan* and *weorþan* also occur.[9]

(22)   a. and he ne mot na   beon eft   gefullod
           and he not may never be   later baptized
           'and he may never be baptized later'   (*ÆLS*(AshWed) 141)
        b. biterlice scel hit him   wyrþan forgolden on þam toweardan life
           bitterly shall it on-him become revenged in the future   life
           'bitterly it shall be revenged on him in the life to come'
                                                         (*HomU* 42(Nap 52) 7)

There is some discussion in the literature as to whether the passive infinitive after modals was a native construction or not. Callaway (1913: 83, 194, 238) inclines to the view that the construction was Latin-influenced, while Mitchell (1985: § 922) is far more guarded. Bock (1931: 200) believes that in general the passive infinitive in Old English is a Latin-inspired phenomenon, except possibly after modals. It is only after modals that the passive infinitive occurs more frequently in native than in Latinate prose. And in this position it even occurs in poetry (albeit not frequently) (for more details see Callaway 1913 and Fischer 1991: 143–6).

Although we cannot conclusively settle the question of Latin influence, some things are clear. First of all, the passive infinitive found after modals presents the only position in which it is frequent in native Old English; in all other positions it is rare, and if it does occur, it occurs mainly in Latinate prose (see Fischer 1991: 145). Secondly, even if the passive infinitive after modals is modelled after Latin, it is an understandable development because the resulting construction resembled existing ones in which a modal was followed by the copula *beon* and an adjective.[10] Thirdly, the passive infinitive filled a paradigmatic gap in that all other tenses and moods of the verb in Old English had active as well as passive forms. And finally, there was a much greater need for passive infinitives after modals than in other positions because an active infinitive could not be used here. This last factor needs some explanation. In most cases where present-day English uses a passive infinitive (see below for examples), Old English would use an active one. This did not present an interpretive problem because the NP preceding the infinitive would not be interpreted as the subject of that infinitive but rather as its object because of the verb-final character of Old English subordinate clauses. It is clear from the (made-up) active variant of (22a) given in (22a′), that an active infinitival form after a modal yields a completely different sense than when a passive infinitive is used there.

---

[9] For possible differences between these auxiliaries, see Mitchell (1985: § 786 ff.).
[10] The *beon* + adjective construction had stative meaning, and it seems quite likely that the earliest passive constructions were also stative, with the past participle used and declined like an adjective.

(22a′)   and he ne mot na eft gefullian
        'and he may never again baptize'

The reason is that what should serve as the object of *gefullian* (i.e. *he* both in (22a) and (22a′)), can only be interpreted as subject in (22a′) because of its sentence-initial position before the finite verb.

Let us now consider the various cases where present-day English regularly uses or has to use a passive construction, but where Old English has an active one. They are given in (23).

(23)   i.   *after semi-modal* be
                þas þing   sint to donne
                these things are to do
                'these things can/must/ought to be done'   (*Lch* II(2)22.1.8)

      ii. *as adjunct to an adjective*
                Ne bregden ge no ða stengas of   ðæm hringum, ðylæs sio
                not remove you not the poles   from the   rings,   lest   the
                earc si ungearo to beranne
                ark be unready to carry
                'Do not remove the poles from the rings in case the ark may not be ready yet to be carried'   (*CP* 22.173.9)

     iii. *as adjunct to a noun*
                næs   þær . . . wæteres drync to bruconne
                not-was there   of-water drink to use
                'there was no drink of water that could be used'   (*And* 21)

     iv. *in combination with a main verb*
         a. *as an adverbial adjunct of purpose*
               7   rice men sendon heora dohtor   þider to læranne
               and rich men sent   their   daughters there to teach
               'and rich men sent their daughters there to be taught'
                                   (*Bede* 3.6.172.16)

         b. *in an AcI construction after perception verbs and causatives*
               he het   hine mid strælum ofscotian
               he ordered him with arrows off-shoot
               'he ordered him to be shot to death with arrows'
                        (*Mart* 5(Kotzor) 211[JA20])

Note, too, that present-day English does not use a passive infinitive all the time in all these positions. There is quite a bit of variation here. Compare the examples of (23) to those in (24) (a–d refer to the same functions),

(24)   a. What is to be done next?
          They are to blame/to be blamed for this mishap
     b. John is easy to please
          The castle is beautiful to look at
          It seemed to them too funny to be endured
                       (Visser 1963–73: § 1921) / ? to endure

> Your room is not fit to be seen
> He is fit to serve as a captain in the army
> c. It is time to finish the work
> It is time for the work to be finished
> This is a possibility to be gravely considered / ? to gravely consider
> d. Jesus came to John to be baptized
> It is terrible to see a foreigner be treated like that

We will not here consider the causes of the rise of the passive infinitive in these positions in great detail (we instead refer the interested reader to Fischer 1991), but the variation in this area tells us something about why the passive infinitive was introduced in positions other than the post-modal one, from Middle English onwards. Very briefly, the need for a passive infinitive seems to depend on quite a number of factors such as the position and the type of NP that functions as the semantic object (i.e. the NP that bears the θ-role of 'patient') of that infinitive. If the object is placed after the infinitive (as in the first example of (24c)), the active infinitive is the rule in Modern English. If the object can be moved to the matrix clause syntactic subject position, the active infinitive is usually preferred. This is particularly true when there is an adjective in the matrix predicate which has a thematic (subject) relation with this NP, as in the first two examples of (24b), and the second example of (24a), where *to blame* is similar to *blameworthy*. It is interesting to note that when the thematic relation between adjective and subject is less strong, there is a tendency to use the passive infinitive, as in the third instance of (24b), where *too funny* has as strong a semantic relation to the verb as it has to the subject. This is even clearer when the adjective is in an adverbial form and therefore related only to the verb and not to the subject; in that case a passive infinitive must be used, as in *Jack Rapley is not easily to be knocked off his feet* (Visser 1963–73: § 1921). When the object that has to be raised to matrix subject position is inanimate, a passive infinitive is usually preferred, perhaps because inanimate NPs are dispreferred as subjects, which are generally animate in English, hence the differences between the examples of (24a) and the difference between the *fit* examples of (24b). An additional reason here, of course, is that *fit* is ambiguous, and the difference in infinitives is needed to distinguish the passive ('suitable') and active ('appropriate, capable') meanings of the adjective *fit*.[11] It is only when the NP in question has not been raised to the

---

[11] This is also the reason why in (23b) a passive infinitive must be used after *ready* in the Modern English translation. Like *fit*, *ready* has both an active and a passive sense, since it can mean both 'willing', 'showing readiness' or 'made ready, ready to be used'. In the active sense, an active infinitive is obligatory, as in *I am ready to suffer torments*. For more information on how these 'two-faced' adjectives came into the language (they were very rare in Old English), see Greenough and Kittredge (1902: 272); for how they combine with infinitives, see Fischer (1991: 175–9).

matrix subject position and appears right in front of the infinitive (as in the last two examples of (24c) and the last of (24d)) that the passive infinitive has become obligatory.

From these brief observations, it can be concluded that the form of the infinitive depends heavily on the position of the NP object of the infinitival verb, and that therefore the cause of the change must once again be sought in word order changes as described above. From Middle English onwards, as the SVO order became fixed in every clause type, a NP–V sequence became as it were automatically interpreted as subject–verb. We will now return to our earlier concern, the AcI construction.

7.2.4 The AcI and the passive infinitive

In the previous section, it became clear that the so-called object-infinitivals, i.e. the (b) structures in (21), must have become more and more opaque to learners who were increasingly confronted in the surrounding data with SVO surface structures. This is corroborated by the data emerging from the corpus, which was investigated with a view to discovering the spread of the AcI in English. Table 7.1 shows clearly that object-infinitivals decreased fast: in the corpus sixty-two examples are found,[12] but they are mainly from early texts. By contrast, subject-infinitivals continue to be highly frequent (2,056 examples were found). The investigation of the data also shows that there were various ways of avoiding the increasingly 'awkward' object-infinitival, as listed and discussed below.

(i) First, instead of an infinitival construction, a *that*-clause could be used. This was an option with all verbs except with some of the causatives, notably *let*. There are, however, some problems with this option. First of all, *let* was one of the most frequent verbs in the object-infinitival. Second, if the *that*-clause contained an active verb, the agent of the activity would have to be made explicit with some verbs (see iii below). Third, *that*-clauses and infinitives are not always semantically equivalent (cf. van der Leek 1992). Fourth, we saw above that there was a substantial increase in the number of infinitives in Middle English accompanied by a decrease in *that*-clauses.

(ii) In order to resolve the ambiguity of the NP object between its function as an object of the infinitive and of the matrix verb, a speaker used to

---

[12] In table 7.1 only object-infinitivals that showed surface V_{fin} NP_o V_{inf} word order have been counted. Structures where the NP has been moved were not included because it is not clear what position they have been moved out of, i.e. pre- or postinfinitival position.

SVO structures might also place this object after the infinitive. This indeed occurs, as the Appendices show, most frequently with *let* (194 instances) and much less with the other verbs (a total of 131 instances was found for all other verbs).

(25)   a. He lette blauwen bemen;   and nam al þa burhwes . . .
           he let blow   trumpets, and took all the strongholds
           'He caused the trumpets to be blown and took all the strongholds . . .'
                                                    (Layamon *Brut* (Clg)2227)
        b. And kyng Arthure with the two kyngis lette departe the seven
           and King Arthur with the two kings let   split up the seven
           hondred knyghtes
           hundred knights
           'And King Arthur with the two kings let the seven hundred knights be
           split up'   (Malory *Works* 23,9)

The reason why this option was not often chosen may be that such a move would result in an infinitival complement introduced by PRO_{arb}, which is a construction that has been losing ground in the history of English (cf. Fischer 1991: 165–71). In fact the new structure V_{fin}–V_{inf} (–NP) resembles that of auxiliary verbs followed by infinitives, which are all cases of subject control. Since auxiliaries were also becoming much more common in the Middle English period, this may have helped to oust the PRO_{arb} construction, which was similar on the surface. It is therefore perhaps not surprising that this 'solution' is most frequently encountered with the verb *let,* which of all the verbs considered in the corpus comes closest to an auxiliary (for more information on the 'auxiliarization' of *let,* see Fischer 1992b: 39–41).

(iii) A third way of avoiding the object-infinitival was to add an overt subject for the infinitive. (26) contains an interesting example from the *Brut,* which has an object-infinitival in the more archaic Caligula Ms., while an overt subject is added in the linguistically more modern Otho Ms.

(26)   a. And hæhte   heo wite   wel faste
           and commanded her guard well firmly   (Layamon *Brut* (Clg)4801)
        b. and hehte   ʒam hine witie   faste
           and commanded them him to guard firmly
           'And commanded it [=the castle] to be guarded securely'
                                                    (Layamon *Brut* (Otho)4801)

This, however, cannot always have been a suitable option, because it forces one to make the agent explicit when it is intended to be generic. This is the case, for instance, in the awkward example in (27): *the knyghtes* mentioned there appear quite out of the blue, and play no further role in the rest of the narrative.

(27)   He [Sir Cadore] alyght off his horse and toke hym in his armys and there
        commaunded knyghtes to kepe well the corse.
        'He dismounted from his horse and took him in his arms and commanded
        knights to guard his corpse well there.'   (Malory *Works* 215.6)

The possibility of leaving the agent implicit indeed may have been one of the
reasons why the object-infinitival was used in the first place.

(iv) A fourth method of avoiding the use of the object-infinitival was a
lexical one, and was restricted to only a small number of verbs that could be
reinterpreted as intransitive, with the pre-infinitival object reinterpreted as a
subject. An example of this is (25a). In Old English *blawan* was intransitive
only if the subject was animate. This changes in Middle English, a development which may well have been helped along by the frequent occurrence of
original object-infinitivals such as *He heard the horns blow*. Another example
comes from Chaucer:

(28)   And now to loke on every side,/ A man may se the world divide, The werres
        ben so general . . .
        'And now a man only has to look around him and he will see the world
        divide/be divided, wars being so general . . .'   (Chaucer *Gen. Prol.* 895)

According to the *OED* the intransitive (reflexive) meaning of *divide* only
became available from 1526 onwards, so this may be either a late example of the
old object-infinitival or a very early instance of the intransitive use of this verb.

(v) A final option was the use of a passive infinitive. This had some advantages over the others in that the possibility was not restricted to a small
number of verbs, as in (iv); an agent subject need not be added, as in (iii); it
avoided the V_{fin}–V_{inf} order of (ii) because the original object, now a subject,
intervened between the two verbal forms; and finally it could be used with all
verbs and was semantically closer to the active infinitive than the *that*-clause,
cf. (i). The use of a passive infinitive may have represented a somewhat more
formal style, but it must be noted that the passive infinitive occurs in all the
texts of the corpus. Some examples are given in (29).

(29)   a. þa lette he his cnihtes; dæies & nihtes. æuere beon iwepned
          'then he made his knights always be armed day and night'
                                                         (Layamon *Brut* (Clg)8155)
        b. I prey yow let them be sealyd and sent me by Radley wyth the deedys
          ther-in
          'I pray you let them be sealed and sent to me via Radley with the deeds
          contained in it'   (*Paston Letters* 349.8)
        c. That with his doghter scholden go,/ To se the Souldan be converted
          'Who should accompany his daughter to witness the conversion of the
          Sultan'   (Gower *Confessio Amantis* 2.637)

Table 7.1 shows that indeed the use of the passive infinitive rises steeply in this period, whereas it was quite rare with these verbs in native Old English, as we saw in section 7.2.3. In the earliest text, Layamon's *Brut*, only two instances were found, in late Middle English rising to fifteen (*Confessio Amantis*), seventy-five (*Paston Letters*) and fifty-four (Malory). The passive infinitives (a total of 146) had also clearly become more frequent than the object-infinitivals (only sixty in this period). The use of the passive in these constructions was in turn of course aided by the fact that the passive had also, from the twelfth century onwards, come to be used in other positions, for instance after nouns, adjectives and semi-modal *to be to*, as we saw in the previous section.

Although the Middle English data strongly suggest that the change in word order was a necessary condition for the development of the passive infinitive in these verbal complements, we do not wish to suggest that it was a sufficient condition. The Scandinavian situation makes this quite clear. Swedish, Norwegian and Danish show surface SVO both in main and in subordinate clauses, but they still allow the so-called passival infinitives, which is the type represented by the Old English examples given in (21b) and whose loss was discussed under (iii) above. Further contributing causal factors in English may have been the general spread of the passive infinitive in English in other positions coinciding with this new development, and the rigidity of SVO order in English. In this second respect, English differs from the Scandinavian languages, where the Verb-Second rule is still a firm feature of main clause syntax; for discussion, see Holmberg and Platzack (1995). Furthermore, it is often suggested in the literature that a prerequisite for the passival infinitive is an overt infinitival ending on the verb. In work in which the passival infinitive is interpreted as passive, this ending is then assumed to be ambiguous between passive and infinitival morphology (Vanden Wyngaerd 1990); those who analyse the passival infinitive as active take this morphology to license the phonetically empty subject of the infinitive (Petter 1994, 1998). Either way, the loss of the passival infinitive might fit in with the loss of the infinitival ending -*en* in English, but there is clearly room for more work here.

So far, we have considered what happened to two types of infinitival constructions, i.e. the ones occurring after perception verbs and those after causatives (types (i) and (ii) mentioned in (21) above). Old English had yet another infinitival type, i.e. the object-control constructions of (21iii). What happened with these in the Middle English period? We have seen that object-control verbs typically have an animate indirect object, while the infinitive functions as its direct object. In this respect, object-control verbs are different from causative and perception verbs, which are monotransitive: the accusative NP and the infinitive together form a clausal object. Since with object-control verbs the animate indirect object also controls the PRO subject of the infinitive, no opacity problem presented itself to the language learner when SVO surface order became generalized. While before, the indirect object could also precede the matrix verb, it would now always follow it, which makes no difference to the interpretation of PRO.

It was, however, noted in connection with the examples of (21) that a number of verbs were ambiguous between types (21ii) (the causatives) and (21iii) (the object-control verbs). In Old English, such a verb was *hatan*, which could mean 'to command, to order', or function more purely as a causative verb, used in the sense of 'let'. For object-control verbs with the meaning of 'order' to develop into causatives is not unusual; for example, classical Latin *iubere* became a pure causative in later times. With a causative the emphasis is on the completion of an order, i.e. it has perfective or resultative aspect, whereas with an object-control verb like *order*, the emphasis is on the process of ordering itself, and the person who is being ordered to do something is the focus of attention.[13] It is not surprising therefore that there should be some overlap between these categories, and indeed that 'order' verbs should be amenable to an interpretation as causatives with the emphasis on the activity rather than the person ordered. Thus, in Old English we find *hatan* and *biddan* constructions both with and without the 'orderee', and similarly in Middle English we find object-control verbs like *command* also without an indirect object, as shown in (30).

(30)   . . . therefore the lorde commaunded to sle hym, and for thys cause ys he slayne
'. . . therefore the lord commanded to kill him, and for this reason he is killed'   (Malory *Works* 811.20)

Since we find constructions like (30), it is likewise not surprising that the passive infinitive begins to be used after object control verbs with this causative flavour. Table 7.1 shows that here, too, the passive infinitive began to make inroads in Middle English. We have found nineteen such instances in our corpus, all with causative types of control verbs; some of them are given in (31).

(31)   a. And when he had used hit he ded of hys crowne and
          and   when he had used it   he did off his crown   and

---

[13] For the relation between causativity and perfective aspect see also Royster (1918), Denison (1985) and, most explicitly, van Dijk (1999).

commaunded the crowne to be sett on the awter
commanded   the crown   to be set on the altar
'And when he had used it he took off his crown and commanded the
crown to be set on the altar'   (Malory *Works* 908.11)

b. And as for all oþer erondys that ye haue commandid for to be do, þey
shall be do als sone as þei may be do
'And as for all the other errands that you have given orders to be done,
they shall be done as soon as they can be done'   (*Paston Letters* 148.17)

c. . . . and Debunham ded charge an other court ther þe Sunday next after
to be holde
'. . . and Debenham ordered another court session to be held there next
Sunday'   (*Paston Letters* 192.35)

The appearance of passive infinitives after object-control verbs is syntactically much more remarkable than their appearance after causatives and
perception verbs, because after object-control verbs, it involves a new
construction. The structure of an active sentence is different from that of a
passive in the manner shown in (32).

(32)   i. He commanded him to set the crown on the altar
NP$_S$ V$_{fin}$ NP$_i$ [PRO$_i$ to infinitive]
ii. He commanded the crown to be set on the altar
NP$_S$ V$_{fin}$ [NP to infinitive]

In (32ii) the relevant NP has now become part of the clausal object of the
matrix verb. But the construction is clearly different from the type of AcI used
after causatives and perception verbs. There is no bare infinitive but a *to*-
infinitive, and the tense domains of infinitive and matrix verb are not clearly
simultaneous. In fact, this type looks very much like the Latin type of AcI (i.e.
the AcI following 'believe' verbs), which did not yet occur in Old English (as
noted above in (21)). How do we explain this development? It seems to us that
the cause here must be analogical extension, the passive infinitive spreading
from causatives to (causative) object-control verbs.

At more or less the same time (second half of the fourteenth century) that
we see these passive AcI's occurring after object control verbs, we witness the
appearance of Latin-type AcI constructions after the so-called *verba cogitandi et declarandi* (verbs expressing a claim, expectation, belief etc.).
Borrowing from Latin indeed plays an important role in the introduction of
these constructions, as shown by Warner's (1982: 134–57) comparison of two
versions of the Wycliffite Bible (the so-called Early Version being a very literal
translation, the Late Version being much more free). Warner (1982: 134) also
notes that the Latin AcI was 'at first adopted principally where surface (NP

to VP) is avoided, or where it contains TO *be* and is potentially an extension of the previously available sequence NP–PRED [as in *I consider him beauti-ful* > *I consider him to be beautiful*], so that the change appears first where "least salient", or where only a "minimal alteration of previous structures is concerned"'.

We will come back to the idea of 'least saliency' later, but here we note that the use of *to be* as the infinitive in the AcI is indeed remarkable, not only as an extension of a sequence NP–PRED. In our investigation of the corpus of AcI examples after verbs like *believe* (see Appendix C), we found again that the passive infinitive plays an important role. The use of the passive is not included in Warner's 'minimal alteration' scheme (Warner 1982: 148–50), but our data show that one fifth of the Latin-type Ac's found in the corpus (thirty in all) involve passive infinitives. When we discount the ambiguous AcIs (see note 3 in Appendix C), they even make up almost one third of the AcIs. This could hardly be coincidental. Some examples are given in (33).

(33)   a. . . . the weche xx^{ti} marke she hath delyuerd to me in golde for you to haue
         at your comyng home, for she dare not *aventure here money to be brought*
         vp to London for feere of robbyng for it is seide heere that there goothe
         many thefys be-twyx this and London . . .
         '. . . the which twenty marks she has delivered to me in gold for you to
         have at your home-coming, for she dare not venture her money to be
         brought up to London for fear of robbing; for it is said here that there go
         about many thieves between here and London'   (*Paston Letters* 156.7)
    b. . . . and in lyke wyse may ye do, and ye lyst, and take the quene knyghtly
         away with you, if so be that the kynge woll *jouge her to be brente*
         '. . . and in like wise you may do, if you please, and like a real knight take
         the queen away with you, if it is the case that the king will judge her to be
         burnt'   (Malory *Works* 1173.3)

Another point of interest is that quite a few of these matrix *believe*-verbs carry a causative connotation (as also in (33)), just like the object-control verbs that acquired a passive infinitive. So it looks, once again, as if the AcI has spread here through analogical extension. The above discussion shows, we think, that the introduction of the ECM construction results from a delicate interplay of grammar-internal factors (word order change, and the loss of case distinc-tions, the rise of the passive infinitive), analogical factors and external ones, primarily borrowing.

Let us now briefly consider another explanation that has been given for the developments discussed here. Lightfoot (1991) ascribes the new lexical subject constructions to a change taking place in the grammar in the status of *to*, invoking the coalescence of *to* with the governing verb, in which *to* enables the governing verb to transmit its head-government and case properties (Lightfoot 1991: 89, 91).[14] As we see it, there are a number of problems with this proposal. First of all, the notion of coalescence itself is somewhat abstract, and in the more customary sense of coalescence somewhat unusual because the elements that coalesce (*to* and the governing verb) are not adjacent, nor do they have a semantic relation with one another. Cases of coalescence in the literature are motivated either by adjacency or by a semantic relation between the two elements that become coalesced. If coalescence were to occur in this case, one would expect it to have involved *to* and the infinitive, which *are* adjacent and form a semantic unity.[15] However, in Lightfoot's scenario, the coalescence of *to* with the governing verb is necessary so that *to* can be said to transmit case in constructions like (31a). A more serious problem, however, is the way Lightfoot relates the word order change to the change in *to*. He first discusses how a construction like (21i b), *Ic seah turf tredan*, becomes, *I saw turf be(ing) trod*. This is due to the SOV > SVO change (the basic word order change postulated here), because the Middle-English-speaking (SVO) child will interpret the NP *turf* before the verb *tredan* as a subject rather than an object. The use of the passive infinitive will then automatically follow because the child has no access to anything beyond the embedded subject position (according to Lightfoot's degree-0 learnability hypothesis). Next, Lightfoot argues that object-control verbs (of the type given in (21iii)) undergo the same reanalysis. This is also our argument here. We have shown that object-control verbs follow the causative verbs in taking a passive infinitive through analogical extension, the *causative* control verbs being

---

[14] The change in the status of *to* is important because it opens up the possibility of explaining a number of new infinitival constructions in Middle English together (so in Lightfoot's case also the structure given in (3iii) and some others) as the result of one and the same parameter shift.

[15] Cases of coalescence invoked in the literature are, for instance, the rebracketing of *want + to*-infinitive and *(to be) going + to*-infinitive into *want to + infinitive* and *going to + infinitive*; that coalescence has occurred becomes evident from the later, alternative forms *wanna* and *gonna*. This coalescence was motivated by the fact that these verbs and the *to*-infinitives were adjacent, but also because 'purposive' *to* was semantically compatible with the future intention implied in verbs like *want* and *go* (cf. Hopper and Traugott 1993: 82–93). Another well-known example of coalescence is the reanalysis of verb + particle into phrasal verbs, which is the topic of chapter 6. It is clear from the discussion there that it was the change in particle position that took place in Middle English, i.e. the development of a fixed position of the particle after the verb, that enabled particle verbs to develop into what are now called phrasal verbs.

affected first. Lightfoot's (1991: 94) own (made up) example of such a control structure is, *I order $_{S'}[COMP$ $_S[PRO$ $_{VP}[grass$ $cut]]]$*, which becomes through reanalysis, *I order $_{S'}[COMP$ $_S[grass_i$ to $[be$ cut $e_i]]]$*. In Lightfoot's account, however, it is not analogy that makes the new passive construction possible after control verbs. Lightfoot (1991: 94) writes, '[s]ince *order* is not a causative or perceptual verb which may take a headless complement, case could be assigned to *grass* only indirectly; therefore, the coalescence option was invoked and the *to* marker became necessary'. He suggests, in other words, that *to* came to be *actively* selected, in order to transmit government. The fact is, however, that when *to* is found in passive infinitive constructions like (31a) and in the above example with *order*, this *to* was already there in the corresponding Old English active construction. The data in the Appendices show very clearly that active bare infinitives acquire passive bare infinitives in Middle English, and active *to*-infinitives acquire passive *to*-infinitives. So one cannot really maintain that *to* is selected, only perhaps that *to* came to be reanalysed as a result of the use of passive infinitives after object-control verbs. In other words, the parameter shift involving *to* cannot be the cause of the change. As we see it, it was the use of the passive infinitive, which in itself was caused by the word order changes, which promoted further change. In Lightfoot's view, the passive infinitive itself cannot play a causal role because the child has no access to this embedded infinitive. Therefore he sees the use of the passive form of the infinitive as 'an effect and not a cause of anything' (Lightfoot 1991: 94), whereas in our view, it is the use of the passive infinitive itself that causes the NP in constructions like (31a) to be reanalysed as part of the embedded clause: from an NP governed and θ-marked by the matrix verb, it becomes the lexical subject of the infinitive.

A second problematic factor in Lightfoot's analysis is the replacement of the bare infinitive by a *to*-infinitive. Lightfoot himself writes that his 'coalescence'-analysis of *to* 'is likely to involve understanding the conditions under which the *to* form of the infinitive came to take over from the plain form of the infinitive without the *to* marker', adding that this is 'a difficult matter and has never been properly understood, despite being subjected to much energetic attention by generations of anglicists' (Lightfoot 1991: 90). As we stated in the introduction it was indeed the traditional belief that the increase of the *to*-infinitive in the Middle English period was due to the fact that the marker *to* was added to the bare infinitive in order to characterize it clearly as an infinitive (the bare form had become opaque due to the general loss of inflections). However, evidence has been building up in the past few years that the *to-* and the bare infinitive remained semantically and syntactically distinct (cf. Fischer 1995, 1996b, 1997b), and that the sharp increase in the use of the *to*-infinitive must be linked with the decrease in the use of *that*-clauses rather than a decrease in bare infinitives (cf. Los 1998).

Some concluding remarks. We have oversimplified the development somewhat here, because it is clear that there must have been further contributory factors. One may have been the ambiguity arising through the fact that the bare infinitive cannot always be distinguished from finite forms, connected with the fact that the complementizer *that* could be left out.[16] Another factor, which we return to below, was the use of the reflexive pronoun as the 'accusative' NP. But the point still stands that the Latin AcI's could only be taken into the language successfully because their bed had been prepared, so to speak.[17] They no longer represented a construction alien to the language system. Once causatives and object-control verbs had developed passive AcI's, there was nothing really that could stop the Latin-type AcI from entering, since the structure was already there. No such cosy bed had been prepared for the construction in Dutch, to which we will now turn.

7.3   Borrowing and internal factors: the Latin AcI in the history of Dutch

We have so far concentrated on the grammatical factors leading to the establishment of the Latin-type AcI structure (especially the word order

---

[16] I.e. in examples such as,

  I deeme anon this cherl his servant have   (Chaucer *Physician* 199)
it is not always clear whether a finite or a non-finite clause is intended because *have* could be infinitive as well as subjunctive. For more details, see Fischer (1989: 168–74).

[17] Harris and Campbell (1995) show that it is not necessarily the case that borrowed structures must fit into the borrowing language: 'contrary to opinions expressed by many, borrowing and language contact can introduce structures to a language which are not harmonious with existing structures' (p. 150). They write that 'given enough time and intensity of contact, virtually anything can (ultimately) be borrowed' (p. 149). It does seem, however, that syntactic borrowing is subject to stricter constraints than lexical borrowing, i.e. that the contact either has to be more intensive or that the new structure has to harmonize with existing structure for borrowing to be possible. In the case of Latin, harmony is likely to be a necessary condition since the contact situation only applied to the very small part of the population familiar with Latin.

change and analogical extension). We will now consider the role of Latin more closely. Many linguists in the past have considered the introduction of the Latin-type AcI into English a case of pure borrowing (see, for instance, Krickau 1877: 4, 34; Jespersen 1905: 127; Mustanoja 1960: 526–7; Scheler 1961: 92 ff.; Lightfoot 1981b). It is therefore of some interest to tease apart the grammatical causes of the change from external causal factors such as borrowing from Latin. In this section we will consider in some more detail the development in Dutch, since Dutch did not share the rigidification of VO word order that English underwent in the period of the introduction of the AcI, while, at the same time, the influence of Latin was as strong as it was in English, and indeed a Latin-type AcI is found in Dutch during the medieval, and especially the Renaissance period. We will first explore the role played in Dutch by the factors discussed above for English. Does the path of the AcI resemble that of 'least saliency' or 'minimal alteration', discovered in the Middle English Latin-influenced writings by Warner (1982)? Does the passive infinitive play a role as in English? Was analogical extension of any importance? An answer to these questions will help us to find out more about the relation between internal and external factors, and may enable us to constrain the factor of borrowing in syntactic change.

Fischer (1994b) studied the types of AcI used in Middle Dutch and seventeenth-century Dutch.[18] Both native AcI's (after physical perception verbs and causatives, i.e. the ones that occur in native Old English as well) and Latinate ones (after the *verba cogitandi et declarandi*) were found. In Middle Dutch, however, most AcI's were of the native type. Some examples are given in (34).

(34)   a. Gheselle   Roelant, nu   moogdi hier merken enen wijch gescien
           companion Roelant now can-you here see   a   battle happen
           'my friend Roelant, now you can see a battle taking place here'
                                                                                       (Stoett 1923: 128)

          b. Hi sach mi driven groot misbaer
              he saw me make   great clamour
              'He saw me making a great outcry'   (*Rein.*II,4416, *MNW* VII: 1077)

---

[18] For more information on the data, see Fischer (1994b). The Middle Dutch data are from secondary sources, such as Stoett (1923), the Dictionary of Middle Dutch (*MNW*) and the OED-type dictionary of Dutch (*WNT*). For the seventeenth century were used: extracts from Hooft's *Nederlandsche Historien* (1642), a history of the Netherlands written in the style of Tacitus' *Annales*; three grammars of seventeenth-century Dutch, van Helten (1883), Overdiep (1935) and Koelmans (1978); and the *WNT*.

c. Over hondert milen daer wetic   enen wilden wenen . . .
   over hundred miles there know-I a   wild   live
   'I know [by experience] where a wild man lives a hundred miles away'
                                             (*Wal.* 5938, *MNW* IX: 2383)

These native AcI's are recognizable (as in Old English; cf. 7.2.2) by the nature of the matrix verb (perception verbs and causatives); the absence of *te* (the cognate of *to*) preceding the infinitive; the frequent preference for the present participle over the infinitive; the presence (usually) of a locative phrase; the simultaneity of the actions expressed by the matrix verb and the infinitive; and the concreteness of the activity expressed by the infinitive. Note that (34c) with the matrix verb *weten* (a cognate of OE *witan*) is similar to the OE *witan* examples discussed in (18). When we look at some of the Latinate AcIs found in Middle Dutch, as in (35), we see that these indeed do not share the above characteristics.

(35)   a. Si vinden di te wesen een haven des vreden
          'They find you to be a harbour of (the) peace'   (Stoett 1923: 137)
     b. Een jonglinc dien   wi horen geboren zijn van   Ragusia
        a   youth   whom we hear born   be from Ragusa
        'A youth of whom we hear that he was born in Ragusa'
                 (Stoett 1923: 136; also in Duinhoven 1991: Franc 8637)
     c. Si   kennen di   te sijn die camer eens machtigen meesters
        they know   you to be the servant of-a powerful   master
        'They know that you are the servant of a powerful lord'
                            (Stoett 1923: 129)

In these examples the infinitive is usually preceded by *te*; it does not convey any concrete activity (in fact, the verb usually is the Dutch equivalent of *to be*); present participle constructions are as good as absent; and when a perception verb is used, as in (35b), the action expressed in the infinitive is not perceivable and not in the same temporal frame as the matrix verb. In other words, the two types seem to be structurally different.

The same is true for the AcI examples from seventeenth-century Dutch. In the data examined, there is a sharp division between the native AcIs, which are very common, and the Latinate AcIs, which are rare. What is striking in the Latinate examples from both Middle and Renaissance Dutch is that the factors identified by Warner (1982) for AcIs in Middle English are observed here too. Warner found that the AcI occurs very often in constructions that show a 'minimal alteration' of existing structures. Thus, it occurs often in constructions in which the accusative NP has been moved (e.g. in passive constructions like (36d), cases of topicalization or heavy NP movement as in

(36a) or wh-movement as in (35b) and (36c)), and as an expansion of a NP PREDICATE construction by means of the verb *sijn/wesen* 'to be', as in (35a, c) and (36b, c).[19] Some examples showing these parameters from Renaissance Dutch are given in (36).

(36)   a. In dus   een zee van zorgen, vernam   zij, onder 't   volk   gezaaid
        in thus a   sea of worries perceived she under the people sown
        te zijn zeker   boek, getiteld . . .
        to be   certain book entitled
        'Thus surrounded by worries, she learned that a certain book, entitled . . .
        had been dispersed among the people'
                            (Hooft *Historien* a.1581, Nijhoff 1947 [1978]: 311)
        b. Men   waande   hen   opgeruid te zijn door Rennenbergh . . .
        one [people] considered them instigated to be by   Rennenbergh
        'They were considered to be instigated by Rennenbergh . . .'
                            (Hooft *Historien*, Nijhoff 1947 [1978]: 269)
        c. 'T geen ghy in andren meynt bestraffelijck te wesen
        which you in others think punishable   to be
        'Which you consider to deserve punishment in others'
                            (van Helten 1883: 53)
        d. Al hunne goederen werden verklaard, aan den koning, vervallen te
        all their goods   were   declared   to the king   forfeited to
        zijn
        be
        'All their goods were declared to be the property of the king'
                            (Hooft *Historien*, Nijhoff 1947 [1978]: 79)

The Latinate AcI is frequent in two other types of syntactic constructions. In the first, the 'accusative' NP is a reflexive pronoun (37a). This was also found by Warner (1982: 144), but not considered to be significant since it only occurred with two verbs. The second is a construction with *men*, as in (37b, c) and also (36b), and is not found in Middle English, since Old English *man* had, by late Middle English, been replaced mainly by passives.

(37)   a. Den 1   May gisten   ons ontrent 8 mylen buyten de Oostelyckste
        the 1st May guessed us about   8 miles outside the most-eastern
        eylanden van Macou te wesen
        islands   of Macou to be
        'The 1st of May [we] guessed (ourselves) to be about 8 miles away from
        the most eastern isles of Macou'   (Bontekoe 88/23, Overdiep 1935: 408)
        b. Men   kan immers niet gelooven al gantsch Israel soo puyr sot
        'Man' can indeed not believe   all whole   Israel so pure foolish
        te zijn gheweest
        to be been

---

[19] For more details, see tables 1 and 2 in Fischer (1994b).

'Indeed it cannot be believed that all of Israel would have been so utterly foolish'   (Coornhert 1,46, *WNT* IV, 1271)

c. Men   hiet   my doe ter   tijt   geluckigh te wesen
'Man' called me then in-the time happy   to be
'People considered me happy in those days'
(Florian, Ovid.Hersch 227, *WNT* VI, 406)

It is clear in these two latter construction types that Warner's 'minimal alteration hypothesis' does not work, because the 'accusative' NP appears in its base
generated position, and should therefore be considered 'awkward' for both the
Middle English and the Dutch grammatical system. Indeed, the instances in
(37) are syntactically quite salient. Notice, however, that semantically they are
on a par with, for instance, the passive construction types in that the accusative
NPs in (37) do not constitute an *additional* NP argument in semantic terms.
Thus, the reflexive pronoun has the same referent as the matrix subject NP,
and in the *men*-construction the matrix predicate is to all intents and purposes
passive, because *men* has no reference to any semantic entity. So it looks as if
the Latinate AcI crops up in Latin-influenced texts in both Middle English and
Dutch in contexts where it is least salient. Nevertheless, the Latin AcI does not
gain a real foothold in Dutch: the older Dutch instances given above are no
longer possible in Modern Dutch.

There are, furthermore, two notable differences between the use of the
Latinate AcI in older Dutch and in Middle English. First of all, no instances
were found of object-control verbs followed by an AcI construction in Dutch,
a fairly common phenomenon in Middle English, as we saw above (cf. (31)).
Secondly, the passive infinitive does not really play a role in the spread of the
AcI as it was seen to have done in Middle English. Only three examples in all
were found with a passive infinitive (with the verb *worden* in Dutch). Two
instances occur after the verb *geloven* 'to believe', and one after the causative
verb *maken*:

(38)   a. van soo vreught haetende gemoet dat hij niet gelooft hadde in
of so joy   hating   mind   that he not believed had   in
de gantsche werelt gevonden te werden
the whole   world found   to be
'of a nature that so abhorred joy that he had not believed it could be
found anywhere in the world'   (Bat.Arc.71.4; Overdiep 1935: 410)

b. en   desen sotten en onsinnigen mensch, ghelooft sulcx door
and this   foolish and mad   man,   believes such through
sijne woorden verricht te worden
his words   achieved to be
'and this foolish and mad human being believes that this can be brought
about by his words'   (Koelmans 1978:35)

c. Ick . . . salse . . .   maken verstroyt te worden
I   shall them make   dispersed to be
'I shall cause them to be dispersed'   (Ezech.6, Kantt.11, *WNT* IX,123)

The example in (38c) is especially interesting because it occurs with a caus-ative. Since in Dutch SOV structures were retained in subordinate clauses, the old active type of infinitive construction, common also in Old English (cf. (21i b and 21ii b)), remained the rule, and indeed we usually find the active infinitive there all through the history of Dutch. Thus, (38c) would be in Modern Dutch:

(38′)   c. Ik zal ze laten (= maken) verstrooien
            'I will them let disperse'

An example from seventeenth century Dutch is given in (39).

(39)   De welke [de preek]   geeindigd zijnde; deed hij den brief ter
        which   [the sermon] ended   being   did he the letter from-the
        stoel   aflezen
        pulpit off-read
        'And after it had ended, he let the letter be read from the pulpit'
                                          (Hooft *Historien,* Nijhoff 1947 [1978]: 180)

The evidence from Dutch thus seems to suggest quite strongly that the strat-egy of least salience by itself was not sufficient to gain the Latinate AcI a foot-hold in the language. The extra NP argument that the Latin construction introduced before the infinitive remained an awkward element, apparently even when put in a less awkward position. The data from Dutch and English rather seem to show that the borrowing of a foreign construction was made possible ultimately by (the changes in) the syntactic structure of the receiving language, and that therefore, although internal and external factors were both responsible for the introduction of this AcI, it is the internal grammatical factors in this case of change which play the more crucial role.

Reconsidering the factors promoting the acceptance of the ECM in English, we find that a chain of changes was set in motion by the word order change (involving the constructions given in (3i, 3ii), involving reanalysis and analogical extension of the infinitival construction after causatives and per-ception verbs, and of the *(for) NP to V* construction. The influence from Latin was present all along, but only became effective when the syntactic structures of English had been altered in such a way that Latin AcI's resembled the new native AcI's. This case also suggests that for borrowing on the syntactic level, length and intensity of contact alone may not be sufficient. Linguists rather differ in their opinions on how permeable the syntactic level is compared to other (phonological, lexical) levels of language. Birnbaum (1984: 34), for instance, believes that the syntactic component is as susceptible to foreign elements as the lexical component (see also note 17), and cf. also Danchev (1984: 50), who voices a similar opinion. Others support the conclusion drawn here (e.g. Bock 1931: 116; Sørensen 1957: 133; Aitchison 1991: 114–17; Mithun 1992).

Appendix A (all appendices are taken from Fischer 1992b)

Verb (cat. in Visser)	corpus	full verb	subject constr. an.	subject constr. in-an.	Ø inf	to inf	for to inf	ing	object constr.	V + NP + inf	V + inf + NP cl.	V + inf + NP rest	NP + V + inf pron	NP + V + inf wh topic	Ø inf	to inf	for to inf	pure inf	pass. inf subj. constr.
bid[2] / IV + VIII	Br	36	24		23	1			2	2					x			7	1
	CA	60	67		47	14	6		11	4		6		1	9	1	1		
	PL	5	24		23	1													
	MA	2	21		18	3													
do / II	Br	376	7		x														
	CA	531	33	5	13	12	13		19	6	2	5	2	4	x				1
	PL	829	20		14	5	1		56	5	1	48		2	x				10
	MA[4]	1446	7		1	6			6[3]			6			x				
cause / II	CA	13	2		x				1			1					x	1	
	PL	8	58	3		58	3		1			1					x		16
	MA	16	35		x				1			1						1	3
haten / VIII	Br	11	32		x				11	4		6		1	x				
	CA	1	all other instances of 'hoten' in CA involve the meaning 'to be called'																	
let / II + V	Br	9	33	15	x				96	23	4	50	19		x			9	1
	CA[4]	20	24	37	60	1			32	7	2	16	1	6	x			2	6
	PL	11	213	13	225	1			9			9			x				42
	MA	23	216	13	x				149		25	119		5	x			26	19
make / II	Br	122																	
	CA	503	93	13	62	27	17		3	3					x			1	2
	PL	574	36		10	26													3
	MA	906	119	3	23	96	3		13		1	12			5	8			19
suffer / V	CA	42	13	2	7	7	1												1
	PL	—	13	1	x														2
	MA	55	76		x													2	9
hear / I	Br	71	1		x				12	2	6		3	1	x				
	CA	286[5]	29	3	29	1		2	31	3	9	2	7	10	x				
	PL	41[5]	6		x				26	1	18	1		6	x				
	MA	158[5]	65	4	x				35		27			8	x				
see / I	Br	49	9	(1)	x				1?						x				
	CA	390	46	29	67	1?		16	4						x				5
	PL	126	2		1			1											2
	MA	709	175	23	171	4		23											4

Notes to Appendix A:

[1] This category contains the following subtypes indicated by square brackets:
[a] equivocal between a subject and object construction, i.e., the verb may be transitive as well as intransitive;
[b] equivocal between an imperative and a bare-infinitive subject construction; [c] hybrid of the type: *she hath do slain him, I have herd you seid* with a past participle instead of the expected infinitive; [d] equivocal between periphrastic and emphatic *do* and in some cases also causative *do* (if the latter, the construction would be an object construction); [e] equivocal between a bare-infinitive subject construction and a (*that*)-clause; [f] hybrid of the type: *he now late toke Roger Cherche* with a past tense form instead of the expected infinitive; [g] equivocal between a bare-infinitive object construction and a construction with a past participle.

Ø inf	to inf	for to inf	past partic.	verb +NP obj. +adj.	that cl.	NP+ that cl.	(that) cl.	NP+ (that) cl.	how cl.	NP+ how cl.	wh-/if cl.	NP+ wh/if cl.	pro-verb DO	hybrid/ equivocal[1]	second pass.	imperative
	x			28	22	10								1[a]		1
					2											
						6										
						1								3[b]		2
													26			
x					2								91	2[c]	1	
1	9												227	3[c]	1	
							1						189	41[d]		
			1		1											
	15	1	1	1	1	2										
x						1		2								
					3	3										
x			1											9[a]		
x														7[a]		
41	1		1											4[f]		
														2[a, g]		
				24												
1		1	4	111	5?	2?								4[a]	4(1)	
	x		2	56												
	x		6	201	1?									4[g]	3	
x				2							1					
	x														1	
	x						1									
					4	13			1	3	1	1				
		1			2		2		13	4	16			5[c]		
		1							1		1					
					13		1		8		4			8[a]	1	
					6	1				2	2	2		1[a]		
3	2		20	39 (15)[6]	26		28	1	23	6	24	4		9[a]		
x			10	4 (1)[6]	24	1?	1		2		4					
	x		63	26	66	3	50		66		3			3[c, e]	1?	

Notes to Appendix A (cont.)

[2] The count does not include *bid* in the sense of 'to say one's prayers'.

[3] All these examples are marked by an *extra* causative verb.

[4] Combinations of *let* and *do* are also found. In *Gower* there are fifteen examples of constructions with *let do*; in *Malory* there are three examples of constructions with *do let*.

[5] Instances of *to hear of* are not included. In *Gower* and the *Paston Letters* I have not counted the bare infinitive form here. This would have taken too much time since this form is also used for the personal pronoun *her* and the place adverb *here*.

[6] The instances in brackets represent examples with present participles instead of adjectives.

Appendix B

Verb (cat. in Visser)	cor-pus	full verb	subject constr. an.	subject constr. in-an.	Ø inf	to inf	for to inf	ing	ob-ject con-str.	V + NP + inf	V + inf + NP cl.	V + inf + NP rest	NP + V + inf pron	NP + V + inf wh topic	Ø inf	to inf	for to inf	pure inf	pass. inf subj. constr.
ask IV	Br	13																	
	CA	79						2	2							1	1	2	
	PL	66																8	1
	MA	157	1			x													
charge VIII	CA	3	2			x													
	PL	14	8			x													1
	MA	12	13			x												1	
command VIII	CA	5	2			x												2	
	PL	12	22			18	4		1			1					x		1
	MA	33	43	1?		42	2		2			2					x		5
desire VI	CA	33							3	1		1	1			1	2	6	
	PL	32	48			x			19		3	13	3			x		15	4
	MA	30	6			x			11			9	2			x		12	
grant V	CA	30	3			x	x											1	
	PL	43	7			x			7			6	1			x			1
	MA	46	4			x			3			3				x		3	
license V	PL	1	2			x												1	1
order VIII			does not occur as such in any text, in the PL only in the sense of 'arrange'																
ordain IV	CA	48	2			1	1												
	PL	14	1	1		x													1
	MA	34	5	1?		x			3			3				1	2		
pray[2] IV	CA	69	18			13	5		4	1	2	1				x		5	
	PL	13	120			117	3		5		2	3				4	1		
	MA	28	132			127	5												
require IV	PL	20	6			x													1
	MA	32	39			38	1		1			1				x			1
warn XI	CA	7																	
	PL	9	6			x													2
	MA	22	3			x													

Notes to Appendix B:

[1] This category contains the following subtypes indicated by square brackets:
   [a] equivocal between an imperative and a bare-infinitive subject construction;
   [b] equivocal between an imperative, a bare-infinitive subject construction, and a *(that)*-clause;
   [c] hybrid: *that*-clause and *to*-infinitive combined;
   [d] hybrid: combination of the infinitival marker *to* and a finite verbal form;
   [e] equivocal between an imperative and a bare-infinitive object construction;
   [f] hybrid of the type: *I prey to Jesu preserve you and yours.*

[2] The count does not include *pray* in the sense of 'to say one's prayers'.

[3] The NP *God* or *to God* is frequently found as a kind of interjection between *pray* and the clause.

Ø inf	to inf	for to inf	past partic.	verb +NP obj. +adj.	that cl.	NP+ that cl.	(that) cl.	NP+ (that) cl.	how cl.	NP+ how cl.	wh-/ if cl.	NP+ wh/ if cl.	proverb DO	hybrid/ equivocal[1]	second pass.	imperative
				1					1		1	2				
					4				2	6	26	19				
	x									2	2	22				
					1	2			3	11	29	117				
						3										
	x					11	1							1[a]	5	(1)
					2	20								7[a, b]	1	1
					2	1										
		x			1	4								1[c]	3	
	x				8	3									4	
	x				13	18	1	4						1[d]	2	
					2	2						1			1	
					2	1	3									
	x				6	1								1[c]		
					1	1		1			1					
	x															
					7						2				1	
	x				5											
					4	1		1			1				6	
					29	33	8	1		1				8[a, c]		1
					9³	145	8	1						331[a, b e, f]		2
					6³	44	3							97[a, b f]		2
	x					7								1[a]	2	
	x					18								43[a, b]	2	
						3				1						
	x					3									2	2
						10		13		1						1

Appendix C

Verb (cat. in Visser)	corpus	no. (if lim)[1]	type of inf.			predicate			clause					aci	type	instances found
			∅	to	for to	adj.	p.p.	NP	that	(that)	if	how	wh-			
accord XI	CA			x					x			x	x			
	PL								x			x				
	MA								x							
adventure VI	CA	2		x	x											
	PL	1												1	p. inf.[2]	156,8
	MA	3		x												
affirm XI	CA								x							
	PL					x			x					1	refl.	2.4-5
allege XI	CA															
	PL													2	p. inf.[2]	252,20, 253,35
assure XI	CA			x					x							
	MA			x					x							
avaunt XI	CA								x							
	PL	2														
believe IX	CA			1					x							
	PL								x							
	MA								x							
comprehend IX	CA															
	PL															
condemn XI	PL	1														

confirm	CA	3														
XI	PL	1														
	MA	3						x								
covet VI	CA															
declare	CA											x	x			
XI	PL								x					1	p. inf.[2]	60,59
deem	CA								x		x		x	1	ambig.[2]	8: 1948
XI	PL			1			x		x	x			x	1	ambig.[2]	300,18
	MA			x		x		x	x	x						
deny XI	PL	2														
devise	CA			x								x	x			
XI	PL															
	MA								x				x			
dread	CA								x							
VII	PL															
	MA			x					x	x				3	refl. p.	142,33; 299,4; 307,8
guess IX	CA					x							x			
hold	CA					x	x	x								
IX	PL					x	x	x								
	MA					x	x	x	x				x			
judge	CA	2														
IX	PL	1														
	MA							x						1	p. inf.[2]	1173,5
know	CA					x			x	x	x	x	x			
IX	PL					x	x	x	x	x	x	x	x	1		260,13
	MA					x[4]		x[5]	x	x		x	x			

Appendix C (cont.)

Verb (cat. in Visser)	corpus	no. (if lim)[1]	∅	to	for to	adj.	p.p.	NP	that	(that)	if	how	wh-	aci	type	instances found
(ac)knowledge IX	PL	4		2			x		x			x		1		118,2
pretend XI	PL	3		2												
prove XI	CA					x			x	x			x			
	PL					x			x	x				1	ambig.[3]	8,32
	MA		x			x			x	x			x			
say XI[6]	CA								x	x		x	x			
	PL			x					x	x	x		x	1	p. inf.[2]	97,21
	MA			x					x	x		x	x			
suppose IX	CA								x	x			x	1	ambig.[3]	8: 1236
	PL			x					x	x				2	ambig.[3]	77,145; 273,9
	MA			x					x	x						
surmise IX	MA	1														
think IX	CA		x	x	x	x	x		x	x		x	x			
	PL			x	x	x	x		x	x		x	x			
	MA			x	x	x			x	x			x			
trow IX	CA								x	x				1	ambig.[3]	5: 1888
	PL			x					x	x				1	ambig.[3]	354a.12
	MA								x	x				1	ambig.[3]	279,3
trust IX	CA															
	PL								x	x						
	MA			x	x				x	x						

																Count	Ambig.	References
understand IX	CA										×	×		×					
	PL				×		×		×	×	×	×	×	×					
	MA						×		×	×	×	×	×	×	×		2	ambig.[3]	380,9; 1212,20
ween IX	CA	×	×	×	×					×	×						5	ambig.[3]	1: 502; 1603; 2607 5: 439 8: 1511
	PL	×	×																
	MA		×						×	×	×								
wit IX	CA				×				×	×	×		×	×	×		1	ambig.[3]	465,20
	PL								×	×	×	×	×	×	×		1		2: 259
	MA		×		×				×	×	×	×	×	×	×				

Notes to Appendix C:

[1] If no number is given in this category it is implied that the verb in question appears a fair number of times in each given corpus. When all the categories are left blank for a given verb, the verb appears with or without a NP object but never with any type of clausal (finite or non-finite) complement.

[2] p. inf. = passive infinitive.

[3] ambig. = the construction is ambiguous. This means that the construction may be interpreted as an aci or otherwise; e.g., as a subjunctive with the complementiser *that* left out, as a tertiary infinitive, etc.

[4] Only with the adjective *lywyng*.

[5] Only with *for NP*.

[6] *Say* occurs in addition with clausal complements introduced by NP *that*, *(un)to* NP *that*, NP *(that)* and with indirect speech.

8

The history of the 'easy-to-please' construction

8.1 Introduction

In this chapter we consider in detail the history of a specific construction, the so-called 'easy-to-please' construction or 'tough' movement. Some modern examples are (1)–(3).

(1)   John was easy to convince.

(2)   The problem was tough to deal with.

(3)   He is hard to get a straight answer from.

In each of (1)–(3), there is a sequence of an adjective plus an infinitival clause which is predicated on a noun phrase. The infinitival clause contains a non-subject gap (in (1), the gap functions as direct object, in (2) and (3) as complement of a preposition), and the noun phrase in the superordinate clause provides the interpretation for this gap. Thus in (1), the speaker is talking about convincing John, not someone else, and (2) and (3) are about dealing with the problem and getting a straight answer from him, respectively. Although (1)–(3) all have the relevant NP functioning as subject of the verb *be*, this is not a necessary characteristic of the construction. Instead of *be*, the verb may also be another copula, like *seem*, *appear*, *turn out* or *become*, and there are also examples like (4).

(4)   I consider Mary impossible to get along with.

In this sentence, although there is no copula between the noun phrase *Mary* and the sequence adjective–*to*-infinitive, it is nevertheless common practice to say that there is a subject–predicate relation holding between *Mary* and *impossible to get along with* (in terms of the analysis of Stowell 1981, 1983 and a great deal of subsequent work, the two elements would form a small clause). If we adopt this view, we can say that the 'easy-to-please' construction, as manifested in all of (1)–(4), has as its essential characteristic that it consists of a subject followed by a predicate formed by an adjective plus an infinitival clause with a non-subject gap. The interpretation of this gap is provided by the subject.

Although this construction as such is attested from the Old English period to the present day, two major changes in its surface manifestations can be traced over the centuries. One of these changes concerns the status of the non-subject gap in the infinitival clause, and its exact relation to the subject NP (as we shall see, this can be interpreted as reflecting a change in the nature of the movement processes operative in the construction) and the second change concerns the form of the infinitive in the subordinate clause (active, as in (1)–(4), or passive, which is no longer allowed in present-day English but was in earlier English).

After presenting the empirical data showing these different changes, we shall discuss in detail the appropriate analysis for the data and the possible reasons for the changes that they manifest, emphasizing their relation with other syntactic changes in English. As a preliminary to these historical matters, we will begin by briefly reviewing some of the basic issues which loom large in theoretical analyses of the construction in present-day English and which will also inform our discussion of the historical data.

8.2   Theoretical issues in the analysis of 'easy-to-please'

In the generative literature on 'easy-to-please' in present-day English, the general view is that the construction instantiates wh-movement (or, to use the more general term, A-bar movement). That is, it is assumed that the sentence in (1) has a basic structure as in (5).

(5) $John_i$ was $[_{AP}$ easy $[_{CP}$ OP_i $[_{IP}$ PRO to convince $t_i]]]$

The adjective *easy* takes a clausal CP complement with a specifier position filled by the empty operator OP, which can be regarded as the non-overt counterpart to an overt wh-phrase. OP has moved to the specifier of CP from the object position inside the embedded IP, leaving a trace; a further mechanism ensures that the matrix subject NP *John* is interpreted as supplying the referential value of the operator, expressed in (5) by coindexation of the two elements. The subject position of the embedded infinitival clause is filled by the non-overt pronoun PRO, which in this case has an arbitrary interpretation.

Various distributional arguments for assuming a structure as in (5) have been put forward by Chomsky (1977), who first proposed the wh-analysis of 'easy-to-please', and Chomsky (1981, 1982), Browning (1987), Foldvik (1989), Massam (1992) and Mulder and den Dikken (1992), who have further developed it. One such argument concerns the variety of functions that the non-subject gap in the infinitival clause can have. To see this, consider the schematic representations of (1), (2) and (3) given in (6), (7) and (8). In (6), the gap, represented by a trace, is in direct object position, in (7) it is contained within a prepositional phrase that is adjacent to the verb, and in (8) the prepositional phrase containing the trace is separated from the verb by an intervening object NP.

(6)   NP$_i$ be Adj   [to V   t$_i$]   structure of (1)

(7)   NP$_i$ be Adj   [to V   P t$_i$]   structure of (2)

(8)   NP$_i$ be Adj   [to V   NP P t$_i$]   structure of (3)

In determining the nature of the gaps in (6)–(8), a choice needs to be made between NP-movement (or A-movement) and wh-movement (A-bar movement), since these are the two main types of movement that can be responsible for a gap in complement position. Now the structures in (6) and (7) might be the result of NP-movement: examples (9) and (10), corresponding to sentences (1) and (2), show that the structures [V t] and [V P t] can arise in passives, which are unambiguous instantiations of NP-movement.

(9)   John$_i$ was finally convinced t$_i$ by our arguments.

(10)   The problem$_i$ has been dealt with t$_i$.

However, in 2.6 we noted that, with the exception of a number of idiomatic expressions such as *to take advantage of* and *to keep tabs on*, the sequence [V NP P t] which we find in (8) is not possible in passives: there is nothing like (11) corresponding to (3).

(11)   *He$_i$ was not got a straight answer from t$_i$.

Under the standard generative analysis of passive (see Chomsky 1981, van Riemsdijk 1982 and Baker, Johnson and Roberts 1989), the past participle in (9) and (10) would be said to absorb the Case that, in the active counterpart, would be assigned to the internal argument. Hence in (9) and (10) the internal argument (*John, The problem*) moves to the subject position to receive Case. Note that in (10), the phrase *dealt with* appears to function as a unit with respect to Case assignment, perhaps through reanalysis of verb + preposition into a single verb (see Hornstein and Weinberg 1981) or some equivalent like incorporation of the preposition into the verb; whatever the exact mechanism is, the result is that the internal argument *The problem* has to move to the subject position to receive Case. In (11), the process of reanalysis/incorporation is blocked by the presence of the intervening NP *a straight answer*, and movement of the NP *He* is therefore disallowed (technically, it would result in a doubly Case-marked NP, which is forbidden).

If we want to classify the examples of 'easy-to-please' in (1)–(3), with their configurations as in (6)–(8), under one type of movement process, NP-movement does not appear to be a good candidate, since it cannot account for all of the data. It would predict a split between (6) and (7) on the one hand and (8) on the other, but the 'easy-to-please' construction shows no such split. The wh-analysis given in (5) does not face this problem, since wh-movement, whether of an overt wh-phrase or of an empty operator, does not correlate with Case absorption and is therefore not blocked by an intervening object NP. As the simple examples in (12)–(14) show, wh-movement can indeed yield all three configurations shown in (6)–(8).[1]

(12)   Who$_i$ did you convince t$_i$?

(13)   Who$_i$ did you deal with t$_i$?

(14)   Who$_i$ did you get a straight answer from t$_i$?

A further distributional argument for assuming that the 'easy-to-please' construction in present-day English features wh-movement is the possibility of 'long' movement, whereby the gap is located in a more deeply embedded clause, as shown in (15) and (16).[2]

(15)   John will be easy [OP$_i$ to convince Bill to do business with t$_i$].

(16)   A book like that is tough [OP$_i$ to claim you've read carefully t$_i$].

These more deeply embedded structures can again be paralleled in unambiguous wh-tokens like (17) and (18).

(17)   Who$_i$ did you convince Bill to do business with t$_i$?

(18)   What book$_i$ did he claim he'd read t$_i$ carefully?

A final piece of evidence that has been adduced in favour of the wh-analysis is the fact that 'easy-to-please' can license a parasitic gap (pg), as in (19).

(19)   This book is difficult OP$_i$ to understand t$_i$ without reading pg carefully.

---

[1] Although it allows all three configurations [$_{VP}$ V (NP) (P) t], this is not to say that wh-movement is completely free of restrictions; see Hornstein and Weinberg (1981) for descriptive details.

[2] The evidence of these sentence types is not crystal-clear. Some writers confidently label examples like this 'fully acceptable', but others call them 'not completely unacceptable', 'marginal' or even 'ungrammatical'. See van der Wurff (1990b: 65–6) for a review of the different opinions.

Here the gap t_i following the verb *understand* is the result of moving OP_i, just as in (5), but the verb *reading* in the adjunct clause also has an object gap. Parasitic gaps like this can occur under certain conditions if a sentence features an instance of wh-movement, as in (20). NP-movement, as in the passive in (21), does not license parasitic gaps.

(20)   What report$_i$ did they file t_i without reading pg carefully?

(21)   *This report$_i$ was filed t_i without reading pg carefully.

Using parasitic gaps as a diagnostic for the type of movement that a 'real' gap is due to, we may conclude from the presence of the parasitic gap in (19) that 'easy-to-please' must indeed be an instance of wh-movement.[3]

The present-day English evidence therefore suggests that (5) gives a reasonable representation of the structure of the infinitival clause in the 'easy-to-please' construction.

(5)   John$_i$ was [$_{AP}$ easy [$_{CP}$ OP$_i$ [$_{IP}$ PRO to convince t_i]]]

What remains a thorny issue is the status of the matrix subject in this construction, i.e. *John* in (5). The point is that the relevant adjectives (the members of what may be labelled the *easy*-class of adjectives) can also take a dummy subject *it,* as in (22).

(22)   It was easy to convince John.

In other cases, such as that of the verb *seem,* as given in (23) and (24), the possibility of having the dummy subject *it* is generally taken to show that the predicate does not theta-mark its subject.

(23)   It seems John has eaten all the bread.

(24)   John seems to have eaten all the bread.

According to the theta-criterion of Chomsky (1981), a noun phrase, and also a chain consisting of a moved NP and its trace(s), must have one and only one theta-role, i.e. it should have one of the roles AGENT, THEME, RECIPIENT, etc., but not two of them. The dummy subject *it,* however, as its name implies, does not need a theta-role. A sentence like (23) is therefore taken to show that *seem* does not assign a theta-role to its subject. Hence, it is standardly assumed that in (24) *John* has moved into the matrix subject position from the position of the subject of the infinitival clause, which has a theta-role (specifically, the

---

[3] Since we are only using parasitic gaps as a diagnostic to decide between NP-movement and wh-movement, we merely note that (19) patterns with (20) rather than (21), leaving aside the precise analysis and status of parasitic gaps (they are often felt to result in sentences that are less than perfect). For various ideas and suggestions, see Chomsky (1982, 1986) and references given there.

role of agent assigned by *(have) eaten)*. In (24), there is therefore movement from a theta-position to a non-theta-position, creating a chain with one theta-role, which is fine. But if in (5) *John* is base-generated as matrix subject, where does it get its theta-role from? The possibility of having dummy *it* as subject, as in (22), suggests that *easy (to convince)* does not theta-mark its subject.

At the present stage, some scholars maintain that in (5) the adjective does theta-mark its subject position (see for example Bennis 1990, Wilder 1991). This of course leaves us with the question why in (5) the predicate assigns a theta-role, while in (22) it does not. Other scholars assume that the pair (5) and (22) should, as far as possible, be dealt with in the same way as the pair (23) and (24). This means that, for (5), they have to appeal to some special mechanism to combine or join the wh-chain (OP_i, t_i) with the main clause subject *John*, in order to provide *John* with a theta-role (for specific proposals, see Chomsky 1981: 308–10, Browning 1987, Foldvik 1989 and Massam 1992).

These then are some of the issues and considerations that have informed the (generative) discussion about the structure of the 'easy-to-please' construction. As we shall see in the following sections, the same kinds of considerations again play a role when it comes to determining the structure of the 'easy-to-please' construction and related phenomena as they existed in Old and Middle English.

8.3   Data and analysis for Old English

Since the 'easy-to-please' construction is much less frequent than some of the constructions discussed in the preceding chapters, we need to tread carefully in making descriptive generalizations about it. It is therefore necessary to devote some special attention here to empirical matters (though this is of course nothing unusual in dealing with historical data, as the general remarks in 1.3 and the case studies in the earlier chapters will have made abundantly clear). The material to be discussed in this section is drawn from van der Wurff (1992a), which reports on the results of a search through the Old English microfiche concordance of Healey and Venezky (1980) for combinations of an adjective with an infinitival clause. Since this concordance contains all Old English texts that have survived, and since the search through it was designed to be exhaustive, we can be fairly confident that what we are looking at is all that there is to look at in the way of Old English 'easy-to-please' examples.[4] The problem is to draw from the limited material the

---

[4] Earlier collections of data can be found in Callaway (1913), van der Gaaf (1928) and Visser (1963–73: §§ 940, 1388). The empirical investigation carried out in van der Wurff (1992a) was explicitly designed to supersede these rather spotty collections.

correct descriptive generalizations about the construction in the grammar of Old English, and to propose a structural analysis incorporating these generalizations.

Among the 286 attested Old English examples with an adjective combined with an infinitival clause which has a non-subject gap, there are 46 that feature an adjective with the meaning 'easy', 'hard' or 'difficult'. A complete list, with the number of attestations in the 'easy-to-please' construction, is given in (25) and three example sentences are provided in (26)–(28).

(25)   adjective   'easy-to-please' tokens

earfoð   15
earfoðlic   3
eaðe   12
uneaðe   4
eaðelic   5
hefig   2
hefigtyme   3
leoht   2

(26)   þæt him wære eaðelic se   wifhired to healdanne
        that him was   easy   the nunnery   to hold
        &   to rihtanne
        and to rule
        'that the nunnery was easy for him to lead and to rule'   (*GD* 1(C) 4.27.4)

(27)   ðis me   is hefi to donne
        this for-me is hard to do
        'this is hard for me to do'   (*Mart* 5(Kotzor) 2035[SE 16/A/14])

(28)   ælc ehtnys   bið earfoðe to þolienne
        each persecution is   hard   to endure
        'every persecution is hard to endure'   (*ÆCHom* II, 42.313.110)

A comparison with Mair (1987), an empirical study of the construction in the modern Survey of English Usage corpus, shows that 'easy-to-please' is about three times more frequent in present-day English than in Old English (one token per 15,000 words in the modern material, one token per 50,000 words in the Old English material). Judging by the available data, the construction also appears to be grammatically more restricted in Old English than in present-day English: the gap in the infinitival clause in (26)–(28), and also in the other forty-three Old English examples of the construction, functions as the object of a verb (*healdan, rihtan, don, þolian*) that would assign accusative case to an overt NP object. As already noted in Allen (1980: 383 n.25), there are no attested examples like (2), (3) or (4), with preposition stranding in the 'easy-to-please' construction, in Old English.

If the absence of such data indeed means that this option was ungrammatical, there is a clear difference between the Old English and present-day forms of the construction. It is therefore important to consider the evidence in some more detail, with the aim of establishing what generalizations can or cannot be based on it. Let us first examine the following example:

(29)   ne bið þær eþe þin spor   on to findanne
        not is there easy your footstep on to find
        'your footstep is not easy to find on it'   (*PPs* 76.16)

Demske-Neumann (1994: 102) suggests that this sentence might be regarded as an instance of preposition stranding with an *easy*-adjective.[5] However, this suggestion must be based on a misreading, since it entails a very strained interpretation ('Your footstep is not easy to find on'). The correct reading is more likely to be that given in the translation to (29), where the preposition *on* is taken to be stranded due to movement of the locative element *þær*. As we saw in 2.6, the Old English locative pronoun *þær* regularly surfaces in a position separated from the preposition that it is associated with, and (29) appears to be just one more example of this phenomenon. The subject *þin spor* is associated not with the empty complement position of *on* but with the empty direct object of *findanne*, making this sentence similar to (26)–(28) as far as the relation between the subject and the infinitive clause is concerned.

What may be another apparent example of preposition stranding in the Old English 'easy-to-please' construction is given in (30).

(30)   for þam þe leohtre is þam   bearnum maga
        because   lighter is for-the children kinsmen's
        swingcela to geþolianne þonne Godes yrre on to
        lashes   to suffer   than God's anger on to
        beyrnanne
        run
        'because it is lighter for the children to suffer the lashes of kinsmen,
        than ? ? ?.'   (*ThCap* 2 (Sauer) 33.369.8)

Here, the second part of the sentence might conceivably have a meaning paraphrasable as 'God's anger is not so light to run into (i.e. to incur)', which would make it into an example of 'easy-to-please' with preposition stranding. However, in 7.2.1, where we also gave this example, we implicitly adopted a different interpretation, and consideration of some further data shows that the

---

[5] Demske-Neumann (1994: 104) actually suggests that apparent stranded prepositions like *on* should be interpreted as particles. It is clear, however, that she is talking about what we are here calling stranded prepositions.

reading adopted there is a more plausible one. The relevant data consist of Old English examples like (31).

(31)   leahter   we onbeyrnað
        reproach we incur
        'we incur reproach'   (*LibSc* 37.11)

Here *onbeyrnan* functions as a transitive verb taking a direct object. As far as we have been able to establish, it only occurs in glosses, where it always corresponds to the Latin verb *incurrere*. For (31), the Latin reads:

(32)   crimen   incurrimus
        reproach we-incur

Apparently, to gloss the Latin verb *incurrere*, the Old English verb *onbeyrnan* was formed from the existing verb *beyrnan* and the particle *on*, resulting in a transitive particle verb of the type discussed in chapter 6. Example (30) can plausibly be interpreted as featuring the same use of this verb *onbeyrnan*. Although the text in which (30) appears, *Theodulphi Capitula 2*, is not a gloss, it is a translation; its editor calls it 'eine ziemlich wörtliche, oft beinahe mechanische Übersetzung' (Sauer 1978: 119). In (33), we give the Latin sentence to which (30) corresponds; note that it also has the verb *incurrere*.

(33)   quia   leuius est filiis   parentum
        because   lighter is   for-children parents'
        flagella suscipere, quam dei   iram   incurrere
        lashes   undergo   than God's anger incur

Unlike the other attested examples with *onbeyrnan* in Old English, (30) has the element *on* separated from the verbal stem by the infinitive marker *to*, which may make it somewhat difficult to recognize but, as shown in 6.2.2, this type of formation is the usual one for Old English particle–verb combinations. For example, (34) and (35) are different versions of the same sentence, with *on to gebringenne* in (35) clearly corresponding to the undoubtedly transitive verb *to donne* in (34), and therefore best interpreted as the inflected infinitive of the existing (transitive) particle verb *ongebringan*.

(34)   se þe naht unstrang nis   wræce   to donne
        he who not weak   is-not vengeance to do
        'he who is not weak to take vengeance'   (*GD* 1(C) 9.63.13)

(35)   se þe nis   na unstrang wrake   on to gebringenne
        he who is-not not weak   vengeance on to bring
        'he who is not weak to bring about vengeance'   (*GD* 1(H) 26.63.13)

We may conclude that the interpretation of (30) given in 7.2 is correct: the second infinitival clause in (30) parallels the first one and the whole sentence means: 'it is lighter for children to suffer the lashes of kinsmen, than to incur God's anger'. The sentence therefore does not contain an example of the 'easy-to-please' construction, let alone one with preposition stranding.

The upshot is that all forty-six attested examples of the 'easy-to-please' construction in Old English have the configuration given in (36).

(36) $NP_i \ldots$ to $V_{acc} \, t_i$

Here V_{acc} indicates that the verb is always one that assigns accusative case to an overt NP object.

While this looks very neat and tidy, there still is the possibility that the absence of cases with preposition stranding in this construction is merely a matter of chance. Perhaps this option did exist in the grammar of Old English, but no recorded examples happen to have survived. This possibility cannot be ruled out altogether, but there are several empirical arguments for assuming that (36) does represent the correct generalization for the grammar of Old English, as we will be able to demonstrate after we have presented some further relevant Old English data.

Apart from the 'easy-to-please' construction itself, Old English also has sentences comparable to present-day English (22), i.e. with dummy *hit*. (37) is an example.

(37)   hit bið swiðe unieðe ægðer to donne
         it is very difficult either to do
         'it is very difficult to do either'   (*CP* 46.355.19)

A variant of the pattern in (37) has no overt subject. (38) is one of the many examples of this very frequent construction.

(38)   nis   me   earfoðe to geþolianne þeodnes willan
         not-is for-me difficult to endure   lord's   will-ACC
         'it is not difficult for me to endure the lord's will.'   (*Guthlac*A,B 1065)

In (39), we summarize the three constructions with an *easy*-adjective and a following infinitive that occur in Old English.

(39)   a. this is easy to do   ('easy-to-please' type)
         b. it is easy to do this ('it'-type)
         c. is easy to do this   (zero-type)

Besides *easy*-adjectives, two other classes of adjectives also occur with a following *to*-infinitive in Old English. One corresponds to what in present-day English is usually called the *eager*-class; in Old English it has as its members words like *fus* 'eager', *gearo* 'ready' and *geornful* 'eager'. This class differs from the *easy*-class in not allowing the subject position to be empty or to be filled by dummy *hit*. Furthermore, the infinitival clause never has an empty object position; it only has an empty subject position, for which the interpretation is provided by the subject of the adjective. An example of this Old English 'eager-to-please' construction is (40).

(40)   þæt þu swiðe geornfull wære hit to gehyranne
        that you very   eager   were it to hear
        'that you were very eager to hear it'   (*Bo* 22.51.6)

Here, the element *þu*, which functions as the subject of the adjective, is also the understood subject of the infinitival clause *hit to gehyranne*, which has no non-subject gap.

A third class of adjectives that can be followed by an infinitival clause consists of words meaning 'pleasant', 'pretty', 'beautiful' and the like; we shall label them the *pretty*-class. Examples are given in (41) and (42).

(41)   his song &   his leoð wæron swa wynsumu to gehyranne
        his song and his poem were   so pleasant   to hear
        'his song and his poem were so pleasant to hear'   (*Bede* 4.25.346.3)

(42)   Wæs seo wunung   þær swyþe wynsum on to wicenne
        was the dwelling-place there very pleasant in to live
        'The dwelling-place there was very pleasant to live in'   (*LS*8 (Eust) 315)

At first sight, the construction in (41) looks just like the 'easy-to-please' construction, except that the meaning of the adjective is slightly different. However, as (42) shows, *pretty*-adjectives differ from the *easy*-class in being attested in a pattern with preposition stranding. A further difference is that *pretty*-adjectives do not occur in either the 'it'-type or the zero-type, i.e. patterns (39b) and (39c), even though these patterns are much more frequent in Old English than pattern (39a). There is also a semantic difference, in that *pretty*-adjectives can be said to describe directly the referent of their NP subject, i.e. they theta-mark the subject, while *easy*-adjectives are always amenable to an interpretation in which they describe or characterize an action, rather than the referent of a NP, with the resultant problems for determining their thematic structure noted in section 8.2. For the distinction between the two types of adjectives in present-day English, see Lasnik and Fiengo (1974).

Having seen that preposition stranding in the adjective–infinitive pattern is attested in Old English, we can now return to the question whether perhaps this pattern was also possible with *easy*-adjectives, but happened not to get written down in any of the surviving texts. How to decide this? One relevant observation here may be that of the total of 286 Old English examples featuring an adjective plus an infinitive clause with a non-subject gap, thirty-seven have preposition stranding as in example (42). If we take this proportion to be the rate at which the adjective–infinitive construction might show preposition stranding in Old English texts, the forty-six examples with an *easy*-adjective could be expected to yield five or six tokens with preposition stranding. But they yield none.

Secondly, data from modern English corpora can be used to strengthen this argument. Mair (1987) discusses the 'easy-to-please' construction in the Survey of English Usage corpus. Although he does not give figures for the frequency of cases with preposition stranding, inspection of the example sentences that he cites in the course of his article shows that five of them have preposition stranding, which means that they represent at least six per cent of the 'easy-to-please' tokens found by Mair. We have obtained roughly similar results in an exploratory examination of the written Brown and London–Oslo–Bergen (LOB) corpora: the proportion of 'easy-to-please' tokens with preposition stranding in both corpora is nine per cent. Assuming a frequency of roughly the same magnitude in Old English, this would mean that we might expect four or five such tokens in the Old English material, provided that this option existed in the first place.

Thirdly, although there has been no exhaustive empirical work on the 'easy-to-please' construction in early Middle English, examination of the lists of examples of the construction given in van der Gaaf (1928), Visser (1963–73: §§ 940, 1388) and the *Middle English Dictionary*, complemented by cursory reading of a large number of early Middle English texts, has thrown up many examples of 'easy-to-please' from this period, but none with preposition stranding. It is only in texts written down around 1400 that such examples are first found (see section 8.4 for further details).

On the basis of these considerations, we are led to believe that the pattern in (36) provides the correct generalization about the 'easy-to-please' construction in Old English, and that the type with preposition stranding, as in *this is easy to deal with*, was not possible at that time. In chapters 2 and 3, it was noted that Old English did not have preposition stranding in several constructions and sentence types which acquired this possibility during the Middle English period. If the reasoning above is correct, as we shall assume in what follows, 'easy-to-please' is one more of these constructions.

Let us now turn to the question of how the Old English 'easy-to-please' construction ought to be analysed. What we shall argue is basically that the infinitive in this construction has properties usually associated with passives, an idea first developed in the generative framework by van der Wurff (1987, 1990a), from earlier hints by Callaway and Jespersen.[6] An important clue to

---

[6] A similar analysis is assumed in Kageyama (1992) and Demske-Neumann (1994: 85–100).

this analysis is the fact that the subject position of *easy*-adjectives can remain empty in Old English, as shown by examples like (38). This suggests that these adjectives do not theta-mark their subject because, apart from some special cases, Old English only allows a null subject if it has no theta-role (see also 2.2.1). Some examples of such non-thematic empty subjects are given in (43)–(45).

(43)   us ne gebyrað to ameldigenne ða scyldigan
        us not befits   to betray   the guilty
        'it does not befit us to betray the guilty ones'   (*ÆCHom* II, 38.284.167)

(44)   Wel ys gelyfed þæt hyt þæt yfel gehæle
        well is believed that it   the evil heals
        'It is truly believed that it heals the malady'   (*Lch* I (Herb) 40.1.3)

(45)   fram þysum weorcum is to gelyfanne þæt God
        from these   works   is to believe   that God
        Zosimus on   þæt mynster   gelædde
        Zosimus into the monastery led
        'because of these things it can be believed that God led Zosimus into the
        monastery'   (*LS*23 (MaryofEgypt) 2.107)

In (43) *gebyraþ* is a so-called impersonal verb. It is usually thought that verbs of this type do not theta-mark their subject position, either generally or at least when no overt NP occurs in that position. The advantages of assuming this are described in detail in Fischer and van der Leek (1983); compare also section 2.2.2. In (44), *(ys) gelyfed* is a passive, which is standardly taken not to theta-mark its subject, and if *to gelyfanne* in (45) is also regarded as passive in nature (see below), the main clause subject position in that sentence is not theta-marked either. The theoretical ramifications of this correlation between lack of a theta-role and occurrence of a null subject (or expletive *pro*-drop) are further explored by Bennis (1986: 275 ff.) and Hulk and van Kemenade (1993); in line with the general approach described in 1.3.3, these studies also compare the Old English facts with modern Dutch, which is quite similar in this area of grammar.

If *easy*-adjectives do not theta-mark their subject in Old English, it might be the case that a NP such as *ælc ehtnys* in the 'easy-to-please' construction (28) has undergone NP-movement.

(28)   ælc ehtnys bið earfoðe to þolienne
        'each persecution is hard to endure'

Movement of *ælc ehtnys* must then have taken place from the object-position of the infinitive, making the movement concerned very much like that in passives, which also have movement from object to subject position. Such an analysis indeed appears to be feasible for Old English and in fact may even be preferable to one in which there is wh-movement (or A-bar movement) in the infinitival clause, which would be the major alternative approach to the facts. As discussed in 2.6, Old English allows preposition stranding with pronouns and in various wh-constructions, but not in passives. Above, we argued in detail that the Old English 'easy-to-please' construction did not allow preposition stranding, and this would follow directly if the construction was actually passive.

Let us look more closely at the details of passive in Old English to see if such an analysis can indeed be maintained. The pattern for 'easy-to-please' found in all attested examples in Old English, given in (36), contains a trace adjacent to a verb that would assign accusative case to an overt object.

(36) $NP_i \ldots$ to $V_{acc} \, t_i$

This is exactly like the pattern that is found for Old English passives with an overt subject, such as (46).

(46)   he$_i$ wæs fram mannum forsewen t$_i$
         he   was   by   men   despised
         'he was despised by men'   (*ÆCHom* I, 23.330.21)

The relevant part of the structure for this sentence is just as in (36), except that the verb is a participle rather than a *to*-infinitive.

Another construction in Old English with a trace adjacent to a verb that assigns accusative case is (47). In this example, *hit* is a referential pronoun rather than a dummy subject.

(47)   hit$_i$ nis   no   to forseone t$_i$
         it   is-not not to despise
         'it is not to be despised'   (*Bo* 24.56.2)

Such examples are comparable to the modern Dutch sentence type seen in (48).

(48)   dit$_i$ is niet te doen t$_i$
         this is not   to do
         'This cannot be done'

The Dutch construction is often referred to as a modal passive and it is analysed as involving NP-movement by van Riemsdijk (1982), Bennis (1990) and others (see also Demske-Neumann 1994 for a similar approach to the corresponding construction in German). If the verb indeed has passive properties, the construction should not allow preposition stranding, since this is impossible in Dutch passives generally. The ungrammaticality of (49) shows that this is correct.

(49)   *Dat onderwerp is niet met hem over te praten
          that subject   is not with him about to talk
          'That subject cannot be discussed with him/That subject is impossible to
          talk about with him'

The same reasoning can be applied to the corresponding Old English construction in (47). This sentence type is attested plentifully in texts, but none of the many examples has preposition stranding. Just like the 'easy-to-please' construction and passives with an overt subject, it only occurs with a trace adjacent to a verb that assigns accusative case if it has an overt object, i.e. it can be regarded as one more instance of pattern (36).

Given the fundamental distinction between NP-movement and wh-movement (or A-movement and A-bar movement), and using the (im)possibility of preposition stranding as a diagnostic to distinguish between instances of these two types of movement in Old English, we are led to the conclusion that all three constructions listed in (50) are cases of NP-movement, with a lexical NP, base-generated as the object of a non-finite verb form and moving from that position, via several intermediate steps, into the subject position.

(50)   NP-movement in OE
       'easy-to-please'   (example (28))
       personal passive   (example (46))
       modal passive   (example (47))

On this view, the *to*-infinitive in the OE 'easy-to-please' construction has passive properties, even though it does not have passive morphology. We are aware that this suggestion is not uncontroversial, since there is widespread disagreement in the literature on the general question of whether the *to*-infinitive in Old English could ever be passive in nature; a review of the opinions is given in Fischer (1991). Our position here is that, within the theoretical framework adopted in this book, both the modal passive and the 'easy-to-please' construction must be analysed as involving a movement process, and that there are some facts that appear to point in the direction of NP-movement rather than wh-movement, while there are none to suggest wh-movement. In the present state of the overall theory and our knowledge of the Old English facts, we therefore think that the classification of (50) is a reasonable one.

As far as the technical details are concerned, in the case of 'easy-to-please' at least one intermediate landing-site in the operation of NP-movement can be assumed. If the *to*-infinitive in (28) is passive-like, it will not assign a theta-role to its own subject position, and *ælc ehtnys* could touch down there on its way to the main clause subject position. The structure of (28) could therefore be as in (51), in which we simply use the label IP for the infinitival clause, disregarding the possible presence of further functional projections.

(51)   ælc ehtnys$_i$ bið earfoðe [$_{IP}$ t$_i$ [$_{VP}$ to þolienne t$_i$]]

Here, *ælc ehtnys* starts out as object of *to þolienne*, and receives a theta-role from this verb, but no case since the verb is passive in nature. It therefore moves via the subject position of the infinitival clause to the matrix subject position, where it receives nominative case. The passive character of the verb *to polienne* in (51) can be attributed to absorption, by the infinitival morphology, of the subject theta-role and the case that it would normally assign, in a manner often postulated for regular passives (see 8.2).[7]

We have seen that *pretty*-adjectives in Old English are different from *easy*-adjectives in that they can be followed by an infinitival clause with a gap either in direct object position or in the complement of a preposition, as shown by examples like (41) and (42). This distributional fact makes the *pretty*-construction similar to Old English instances of wh-movement since – provided the wh-element is non-overt (see 2.6) – these can result in clauses with an empty object or an empty complement inside a prepositional phrase. Examples of relative clauses with the two patterns are given in (52) and (53); for further details, see 2.5.1.

(52)   ðæs   yfeles ðe   he worhte
        of-the evil   that he did
        'of the evil that he did'   (*CP* 25.2)

(53)   ða upahefednysse þe   he ðurh   ahreas
        the presumption   that he through fell
        'the presumption because of which he fell'   (*ÆCHom* I, 13.192.17)

On the basis of this similarity, we can analyse the *pretty*-construction in Old English as an instance of wh-movement, as first suggested in van Kemenade (1987). For a sentence like (42), a structure as in (54) may therefore be assumed, with OP again standing for an empty operator that has moved to the specifier position of the infinitival CP.

(54)   Wæs seo wunung . . . wynsum [$_{CP}$ OP$_i$ [$_{IP}$ PRO on t$_i$ to wicenne]]

In Middle English, the *pretty*-construction continues without change. The 'easy-to-please' construction, however, undergoes several changes, to which we now turn.

8.4   Data and analysis for Middle English

Throughout the Middle English period, the simple type of 'easy-to-please', featuring an empty object in the infinitival clause, continues to be attested, as illustrated in (55) and (56).

---

[7] In Kageyama (1992), a different proposal is put forward for the nature of the absorption process in the Old English *to*-infinitive; see 7.1 for an evaluation.

(55)   pouerte wið menske is eað for to þolien
        poverty with honour is easy for to endure
        'poverty with honour is easy to endure'   (*Wooing Lord* 279.12)

(56)   oþer namys . . . the which byn
        other names   the which are
        herdur to vndurstonde
        harder to understand
        'other names, which are harder to understand'   (Bokenham *MAngl.* 16/15)

But around 1400, examples of the 'easy-to-please' construction start appearing which have preposition stranding just like present-day English (2) and (3). Two examples are given in (57) and (58). Note that in (57), *hit* is a referential pronoun rather than a dummy element.

(57)   þei fond hit$_i$ good and esy
        they found it   good and easy
        to dele wiþ t$_i$ also
        to deal with also
        'they found it good and also easy to deal with.'
                                (*Cursor Mundi* (Trinity & Laud MSS) 16557)

(58)   þe gospel$_i$ . . . is . . . most esi
        the gospel   is   most easy
        to wynne heuene by t$_i$
        to gain heaven by
        'the gospel is easiest to gain heaven by'   (Wyclif *Leaven Pharisees* 2.22)

Altogether, we have so far found six Middle English examples of 'easy-to-please' with preposition stranding, all from fifteenth-century manuscripts, and many more from later centuries. Since no examples at all have been found from any of the preceding centuries, it seems safe to conclude – in spite of the undoubted incompleteness of all the data from the Old and Middle English periods – that both (57) and (58) are innovations that first became possible at some time in the late Middle English period. The robustness of the fifteenth-century evidence for preposition stranding (six tokens among a total of some fifty instances of 'easy-to-please' that we have collected so far) thus supports the line of reasoning pursued in the previous section, where we argued that there was a sufficient number of 'easy-to-please' instances in Old English (and also early Middle English) for preposition stranding cases to be attested if they were possible at all.

   The theoretical significance of the occurrence of preposition stranding in the 'easy-to-please' construction is of course that it can be used as a diagnostic for determining whether the construction instantiates wh-movement or NP-movement. However, this diagnostic cannot be applied in precisely the same way in Middle English as in Old English, since there was an important change in the area of preposition stranding in Middle English: in the thirteenth century, stranding begins to occur in passive constructions like (59), where the stranded preposition is adjacent to the lexical verb, and from around 1400, it is also found in passives like (60), which have a direct object in between verb and stranded preposition. As in present-day English, cases like (60) are only found with fixed idiomatic expressions such as *take heed to/of*. For further details and full discussion of the rise of preposition stranding in passives, see Denison (1993: 124–62), from which we have also taken the two examples given here.

(59)   &   how it$_i$ may not be comen to t$_i$
         and how it may not be come   to
         'and how it cannot be attained'   (*Cloud* 3.20)

(60)   and [þes oþer wordis of þis bischop]$_i$
         and these other words of this bishop
         ouȝte to be taken hede to t$_i$
         ought to be taken heed to
         'and these other words of this bishop ought to be taken heed of'
                                                (Wycl *Clergy HP* 369.1)

The occurrence of preposition stranding in passives like (59) entails that the 'easy-to-please' example in (57) (*they found it easy to deal with*) can be analysed as an instance of NP-movement, similar to the 'easy-to-please' tokens found in Old English. This also holds for the simple Middle English cases in (55) and (56), yielding the following representations for the relevant parts of these three sentences:

(61)   pouerte$_i$ is eað [$_{IP}$ t$_i$ [$_{VP}$ for to þolien t$_i$]]

(62)   the which$_i$ byn herdur [$_{IP}$ t$_i$ [$_{VP}$ to vndurstonde t$_i$]]

(63)   hit$_i$ esy [$_{IP}$ t$_i$ [$_{VP}$ to dele wiþ t$_i$]]

As in the Old English period, the Case and external theta-role of the lexical verb can be said to be absorbed by the infinitival morphology, forcing movement of the complement NP (*pouerte, the which, hit*) to the matrix subject position.

Support for the passive analysis of Middle English *easy to deal with*, as given in (63), can be found in the fact that, around 1400, the modal passive too starts appearing in sentences with preposition stranding; an example is given in (64).

(64)   ye$_i$ be nat to trust to t$_i$
         you are not to trust in
         'you cannot be trusted'   (*Tale of Beryn* (Northumberland MS) 343)

This then would provide us with a simple and unified analysis for each of the following constructions in Middle English: ordinary passives, modal passives and 'easy-to-please' constructions. They would share the configuration in (65), in which the subject NP has undergone NP-movement from the position marked with a trace and there is Case absorption by the participial or infinitival morphology.

(65) NP_i be (ADJ) $V_{part/inf}$ (P) t_i

However, this cannot be the whole story for the 'easy-to-please' construction. An analysis in terms of NP-movement will not work for the innovative pattern in (58), i.e. *the gospel is easiest to gain heaven by*, in which the stranded preposition is separated from the infinitive by an object NP. Unless the predicate contains an idiomatic expression of the sort seen in (60), passives of this type do not exist in modern English nor have they been possible at any point in its history. The sentence in (66) is clearly ungrammatical.

(66)   *This can be gained heaven by.

Disregarding the special case of idioms, the configuration [V + NP + P + t] can only result from wh-movement, as in the following Middle English example:

(67)   a sheete [$_{CP}$ which$_i$ that [$_{IP}$ they myghte wrappe hem inne t_i]]
        'a sheet that they could wrap him in.'   (Chaucer *Canon's Yeoman* 879)

This means that examples like (58) must have the following structure, in which the infinitival CP has a gap due to wh-movement of the empty operator OP to Spec, CP.

(68)   þe gospel$_i$ is most esi [$_{CP}$ OP$_i$ [$_{IP}$ PRO to wynne heuene by t_i]]

In other words, (68) is an example with the same structure as the 'easy-to-please' construction in present-day English, as discussed in 8.2.[8] From this analysis, we can derive several predictions, based on the properties of the present-day construction: other things being equal, we predict that, in the course of the fifteenth century, 'easy-to-please' should also become possible in sentences with 'long' movement (*He$_i$ was easy to convince Bill to do business with t$_i$* or *A book like that$_i$ is tough to claim you've read carefully t$_i$*) and with parasitic gaps (*this book$_i$ is difficult to understand t$_i$ without reading pg very carefully*). This definitely looks like an exciting challenge, because it appears as if we have here one of the all-too-rare occasions when a historical linguist

---

[8] The late Middle English structure therefore raises the same problem concerning theta-assignment by the adjective as it does in modern English. For a possible solution for the Middle English cases, see van der Wurff (1990a).

can feel that s/he is engaged in the pursuit of crystal-clear empirical observations that are waiting to be made and then used to support or falsify explicit and clear-cut hypotheses.

Unfortunately, linguistics (even historical linguistics) resembles life in not being as easy as we might like: the predictions formulated above are certainly clear-cut, but they turn out to be rather difficult to check. As observed in footnotes 2 and 3 above, the relevant sentences are not judged fully grammatical by all present-day speakers and in the modern Brown and LOB corpora we have not found any examples of these types. This makes it less than likely that any could be found in Middle English, for which the material – though relatively speaking plentiful as far as historical texts go – is quite limited in comparison with present-day English.

Nevertheless, we do not think the prediction that these sentence types should have been possible is meaningless. Further work on the mammoth corpora that are being compiled for present-day English will no doubt yield modern attested examples of the relevant sentence types, and if a fifteenth-century example should ever turn up (and in view of the somewhat under-developed state of the study of Middle English syntax, this is not altogether unlikely), our analysis will be supported. If, on the other hand, an Old English or early Middle English example were found, our analysis would be dis-confirmed. Either way, the data would in principle have clear implications for our hypotheses, which we take to be a desirable state of affairs.

Apart from the empirical predictions following from the wh-analysis of the 'easy-to-please' construction in (68), it raises a theoretical issue. If a wh-analysis is adopted for a subtype of this construction after c. 1400, it may be possible and preferable to derive all of the late Middle English examples of the construction by means of wh-movement. That is, instead of the passive-like structures given in (62) and (63), the structures could be as in (69) and (70), which have wh-movement of an empty operator.

(62)   the which$_i$ byn herdur [$_{IP}$ t$_i$ [$_{VP}$ to vndurstonde t$_i$]]

(63)   hit$_i$ esy [$_{IP}$ t$_i$ [$_{VP}$ to dele wiþ t$_i$]]

(69)   the which$_i$ byn herdur [$_{CP}$ OP$_i$ [$_{IP}$ PRO to vndurstonde t$_i$]]

(70)   hit$_i$ esy [$_{CP}$ OP$_i$ [$_{IP}$ PRO to dele wiþ t$_i$]]

Whether (69) and (70) are correct depends, we think, on details of timing, in particular on when sentences with 'simple' preposition stranding like (63)/(70) became possible, and when sentences with an intervening object, as in (68), first arose. If we assume that the former preceded the latter, as seems likely, an analysis in terms of NP-movement, as given in (62) and (63), would be appropriate during the period when (68) did not exist yet. Afterwards, a wh-analysis as in (69) and (70) might be more plausible. In the following section, we come back to this issue.

Our late Middle English data show one more innovation in the 'easy-to-please' construction, at about the same time that examples with preposition stranding start appearing. This innovation involves the use of a morphologically passive infinitive; (71) is an example. Note that it features an adjective in the superlative (*hardest*), which is one of the contexts in which many of the examples with a passive infinitive are found (see Fischer 1991 for further discussion).

(71)   þe blak   of þe yȝe ... is ... hardest to be helid
        the black of the eye   is   hardest to be healed
        'the black of the eye is hardest to cure'
                                                      (Trevisa *De Proprietatibus Rerum* 42a/b)

The occurrence of such sentences seems to indicate that in late Middle English, 'easy-to-please' could be due to either wh-movement, as is unambiguously the case in (68), or NP-movement, as the use of the passive infinitive in (71) suggests. For (71), the structure could be as in (72), where the main clause subject has been NP-moved from its underlying object position in the infinitival clause.

(72)   þe blak$_i$ is hardest [$_{IP}$ t$_i$ [$_{VP}$ to be helid t$_i$]]

We saw above that Middle English allows preposition stranding in passives, and we might therefore expect to find this option realized also in the 'easy-to-please' construction with a passive infinitive. As it happens, we have found two late Middle English instances of this, given in (73) and (74).

(73)   þe souereinnest   pointe of contemplatife leuing
        the most-sovereign point of contemplative living
        þe whiche is possible by grace
        the which is possible by grace
        for to be comen to
        for to be come to
        'the most sovereign stage of contemplative life which can be reached by
        grace'   (*Cloud* 2.3)

(74)   Fleschly leuyng men of þe woreld, þe whiche
        worldly living men of the world the who
        þinkyn þe statutes of Holy Chirche ouer
        think   the statutes of Holy Church overly
        harde to be amendid by
        hard to be amended by
        'Men living the life of this world, who think the statutes of Holy Church
        overly hard to amend themselves by'   (*Cloud* 104.12)

The interpretation of (73) that is given in the translation seems the most natural one; the sentence then clearly illustrates preposition stranding with a passive infinitive (also note that the same verb–preposition combination *be comen to* is used in the undoubtedly passive example (59), found in the same text). An alternative reading would make the construction in (73) an example of the zero-type, and the auxiliary *be* a marker of the perfect rather than the passive; this would result in the meaning 'The most sovereign stage of contemplative life which it is possible to have reached by grace'. This reading would entail that *be* combines with a perfect infinitive, which according to Denison (1993: 361–3) is probably a development postdating the early fifteenth century. The resultant reading is also less than natural since the context of (73) is about a present or potential rather than a past accomplishment. Altogether, it therefore seems better to interpret (73) as a *bona fide* example of preposition stranding with a passive infinitive.

To sum up, we can say that the derivation of (late) Middle English 'easy-to-please' sentences could involve either NP-movement (most clearly in the instances with a passive infinitive) or wh-movement (clearly in the instances with a stranded preposition following verb + object). If we accept that the Old English 'easy-to-please' construction always involved NP-movement, as argued in 8.3, the question arises of what caused the introduction of the derivation with wh-movement in Middle English. In concrete terms: what caused the appearance of sentences like (58)? Furthermore, we would also like to know what factors were responsible for the innovative use of the passive infinitive, as in sentences (72)–(74), in this construction.

8.5   Explaining the changes in Middle English

A possible answer to the first question posed at the end of 8.4 might run as follows: the wh-derivation of 'easy-to-please' was a result of the introduction of preposition stranding in this construction on the analogy of *pretty*-adjectives, which allowed preposition stranding even in Old English (witness examples such as (42)). This could be formulated as an instance of (syntactic) proportional analogy, in the manner of (75).

(75) $$\frac{NP_i \text{ is pretty to V } t_i}{NP_i \text{ is pretty to V P } t_i} = \frac{NP_i \text{ is easy to V } t_i}{X}$$

$\Rightarrow X = NP_i$ is easy to V P t_i

In terms of a child acquiring these constructions, this would mean that, having acquired simple cases like *This is very pretty to see* and *This is easy to do*, she was exposed to sentences like *This is pretty to look at* and would conclude from

these that *This is easy to deal with*, with the same wh-derivation, was also possible. Although such influence from a similar construction seems plausible
enough, this answer is not entirely satisfactory. First, it suffers from the same
drawbacks as any other appeal to the notion of analogy which does not specify
why the analogical change took place at the particular time that it did, and not
earlier or later. In this case, the question would be why the introduction of
preposition stranding in 'easy-to-please' did not take place already in Old
English. This problem could perhaps be solved by saying that analogical
factors may lie dormant for a certain period of time without actually giving
rise to change. But the explanation then implies that the change in 'easy-to-
please', which took place in late Middle English, might just as well have happened in the Old English period, or not at all. Obviously, such explanations
cannot be considered completely satisfactory. Although the *pretty*-construc-
tion may have exerted some anological pressure on the 'easy-to-please'
construction, the Old English data show that this pressure by itself was not
strong enough to bring about the change that we are considering.

Moreover, there is a much more plausible source for the rise of preposition
stranding in the 'easy-to-please' construction. Several times now, we have
noted that in Middle English, passives with preposition stranding became possible; we have given examples in (59) and (60). Since 'easy-to-please' was also
an NP-movement construction (see 8.3), it developed the possibility of
preposition stranding as well. That is, the infinitival clause came to allow the
configuration [*to* V P t], with t as the trace of NP-movement. (57) is an
example. Its development can be explained fairly simply by the rise of preposition stranding in regular passives.

The appearance of the pattern in (57), i.e. *This is easy to deal with*, once it
is viewed as being due to the prior change in ordinary passives, can be
exploited to account for the appearance of sentences like (58), i.e. *This is easy
to gain heaven by*, with the configuration [V NP P t], in which wh-movement
must have applied. We can hypothesize that (57), although originally an
instance of NP-movement, as shown in (63), was reanalysed at some point as
an example of wh-movement, as shown in (70). If a language acquirer interpreted (57) as involving wh-movement, then she would automatically be led to
assume that examples like (58) were also possible. This may have been the way
such sentences first started.

A valid objection to this scenario could be that there was apparently nothing
forcing the language acquirer to reanalyse the relevant sentences as cases of
wh-movement: they could have remained instances of NP-movement. Clearly,
from a theoretical point of view, it would be better if, having demonstrated that
the wh-movement analysis for the construction in (57) was possible, we could

also show that, in some cases at least, it was necessary. A first approach to doing so, found in van der Wurff (1990b, 1992b), tries to further develop the scenario in terms of two different varieties or dialects of English influencing each other. In that way, synchronic variation is made to play a role in the change. Such an interpretation can be based on the fact that there is a time difference in the occurrence of preposition stranding with the various passive constructions that we have looked at: examples like (59), with a personal passive, are found from about 1250, but cases like (64), with a modal passive, and also (57), with 'easy-to-please', start only around 1400 (see Denison 1993: 124–62 and Visser 1963–73: § 1384 for examples and details on the first two categories). (76) summarizes these facts.

(76)   Grammatical spread of preposition stranding in passives
         a. personal passive   (past participle)   1250
         b. modal passive   (*to*-infinitive)   1400
         c. 'easy-to-please'   (*to*-infinitive)   1400

This simple table of course needs to be refined for a complete picture of the spread of preposition stranding through the various passive constructions to be obtained. A beginning on this is made by Denison (1985), who puts forward the interesting suggestion that stage (76a) proceeded by a process of lexical diffusion. Unfortunately, the frequency of the 'easy-to-please' construction in Middle English is not high enough to demonstrate the relevance of this process for stage (76c). We will therefore have to settle, at least for the time being, for the major outlines of the change as represented in (76).

As (76) suggests, the reason for the differential spread of preposition stranding may lie in the nature of the verb – past participle or infinitive; obviously, there is scope for further theoretical work to determine the structural causes of the difference. Here, we focus on the distribution of the three constructions of (76). Unless they were distributed entirely at random, it must be supposed that around 1400 some 'progressive' varieties of English already allowed preposition stranding in the modal passive and 'easy-to-please', while other, 'conservative' varieties did not. Data for locating such varieties in time and space are not available, but this is likely to be due more to limitations on the survival of the Middle English data than to anything else. In such a situation, borrowing of sentences like (57), i.e. examples of (76c) (*This is easy to deal with*), from a 'progressive' variety to a 'conservative' variety could lead to the crucial reanalysis. In the 'conservative' variety, the modal passive did not yet have preposition stranding (i.e. *This is to deal with* did not occur), and the cases of 'easy-to-please' with preposition stranding that speakers were being exposed to could therefore not be analysed as being due to NP-movement.

They were therefore forced to analyse such sentences as involving wh-movement. A result of the new analysis would be that (58) (*This is easiest to gain heaven by*) would come into existence; it could then spread out from the variety where it originated to other varieties.

In this way, we now have a scenario in which the new wh-analysis was not only possible, but also necessary. Obviously, the empirical claims inherent in the scenario are difficult to prove: there is a lack of data for the period in question, and the construction is not frequent anyway. This in itself may be a problem, since the modal passive appears to be more frequent throughout the Old and Middle English periods than the 'easy-to-please' construction, making it somewhat difficult to see why the latter rather than the former underwent social or regional diffusion. However, it may not be frequency in itself that determines whether an item or construction will get diffused: much must depend on the types of occasions on which it is used and the functions it has. Again, these are factors that seem to be beyond recovery in this specific case.

We now turn to the second question posed at the end of 8.4: what factors caused the appearance of the passive infinitive in 'easy-to-please' in late Middle English? In Fischer (1991), several factors are identified which may have played a role. First of all, this development should be viewed in relation to the rise in early Middle English of the verbal form consisting of *to be* followed by a past participle (i.e. *to be V-ed*, a form that does not occur in Old English, where bare *be* + past participle, i.e. *be V-ed*, is attested), and the spread of this new passive infinitive through various constructions in the language, some of which were discussed in chapter 7. For the introduction of this form in the 'easy-to-please' construction, several reasons can be given. For one, the new use of the passive infinitive after *eager*-adjectives may have promoted its use also with adjectives belonging to the *easy*-class. An example of a passive infinitive with an *eager*-adjective is (77).

(77)   the quene was aferde to be schente
        'the queen was afraid of being ruined'   (*Syr Tryamowre* 364)

Second, in late Middle English several adjectives (among them *light, hard*) appear both in the 'easy-to-please' construction and in the 'eager-to-please' construction. This may have started with Romance adjectives that were borrowed into English with two slightly different meanings, reflecting a systematic property of Latin vocabulary having to do with mental concepts. The word *profitable*, for example, could mean 'able/competent' (and hence occur in the 'eager-to-please' construction) as well as 'useful' (leading to the use of the 'easy-to-please' construction). In (78) and (79) we illustrate this property with the native word *eth* 'easy'.

(78)   a fool is eythe to bigyle
        'a fool is easy to mislead'   (*RRose* 3955)

(79)   how freel he was and eþ to falle
        'how frail he was and easy (apt) to fall'   (Audelay *Poems* 88/201)

As pointed out in 8.3, the main-clause subject in the 'eager-to-please' construction is interpreted as coreferential with the empty subject of the infinitive clause. In (80), for example, the subject of *to go* is understood to be *they*.

(80)   They were all eager to go home.

Since this results in a very different interpretation than the 'easy-to-please' construction, the occurrence of one and the same adjective in both sentence-types might lead to ambiguity, which could be resolved by using passive morphology in the 'easy-to-please' construction. In support of this idea, Fischer (1991) cites the fact that (81), the only Old English example outside glosses of an adjective followed by a passive infinitive, features an adjective that occurred in both 'easy-to-please' and 'eager-to-please' structures.

(81)   we ðe   næron   wurðe beon his wealas gecigde
        we that were-not worthy be   his slaves called
        'we who were not worthy to be called his slaves'   (*ÆCHom* II, 21.181.49)

Further support can be found in present-day English cases such as (82), a classic example of syntactic ambiguity:

(82)   The lamb is ready to eat.

One of the ways of resolving the ambiguity of this sentence is to use a passive infinitive, as in (83), for the reading in which *the lamb* is to be interpreted as the object of *eat*.

(83)   The lamb is ready to be eaten.

If the same kind of mechanism was operative in the 'easy-to-please' construction in Middle English, we would expect the passive infinitive to be most frequent, initially at least, in sentences that were indeed potentially ambiguous. This means that they should feature verbs such as *eat* or *please*, which have two subcategorization frames, one with and one without a (referential) object. The Middle English example given in (71), *the blak of the yȝe is hardest to be helid*, is indeed of this type, since *heal* could mean either 'become healthy' or 'make healthy'. It would be worthwhile to try and test this prediction on further data for the 'easy-to-please' construction in (late) Middle English.

    Yet another route by which the passive infinitive may have been introduced into the 'easy-to-please' construction was its use in the modal passive, i.e. in sentences like (84).

(84)   hyt ys to be forȝyue
        it   is to be forgiven
        'it should be forgiven'   (Manning *HS* 12096)

This construction is found next to the older type (*It is to forgive*), from about 1300 onwards. Addition of an adverb to this construction might result in a sentence like *This is most easily to be done*, and if the adverb did not have the ending -*ly* (a common enough phenomenon in Middle English), the sentence would be *This is easiest to be done*. Although there may have been some semantic differentiation of the two constructions, this is clearly a route by which 'easy-to-please' could have acquired the option with a passive infinitive. All in all, we may conclude that, since the infinitive in the 'easy-to-please' construction in Old English and (early) Middle English was passive-like anyway, it is not surprising that the passive infinitive also spread to this sentence-type, especially given the further factors promoting this that Fischer (1991) identifies.

A final crinkle that remains is the somewhat puzzling simultaneity of the new wh-pattern (*This is easiest to gain heaven by*) and the new passive infinitive (*The eye is hardest to be healed*). Both of them are first attested around 1400, but in the account given above this is entirely due to the fortuitous simultaneity of the various causative factors that played a role. A more principled explanation for the simultaneity, which ties in these two new patterns with a sound change operating in late Middle English, would run as follows:[9] when the infinitival ending -*en* was lost in late Middle English, there was no infinitival morphology left to absorb the Case and external theta-role of the verb, making a passive interpretation of the infinitive by language learners more and more difficult.[10] Yet these language learners would still be exposed to tokens of the 'easy-to-please' construction. For the older generation, such tokens would instantiate NP-movement, as in (62) and (63).

(62)   the which$_i$ byn herdur [$_{IP}$ t$_i$ [$_{VP}$ to vndurstonde t$_i$]]

(63)   hit$_i$ esy [$_{IP}$ t$_i$ [$_{VP}$ to dele wiþ t$_i$]]

The younger generation would be faced with the task of devising a structure that could yield surface strings like this, but the decline of the infinitival ending meant that the NP-movement analysis was not an option for them. One response to this situation could be a reanalysis of (62) and (63) into the structures of (69) and (70), which would yield the same sentences but derived by means of wh-movement. The appearance of the further pattern with preposi-

---

[9] We would like to thank Anthony Warner for suggesting this approach to us.
[10] Lass (1992: 97–8) provides figures showing clear decline in fifteenth-century texts; in speech, the loss must have been more advanced.

tion stranding (*This is easiest to gain heaven by*) would be a direct result of the introduction of this new wh-option.

(69)   the which$_i$ byn herdur [$_{CP}$ OP$_i$ [$_{IP}$ PRO to vndurstonde t$_i$]]

(70)   hit$_i$ esy [$_{CP}$ OP$_i$ [$_{IP}$ PRO to dele wiþ t$_i$]]

Another response to the situation might consist in the use of a passive infinitive, yielding *they are harder to be understood* and *it is easy to be dealt with*, in which the participial morphology would absorb the Case and external theta-role of the lexical verb, and in that way provide a possible derivation for these sentences. This response implies that there was a rather abrupt change in forms, rather than the superficially more gradual process of reanalysis by which the wh-derivation arose. It is possible that this correlates with the locus of the change, where perhaps language learners were responsible for the introduction of the wh-analysis, while adult speakers reacted to the ongoing loss of the infinitival ending by adapting the form of the verb in what for them remained a basically passive derivation; the factors discussed above would make the adaptation employed a natural one for them. Alternatively, this abrupt innovation may be taken to lend support to Lightfoot's (1991) hypothesis that language learners take their cues from main clauses (degree-0 domains) only, which can lead to rather drastic changes in embedded domains; see 1.1.3.1 for a description of this approach.

The explanation that we have now arrived at has several attractive properties. First, it may help us understand why the two major Middle English changes in the 'easy-to-please' construction took place at roughly the same time: it views them as alternative responses to the certain features in the primary data confronting language learners around 1400. Furthermore, the explanation provides a clear trigger for the changes, in the form of the reduction of infinitival morphology that is known to have been underway in this period. The explanation can be integrated with the other factors discussed in this section, as pointed out above for the appearance of the passive infinitive. The borrowing scenario can also be made more precise by noting that the diffusion of *It is easy to deal with* would result in reanalysis specifically if the borrowing variety had more advanced decline of the verbal endings; in such a variety, moreover, borrowing of the perhaps more frequent modal passive pattern *This is to deal with* would not be possible, since there would be no infinitival morphology to absorb Case and the external theta-role, and no alternative wh-derivation existed for this sentence type (hence also the eventual disappearance of the modal passive).

9

Grammaticalization and grammar change

9.1   Introduction

In this chapter we will discuss two cases of long-term change in the history of English which have been interpreted by a number of linguists as cases of grammaticalization. We will present an account of the historical development of the periphrastic construction with *have to* and of the development of sentential negation, better known as Jespersen's negative cycle. We will, in the spirit of this book, analyse these cases explicitly in terms of grammar change. We want to show what role the (synchronic state of the) grammar and the language acquisition process play in a development which grammaticalization theorists – looking at it from a language-historical rather than a grammar-theoretical angle – generally regard as a universal, gradual, long-term development with an impetus of its own. This is a view that, as such, is foreign to the general approach adopted in this book, and we shall therefore propose reanalyses of the two changes, suggesting that they can be understood using the notion of grammar change that we also employed in analysing the empirical developments dealt with in the earlier chapters.

Before explicating the differences between these two approaches, we should say that the term 'grammaticalization' itself is used in two different ways, which is potentially confusing. According to the most traditional use of the term, grammaticalization is an empirical phenomenon, for which Meillet's (1912: 13) definition is appropriate: it involves the '[a]ttribution du caractère grammatical à un mot jadis autonome' (the attribution of grammatical character to an erstwhile autonomous word). Grammaticalization in this sense refers to the countless instances of language change whereby lexical elements lose their lexical status and come to be employed as grammatical function words. A good example of grammaticalization in this sense in the history of English is the sequence of changes that the modal verbs underwent, as discussed in chapter 1. In this view, grammaticalization is a term for a phenomenon that can in principle be analysed in a variety of approaches, just like any other case or type of language change.

From being a term confined to morphological processes and specifically tied to historical change, the study of grammaticalization became considerably broadened in the 1970s and 1980s through the work of scholars like Givón (1971, 1979), Lehmann (1982, 1985), Heine and Reh (1984), Traugott (1982) and others. In their hands, the term grammaticalization has come to be associated with a particular approach to the study of language, and it seems reasonable to characterize this approach as 'grammaticalization theory'. Grammaticalization theorists are primarily interested in the cognitive mechanisms that drive grammaticalization, and they tend to stress the long-term, diachronic aspects of this type of change; indeed, they speak of diachronic processes, and there is an emphasis on language as a changing object in time. Here one can still see a link with the more concrete aspects of grammaticalization that we have just touched upon. However, grammaticalization theory in a more general sense also refers to a framework that focusses on how grammatical forms arise. It calls into question a number of the basic axioms of structural linguistics, such as the notion of the discreteness of categories, the strict separation of diachronic and synchronic dimensions in language, the independence of the domains of grammar/language (e.g. the autonomy of syntax), the split between competence and performance, *langue* and *parole*, etc. Through the information gained from concrete cases of grammaticalization, the idea has arisen that the rules and categories of grammar are fluid, that we often have clines rather than discrete categories, and that the notion of a synchronic stable stage is unwarranted even as an idealization. Another aspect that is stressed is that grammar arises out of discourse, and that therefore discourse factors must be taken into account much more seriously than is done in theories that advocate a strict separation between the grammatical system and language use.

Although different practitioners of grammaticalization theory emphasize different aspects of the general picture sketched above, any approach of this type is clearly not readily compatible with the one adopted in this book. Our approach is essentially synchronic, with emphasis on the formal structure of the grammar of the speaker/language learner, a grammar which has discrete rules and formally defined categories. Looking at grammaticalization from the learner's point of view requires a different approach because all language learners build up their grammars afresh; they do not take account of 'processes' that started long before their lifetime but they proceed on the basis of the language spoken around them. Grammaticalization phenomena, which are typically cases of long-term change involving greater fluidity, might therefore seem to be a problem for a synchronic and formal approach such as ours. But this is not necessarily the case, as we shall show.

The case studies we discuss in this chapter are both typical cases of grammaticalization as an empirical phenomenon. In the case of the development of the *have to* periphrasis, we see a reanalysis of constructions with *have* as a main verb followed by an object and a *to*-infinitive to its use as a periphrastic auxiliary expressing obligation. In the case of the development of negation, we see the rise and fall of multiple sentential negation. Both are gradual long-term changes and both are said in the literature to be semantically driven. We will show in our case studies, however, that at crucial stages in the development, the changes are shaped by the structure of the synchronic grammar that is being acquired by the speaker/learner. In other words, our case-studies do not show one conglomerate diachronic process, but rather a sequence of steps that can be characterized structurally, in terms of the synchronic grammar, with a good deal of precision. Our conclusion will be that the theoretical approach adopted in this book illuminates important aspects of grammaticalization phenomena.

Given that our approach is different from the one usually adopted by grammaticalization theorists, we will first outline in section 9.2 what the corner stones of grammaticalization theory are, as it is understood in the literature. We will show how grammaticalization is generally understood, by means of some examples and a discussion of the most relevant literature from the perspective of grammaticalization theory (9.2.1). We will briefly discuss the stages (or parameters) that are distinguished in the process of grammaticalization (section 9.2.2). In section 9.2.3, we will have a closer look at the notions of unidirectionality, gradualness and the idea that grammaticalization is semantically driven, which are basic tenets of the theory, but which may create problems for the essentially synchronic view adopted here. In section 9.2.4, we give an explicit outline of our own approach. In section 9.3, we present two case-studies of grammaticalization in the history of English in which grammar change stands central: in 9.3.1, we will discuss the development of the verb *have* followed by a *to*-infinitive from a fully lexical verb (with the sense of 'possession' as in *I have this job to do*) into a semi-modal verb expressing obligation, as in *I have to do this job*, and in section 9.3.2, we look at Otto Jespersen's 'negative cycle' and consider how synchronic structural steps are manifested in the history of negation in English. In section 9.3.3, we will sum up our findings.

9.2   Grammaticalization theory

9.2.1   What is grammaticalization?

Grammaticalization is generally seen as a process whereby a lexical item, with full referential meaning, develops into a grammatical marker. This is accompanied by a reduction in or loss of phonetic substance, loss of syntactic independence and loss of lexical (referential) meaning. In formal terms the reduction is described by Hopper and Traugott (1993: 7) as follows:

content item > grammatical word > clitic > inflectional affix > (zero)

A well-known illustration of this process is adverb formation in Romance languages, e.g. in French or Italian (cf. Hopper and Traugott 1993: 130–1). We can roughly distinguish the following stages,

(1)   i.   (Latin) *humile mente*: 'with a humble mind'
        ii. a. (Old French) *humble(-)ment*: 'in a humble(-)way'
             b. *lentement*: 'in a slow-way'
             c. *humble e doucement*: 'in a humble and gentle-way'
        iii. *humblement*: 'humbly'
             humblement et doucement: 'humbly and gently'

At stage (i) the Latin feminine noun *mens* (ablative *mente*) could be used with adjectives to indicate the state of mind in which something was done. At a next stage, the phrase acquired a more general meaning (iia), and *mente* came to be used also with adjectives not restricted to a psychological sense (iib). However, *mente* retained some of its independence in that in a conjoined adjectival phrase the morpheme did not need to be repeated (iic). Finally during stage (iii), the noun developed into an inflectional morpheme, the only remnant of the original construction being the feminine ⟨e⟩ ending after the adjectival stem, which now serves mainly as a kind of epenthetic vowel to ease pronunciation.

   An illustration of a still ongoing grammaticalization process can be given from English (cf. Hopper and Traugott 1993: 2–3).

(2)   a. *I am going (to Haarlem) to visit my aunt*
        b. *I am going to marry (tomorrow)*
        c. *I am going to like it*
        d. *It is going to rain*
        e. *I am going to go there for sure*
        f. *I'm gonna go*

In the first example *go* is used as a concrete directional verb (i.e. the verb is fully lexical) and the infinitive has a purposive function (syntactically it is an adjunct). In contexts where finite verb and infinitive are adjacent, the directionality of the verb could change from a locative into a temporal one, expressing futurity, as in (2b). The meaning of each particular case depends quite heavily on context; e.g., the addition of *tomorrow* in (2b) makes a purely temporal interpretation much more likely. Once this non-directional sense has developed, the verb *go* also begins to be found with infinitives which are incompatible with a purposive meaning as in (2c), and from there it may spread to other structures like (2d–e), losing ever more of its concrete directional sense. These semantic changes go hand in hand with a categorial change: in (2e–f) the verb *go* has changed from a full verb into an auxiliary.[1] As a result of the loss of directional content, the verbal structure also frequently undergoes loss of phonetic substance, which is shown in (2f). It is to be noted that this particular grammaticalization process reflects a diachronic development as well as synchronic variation. This situation is quite usual: the forms reflecting various stages of grammaticalization and the non-grammaticalized forms often continue to occur side by side. This phenomenon has been called 'layering' (cf. Hopper 1991: 22–4; Hopper and Traugott 1993: 123 ff.). When the grammaticalized and non-grammaticalized forms go their own separate ways, the term 'divergence' can be used. An example of this would be the indefinite article *(a)n* and the numeral *one*, which both go back to the same Old English form *an* (cf. Hopper and Traugott 1993: 116 ff.; Hopper 1991: 24–5).

9.2.2   Parameters of grammaticalization

In grammaticalization theory a number of principles or parameters have been distinguished that serve to characterize the process. The clearest discussion of this is found in Lehmann (1985), whose parameters can be used to represent stages in the development; Hopper (1991) presents a number of further generalizations that can be made regarding the process.

Lehmann (1985: 306) presents the following table (slightly adapted in order to indicate the *processes* taking place):

Table 9.1. *Diachronic stages in the process of grammaticalization*

Parameters	Paradigmatic processes	Syntagmatic processes
Weight	(loss of) integrity	(reduction of) scope
Cohesion	(increase in) paradigmaticity	(increase in) bondedness
Variability	(loss of) paradigmatic variability; increase in obligatoriness	(decrease in) syntagmatic variability

---

[1] We use the term 'auxiliary' in a purely descriptive sense here, i.e. the term refers to a verb that has lost some of its main verb syntactic characteristics. In the case of *going to*, for example, the form *gonna* can no longer occur on its own but must be accompanied by an infinitive (significantly, this has to be the bare infinitive, the usual form after the core auxiliaries of English). Warner (1993: 9–10) discusses some of the problems involved in the determination of Aux as a word class. The two cases discussed in this chapter, *going to* and *have to*, are both classified (in present-day English) as auxiliaries by him.

The 'weight' or substance of a lexical item involved in a grammaticalization process is reduced (in contrast to similar, but non-grammaticalized items within the same field or paradigm), through semantic and phonetic erosion. As a result, the element becomes syntactically less dominant, e.g. a full lexical verb such as *be going* in example (2) becomes an auxiliary, a modifier of the VP headed by the infinitive. Similarly, in (1), *mente* could at first have two coordinated adjectives in its scope (as shown in stage (iic)), but at stage (iii), it needs to be repeated, indicating that its scope has been reduced to the immediately preceding element; it has in fact become a bound morpheme.

Concerning 'cohesion', the more grammaticalized a linguistic element is, the less choice there is within the paradigm of forms that have a similar function. Thus, in the expression of a thematic role, a case ending is more paradigmatized than a preposition because usually only one choice exists within the paradigm of case forms, whereas often more than one preposition can be used to express the same function. Syntagmatically, cohesion is increased in that the grammaticalized item fuses with other linguistic elements, e.g. *mente* in example (1) becomes a suffix.

'Paradigmatic variability' refers to the degree to which a linguistic element is obligatory within the clause. Thus, the past tense marker in English is a highly grammaticalized element because it is obligatory within the clause, whereas adverbial markers of time can occur much more freely, their presence being determined by discourse rather than grammar. Syntagmatically, a grammaticalized element becomes less variable because it takes up a fixed position in the clause. For example, the tense marker must follow the matrix verb, while the adverbial marker of time can occur in quite a number of positions within the clause.

In this way, the parameters in table 9.1 provide some further elaboration of the notion of grammaticalization. More specifically, they can be used to determine the degree to which a particular linguistic item has grammaticalized, making a comparison of different cases possible.

9.2.3   Some core concepts of grammaticalization theory

Grammaticalization is generally seen as a *gradual* and *unidirectional* process, i.e. it always shows the 'evolution of substance from the more specific to the more general and abstract' (Bybee et al. 1994: 13). The unidirectionality is said to apply at all levels: the semantic, the syntactic and the phonological. Unidirectionality is most strongly defended in Haspelmath (forthcoming), who indeed suggests that it is exceptionless. However, we have some doubts about the *necessity* of unidirectionality in grammaticalization. Haspelmath (1999), for instance, is only able to adhere to this strong version of irreversibility by taking less than full account of potential counterexamples, i.e. cases advanced in the literature as instances of de-grammaticalization, where linguistic elements have developed from functional into more lexical items (this is also often termed 'lexicalization'). Where such cases do occur, e.g. a particle like *up* developing into a fully lexical verb, as in *They upped the costs to the public*, Haspelmath dismisses them as cases of 'conversion'. However, it may be argued that the change from particle 'up' to verb 'up' follows some of the parameters described in table 9.1 in reverse order, i.e. the verb 'up' shows less syntactic bondedness and more scope than the particle 'up', and that it can therefore be considered to instantiate grammaticalization in reverse (see also Hopper and Traugott 1993: 49).

Virtually all writers on grammaticalization view the process as being *semantically driven*, with semantic bleaching playing a primary role. Rubba (1994: 81), for instance, describes it as primarily a process of semantic change. Bybee et al. (1994: 17–18) even suggest that we can reconstruct the path of grammaticalization with the help of the 'hypothesis that semantic change is predictable'. There is some difference of opinion as to the stage of grammaticalization in which bleaching is most prominent. According to most investigators of the phenomenon, the bleaching of source concepts sets off the process (cf. Givón 1975, Lehmann 1982, Heine and Reh 1984, Bybee and Pagliuca 1985: 59–63, Heine et al. 1991a), but according to some others (notably Traugott 1982 and Hopper and Traugott 1993: 87–93), bleaching is a process that occurs in the later stages of grammaticalization, the semantic shift at the beginning being one of pragmatic enrichment rather than loss.

The notion of graduality implies that grammaticalization is seen as 'an evolutional continuum. Any attempt at segmenting it into discrete units must remain arbitrary to some extent' (Heine and Reh 1984: 15; see also Heine et al. 1991a: 68, 165 and *passim*). Heine et al. (1991b) indeed refer to the process as a 'chain'. The idea of graduality is also closely connected with the prominent position of semantic change in grammaticalization theory. Grammaticalization is usually seen as the result of 'conceptual manipulation' (Heine et al. 1991b: 174), a process in which semantic change is intertwined with and followed by grammatical restructuring. In other words, semantic and grammatical changes are usually seen as interdependent, with semantic change leading to grammar change almost automatically, as it were. We should bear in mind, however, that semantic change takes place at the lexical level, that it depends on context, connotation and discourse and that it involves individual expressions. Grammar change, on the other hand, involves an abstract constructional level, and involves rules and categories. Changes in grammatical behaviour are constrained by the structure of the grammar; some restructurings are therefore more likely than others. For this reason we do not believe that there is universal, semantically driven unidirectionality. Our misgivings on this point will be illustrated by our discussion of the case studies in section 9.3. For instance, concerning Jespersen's cycle in section 9.3.2, it will be argued that, although the bleaching of the negative adverb (*not* and its precursors in Old and Middle English) is part and parcel of the sequence of changes involved, the history of English negation may be considered a pure example of a morphosyntactic change; nothing whatever changes in the semantics of the construction.

The emphasis on unidirectionality and on the graduality of a process that cannot be cut up into segments has also led to the idea that the process is mechanistic, that it is itself a mechanism or cause for change. Bybee at al. (1994: 298), for instance, write: 'Thus our view of grammaticization is much more mechanistic than functional: the relation between grammar and function is indirect and mediated by diachronic process. The processes that lead to grammaticization occur in language use *for their own sakes*; it just happens that their cumulative effect is the development of grammar' (emphasis added). Most investigators of grammaticalization describe it vaguely as a 'phenomenon', a 'process' or an 'evolution'. However, the fact that for most linguists its intrinsic properties are graduality and unidirectionality suggests to us that in their view the process must have some independence. Heine et al. (1991a: 9) write that 'Meillet followed Bopp rather than Humboldt in using grammaticalization as *an explanatory parameter* in historical linguistics' (emphasis added), and the authors themselves seem to follow this line. Interestingly too, Vincent (1995: 434) writes, in an article which challenges the pre-eminence of grammaticalization as a source of new patterns, that he still does not 'wish . . . to deny the power of grammaticalization as an *agent* of change' (emphasis added).

A rather different point of view is presented in Harris and Campbell (1995), who write:

> Examples of grammaticalization are important in the broad database of grammatical changes, and instances occur in most of the subsequent chapters of this book. As will be seen in those chapters, however, we find that grammaticalization cases can be explained adequately by the other mechanisms of syntactic change . . . and we therefore attribute to grammaticalization no special status in our approach   (Harris and Campbell 1995: 20)

> Grammaticalization is one type of macro change, consisting minimally of one process of reanalysis, but frequently involving more than one reanalysis . . . Grammaticalization is often associated with 'semantic bleaching,' and this 'bleaching' is the result of reanalysis or, perhaps better said, it is the essence of the reanalysis itself   (ibid. p. 92)

Thus, their proposal cuts up the process of grammaticalization into a series of reanalyses, thereby loosening the links in the chain of grammaticalization, which is usually seen as unsegmentable.

9.2.4   *Grammaticalization and grammar change*

After this brief presentation of the basic notions that play a role in grammaticalization theory, we will lay out explicitly our own approach for this chapter. In this book, the focus is on grammar change in the history of English, and we believe that the locus of grammar change is, to an important extent, part of the language acquisition process of each new speaker/learner. The language acquisition process and communication between speakers are by their very nature synchronic, and we therefore cannot see that there is room for a separate and 'independent' process of grammaticalization, since this would imply that speakers and language learners recognize a master plan of long-term change in progress. We will therefore attempt to identify sequences of synchronic steps in the case studies we discuss. After all, even in those cases of grammaticalization that seem to be unidirectional and gradual, we should be able to account for the fact that there is apparently sufficient synchronic evidence for the speaker/language learner to acquire the grammar producing it. In this sense, the fact that this synchronic stage is part of a long-term change is something that the linguist discovers post hoc, with the benefit of hindsight. It would be of considerable interest to look for 'grammaticalization processes' that were aborted, or reversed along the way. The similarities in known cases of grammaticalization may have led to an overemphasis on a common core, leading to the idea that grammaticalization is an explanatory parameter in itself. We believe that it is the subprocesses that explain the change, and agree with linguists such as Lightfoot (1979, 1991) and Joseph (1992) that diachronic processes cannot exist because diachronic grammars do not exist. Each speaker constructs her own grammar on the basis of data surrounding her, and on the basis of her general cognitive abilities or strategies. Our approach to grammaticalization is more in line with that of Harris and Campbell (1995), who, as we have seen, subdivide the process into series of reanalyses.

In the case studies we present in the next section, we will, by concentrating on the synchronic steps in the grammaticalization process, come to question the necessity of the notions of graduality, unidirectionality and semantic triggering. We will argue that at each stage, the language learner simply constructs the optimal grammar fitting the full set of facts, whether these are syntactic and morphological or semantic and pragmatic.

9.3   Two case studies

In this section we will discuss two developments in the history of English which have been generally considered to be typical cases of grammaticalization. In each case we will highlight different aspects of the principles and mechanisms of grammaticalization, as discussed in the previous section, and we will show that the process does not always follow the 'regular' path defined by these basic principles. We believe that the shape of the synchronic grammar, i.e. the grammatical system at each stage of the development, must be taken into account because it may alter the interpretation of the process in question, and as a result also the interpretation of the characteristics or principles of grammaticalization in a more general sense.

9.3.1   The grammaticalization of have to

It has usually been taken for granted that the historical development of English *have to* represents a 'regular' case of grammaticalization from a full verb, possessive *have*, to an auxiliary. Thus, van der Gaaf (1931), followed by Visser (1963–73: § 1396 ff.), accepts the following developmental stages for the construction, *I have my work to do/I have to do my work*:[2]

(3)   • *have* at first is used as a full verb, meaning 'to possess'
       • the NP (*work*) functions as the direct object of *have*
       • the *to*-infinitive is not obligatory
       • the infinitive functions as an adjunct dependent on the NP
       • word order is not relevant; it does not influence meaning

In a subsequent stage of the development, the meaning of *have* is slowly bleached and generalized and it is said to acquire modal colouring in combination with the *to*-infinitive, which now becomes obligatory. The infinitive no longer functions as an adjunct to the NP but as an object complement of the matrix verb *have*, and the original object of *have* becomes an argument of the infinitive. In the final stage, *have* is bleached further before the infinitive and now expresses only duty or obligation. Syntactically *have* has become 'to all intents and purposes' (van der Gaaf 1931: 184) an auxiliary, which resulted in reanalysis or rebracketing from (4a) to (4b).

(4)   a. I have [my work to do]
       b. I [have to do] my work

---

[2] Neither van der Gaaf nor Visser use the term 'grammaticalization', but it is quite clear that this is the process they have in mind.

resulting in a fixed *have* + *to*-infinitive + NP word order (note the sudden shift in word order between (4a) and (4b), which is left unexplained in this proposal).

In this sketch of the putative development of *have to*, grammaticalization proceeds along a path of semantic change; the syntactic changes are subordinate to it, following hard on the heels of the semantic changes. Because the development is seen as gradual (one of the tenets of the grammaticalization hypothesis), it is extremely hard to disentangle the various stages. This is noticeable also from the fact that although van der Gaaf and Visser do distinguish three stages, they do not really indicate the order of these stages in real time. All are said to occur already in Old English, with the proviso that the word order change is clearly later; according to van der Gaaf (1931: 184), 'it is still rare in Middle English; [and] only became firmly established in Modern English'.

It has been noted by Bock (1931: 164–5), Mitchell (1985: § 950 ff.) and Brinton (1991: 19–20) that there are quite a few problems with this account, which all have to do with the fact that the *have* + *to*-infinitive construction is difficult to interpret since the types occurring in the three stages are formally indistinguishable. It is therefore virtually impossible to keep the various stages apart. It is probably not accidental that van der Gaaf attests all three constructions already in Old English. The only concrete indication in the above description of the stages is a change in word order, but as noted by van der Gaaf, this change is relatively late. The interpretation of the object NP as either (i) an argument of *have* or (ii) an argument of the infinitive, and the related interpretation as to which functions as the main verb (i.e. in construction (i), *have* is the main verb, and in (ii) the infinitive) depends ultimately on the interpretation of *have* as conveying either possession or obligation. Quite obviously, we are running around in circles here.

In the literature, two ways of resolving this vicious circle are found: the first is in Bock and Mitchell, who deny that there was such a development; the second is in Brinton, who tries to find additional pieces of evidence which may enable us to break through the circularity of argument. For Bock and Mitchell it is not difficult to ignore the development sketched above, because they are only concerned with Old English. The only hard piece of evidence for the actuality of the grammaticalization development of *have* in Old English would be examples where no object NP is involved, i.e. instances where the infinitive is intransitive. If there is no object NP, *have* can no longer be a full verb of possession and must have developed into some kind of auxiliary. The only two 'intransitives' found in Old English can convincingly be shown to be really transitive (cf. Mitchell 1985: § 953):

(5)   a. teleþ   þa andfengas þe   him   behefe   synt, hwæðer he
         counts the takings   which to-him necessary are   whether he
         hæbbe hine to fullfremmenne
         has   him to finish
         'counts the money which he needs, (to see) whether he has (money) to
         finish it [the tower]'   (*Lk*(WSCp) 14.28)
      b. Gif ge   noldon   Gode   lybban on cildhade,   ne   on geogoðe,
         if   you would-not for-God live   in childhood, nor in youth,
         gecyrrað nu   huruðinga on ylde   to lifes   wege, nu   ge
         turn   now at-least   in old-age to of-life way   now you
         habbað hwonlice to swincenne
         have   but-little to work
         'If you wouldn't follow God's example in childhood, nor in youth, turn
         at least in your old age to the way of life now that you have but little
         work to do'   (*ÆCHom* II, 5.45.123)

Mitchell (1985: 401–2) notes that in (5a) 'the object *andfengas* is to be understood from the previous clause', while in (5b) *hwonlice* functions logically as
the object (cf. also Jespersen 1940: 205). Mitchell (1985: § 953) therefore
follows Bock (1931: 165) in concluding that all Old English cases of *have* followed by the *to*-infinitive are the same syntactically: the NP object is an argument of *have* and is itself followed by an adnominal infinitive.

Brinton (1991: 20–1), on the other hand, adheres more or less to the proposed grammaticalization development, but tries to find support for it by
looking at other cases of grammaticalization and generalizations that can be
extended from those. Thus, she considers parallel developments in Romance
languages with the cognate or close equivalent of *have*, as described in
Benveniste (1968), Fleischman (1982) and especially Pinkster (1987). She uses
these as support for a similar development in English, according to the
method advocated in Hopper (1991: 20): 'The application of such cross-linguistic generalizations about grammaticization is a standard . . . technique to
guide an investigation of grammaticization in a particular language.' The
danger of such a strategy is, as indicated in section 9.2, that grammaticalization itself comes to be seen as a causal factor. We should look in the first place
at the synchronic facts at each relevant stage in the history of English to find
out what caused the grammar changes that are reflected at each stage. This is
indeed Brinton's second point, namely that we need more linguistic detail to
help decide to what stage a particular construction belongs. On the basis of
her investigation (using the Helsinki Corpus as her main data-base), Brinton
recognizes the four stages given in (6), the first three of which roughly correspond to the stages posited by van der Gaaf and Visser. The grammatical correlates of the construction at each stage are listed. Brinton is also much more

precise as to dates: stages (i) and (ii) are attested from Old English onwards, stage (iii) from Middle English and (iv) from early Modern English onwards. We highlight the *new* grammatical details Brinton provides by italicizing them, thus distinguishing them from the features already provided by van der Gaaf and Visser (see (3) above).

(6)   i. **Old English →**
          have + NP + to infinitive: full predicate (Brinton 1991: 22–5)

- *have* functions as a full verb meaning 'possess'
- the infinitive is an adjunct to the NP, which is the direct object of *have*
- the NP is *'normally a concrete object which can be possessed'* (p. 22)
- have *and infinitive have separate subcategorization frames*
- *lack of subject identity (between subject of* have *and infinitive) possible*[3]
- infinitive is not obligatory
- *order invariably* 'have *NP* to-*infinitive' unless NP is fronted*
- have *can be substituted by other verbs of possession*
- *meaning of* have *may have modal colouring*[4]

  ii. **Old English →**
       predicative structure (nb: construction (i) also remains) (Brinton 1991: 26–9)

- the meaning of *have* is generalized; it expresses a combination of obligation and possession
- *the infinitive functions as an object complement*
- *the NP object is frequently 'factitive' or negative, i.e. it denotes something that cannot be possessed*
- *argument structure determined by the infinitive*
- *subject identity between subject of* have *and infinitive*
- *infinitive is obligatory*
- order still as in (i)

  iii. **Middle English →**
        periphrastic structure (a further development of (ii); (i) and (ii) also remain) (Brinton 1991: 32–8)

- semantically, the meaning of possession is no longer possible
- syntactically, *have* is developing into an auxiliary
- *increase in 'quasi-objects' and factitive objects; appearance of* it, *reflexive pronouns and clauses as object*

---

[3] E.g. in an examples such as,
        hæfst ðu   æceras to erigenne
        have   you acres to plough   (*ÆGram* 135.2)
     the ploughing does not necessarily have to be done by the main verb subject *ðu*.
[4] I.e. modal colouring may but need not be present in the clause containing *have* and a *to*-infinitive; if present, it may involve obligation but also, as we will see, possibility (cf. (10a)) or ability (cf. (10b)).

- *appearance of inanimate subjects (with the beginning of a shift from deontic to epistemic meaning)*
- *appearance of intransitive infinitives*
- development of new word order '*have* + *to*-infinitive + NP' but not yet fixed
- have to *begins to occur after modals, in non-finite form and in the perfect*

iv. **Early Modern English →**
have as 'operator' (Brinton 1991: 39–41)

- *integration of* have *into modal paradigm; epistemic meaning fully developed*
- syntactic rebracketing to 'I [have [to write a paper]]'
- word order completely fixed
- *contraction of* have *with* to

The first stage looks similar to that of van der Gaaf and Visser, except that Brinton looks more carefully at the type of object that can be 'possessed'. If it is true that the object NP is normally concrete, it would be 'high' in the categorial hierarchy used in grammaticalization studies to ascertain the degree of grammaticalization (cf. Heine et al. 1991a: 157), and it would indeed indicate that OE *habban* fully functions as a lexical verb. Similarly the ±animacy of the subject is an indicator of degree of grammaticalization, as we have seen in the *to be going to* example in (2) (where the presence of an inanimate subject in the fourth example indicates that *be going to* has lost its concrete sense of 'directed movement', which requires an agentive (animate) subject). In Old English the subject is animate, high on the so-called 'animacy hierarchy' defined by Hopper and Traugott (1993: 157):

> human > animate > inanimate > abstract

At stages (ii) and (iii) the nature of the object and subject begin to change according to Brinton, going down the 'category' and 'animacy' hierarchy respectively. Further formal evidence in stage (iii) is the appearance of intransitive infinitives, and in stage (iv) the contraction of *have* and *to,* and the development of epistemic meaning. Other evidence, not mentioned by Brinton, would be the appearance of 'double *have*', indicating that the first *have* must be an auxiliary (cf. 'double' *go* in example (2), *I'm going to go there*).

It is evident from Brinton's use of incremental terms (*is developing, increase,* etc.) that she still sees the development as essentially gradual, with the semantic changes leading the way for the later syntactic ones. This is indeed a possible scenario, on which the semantic changes themselves are gradual, and the syntax is adapted to them. We believe, however, that the most important syntactic change (the fixed word order that emerges and the change-over to auxiliary status) is not in itself an *automatic* consequence of the preceding semantic changes. There are two types of evidence, internal and comparative, to suggest that the syntactic change itself may have been forced by other factors. Both have to do with word order changes taking place in the construction.

Let us look at the internal evidence first, which means having a closer look at the developments sketched by van der Gaaf, Visser and Brinton. We will look in turn at the nature of the NP object, the presence of modal colouring, the occurrence of intransitive infinitives, the bleaching of *have*, and the word order.

It is difficult to establish that the object of *have* was really any more concrete in the Old English period than it was later. Non-concrete, 'factive' objects are found early:

(7)   nu   ic longe spell hæbbe to secgenne
       now I long story have to tell
       'now that I have a long story to tell you'   (*Or* 2.8.53.4)

In (7), the object is factive, i.e. it refers to something 'which has no prior exis-tence but is brought about by the action denoted by the infinitive' (Brinton 1991: 28). There is no difference with later examples from the Middle English period, as for instance in:

(8)   That Nature had a joye her to behelde   (Chaucer *Anelida & Arcite* 80)

Here too, the nature of *joye* is specified by the infinitive, just as the *spell* is actualized in (7) by the verb *secgenne*. Similarly, objects referring to 'time' appear with *have* in Old English too:

(9)   a. Hwilum   him ðyncð ðæt he hæbbe fierst genogne to hreowsianne
          sometimes him seems that he has   time enough to repent
          'Sometimes it seems to him that he has time enough to repent'
                                                                     (*CP* 53.415.34)
       b. Ond þa   hi   þa tid   hæfdon ymb þæt to spreconne
          and when they the time had   about that to speak
          'And when they had time to speak about that'
                                                 (*Mart* 5(Kotzor)446[MA20]B/20)

It is difficult to establish whether there has been an increase in the number of such objects. Fischer (1994a) considers the different types of *have + to*-infinitive constructions in the Helsinki corpus, covering the Old, Middle and early Modern English periods (see the Appendix, reproduced at the end of this chapter). Although there is an absolute increase of such objects in the later period, there is no relative increase, and there really seems to have been no change in this respect.

Likewise, the possibility of modal colouring is present from the very begin-ning, but the colouring is not necessarily 'obligative':

(10) a. þe Sægeatas selran   næbban to geceosenne cyning ænigne
         the Sea-Geats better [ACC] not-have to choose   king   any [ACC]
         '[that] the Sea-Geats would not have any better man to choose as
         king/whom they *may* choose as king'   (*Beo* 1845)
      b. Geswiga þu earmingc, ne hæfst ðu nan ðingc on   me to
         be-silent you wretchling not have you no   thing against me to
         donne
         do
         'Be silent you wretch, there is nothing that you can do against me'
                                                    (*LS*14(MargaretAss 15) 147)

It is also not correct to suggest, as the above grammaticalization stages of van
der Gaaf and Brinton do, that modal colouring becomes more prominent over
time, as the Appendix again clearly shows. Also, *to*-infinitives do not contain
explicit tense, voice, modality or aspect (at least not in Old English). This has
to be inferred from context. Moreover, this is true for any *to*-infinitive, not just
the ones after *habban*: any *to*-infinitive may carry implicit modality.

Concerning the occurrence of intransitive infinitives, which are said to
appear in stage (iii), the Middle English period, it can be said that all the early
examples can be explained differently, like the Old English ones discussed in
(5). Brinton provides one from Chaucer:

(11)   I moot go thider as   I haue to go
        I must go there   where/that I have to go   (Chaucer *Pardoner* 749)

This could also be interpreted with *as* as a relative and functioning as the
object of *go*, meaning, 'I must go there, (the way) that I have to go'. This quasi-
transitive use of *go* is found elsewhere, as in the following example from van
der Gaaf (1931: 185):

(12)   Qua has to ga any way, gode es þai   ga bi þe light of day [sic][5]
        who has to go any way   good is they go by the light of day
        'Whoever has any distance to travel, it would be good for him to go during
        day light'   (*Cursor Mundi* (F)14194)

Here the verb *go* (in the first, relative clause) also has a quasi-object, and it is
interesting to observe that in spite of the word order (*have* + *to*-infinitive +
NP), the sentence has no clear obligative meaning; rather, the modality
implicit in the infinitive is of a general nature. Similarly, the early examples in
Visser are not truly intransitive. In the following example from *Layamon*, for
instance, the object (*þa*) has been left out in Visser (1963–73: § 1408); the complete quote is:

[5] Van der Gaaf mixes up two ms. versions in his example so that this particular
configuration of clauses does not in fact occur in one ms. However, this confusion
does not affect our argument here.

(13)   þa   comen þer   uaren. fif   þusend   rideren./ þa   Aurelie   hafde
        then came   there ride   five thousand riders   who Aurelius   had
        an horse to fihten
        on horse to fight
        'then there came riding five thousand knights whom Aurelius had (dealings
        with) to fight on horseback'   (Layamon *Brut* (Clg) 8221)

In examples such as (13), the verb *have* expresses a 'relation' between the subject and object, and the infinitive expresses additional details of the relation. It is clear that *have* is not strictly possessive here: it has been bleached of meaning. But this bleaching in fact has been there from the very beginning. Again no development is visible. Thus, the following Old English example shows that in that period too, *habban* could be used to express a relation between subject and object, a relation that was unspecified and that could equally well be expressed by the existential verb *be* (for the close relation between the verbs 'be' and 'have' in this respect in many languages, see Allan 1971),

(14)   And *her   beoð* swyþe genihtsume weolocas ... *Hit hafað* eac þis   land
        and here are   very   abundant   whelks   it   has   also this land
        sealtseaþas, &   *hit hafaþ hat wæter*
        salt-springs and it   has   hot water
        'And here there are abundant whelks ...
        This country also has salt-springs and hot water'   (*Bede* 1.0.26.12)

So far, we have not found any evidence for the changes that have been proposed as markers of distinction between the various stages. As noted above, the change that may provide firm evidence is the word order change. In the present-day construction the auxiliary status of *have to* and the concomitant sense of obligation are clearly only present when the order is strictly auxiliary-–infinitive (–NP), as in *I have to do nothing*, which is different from *I have nothing to do*. It is time now to have a closer look at the word orders that could appear in this construction in the earlier stages. Brinton (1991) dates the first indications of a change in word order to stage (iii), the Middle English period. But in all the examples she quotes of the new word order, there is only an *accidental* connection between *have* and the infinitive. (15) illustrates this (the fuller context, not quoted in Brinton, is given in brackets),

(15)   (but full lytyll undirstood they that travayle that) Sir Launcelot had to
        endure hym   (Malory *Works* 1217.21; Brinton 1991: 38d)

It is evident that *have* and the infinitive belong to two different clauses. In these examples *have* clearly has no obligative sense. According to Brinton (1991: 38), however, the *new* order is exclusively modal in meaning.

Fischer (1994a) provides a more detailed study of the role of word order, and of the different word order types that appear throughout the period under investigation. All the occurrences in the Helsinki corpus of *have* followed by a *to*-infinitive were checked (see the Appendix). A distinction was made between constructions where only *have* has an object (A1, see (16) below and the Appendix); where both *have* and the infinitive have their own separate objects (A2); where the infinitive is an adjunct with the object of *have* as the 'antecedent' (here the object NP is generally found between *have* and the infinitive, unless topicalized or wh-moved; at the OV word order stage, the object could be ambiguous between being an object of *have* or of the infinitive) (A3); and, finally, where *have* is followed immediately by the infinitive, either without an object (B1) or with an object (B2). (16) illustrates the various types.

(16)   A1: *object governed and theta-marked by* have
            þæt he stowe hæfde in ðæm streame to standenne
            that he place had in the   stream to stand
            'that he had a place to stand in the stream'   (*Bede* 5.13.436.5)

         A2: *both* have *and the infinitive govern their own objects*
            Ic hæbbe anweald mine sawle to alætane
            I have   power   my   soul to leave
            'I have power to lay down my life'   (*Jn*(WSCp) 10.18)

         A3: *there is an NP object, which could be theta-marked by both* have *and the infinitive*
            By ny3gte, whanne he hadde no man to teche
            'By night, when he had no one to teach'   (Trevisa *Polychr.* 225)

         B1: have *and the infinitive are consecutive but there is an implied object 'shared' by both* have *and the infinitive*[6]
            . . . he js wel avysyd þat sche seyd sche wuld neuer have to done wyth all
            '. . . and he is well advised that she said she would never have [anything] to do [with this] at all'   (*Paston Letters* 128.75)

         B2: have *and the infinitive are consecutive but only the infinitive governs an object*[7]
            It is to weten þat auturs [who] tretyn of causon [= kind of fever] commaundeþ not mynuschynge [= bloodletting] to be don . . .

[6] In the data of the Helsinki Corpus only one example was found of *have* and a consecutive infinitive without such an implied object, so with a true intransitive infinitive. This example is from early Modern English, so quite late:
   He went in his coach because Jug has to goe gett hir a payer of bodis
                    (E2 Barrington Family Letter (Searle 1983: 78))
[7] Most of the examples with this 'new' word order in the corpus (fifteen in all, see the Appendix) have a clausal object, which presumably accounts for their position after the infinitive. Three examples may have late NP position for stylistic reasons. The earliest non-ambiguous instance is the one given here.

[because] if þer were made mynuschyng þe heet scholde be more scharped for þe habundance of blod ymynushed, **weche haþ to represse þe efecte of drynes** & to scharpe het is þat þat is moste dred in causon.

(*Phlebotomy* 49)

The data, given in the Appendix, show the following. The first unambiguous example of the modern order is found at the end of the Middle English period (cf. 16 B2); the first example with an intransitive infinitive dates from the middle of the modern period (see note 6). Both of these have clear obligative meaning. When we look at the other constructions, we find that A1 and A2 do not normally carry a sense of obligation (there are no examples among the 101 instances of A1, and only 2 among the 238 instances of A2), whereas with A3, this connotation is not at all unusual (39 out of 122 can be interpreted obligatively). However, the sense of obligation in A3 constructions is no more frequent (relatively speaking) in early Modern English than it is in Old or Middle English (25 out of 80, compared to 4 out of 9 and 10 out of 33 respectively). In other words, there is no progression from less to more obligation, as the schemes of Brinton and van der Gaaf would lead one to expect.

The data suggest the following tentative scenario. There was an equilibrium in the *have + to*-infinitive constructions up to the late Middle English period, when the first examples of the new order begin to appear. This new word order (i.e. the order Aux–V, typical with core modal auxiliaries) led to the reinterpretation of *have* as a modal auxiliary expressing obligation. Once *have to* had become a modal auxiliary, it became possible for *have to* to be followed by intransitive infinitives (because *have*, being no longer possessive, no longer required an object – on which the infinitive in turn depended), to acquire epistemic meaning like other modals and to cooccur with possessive *have* (but these last two stages occur outside the period investigated in the corpus). Since the new auxiliary has an obligative sense, it seems quite natural to look for its origin in those constructions which already often expressed a sense of obligation, i.e. the A3 constructions. Our suggestion is, therefore, that the rise of the auxiliary *have to* is connected with a change in word order affecting the A3 constructions.

This change may have happened as follows: we saw in chapter 5 that during the Middle English period VO word order became increasingly fixed. Even though Old English already had surface SVO structures in main clauses and in some subordinate clauses, the surface word order of infinitival clauses was rigidly OV and this remained so in most dialects until late in the Middle English period (cf. Mustanoja 1985). What happened to the A constructions upon the fixing of VO order? Nothing much happened in the A1 and A2 constructions, except that the object of *have* now normally *followed* the finite verb, and that the object of the infinitive (if present) became positioned after the infinitive (although somewhat later in time) as well. But this had no further consequences for the syntax or semantics of the constructions involved.

The case was different with the A3 construction, however. Recall that we have only one object here. The object is syntactically selected by *have* (the infinitival clause being a relative clause to the NP object of *have*, with a structure $[_{NP}$ no man $[_{CP}$ OP$_i$ [PRO to teach t $_i$]]]. At the OV stage, it can therefore be interpreted as the object of both *have* and the infinitive, i.e. the construction is ambiguous between one where the object receives a θ-role from *have*, and one where it receives a thematic role from the infinitive. In Old English, the position of this object would follow *have* in main clauses (due to Verb-Second) and precede the infinitive. In subordinate clauses it follows *have* because *to*-infinitives are typically clause-final (cf. Los 1999). It is to be noted, therefore, that the NP in A3 constructions normally occupies pre-infinitival position, i.e. the normal position for a syntactic object governed by the infinitive, thus strengthening its thematic link with the infinitive. Since *have* is semantically not a very 'concrete' verb (i.e. its meaning is relational rather than fully referential), it seems likely that thematically the object was closer to the infinitive than to *have*.

What happens to this construction when VO order is firmly established? The earlier ambiguity now had to be resolved: the learner could interpret the object as being theta-selected by *have*, and it would therefore remain in the same surface position and immediately follow *have*. If the learner postulated that its thematic link with the infinitive was stronger, it would shift to postinfinitival position, and be syntactically selected by the infinitive. This is indeed what must have happened in many cases, see (17). The result of this was that *have* and the infinitive became adjacent in constructions where the object was reinterpreted syntactically as an infinitival object. This, more than anything else, must have triggered the slide of *have* towards auxiliary status.

(17)   **Old English: SOV**
        [NP$_s$ have [NP$_o$[OP$_i$ PRO to infinitive t$_i$]]] (main and subordinate clauses)

        Late Middle English: SVO
        [NP$_s$ have [NP [OP$_i$ PRO to infinitive t$_i$]]]   [NP$_s$ have [NP$_o$ to infinitive]]
        I have a letter to write

        [NP$_s$ have to infinitive [NP$_o$]]
        I have to write a letter

What we are in fact suggesting then for this particular case of grammaticalization is that there was a situation of layering all through the Old English period and most of the Middle English period. There were a number of types of *have* + *to*-infinitive constructions with different semantic/pragmatic interpretations depending on context, but all with the same syntactic substructure, i.e. with *have* as a full verb governing an object NP, followed by a relative clause. In this construction the verb *have* could range from fully lexical (as it usually was in the A1 and A2 structures) to almost bleached, and the infinitive could have modal implications (often obligative), again depending on context. This situation lasted for centuries with no visible change until the occurrence of the grammatical reanalysis in the late Middle and early Modern periods. It is therefore difficult to see any *necessary* relationship between the semantic and the syntactic developments in this particular case of grammaticalization. This is further supported by the fact that sister languages like German and Dutch have not witnessed the development of *haben/hebben* (the respective cognates of *have*) into an auxiliary, in spite of the fact that these verbs are used in bleached meanings, just like *have*.[8] Note that both German and Dutch are still SOV languages – in which *have* and the infinitive are not as a rule adjacent on the surface. This may well be one of the reasons why the reanalysis that took place in English was not shared by these languages, and why they are still, as far as this construction is concerned, at the stage that we have described for the Old English and early Middle English periods.

In our view of this case of grammaticalization, therefore, both semantic *and* syntactic changes play a role, and they are partially independent, i.e. the syntactic changes do not simply depend on the semantic ones, automatically following them; they are to a large extent influenced by the grammar acquired by the learner at the moment of the change. It is also of some interest to observe that the construction with *have* and a *to*-infinitive indeed shows a tremendous increase between Old English times and the early Modern period: from 17 occurrences in Old English to 339 in early Modern English counting all categories (see Appendix; length of corpora used is 413,000 words for OE, 608,500 for ME and 551,000 for eModE). Since frequency is considered to be an important factor in grammaticalization theory (because it is considered to be a prerequisite for bleaching to take place, cf. Traugott and Heine 1991b: 9), it must have considerably helped the development that took place. Another syntactic fact that may have aided the auxiliarization of *have* is the development that took place in the existing group of modal auxiliaries. These so-called core modals had been losing most of their non-finite forms (see Lightfoot 1979: 98 ff.; Plank 1984). Thus, the development of new modals (next to *have to*, also *be able to*, *be obliged to*, etc.) must have come in handy to fill a number of paradigmatic gaps. It seems probable that such a chance factor supported the eventual development, but it is unlikely that it provided the trigger for the

---

[8] For a discussion of how the verb *hebben* in combination with a *te*-infinitive is used in contemporary Dutch, see Fischer 1994a: 16–17, note 24.

actual grammaticalization (or rather, the *grammatical* reanalysis leading to further grammaticalization). The trigger must be found in the word order change and the resulting juxtaposition of *have* and the infinitive.

9.3.2   *Jespersen's cycle in the history of English*

In his 1917 work *Negation in English and other Languages*, Otto Jespersen made his seminal observations on the cyclical development of systems of sentential negation. His negative cycle can be summarized as follows:

(18)   i.   negation is expressed by one negative marker
        ii. negation is expressed by a negative marker in combination with a negative adverb or noun phrase
        iii. the second element in stage (ii) takes on the function of expressing negation by itself; the original negative marker becomes optional
        iv. the original negative marker becomes extinct

Jespersen's negative cycle looks like a textbook case of grammaticalization: negative adverbs undergo semantic bleaching and morphosyntactic reduction, up to a point where a new negative adverb is introduced, apparently because the old form is worn out as a linguistic sign. Once this new element is introduced, the old one disappears altogether, upon which the new sign shows the first traces of weakening. And so on. In what follows, this historical cycle will be discussed and illustrated in detail for English. From the point of view of the theoretical issues surrounding grammaticalization, it is of particular interest to look at negation. The fact that the lexical meaning of negative adverbs themselves is fairly straightforward, allows for relatively tight control over the role of semantic change. As a result, we can get the role of syntax and morphology more sharply into focus. We will see that this role is very substantial, and can be analysed very precisely.

We will also see that the sentential structure that has recently come to be adopted in the Principles and Parameters framework, in which negation is represented in a separate phrase according to the standard X′ phrase structure format, yields a particularly insightful account of this sequence of changes. Once this analysis is in place, we will see that the history of sentential negation in English is a pure case of morphosyntactic change, which can be regarded as semantically driven only in the sense that the meaning of negative adverbs is weakened over time. But the force that structures this sequence of changes through a millennium of development is the phrase structure format in which negation is expressed. Let us now first make explicit our assumptions for the structural representation of negation before we go on to discuss the historical evidence.

We follow up the sentential representation apparent from the tree diagram (72) in chapter 4, here repeated as (22). In this tree diagram, relevant morpho-syntactic material, including negation, is projected according to a phrase structure format as in (19):

(19)

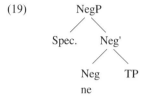

The tree diagram includes the following projections, in this order:

(20)   CP   FP NegP   TP ----- VP

By way of illustration, let us consider a typical sentence in Classical Old English, and how it is derived in the sentential structure that has been discussed in detail in chapters 4–6:

(21)   þonne ne miht þu *na* þæt mot   ut   ateon of ðæs mannes eagan
        then   not could you not the speck out draw of the man's eye
        'then you could not draw the speck out of the man's eye'   (*ÆHom* 14.153)

(22)

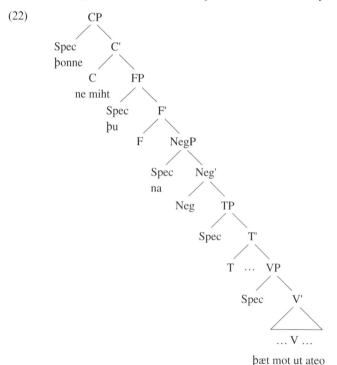

In Classical Old English, the head of NegP is the negative marker *ne*; this is a clitic which is never separated from the finite verb. We will therefore treat it as a prefix to the finite verb, which is checked against the negative head, overtly in clauses with syntactic V-movement such as those discussed in chapter 4, covertly in others.[9] (22) is a clause with syntactic V- movement: *ne miht* is base-generated as the head of the VP, and is moved overtly, to T^0, Neg^0, F^0, and C^0 (negative-initial sentences have V-to-C movement, as the reader will recall from chapter 4). Personal pronouns are checked in Spec,F; we have not further specified the precise checking position for *þæt mot ut*, but following the argument of chapters 5 and 6, we will say that *þæt mot* is checked in Spec,AgrO, and *ut* is perhaps in a predicate phrase. The element *na* in Spec,NegP is the reinforcing sentential negator. We are at stage 2 of Jespersen's cycle here: the original negative marker *ne* has weakened and is reinforced by a second negative adverb *na*. This second negative adverb has a fixed position, as we saw in chapter 4, which is because it is overtly licensed in Spec,NegP. Because it has such a fixed position, it serves as an excellent word order diagnostic, allowing a clear view of possible subject positions: the nominal subject appears on the right of *na*, in Spec,TP, which we therefore assume is the position where nominative case is checked; the pronominal subject, and other non-nominative personal pronouns as well, occur on the left of *na*, we assume in Spec,FP. With respect to the representation of negation, we therefore have clear empirical evidence for a negative specifier *na*, and for a negative head *ne*, which in Old English is an incorporating negative head in the sense that it forms a morphological unit with the finite verb, as we can see from the fact that, in the array of positions that the finite verb can occupy in main and embedded clauses in Old English, as discussed in chapter 4, the negative marker *ne* is always on its immediate left.

The NegP format advocated here allows a principled view of the relative strength or weakness of negative adverbs. As we will see in the material discussed below, negative adverbs 'enter' Jespersen's negative cycle as independent constituents that are checked against a specifier feature in Spec,NegP, just as nominal subjects check nominative case in Spec,TP, nominal objects check a case feature in Spec,AgrOP, and wh-constituents check an interrogative feature in Spec,CP, to name a few parallels. The weaker of the negative adverbs, which in Old English is *ne*, is an incorporating head; this amounts to saying that it is syntactically and morphologically dependent, i.e. proclitic, upon another element, the finite verb. We would expect then that a diachronic pathway in the development of negation systems may be that independent constituents that are checked in Spec,NegP are weakened to negative head

---

[9] We will see below that in early Old English, negation can occur separated from the finite verb.

status, and that subsequently new specifier elements are introduced. In the history of English, this is precisely what we do find. However, from our perspective in this book, it is important to distinguish between the relevant synchronic stages, and to consider at each of them what evidence was available to the language learner. We will see that at each stage, we find structurally identifiable correlates for the status of the elements in question.

Let us now consider in some detail the relevant facts from the various stages of the history of English, beginning with Old English (for general discussion of negation in Old English, the reader is referred to Mourek 1903, Einenkel 1912 and Mitchell 1985: §§ 1596 ff.). Old English is a negative concord language, which means that a logically negative sentence can contain more than one negative marker. As we saw above, negative sentences always have *ne* preceding the finite verb, for which we assume that it is a negative head. We distinguish sentential negation from constituent negation, as motivated in van Kemenade (1999: 148–9). This narrows down our cases to those instances in which no constituent reading is possible, as in, for instance, (21) above. This is even more straightforward in the standard case where sentential negation is predominantly marked by *ne* alone: consider some standard examples as in (23):

(23)   a. *ne* sende se   deofol ða fyr of heofenum, þeah   þe hit ufan
           not-sent the devil   the fire of heaven   though it   from-above
           come
           came
           'the devil did not send fire from heaven, though it came from above'
                                                                        (*ÆCHom* I(Pref) 6.13)
        b. *N*olde   se Hælend for his bene   swaþeah hym fram gewitan
           not-wanted the Lord   for his prayer however him from depart
           'The Lord did not want to leave him because of his prayer'
                                                                        (*ÆHom* 15.199)

In these examples, which are run of the mill cases of negation with *ne* alone, negation negates the sentence as a whole: there simply is no constituent negation reading available.

Let us now look at some negation patterns. We will take Classical Old English as our starting point. This will give us a perspective from which to consider the oldest English of the early poetry, where the evidence is somewhat patchy. After that, we build up the picture into Middle English and beyond, concluding with a discussion of the diachronic scenario from the point of view of the issues under discussion in this chapter.

The dominant and extremely common pattern of sentential negation in Classical Old English is, without a doubt, that in which sentential negation is expressed by *ne* alone. In the vast majority of cases, such sentences are negative-initial, as in (23) above.

Negative sentences with *ne* alone can also be subject-initial, as in (24).

(24)   þæt cild   ne mihte na ða gyt mid wordum his hælend gegretan
        the child not could not yet   with words   his Lord   greet
        'The child could not yet greet his Lord with words'   (*ÆCHom* I, 13.202.20)

There are some instances of topic-initial negative sentences with *ne* alone, but
they are extremely rare. (25) is an example:

(25)   Be ðæm eac cwæð Dryhten ðurh   Essaias ðone witgan: *ðinra*
        of which also spoke Lord   through Isaiah   the   prophet of your
        synna ne   weorðe ic gemunende, ac gemun   ðu hiora.
        sins   not be   I mindful,   but remember you them
        'Of which the Lord also spoke through the prophet Isaiah: "I will not
        remember your sins, but do thou remember them."'   (*CP* 53.413.20)

There is also sentential negation with more than one negative marker in Old
English, contrary to what is often said. The standard story, implicit in
Jespersen (1917) and explicit in Jack (1978a, b, c), is that multiple sentential
negation is first attested in the Middle English period. But there is, on a very
limited scale, multiple sentential negation in Old English: the most common
second negator in such cases is the standard constituent negator *na/no*.[10] (21)
above is a relevant example of this. Some more examples are given in (26):

(26)   a. Ne het   he us *na* leornian heofonas to wyrcenne
           not ordered he us not learn   heavens   to make
           'He did not order us to learn to make heaven'
                                                  (*ÆLS* (Memory of Saints) 127)
        b. Ne sæde *na* ure Drihten þæt he mid cynehelme oððe
           not said not our Lord   that he with diadem   or
           mid purpuran gescryd, cuman wolde to us
           with purple   clothed come   wanted to us
           'Our Lord did not say that he would come to us with a diadem or clothed
           with purple'   (*ÆLS* (Martin) 762)

Examples like (26) were already discussed in chapter 4, where we based a word
order argument on them, showing that pronominal subjects occupy a position
higher than that of nominal subjects. For our present purposes in this chapter,
they serve to illustrate multiple sentential negation with *na*. These are
instances where there is a potential for confusion between multiple sentential
negation with *na*, and constituent negation with negative concord. However,
as in example (21) above, a constituent negation reading is not available: (26a)

---

[10] There are also some instances where the precursor of present-day English *not*,
nawiht/nowiht, is used as a second sentence negator. But *nawiht/nowiht* is somewhat
variable in its behaviour; it can be used as a negated noun, as an emphatic negator,
meaning something like 'not at all' and as a non-emphatic second negator.

cannot mean 'he ordered us not to learn . . .', nor can (26b) mean 'it was not our Lord who said . . .' Rather, they mean: 'it is not the case that he ordered us . . .' and 'it is not the case that our Lord said . . .' Thus, they constitute real sentential negation.

As in the case of sentential negation with *ne* alone, multiply negated sentences are, in the most typical case, negative-initial in Classical Old English, as in the examples in (26). Subject-initial examples also occur, and it is striking that topic-initial sentences with multiple sentential negation occur with some frequency: out of a total number of 243 cases culled from a number of major prose texts, 182 examples are negative-initial, 29 are subject-initial and no fewer than 32 are topic-initial.[11] This is so striking because such examples are quite rare in the spate of clauses with *ne* alone. In (27), an example each is given of a subject-initial clause and a topic-initial clause with multiple sentential negation:

(27)   a. He ne cuðe na þa Cristes boc   þe us cyð ymbe þæt . . .
           he not knew not the book of Christ that us tells about that
           'He did not know the book of Christ that tells us about that . . .'
                                                                              (*ÆHom* 5.233)

        b. & ðeah ða   his lufe ne sece he no for him selfum, ðylæs . . .
           and yet then his love not seek he not for himself,   lest
           'and yet he must not seek popularity for himself, lest . . .'
                                                                              (*CP* 19.147.15)

The question of why there should be this difference in tolerance of a topic between clauses with single and multiple sentential negation is a puzzling one that will be addressed below; we can make some sense of it once we have looked at the historical development.

Against the background of the theoretical assumptions outlined above, let us consider how a tenth-century child might construe a grammar that accommodates multiple sentential negation: given the standard phrase structure format in (19) above, the child will have no problem deciding that *ne* is a negative head incorporating with the finite verb, since it is positionally covariant with the finite verb. The child will analyse *ne* as a prefix that is covertly checked against Neg; the fixed position of *na* would lead the child to conclude that it is a negative specifier in need of overt checking.

---

[11] These examples have been culled from the following major Old English prose texts, searched in full in the machine-readable version of the Toronto text corpus: *The Old English Orosius* (*Or*); *King Alfred's Version of St. Augustine's Soliloquies* (*Solil*); *King Alfred's Old English version of Boethius' 'De Consolatione Philosophiae'* (*Bo*); *King Alfred's West Saxon version of Gregory's Pastoral Care* (*CP*); the Parker ms. of the Anglo-Saxon chronicle (*ChronA*); vol. I of the Catholic Homilies of Ælfric (*ÆCHom* I); *Ælfric's Lives of Saints* (*ÆLS*); the *Homilies of Ælfric* (*ÆHom*); the *Homilies of Wulfstan* (*WHom*).

9.3.2.1 The earliest Old English[12]

We now turn to some of the earliest Old English, in particular the long heroic poem *Beowulf*, written in alliterative four-stress lines. Although the only manuscript we have of the poem was written sometime in the tenth century, there is some consensus that the version we have must have been composed in the course of the eighth century.[13] This puts the poem rather earlier than any of the large prose texts we have. Moreover, the poem was presumably composed and written up in the form as we know it after centuries of oral transmission, which makes it likely that archaic linguistic features have been preserved in it. Against this background, it is tempting to see the variation in patterns of negation attested in *Beowulf* as a mixture of the Classical Old English patterns of sentential negation, and older patterns that had become more or less obsolete by the time of the earliest large prose texts. Let us look at that variation now. Beside the standard pattern of sentential negation in Classical Old English, illustrated in (28), *Beowulf* has an alternative pattern, which is exemplified by (29):

(28)   Nolde   eorla   hleo   ænige þinga þone cwealmcuman cwicne
        not-wanted of-earls protector any   thing the kill-comer   alive
        forlætan
        release
        'The protector of earls was minded in no wise to release the deadly visitant
        alive'   (*Beo* 791)

(29)   a. No he wiht fram me flodyþum feor fleotan meahte, hraþor on
           not he thing from me on waves far swim   could   quicker in
           holme; no ic fram him wolde
           water not I from him wanted
           'In no wise could he swim far from me on the waves of the flood, more
           quickly on the sea; I would not consent to leave him'   (*Beo* 541)
        b. No ic me   an herewæsmun hnagran talige, guþgeweorca, þonne
           not I myself in war-strength inferior count battledeeds   than
           Grendel hine
           Grendel himself
           'I do not count myself less in war-strength, in battle deeds, than Grendel
           does himself'   (*Beo* 675)

---

[12] The material in this subsection is discussed in more detail in van Kemenade (1997b).

[13] This is based on the content of the poem as well as its linguistic features. There is a marked Christian element in the poem, which indicates that it was composed after the christianization of England, putting it no earlier than about 700. Moreover, it is thoroughly Scandinavian in subject matter, in a way so sympathetic to Danish affairs that it must have been composed before the Scandinavians became the enemies of the English at the end of the eighth century. The morphological and phonological characteristics of the language are consistent with this rough date of composition.

There are several points of note about the facts in (29). First, the sentences are negative-initial, like the standard ones in Classical Old English; second, the initial negative element is not reduced to *ne* or procliticized as *n-*, but has a distinctive vowel; third, the initial negative element is not incorporated with the finite verb: while *no* is in first position, the finite verb, *meahte* in (29a), *talige* in (29b), does not seem to have been moved at all. A final observation is that the patterns in (28) and (29) are in complementary distribution: an unreduced form like *no* (but also *nē, næfre*) does not go together with movement of the finite verb, but the reduced form *ne* or the procliticized form does.[14]

Given the fact that the pattern without V-movement has largely died out by the time of Classical Old English, it is tempting to see the alternation between the two negation patterns in *Beowulf* as the result of a change in progress: the rise of V-movement in negative-initial sentences, one of the two environments (the other being questions) in which English throughout its history has had V-movement to C, as discussed in chapter 4. It is impossible to find conclusive evidence for the idea that this represents the rise of V-movement, because we have no earlier text material, but there are pieces of circumstantial evidence. The first of these is that the 'early' pattern without movement is found with any frequency only in older texts, specifically in the oldest poetry, e.g. *Widsith, Genesis A, Daniel.* The pattern which we think is an older one is not a typical poetic feature: the oldest poems have it in varying degrees, but the one poem which we know is a late one, *The Battle of Maldon,* written up close to its late composition date in the tenth century, soon after the battle it relates (991), does not have the older negation pattern we have identified in *Beowulf* and shows only the Classical Old English pattern. There is also some cross-linguistic evidence in the fact that Latin (as in Adams 1994a, b) and Gothic (as in Ferraresi 1991) have undergone a similar rise of V-movement triggered by negative constituents. This hypothesis has several very interesting implications: the first of which is important from the point of view of grammaticalization. Supposing that the initial negative element in *Beowulf* is a Spec,CP element, and that the finite verb, when moved, is moved to C, then the alternation between the two patterns in *Beowulf* suggests that V-movement and the grammaticalization of the negative element to *ne* or proclitic *n-* are crucially

---

[14] There is only one example of multiple sentential negation in *Beowulf* which is a combination of the *no*-initial pattern and . . . *ne* Vf:

   . . . no ðu ymb mines ne þearft/ lices   feorme   leng   sorgian.
      not you about my   not need   body's disposal   longer worry
   '. . . in which case you will no longer need to trouble (yourself) over the
   disposal of my body'   (*Beo* 448)

related, in other words that the fact that the verb moves to a position next to initial *no* entails weakening of *no* to *ne*, with the possibility of *ne* being pro-clitic. This is an argument for the following formalized representation of the two sentential negation patterns in *Beowulf*, which we hypothesize are succes-sive stages that show overlap in the poem:

(30)   *Beowulf*
        The non-V-movement pattern:

        $[_{\text{Spec,CP}}$ no $[\ldots$ finite verb $\ldots]]$

(31)   *Beowulf* and Classical Old English
        The V-movement pattern

        $[_{\text{Spec,CP}}$ ne $[_{\text{C}}$ finite verb $[\ldots]]]$
            | |
        cliticization

(30) represents the 'oldest' pattern. Sentential negation is expressed by moving *no* to Spec,CP. The finite verb is not moved. In (31), there is again a negative constituent in Spec,CP, but now the finite verb is attracted to C. The question of what triggered the rise of this pattern is of some interest. Why should the learner construct a grammar that yields a novel word order pattern? Presumably there is no positive basis in the language environment on which to construct the grammatical basis for such a pattern. With Lightfoot (1999: 152), we think that the answer must probably come from a UG condition stating that lexical material in Spec,CP must be licensed by a lexically filled C. If this is correct, this innovation is a case of UG-driven change as discussed in chapter 1.

It seems that V-movement to C, the position right-adjacent to the negative element in Spec,CP, entails that *no* is reduced/procliticized to the finite verb. We hypothesize that at the stage represented in (31), this cliticization is phono-logical. By this, we mean that, although *ne* is a prefix/proclitic, it does syn-tactically represent a constituent in Spec,CP. This allows an account for the puzzle discussed above in connection with negative-initial clauses with *ne* alone: topics are extremely rare there. This is straightforwardly accounted for by (30) and (31): syntactically, the negative element is in Spec,CP, hence no other elements can appear there. For the learner acquiring a grammar, the fact that sentences with *ne* alone are always introduced by *ne* + Vfin, is presumably evidence that there is a negative operator associated with Spec,CP. The learner will conclude that no other constituent can appear there.

At the stage of the language represented by *Beowulf*, the negative element seems to be in transition from being an independent constituent, an adverb as far as we can tell, to becoming a negative head. The strategy for sentential negation apparent in *Beowulf* is simply to move *no* or some other negative element like *næfre* to Spec,CP. By the time of Classical Old English, *ne* is firmly in place as a negative head, and we should ask ourselves what it is that triggers the introduction of a reinforcing negative adverb in Spec,NegP as in the structure (22) above, as shown by the pattern of multiple sentential negation with *ne* and *na* already presented and analysed above. We will need to assume that the negative force of *ne* is weaker than that of the earlier independent *no* in *Beowulf*. Against this background, we could say that in Classical Old English, a second sentential negator is introduced, with clear evidence that we have a negative specifier (*na*) and a negative head (*ne*). In the perspective sketched here, it is striking also that in the pattern with multiple sentential negation in Classical Old English, topics do occur with some freqency, as discussed above. Following up further the analysis in (30) and (31), there is a straightforward interpretation of this: the force of *ne* as a negative marker is wearing off, perhaps because of the lexical weakening resulting from its becoming an incorporating negative head procliticized to the finite verb. A second sentential negator is introduced: the element *na* that is already around in the language on a large scale as a morphological constituent negator. The position of this second sentential negator is narrowly defined by the NegP format (19), perhaps also because negative constituents were checked, overtly or covertly, in Spec,NegP (Haeberli 1991, van Kemenade forthcoming). As a result, negation is now expressed predominantly in NegP. New generations of learners will conclude that there is no syntactic negative operator in Spec,CP, and they will construct grammars for negative sentences in which nothing bars movement of a topic to Spec,CP. This is evident from the fact that we now find topic-initial negative sentences with increasing frequency.

(32)   Classical Old English and early Middle English
        the topic–*ne*–finite verb pattern, multiple sentential negation with *ne . . . na*

$[_{Spec,CP}$ topic $[_C$ ne + finite verb [. . .$[_{NegP}$ na . . .] . . .]]]

9.3.2.2 Middle English

Some important changes take place that shape the development of sentential negation in the Middle English period. One of the most noticeable of these is that of the ongoing weakening of *ne*, in line with the discussion in the previous section. This goes hand in hand with the increased use of a reinforcing sentential negator. In the Middle English period, the reinforcing negator is no longer *na/no*, which is no longer found in this use, for reasons that are not really clear. The reinforcing negator is now some spelling variant of *not* (*noht, noȝt, nauht, nawht,* etc), the descendant of Old English *nawiht/nowiht*, which in Old English was used as a negated noun or an emphatic negative adverb. *Not* is clearly a semantically bleached version of its Old English precursor, and is now used as a negative adverb with rapidly increasing frequency, as described in detail in Jack (1978a, b, c). But *not* is deployed in exactly the same syntactic environments as *na/no* in Old English in its use as a sentence negator. This is evident from the fact that its distribution continues the pattern attested in Old English: the subject pronoun precedes *not*, the nominal subject follows it.

(33) a. þet ne   seide he noht
         that not said   he not
         'That he did not say'   (*Ken. Serm.* 214.25)
      b. nule   nawt þi   leofmon þoli   na leas þing ta lihe   þe
         not-will not   your beloved tolerate no false thing to deceive you
         longe
         long
         'your beloved will not allow any false thing to deceive you long'
                                                         (*St. Juliana* (Bod) 33.332)

(34) a. yet ne   wolde   he nat answare sodeynly
         yet not wanted he not answer   suddenly
         'yet he did not want to answer suddenly'   (Chaucer *Melibee* 1032/2222)
      b. also ne   accordith nat the peple   to that   I schal seyn
         also not agreed   not the people to what I shall say
         'the people did not agree to what I shall say'
                                                         (Chaucer *Boece* IV, prosa 4. 219)

It seems reasonable to assume, therefore, that *not* replaces *na/no* as the negative adverb in Spec,NegP in the transition from Old English to Middle English.

Negated preposed verbs now frequently occur with topics preceding them:

(35) a. þer   ne   þerf he habben kare of ʒeve ne   of ʒelde
         there not need he have   care of gifts nor of rewards
         'there he needn't be worried about gifts or rewards'   (*Poema Morale* 45)
      b. for of al his strengðe ne   drede we nawiht
         for of all his strength not dread we not
         'for of all his strength we don't have any dread'   (*Sward* 255.8)
      c. þis ne   habbe ic nauht ofearned
         this not have   I   not   earned
         'this I have not earned'   (*Vices&V* 17.9)

We take this as further confirmation of the ongoing weakening of *ne*. As part of this development, *ne* is beginning to be dropped altogether, which takes us to stage (iii) of Jespersen's cycle: *not* is fast increasing in frequency, and the original negative marker *ne* becomes optional. Indeed, at the close of the Middle English period, it has to a large extent disappeared, as discussed in detail in Jack (1978a, b, c). This takes us to stage (iv) of Jespersen's cycle: the original negative marker becomes extinct.

As soon as *ne* has disappeared, *not* immediately begins to show signs of phonological weakening, and its syntax gives clear evidence that it is becoming a negative head. To see this, we will look at the relative ordering of subjects and *not* during the Middle English period. Recall that the pattern inherited from Old English is one in which *not* has a fixed position, with pronominal subjects preceding it and nominal subjects following it. This was the very evidence that we took to motivate an analysis of *not* as a Spec,NegP element, with *ne* as the negative head. Part of the further motivation for this analysis is that *ne* behaves as an incorporating head, covarying positionally with the finite verb. Once *ne* has disappeared, *not* is beginning to show evidence of being a negative head: it moves along with the finite verb when the latter is moved to C, for instance in negative questions. This is illustrated by (36a), which we analyse as in (36b):

(36)   a. dyd not I send unto yow one Mowntayne that was both a traytor and a
           herytyke . . .?   (*Mowntayne* 210)
         b.

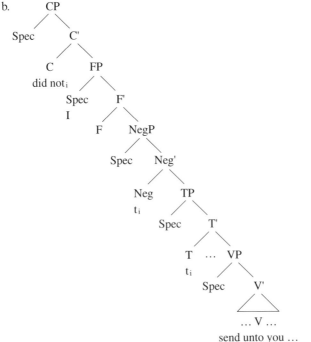

In the grammar producing (36), *not* is a negative head incorporating with the finite verb *did* on its way to C. The innovation is that a new generation of learners is constructing grammars in which *not* is no longer a specifier, but a

Table 9.2. *The relative position of subject and* not *in negative subject–verb inversion sentences in Middle English*

	Spro + *not*	*not* + Spro	*not* + SNP	SNP + *not*[15]
ne + *not*, have/be/modal	68	0	11	6
ne + *not*, main verb	82	0	4	1
not, have/be/modal	68	5	12	3
not, main verb	51	1	4	2

head. Again, we should see what triggers this innovation. There is no shift in the positional evidence: the position of *not* was always fixed. The trigger therefore seems to be the loss of *ne*. This is of some interest, since it is hard to see what would bar *not* from remaining a specifier element. Apparently, the default option for the learner is, in the absence of another head (*ne*), *not* is a head.

There is some independent evidence for this account from the facts in table 9.2. Observe that the new pattern with the pronominal subject following *not* (column 2), which we analyse as movement of the new negative head *not* with the finite verb to C, is first attested when *ne* has disappeared: the pattern does not occur at all in those instances when *ne* is around. This makes sense: as long as *ne* was around, *not* was interpreted by the learner as a specifier element. Once *ne* has disappeared, learners construct grammars in which *not* is a head, moving with the finite verb, which at this stage could be a lexical finite verb, auxiliary or *do*. We are at the last stage of Jespersen's cycle, where we see the cycle coming full circle: in Jespersen's terms, the original negative marker (*ne*) becomes extinct, upon which the new negative marker begins to show the first signs of weakening. Weakening is again narrowly structurally circumscribed: a strong, positionally invariant, negative specifier is reinterpreted as a negative head, and incorporates with the finite verb as a clitic, moving with the finite verb to the C-position.

There are some relics of the old pattern in the present-day language: according to Quirk et al. (1985: 11.7), we have, beside the familiar pattern with negative contraction in negative questions, as in (37), an uncontracted, more formal usage as in (38), in which the old pattern handed down from Old English times is retained. In this pattern, the pronominal subject precedes *not*, while the nominal subject follows it.[16]

[15] This can often be interpreted as a constituent negation; also, the subject is often *mon/men*.

[16] A note of caution: the pattern in the uncontracted variant (38a–b) is not acceptable to some native speakers.

(37)   a. Didn't they warn you?
       b. Isn't history a social science?

(38)   a. Did they not warn you?
       b. Is not history a social science?

The new pattern emerging in table 9.2, with the pronominal subject following *not*, should then be identified as the rise of negative contraction (this insight is due to Rissanen 1994, 1999), resulting from the emergence of *not* as a negative head, hard on the heels of the loss of *ne*.

What we have seen in this section then, is that through the history of English sentential negation, the behaviour of negative adverbs is narrowly structurally circumscribed: in their variation and development, they remain precisely within the structural rigours imposed by NegP. When a negative adverb is a specifier, it is positionally confined to Spec,NegP; when it is a head, it incorporates with the finite verb, and positionally covaries with the finite verb. What is so striking is that the process throughout has tell-tale structural correlates by which we can diagnose the precise morphosyntactic properties at each synchronic stage. We therefore conclude that the history of sentential negation is a prime piece of evidence for seeing that the grammaticalization process consists of a series of synchronies: the gradual development is punctuated by small structural shifts which can be analysed quite precisely in the NegP format assumed in this section. Inasmuch as we see a grammaticalization process here, we see a cycle of lexical bleaching followed by reinforcement. But this development follows a course that is narrowly restricted by grammars at each stage.

9.3.3   Concluding discussion

Above, we have studied in detail two well-known cases of grammaticalization in the history of English, and we have analysed them in terms of grammar change. Along the way, we have tried to show that they cannot be simply analysed as unidirectional, semantically driven, diachronic processes. At each synchronic stage, the syntactic shape of the grammar plays a structurally well-defined role. In both cases, there is semantic bleaching of lexical content, but this does not mean that the development is semantically driven. In the case of *have to*, the general word order change towards fixed VO word order discussed in chapter 5 plays a pivotal role in the sense that it crucially led to the adjacency required for the reanalysis of *have to* from main verb to auxiliary. Similarly, in the development of negation, the NegP format has throughout been a precise structural factor. By this, we do not mean to suggest, of course, that semantic factors do not play a role. Rather, we hope to have shown that in our two case studies, there is no question of the change being exclusively semantically driven, or of it being part of a big overall process that can be regarded as a diachronic driving force.

There remains, of course, the role of semantic bleaching; if anything, this is what tends to be unidirectional in many cases of grammaticalization, and it remains a question what it is that drives a lexical weakening process. For reasons discussed in the introduction to this chapter, we would not want to invoke grammaticalization itself as an agent of change; our essentially synchronic language acquisition perspective precludes the existence of such a diachronic driving force. The weakening process seems to persistently go hand in hand with a particular morphosyntactic dependency: adjacency to and cliticization to the finite verb. In other words, independent constituents become bound morphemes through long-term association with a displaced finite verb. We have seen some evidence that the formal weakening may be earlier than the semantic weakening: recall, for instance, Classical Old English negative-initial clauses, in which *ne* is formally a prefix, but must correspond with a syntactic operator in Spec,CP that precludes the hosting of a topic. Postma (1995) presents the interesting hypothesis that it is the displacement itself that leads to semantic bleaching; in Postma's terminology, displacement resulting from syntactic movement moves a constituent into 'zero semantics'. The result of this is that part of the lexical meaning of an element is lost, and it is the syntactic configuration as a whole that determines the meaning of a construction. Another avenue worth exploring, which is fully compatible with Postma's ideas, is that the nature of functional categories is such that it induces lexical weakening: in many instances of grammaticalization, for instance that of the modal verbs, the final stage of grammaticalization is reanalysis to a functional category, i.e. the head of a functional projection such as T in TP (in the case of tense morphemes), M in MP (in the case of modality), D in DP (in the case of determiners), after a long period in which the element in question was moved to that category. Since functional categories are by their very nature just that, functional, association with such a category invites loss of lexical meaning. Much research remains to be done here. But we hope at least to have shown and illustrated the role of the synchronic grammar at each stage in developments typically analysed as grammaticalization. The conclusion, then, is that our view of synchronic grammatical reanalysis allows us to see that cases of grammaticalization, as much as the other changes discussed in this book, are the stuff of synchronic grammars as acquired by the learner.

Appendix (Fischer 1994a)

period	A1 object of HAVE only	A1 wh-/topic	A1 inf.=DO	A1 object=negat.	A1 quasi object	A1 sense of oblig.	A1 object=NEDE	A1 subj.in-anim	A2 HAVE+object infinitive+object	A2 wh-/topic	A2 inf.=DO	A2 object=negat.	A2 quasi object	A2 sense of oblig.	A2 object=NEDE	A2 subj.in-anim
HO1	2															
HO2	1				1											
HO3							1		1				1			
HO4									2				1			
HM1	6	1(1)			(1)				9	1(1)			2	(1)		
HM2	3	1		1					3	(1)			2	(1)		
HM3	18	2		2			1(2)		33	1		2(1)	2		5(2)	1
HM4	15		(1)	(1)	1		1	1(2)	26	2			2			(1)
HE1	19	1						1	39	1		1	4		1	5
HE2	17	1			1		1		50	1			3(2)		2(2)	4
HE3	20							1	75	2	1		6		2	

Notes:

1 The letters A1, A2, A3 and B in the column headings correspond to the letters used in (16). The numbers given here represent totals. The subcolumns following the main columns (main columns are distinguished by double lines, subcolumns by single ones) indicate the number of each type of construction within the total given. Numbers given in round brackets represent constructions which belong in more than one subcolumn. Thus, for example, in period HM4 a negative object is attested once with construction A1, but the negative object example also shows a feature of another subcolumn, which in this case can only be the example in the subcolumn 'infinitive = DO'. So one out of the 15 instance has a negative object and DO as infinitive.

2 The heading 'quasi object' includes nouns indicating time or space, but also prepositional objects.

period	A3 object shared by HAVE + infin.	wh- / topic	inf. = DO	object = negat.	quasi object	sense of oblig.	object = NEDE	subj. in- anim	B₁ HAVE + to-infin. (no object) [obligatory sense]	B₂ HAVE + to-inf. + object [obligatory sense]	of which, object = clause	causative HAVE + clause	HAD LEVER etc. + to-inf.
HO1													
HO2	3	(2)				(2)							
HO3	6	1				2			2				
HO4				(1)	(1)								
HM1	8	(2)	(2)	1	1(2)	1(1)			1 (TO DO)	1[1]			
HM2	8	1(3)	(2)	1(1)	(1)	1(4)			1 (TO DO)	1			
HM3	13	2(2)		3(1)	(2)	1(1)		3	1	[2]	[1]	1	1
HM4	4		(1)	1(1)	1	1			1 (TO DO)				2
HE1	31	1(11)	(12)	3(3)	(4)	3(8)	(1)		2[1] (3×DO)	[3]	[2]	4+1?	
HE2	15	(3)	(1)	2(1)	2(3)	4(1)			4[1] (2×DEAL)	[6]	[5]	5	2
HE3	34	3(5)	2(1)	4	1(1)	4(5)		(1)	3 (TO DO)	[1]		3	3

References

Adams J. N. 1994a. Wackernagel's Law and the Position of Unstressed Pronouns in Classical Latin. *Transactions of the Philological Society* 92: 103–78.

1994b. *Wackernagel's Law and the Placement of the Copula esse in Classical Latin.* (supplementary vol. 18.) Cambridge: Cambridge Philological Society.

Adamson, Sylvia, Vivien Law, Nigel Vincent and Susan Wright (eds.). 1990. *Papers from the 5th International Conference on English Historical Linguistics.* Amsterdam and Philadelphia: Benjamins.

Aitchison, Jean. 1991. *Language Change: Progress or Decay?* 2nd edn. Cambridge: Cambridge University Press.

Allan, K. 1971. A Note on the Source of *There* in Existential Sentences. *Foundations of Language* 7: 1–18.

Allen, Cynthia. 1977. Topics in English Diachronic Syntax. Dissertation, University of Massachusetts, Amherst.

1980. Movement and Deletion in Old English. *Linguistic Inquiry* 11: 261–323.

1986. Reconsidering the History of *Like*. *Journal of Linguistics* 22: 375–409.

1992. Old English and the Syntactician: some Remarks and a Syntactician's Guide to Editions of the Works of Ælfric. In Colman 1992. 1–19.

1995. *Case Marking and Reanalysis*. Oxford: Clarendon.

1997. The Origins of the 'Group Genitive' in English. *Transactions of the Philological Society* 95: 111–31.

Andersen, Henning. 1973. Abductive and Deductive Change. *Language* 49: 765–93.

Anderson, John M. 1988. The Type of Old English Impersonals. In John M. Anderson and Norman MacLeod (eds.) *Edinburgh Studies in the English Language*, vol. I. 1–32. Edinburgh: John Donald.

1993. Parameters of Syntactic Change: a Notional View. In C. Jones (ed.) *Historical Linguistics: Problems and Perspectives*. 1–43. London: Longman.

1997. *A Notional Theory of Syntactic Categories*. Cambridge: Cambridge University Press.

Baker, Mark, Kyle Johnson and Ian Roberts. 1989. Passive Arguments Raised. *Linguistic Inquiry* 20: 219–51.

Baker, Peter S. and Michael Lapidge (eds.). 1995. *Byrhtferth's Enchiridion*, Early English Text Society, Supplementary Series 15. Oxford: Oxford University Press.

Bauer, Brigitte. 1995. *The Emergence and Development of SVO Patterning in Latin and French: Diachronic and Psycholinguistic Perspectives*. Oxford: Oxford University Press.

Belletti, Adriana. 1990. *Generalized Verb Movement: Aspects of Verb Syntax*. Torino: Rosenberg and Sellier.

Bennis, Hans. 1986. *Gaps and Dummies*. Dordrecht: Foris.

1990. A Note on Modal Passives. In Joan Mascaró and Martina Nespor (eds.) *Grammar in Progress. Glow Essays for Henk van Riemsdijk*. 33–40. Dordrecht: Foris.

1992. Long Head Movement: the Position of Particles in the Verbal Cluster in Dutch. In R. van Hout and R. Bok-Bennema (eds.). *Linguistics in the Netherlands 1992*. 37–47. Amsterdam and Philadelphia: Benjamins.

Benveniste, Emile. 1968. Mutations of Linguistic Categories. Translated by Y. Malkiel and M. M. Vihman, in W. P. Lehmann and Yakov Malkiel (eds.) *Directions for Historical Linguistics*. 83–94. Austin: University of Texas Press.

Besten, Hans den. 1983. On the Interaction of Root Transformations and Lexical Deletive Rules. In Werner Abraham (ed.) *On the Formal Syntax of the Westgermania. Papers from the '3rd Groningen Grammar Talks', Groningen, January 1981*. 47–131. Amsterdam and Philadelphia: Benjamins.

Beths, Frank. 1999. The History of *Dare* and the Status of Unidirectionality, *Linguistics* 37: 1069–110.

Bever, Terence G. and D. Terence Langendoen. 1972. The Interaction of Speech Perception and Grammatical Structure in the Evolution of Language. In R. P. Stockwell and R. K. S. Macauley (eds.) *Linguistic Change and Generative Theory*. 32–95. Bloomington: Indiana University Press.

Birnbaum, H. 1984. Notes on Syntactic Change: Cooccurrence vs. Substitution, Stability vs. Permeability. In Fisiak 1984. 25–46.

Blake, Norman (ed.). 1992. *The Cambridge History of the English Language*, vol. II: *1066–1476*. Cambridge: Cambridge University Press.

Bobaljik, J. D. and H. Thráinsson. 1998. Two Heads aren't Always Better than One. *Syntax* 1: 37–71.

Bock, H. 1931. Studien zum präpositionalen Infinitiv und Akkusativ mit dem to-Infinitiv. *Anglia* 55: 114–249.

Bolinger, Dwight 1967. Apparent Constituents in Surface Structure. *Word* 23: 47–56.

Bosworth, J., and T. N. Toller (eds.). 1898. *An Anglo-Saxon Dictionary*. Oxford: Oxford University Press.

Bradley, S. A. J. 1982. *Anglo-Saxon Poetry*. London: Everyman.

Brinton, Laurel J. 1988. *The Development of English Aspectual Systems: Aspectualizers and Post-Verbal Particles*. Cambridge: Cambridge University Press.

1991. The Origin and Development of Quasimodal *have to* in English. Paper presented to the 10th ICHL, Amsterdam 1991. Unpublished ms. University of British Columbia.

Browning, Maggie. 1987. Null Operators and their Antecedents. *NELS* 17: 59–78.

Burchfield, Robert (ed.). 1994. *The Cambridge History of the English Language*, vol. V. *English in Britain and Overseas: Origins and Development*. Cambridge: Cambridge University Press.

Burrow, J. and T. Turville-Petre. 1992. *A Book of Middle English*. Oxford: Blackwell.

Bybee, Joan and William Pagliuca. 1985. Cross-Linguistic Comparison and the Development of Grammatical Meaning. In Jacek Fisiak (ed.) *Historical Semantics and Historical Word Formation*. 59–83. Berlin: Mouton de Gruyter.

Bybee, Joan, Revere Perkins and William Pagliuca. 1994. *The Evolution of Grammar: Tense, Aspect, and Modality in the Languages of the World*. Chicago: University of Chicago Press.

Callaway, Morgan Jr. 1913. *The Infinitive in Anglo-Saxon*. Washington: Carnegie Institution of Washington.

Campbell, Alistair. 1959. *Old English Grammar*. Oxford: Oxford University Press.

Canale, Michael. 1978. Word Order Change in Old English: Base Reanalysis in Generative Grammar. Dissertation, McGill University.

Cardinaletti, A. and M. Starke. 1996. Deficient Pronouns: a View from Germanic. A Study in the Unified Description of Germanic and Romance. In Thráinsson, Epstein and Peter 1996. 21–65.

Chomsky, Noam. 1977. On Wh-movement. In Peter W. Culicover, Tom Wasow and Adrian Akmajian (eds.) *Formal Syntax*. 71–132. New York: Academic Press.

1981. *Lectures on Government and Binding*. Dordrecht: Foris.

1982. *Some Concepts and Consequences of the Theory of Government and Binding*. Cambridge, Mass.: MIT Press.

1986. *Barriers*. Cambridge, Mass.: MIT Press.

1991. Some Notes on Economy of Derivation and Representation. In Robert Freidin (ed.) *Principles and Parameters in Comparative Syntax*. 417–53. Cambridge, Mass.: MIT Press. Revised version published as chapter 2 of Chomsky 1995.

1993. A Minimalist Program for Linguistic Theory. In K. Hale and S. J. Keyser (eds.) *The View from Building 20: Essays in Linguistics in Honor of Sylvain Bromberger*. Cambridge, Mass.: MIT Press. 1–52. Reprinted as chapter 3 of Chomsky 1995.

1995. *The Minimalist Program*. Cambridge, Mass.: MIT Press.

Cinque, G. 1995. *Italian Syntax and Universal Grammar*. Cambridge: Cambridge University Press.

Clark, Robin. 1990. *Papers on Learnability and Natural Selection*. Technical Reports in Formal and Computational Linguistics, 1. University of Genève.

1992. The Selection of Syntactic Knowledge. *Language Acquisition* 2: 83–149.

Clark, Robin and Ian Roberts. 1993. A Computational Model of Language Learning and Language Change. *Linguistic Inquiry* 24: 299–345.

Collins, Chris and Höskuldur Thráinsson. 1996. VP-internal Structure and Object Shift in Icelandic. *Linguistic Inquiry* 27: 391–444.

Colman, Fran. 1988. Heavy Arguments in Old English. In John M. Anderson and Norman MacLeod (eds.) *Edinburgh Studies in the English Language*, vol. I. 33–89. Edinburgh: John Donald.

(ed.) 1992. *Edinburgh Studies in the English Language*, vol. II: *Evidence for Old English*. Edinburgh: John Donald.

Courtney, Rosemary. 1983. *Longman Dictionary of Phrasal Verbs*. Harlow: Longman.

Cowie, A. P. and R. Mackin. 1975. *Oxford Dictionary of Current Idiomatic English*, vol. I: *Verbs with Prepositions & Particles*. Oxford: Oxford University Press.

Danchev, Andrei. 1984. Translation and Syntactic Change. In Fisiak 1984. 47–60.

1991. Language Typology and some Aspects of the SVO Development in English. In Kastovsky 1991. 103–24.

Demske-Neumann, Ulrike. 1994. *Modales Passiv und* Tough Movement*: Zur struk-turellen Kausalität eines syntaktischen Wandels im Deutschen und Englischen.* Tübingen: Niemeyer.

Denison, David. 1981. Aspects of the History of English Group-Verbs, with Particular Attention to the Syntax of the Ormulum, Dissertation, Oxford University.

1985. Why Old English had no Prepositional Passive. *English Studies* 66: 189–204.

1990. The Old English Impersonals Revived. In Adamson et al. 1990. 111–40.

1993. *English Historical Syntax.* London and New York: Longman.

Diekstra, Frans. 1984. Ambiguous *that*-clauses in Old and Middle English. *English Studies* 65: 97–110.

Dijk, Kees van. 1999. The Verbal Syntax of Early Middle Dutch: the Case of the Perfect and Related Constructions. Ms. University of Amsterdam.

Dikken, Marcel den. 1995. *Particles: on the syntax of Verb–Particle, Triadic, and Causative Constructions.* New York and Oxford: Oxford University Press.

Dikken, Marcel den and Jan-Wouter Zwart. 1996. Very Exceptional Case Marking. In Thráinsson, Epstein and Peter 1996. 85–108.

Duinhoven, Antonius M. 1991. Dat siet men wit ende reine wesen. A.c.i.-constructies in het Nederlands. *De Nieuwe Taalgids* 84: 409–30.

Dunn, C. W. and E. T. Byrnes (eds.). 1973. *Middle English Literature.* New York: Harcourt Brace Jovanovich.

Einenkel, Eugen. 1912. Die Englische verbalnegation. *Anglia* 35: 187–248.

Ellegård, Alvar. 1953. *The Auxiliary* Do*: the Establishment and Regulation of its Use in English.* Stockholm: Almkvist and Wiksell.

Elliott, R. W. V. 1974. *Chaucer's English.* London: André Deutsch.

Ferraresi, Gisella. 1991. Die Stellung des Gotischen Verbs im Licht eines Vergleichs mit dem Althochdeutschen. Tesi di Laurea, University of Venice.

Ferris, C. 1993. *The Meaning of Syntax: a Study in the Adjectives of English.* Harlow: Longman.

Fillmore, Charles. 1992. 'Corpus Linguistics' or 'Computer-Aided Armchair Linguistics', in Jan Svartvik (ed.) *Directions in Corpus Linguistics: Proceedings of the Nobel Symposium 82, Stockholm, 4–8 August 1991.* 35–60. Berlin: Mouton de Gruyter.

Fischer, Olga. 1988. The Rise of the *for NP to V* Construction: an Explanation. In J. Honey (ed.) *An Historic Tongue: Studies in English Linguistics in Memory of Barbara Strang.* 67–88. London and New York: Routledge.

1989. The Origin and Spread of the Accusative and Infinitive Construction in English. *Folia Linguistica Historica* 8: 143–217.

1991. The Rise of the Passive Infinitive in English. In Kastovsky 1991. 141–88.

1992a. Syntax. In Blake 1992. 207–408.

1992b. Syntactic Change and Borrowing: the Case of the Accusative and Infinitive Construction in English. In Gerritsen and Stein 1992. 17–88.

1994a. The Development of Quasi-auxiliaries in English and Changes in Word Order. *Neophilologus* 78: 137–64.

1994b. The Fortunes of the Latin-type Accusative and Infinitive Construction in Dutch and English Compared. In Toril Swan, Endre Mørck, Olav Jansen Westvik (eds.) *Language Change and Language Structure: Older Germanic Languages in a Comparative Perspective.* 91–133. Berlin: Mouton de Gruyter.

1995. The Distinction between Bare and *to*-infinitival Complements in Late Middle English. *Diachronica* 12: 1–30.

1996a. The Status of *to* in Old English *to*-infinitives: a Reply to Kageyama. *Lingua* 99: 107–33.

1996b. Verbal Complementation in Early Middle English. How do the Infinitives Fit in? In Derek Britton (ed.) *English Historical Linguistics 1994: Papers from the 8th International Conference on English Historical Linguistics.* 247–70. Amsterdam and Philadelphia: Benjamins.

1997a. The Grammaticalisation of Infinitival *to* in English Compared with German and Dutch. In Hickey and Puppel 1997. 265–80.

1997b. Infinitive marking in Late Middle English: Transitivity and Changes in the English System of Case. In Fisiak 1997. 109–34.

Fischer, Olga and Frederike van der Leek. 1983. The Demise of the Old English Impersonal Construction. *Journal of Linguistics* 19: 337–68.

Fisher, J. H. 1977. Chancery and the Emergence of Standard Written English in the Fifteenth Century. *Speculum* 52: 870–99.

Fisiak, Jacek (ed.). 1984. *Historical Syntax.* Berlin: Mouton de Gruyter.

(ed.) 1997. *Studies in Middle English Linguistics.* Berlin: Mouton de Gruyter.

Fleischman, Suzanne. 1982. *The Future in Thought and Language: Diachronic Evidence from Romance.* Cambridge: Cambridge University Press.

Foldvik, Sandra. 1989. Easy-adjectives, Tough-movement. *University of Trondheim Working Papers in Linguistics* 8.

Foster, Tony and Wim van der Wurff. 1995. The Survival of Object–Verb Order in Middle English: some Data. *Neophilologus* 79: 309–27.

1997. From Syntax to Discourse: the Function of Object–Verb Order in Late Middle English. In Fisiak 1997. 135–56.

Gaaf, W. van der. 1928. The Post-adjectival Passive Infinitive. *English Studies* 10: 129–38.

1931. *Beon* and *Habban* Connected with an Inflected Infinitive. *English Studies* 13: 176–88.

Geerts, G., W. Haeseryn, J. de Rooij and M.C. van den Toorn. 1984. *Algemene Nederlandse Spraakkunst.* Groningen: Wolters-Noordhoff.

Geoghegan, S. G. 1975. Relative clauses in Old, Middle and New English. *Working Papers in Linguistics* (Department of Linguistics, Ohio) 18: 30–71.

Gerritsen, Marinel and Dieter Stein (eds.) 1992. *Internal and External Factors in Syntactic Change.* Berlin: Mouton de Gruyter.

Givón, Talmy. 1975. Serial Verbs and Syntactic Change: Niger-Congo. In Charles Li (ed.) *Word Order and Word Order Change.* 47–112. Austin: University of Texas Press.

1971. Historical Syntax and Synchronic Morphology: an Archaeologist's Field Trip. *Papers from the Chicago Linguistics Society* 7: 394–415.

1979. *On Understanding Grammar.* New York: Academic Press.

Greenough, J. B. and G. L. Kittredge 1902. *Words and their Ways in English Speech.* London: Macmillan.

Haeberli, Eric 1991. *The Neg Criterion and Negative Concord.* Memoire de Licence, University of Geneva.

Haegeman, Liliane 1994. *Introduction to Government and Binding Theory*. 2nd edn. Oxford: Blackwell.

Haegeman, Liliane and Jacqueline Guéron 1999. *English Grammar: a Generative Perspective*. Oxford: Blackwell.

Harris, Alice C. and Lyle Campbell. 1995. *Historical Syntax in Cross-Linguistic Perspective*. Cambridge: Cambridge University Press.

Harrison, T. P. 1892. The Separable Prefixes in Anglo-Saxon. Dissertation, Johns Hopkins University.

Haspelmath, Martin. 1999. Why is Grammaticalization Irreversible? *Linguistics* 37: 1043–1068.

Hawkins, John. 1990. Seeking Motives for Change in Typological Variation. In William Croft, Keith Denning and Suzanne Kemmer (eds.) *Studies in Typology and Diachrony: Papers Presented to Joseph H. Greenberg on his 75th birthday*. 95–122. Amsterdam and Philadelphia: Benjamins.

Healey, Antonette diPaolo, Joan Holland, David McDougall, Nancy Speirs and Pauline Thomson (eds.). 1994. *Dictionary of Old English, Letter A*. Toronto: Pontifical Institute of Medieval Studies.

Healey, Antonette diPaolo and Richard Venezky. 1980. *A Microfiche Concordance to Old English*. Toronto: Pontifical Institute of Medieval Studies.

Heine, Bernd, Ulrike Claudi and Friederike Hünnemeyer. 1991a. *Grammaticalization: a Conceptual Framework*. Chicago: University of Chicago Press.

1991b. From Cognition to Grammar: Evidence from African Languages. In Traugott and Heine 1991a. Vol. I, 149–87.

Heine, Bernd and Mechthild Reh. 1984. *Grammaticalization and Reanalysis in African Languages*. Hamburg: Helmut Buske.

Helten, Willem L. van. 1883. *Vondel's taal*. Deel 2, Syntaxis. Groningen: Wolters.

Henry, Alison. 1997. Viewing Change in Progress: the Loss of Verb-Second in Hiberno-English Imperatives. In van Kemenade and Vincent 1997. 272–96.

Hickey, Raymond and Stanisław Puppel (eds.). 1997. *Language History and Linguistic Modelling: a Festschrift for Jacek Fisiak on his 60th Birthday*. Berlin: Mouton de Gruyter.

Hiltunen, Risto. 1983. *The Decline of the Prefixes and the Beginnings of the English Phrasal Verb*. Turku: Turun Yliopisto.

Hoekstra, Teun. 1988. Small Clauses Results. *Lingua* 74: 101–39.

Hofstadter, Douglas. 1995. *Fluid Concepts and Creative Analogies: Computer Models of the Fundamental Mechanisms of Thought*. In cooperation with the 'Fluid Analogies Research Group'. New York: Basic.

Hogg, Richard M. (ed.). 1992a. *The Cambridge History of the English Language*, vol. I: *The Beginnings to 1066*. Cambridge: Cambridge University Press.

1992b. Phonology and Morphology. In Hogg 1992a. 67–167.

Holmberg, Anders and Christer Platzack. 1995. *The Role of Inflection in Scandinavian Syntax*. New York and Oxford: Oxford University Press.

Holyoak, Keith J. and Paul Thagard. 1995. *Mental Leaps: Analogy in Creative Thought*. Cambridge, Mass.: MIT Press.

Hopper, Paul. 1991. On Some Principles of Grammaticization. In Traugott and Heine 1991a. Vol. I, 17–35.

Hopper, Paul and Elizabeth C. Traugott. 1993. *Grammaticalization*. Cambridge: Cambridge University Press.

Hornstein, Norbert and Amy Weinberg. 1981. Case Theory and Preposition Stranding. *Linguistic Inquiry* 12: 55–91.

Hulk, Aafke and Ans van Kemenade. 1993. Subjects, Nominative Case, Agreement and Functional Heads. *Lingua* 89: 181–215.

1997. Negation as a Reflex of Clause Structure. In Danielle Forget, Paul Hirschbühler, France Martineau and María-Luisa Rivero (eds.) *Negation and Polarity*. 183–207. Amsterdam and Philadelphia: Benjamins.

Itkonen, Esa. 1994. Iconicity, Analogy and Universal Grammar. *Journal of Pragmatics* 22: 37–53.

Jack, George B. 1978a. Negative Adverbs in Early Middle English. *English Studies* 59: 295–309.

1978b. Negation in Later Middle English Prose. *Archivum Linguisticum* (n.s.) 9: 58–72.

1978c. Negative Concord in Early Middle English. *Studia Neophilologica* 50: 29–39.

1991. The Infinitive in Early Middle English Prose. *Neuphilologische Mitteilungen* 92: 311–41.

Jacobsson, Bengt. 1951. *Inversion in English: with Special Reference to the Early Modern English Period*. Uppsala: Almqvist and Wiksell.

Jaeggli, Osvaldo and Ken Safir (eds.). 1989. *The Null Subject Parameter*. Dordrecht, Boston and London: Kluwer Academic.

Jespersen, Otto. 1905. *Growth and Structure of the English Language*. Leipzig: Teubner.

1917. *Negation in English and other Languages*. Det Kgl. Danske Videnskabernes Selskab. Historisk-filologiske Meddelelser 1. 1–151. Copenhagen.

1940. *A Modern English Grammar*, vol. V. London: Allen and Unwin.

Joseph, Brian D. 1992. Diachronic Explanation: Putting Speakers back into the Picture. In Garry W. Davis and Gregory K. Iverson (eds.) *Explanation in Historical Linguistics*. 123–44. Amsterdam and Philadelphia: Benjamins.

Kaartinen, A. and T. F. Mustanoja. 1958. The Use of the Infinitive in A Book of London English 1384–1425. *Neuphilologische Mitteilungen* 59: 179–92.

Kageyama, Taro. 1992. AGR in Old English Infinitives. *Lingua* 88: 91–128.

Kastovsky, Dieter (ed.). 1991. *Historical English Syntax*. Berlin: Mouton de Gruyter.

Kayne, Richard. 1975. *French Syntax: The Transformational Cycle*. Cambridge, Mass.: MIT Press.

1994. *The Antisymmetry of Syntax*. Cambridge, Mass.: MIT Press.

Kemenade, Ans van. 1987. *Syntactic Case and Morphological Case in the History of English*. Dordrecht: Foris.

1997a. V₂ and Embedded Topicalization in Old and Middle English. In van Kemenade and Vincent 1997. 326–52.

1997b. Negative-initial Sentences in Old and Middle English. In *A Festschrift for Roger Lass on his Sixtieth Birthday. Studia Anglica Posnaniensia* XXXI, 91–104.

1998. Review of Allen 1995. *Journal of Linguistics* 34: 227–32.

1999. Sentential Negation and Clause Structure in Old English. In Tieken-Boon van Ostade, Tottie and van der Wurff 1999. 147–65.

forthcoming. Verbal Syntax and Negation in the History of English. Ms. University of Nijmegen.

Kemenade, Ans van and Nigel Vincent (eds.). 1997. *Parameters of Morphosyntactic Change*. Cambridge: Cambridge University Press.

Kiparsky, Paul. 1982. *Explanation in Phonology*. Dordrecht: Foris.

1997. The Rise of Positional Licensing. In van Kemenade and Vincent 1997. 460–94.

Kitahara, H. 1995. Target: Deducing Strict Cyclicity from Derivational Economy. *Linguistic Inquiry* 26: 47–77.

Klima, Edward. 1964. Negation in English. In J. A. Fodor and J. J. Katz (eds.) *The Structure of Language*. Readings in the Philosophy of Language. 246–323. Englewood Cliffs: Prentice Hall.

Klöpzig, W. 1922. Der Ursprung der *to be to* Konstruktion. *Englische Studien* 56: 378–89.

Koelmans, Leendert. 1978. *Inleiding tot het lezen van zeventiende-eeuws Nederlands*. Utrecht: Bohn, Scheltema en Holkema.

Koopman, Willem. 1984. Some Thoughts on Old English Word Order. In Erik Kooper (ed.) *Current Research in Dutch and Belgian Universities*. Papers read at the fifth Philological Symposium. 2–20. University of Utrecht.

1985. The Syntax of Verb and Particle Combinations in Old English. In Hans Bennis and Frits Beukema (eds.) *Linguistics in the Netherlands 1985*. 91–9. Dordrecht: Foris.

1990. Word Order in Old English. Dissertation, University of Amsterdam.

1994. The Order of Dative and Accusative Objects in Old English. Ms. University of Amsterdam.

1995. Verb-final Main Clauses in Old English Prose. *Studia Neophilologica* 67: 129–44.

1997. Another Look at Clitics in Old English. *Transactions of the Philological Society* 95: 73–93.

1998. Inversion after Single and Multiple Topics in Old English. In J. Fisiak and M. Krygier (eds.) *Advances in English Historical Linguistics (1996)*. 135–50. Berlin: Mouton de Gruyter.

Koster, Jan. 1975. Dutch as an SOV Language. *Linguistic Analysis* 1: 111–36.

Krapp, George Philip. 1931. *The Junius Manuscript*. The Anglo-Saxon Poetic Records 1. New York: Columbia University Press.

Krickau, C. 1877. Der Accusativ mit dem Infinitiv in der englischen Sprache, besonders im Zeitalter der Elisabeth. Dissertation, University of Göttingen.

Kroch, Anthony. 1989. Reflexes of Grammar in Patterns of Language Change. *Language Variation and Change* 1: 199–244.

Kroch, Anthony and Ann Taylor. 1994. Remarks on the VX/XV Alternation. Paper presented at the Third Diachronic Generative Syntax Conference. Amsterdam, Vrije Universiteit.

1997. Verb Movement in Old and Middle English: Dialect Variation and Language Contact. In van Kemenade and Vincent 1997. 297–325.

Kytö, Merja. 1991. *Manual to the Diachronic Part of the Helsinki Corpus of English Texts*. Helsinki: Helsinki University Press.

Lasnik, Howard and Robert Fiengo. 1974. Complement Object Deletion. *Linguistic Inquiry* 5: 535–71.

Lass, Roger. 1992. Phonology and Morphology. In Blake. 23–155.

1997. *Historical Linguistics and Language Change*. Cambridge: Cambridge University Press.

(ed.) 1999. *The Cambridge History of the English Language*, vol. III: 1476–1776. Cambridge: Cambridge University Press.

Leek, Frederike van der. 1992. Significant Syntax: the Case of Exceptional Passives. *Dutch Working Papers in English Language and Linguistics* 27: 1–28.

Lehmann, Christian. 1982. *Thoughts on Grammaticalization: A Programmatic Sketch*, vol. I. Cologne: University of Cologne.

1985. Grammaticalization: Synchronic Variation and Diachronic Change. *Lingua e Stile* 20: 303–18.

Leith, Dick. 1983. *A Social History of English*. London: Routledge and Kegan Paul.

Lightfoot, David. 1979. *Principles of Diachronic Syntax*. Cambridge: Cambridge University Press.

1981a. The History of Noun Phrase Movement. In C. L. Baker and J. McCarthy (eds.) *The Logical Problem of Language Acquisition*. 86–119. Cambridge, Mass.: MIT Press.

1981b. Explaining Syntactic Change. In N. Hornstein and D. Lightfoot (eds.) *Explanation in Linguistics: the Logical Problem of Language Acquisition*. 207–40. London: Longman.

1991. *How to Set Parameters: Arguments from Language Change*. Cambridge, Mass.: MIT Press.

1997. Shifting Triggers and Diachronic Reanalyses. In van Kemenade and Vincent 1997. 253–72.

1999. *The Development of Language*. Oxford: Blackwell.

Los, Bettelou 1998. The Rise of the *to*-infinitive as Verb Complement. *English Language and Linguistics* 2: 1–36.

1999. *Infinitival Complementation in Old and Middle English*. The Hague: Holland Academic Graphics.

MacLeish, Andrew. 1969. *The Middle English Subject-Verb Cluster*. The Hague: Mouton.

McMahon, April M. S. 1994. *Understanding Language Change*. Cambridge: Cambridge University Press.

McNeill, D. 1966. Developmental Psycholinguistics. In F. Smith and G. A. Miller (eds.) *The Genesis of Language: A Psycholinguistic Approach*. 15–84. Cambridge, Mass.: MIT Press.

Mair, C. 1987. Tough-movement in Present-day British English: a Corpus-based Study. *Studia Linguistica* 41: 59–71.

Maling, Joan. 1990. Inversion in Embedded Clauses in Modern Icelandic. In Maling and Zaenen 1990. 71–91.

Maling, Joan and Annie Zaenen (eds.). 1990. *Modern Icelandic Syntax*. San Diego: Academic Press.

Malsh, D. L. 1976. Clauses and Quasi-clauses: VO Order in Old English. *Glossa* 10: 28–43.

Manabe, K. 1989. *The Syntactic and Stylistic Development of the Infinitive in Middle English*. Fukuoka: Kyushu University Press.

Massam, Diane. 1992. Null Objects and Non-thematic Subjects. *Journal of Linguistics* 28: 115–37.

May, R. 1985. *Logical Form: its Structure and Derivation*. Cambridge, Mass.: MIT Press.

Meier, Hans. 1967. The Lag of Relative 'who' in the Nominative. *Neophilologus* 51: 277–88.

Meillet, Antoine. 1912. L'Evolution des formes grammaticales. Reprinted in A. Meillet 1958. *Linguistique historique et linguistique Générale*. 130–48. Paris: Champion.

Mitchell, Bruce. 1978. Prepositions, Adverbs, Prepositional Adverbs, Postpositions, Separable Prefixes, or Inseparable Prefixes, in Old English? *Neuphilologische Mitteilungen* 79: 240–57.

1980. The Dangers of Disguise: Old English Texts in Modern Punctuation. *Review of English Studies* 31: 385–413.

1985. *Old English Syntax*. Oxford: Clarendon.

Mithun, Marianne. 1992. External Triggers and Internal Guidance in Syntactic Development: Coordinating Conjunctions. In Gerritsen and Stein 1992. 89–129.

Miyabe, K. 1956. Some Notes on the Perfect Infinitive in Early Middle English. *Anglica* 2: 13–19.

MNW. 1885–1941. E. Verwijs and J. Verdam (eds.) *Middelnederlandsch woordenboek*. The Hague: Nijhoff.

Mourek, V. E. 1903. *Zur Negation im Altgermanischen*. Prague: Verlag der kgl. Böhmischen Gesellschaft der Wissenschaften.

Mulder, René and Marcel den Dikken. 1992. Tough Parasitic Gaps. *NELS* 20: 303–17.

Mustanoja, Tauno. 1960. *A Middle English Syntax*, part 1: *Parts of Speech*. Helsinki: Société Néophilologique.

1985. Some Features of Syntax in Middle English Main Clauses. In Mary-Jo Arn and Hanneke Wirtjes (eds.) *Historical and Editorial Studies in Medieval and Early Modern English for Johan Gerritsen*. 73–5. Groningen: Wolters Noordhoff.

Neeleman, Ad. 1994. Secondary Predication. Dissertation, University of Utrecht.

Nevalainen, Terttu. 1997. Recycling Inversion: the Case of Initial Adverbs and Negators in Early Modern English. In *A Festschrift for Roger Lass on his Sixtieth birthday. Studia Anglica Posnaniensia* XXXI, 203–14.

Nijhoff, M. (ed.). 1947 [1978]. *P.C. Hooft, Nederlandse Historiën in het kort*. Amsterdam: Elsevier.

Noël, Dirk. 1997. The Choice between Infinitives and that-Clauses after Believe, *English Language and Linguistics* 1: 271–84.

Ohlander, U. 1941. A Study on the Use of the Infinitive Sign in Middle English. *Studia Neophilologica* 14: 58–66.

Ono, S. 1975. The Old English Verbs of Knowing. *Studies in English Literature. English Number* 1975, 33–60.

Overdiep, G. S. 1935. *Zeventiende Eeuwse Syntaxis*. Groningen: Wolters.

Petter, Marga. 1994. On the Dutch Verb *Laten*. In Reineke Bok-Bennema and Crit Cremers (eds.) *Linguistics in the Netherlands 1994*. 163–74. Amsterdam and Philadelphia: Benjamins.

1998. *Getting PRO under Control*. The Hague: Holland Academic Graphics.

Phillipps, K. C. 1965. Asyndetic Relative Clauses in Late Middle English. *English Studies* 46: 323–9.

1966. Adverb Clauses in the Fifteenth Century. *English Studies* 47: 355–65.

Pinkster, Harm. 1987. The Strategy and Chronology of the Development of Future and Perfect Tense Auxiliaries in Latin. In M. Harris and P. Ramat (eds.) *Historical Development of Auxiliaries*. 193–223. Berlin: Mouton de Gruyter.

Pintzuk, Susan. 1991. Phrase Structures in Competition: Variation and Change in Old English Word Order. Dissertation, University of Pennsylvania.

1993. Verb Seconding in Old English: Verb Movement to Infl. *Linguistic Review* 10: 5–35.

1996. Old English Verb–Complement Word Order and the Change from OV to VO. *York Papers in Linguistics* 17: 241–64.

Pintzuk, Susan and Anthony Kroch. 1989. The Rightward Movement of Complements and Adjuncts in the Old English of *Beowulf*. *Language Variation and Change* 1: 115–43.

Plank, Frans. 1983. Coming into Being among the Anglo-Saxons. In Michael Davenport, Erik Hansen and Hans Frede Nielsen (eds.) *Current Topics in English Historical Linguistics: Proceedings of the Second International Conference on English Historical Linguistics held at Odense University 13–15 April 1981*. 239–78. Odense: Odense University Press.

1984. The Modals Story Retold. *Studies in Language* 8: 305–64.

Platzack, Christer and Anders Holmberg. 1989. The Role of AGR and Finiteness. *Working Papers in Scandinavian Syntax* 43: 51–76.

Postma, Gertjan. 1995. *Zero Semantics: a Study of the Syntactic Conception of Quantificational Meaning*. The Hague: Holland Academic Graphics.

Quirk, Randolph, Sydney Greenbaum, Geoffrey Leech and Jan Svartvik. 1985. *A Comprehensive Grammar of the English Language*. London and New York: Longman.

Quirk, Randolph and Jan Svartvik. 1970. Types and Uses of Non-finite Clauses in Chaucer. *English Studies* 51: 393–411.

Radford, Andrew. 1997. *Syntactic Theory and the Structure of English: a Minimalist Approach*. Cambridge: Cambridge University Press.

Reddick, R. J. 1982. On the Underlying Order of Early West Saxon. *Journal of Linguistics* 18: 37–56.

Riemsdijk, Henk van. 1978. *A Case Study in Syntactic Markedness*. Dordrecht: Foris.

1982. A Note on Case Absorption. *Wiener Linguistische Gazette* 27/28: 71–82.

Rissanen, Matti. 1994. The Position of *not* in Early Modern English Questions. In D. Kastovsky (ed.) *Studies in Early Modern English*. 339–48. Berlin: Mouton de Gruyter.

1999. *Isn't it?* or *Is it not?* On the Order of Postverbal Subject and Negative Particle in the History of English. In Tieken-Boon van Ostade, Tottie and van der Wurff 1999. 189–205.

Rissanen, Matti, Merja Kytö and Kirsti Heikkonen (eds.). 1997. *Grammaticalization at Work: Studies of Long-term Developments in English*. Berlin and New York: Mouton de Gruyter.

Rizzi, Luigi 1997. The Fine Structure of the Left Periphery. In Liliane Haegeman (ed.) *Elements of Grammar: Handbook in Generative Syntax*. 281–337. Dordrecht: Kluwer.

Roberts, Ian. 1985. Agreement Parameters and the Development of English Modal Auxiliaries. *Natural Language and Linguistic Theory* 3: 21–58.

1993. *Verbs and Diachronic Syntax: a Comparative History of English and French.* Dordrecht, Boston and London: Kluwer Academic.

1995. Object Movement and Verb Movement in Early Modern English. In H. Haider, S. Olsen and S. Vikner (eds.) *Studies in Comparative Germanic Syntax.* 269–84. Dordrecht: Kluwer.

1997. Directionality and Word Order Change in the History of English. In van Kemenade and Vincent 1997. 397–426.

Rögnvaldsson, Eirikur and Höskuldur Thráinsson. 1990. On Icelandic Word Order Once More. In Maling and Zaenen 1990. 3–41.

Rohrbacher, Bernard W. 1994. The Germanic Languages and the Full Paradigm: a Theory of V to I Raising. Dissertation, University of Massachusetts, Amherst.

Romaine, Suzanne (ed.) 1998. *The Cambridge History of the English Language*, vol. IV: *1776–1997.* Cambridge: Cambridge University Press.

Rosch, Eleanor. 1978. Principles of Categorization. In E. Rosch and B. B. Lloyd (eds.) *Cognition and Categorization.* 27–48. Hillsdale, N.J.: Erlbaum.

1988. Coherences and Categorization: a Historical View. In F. Kessel (ed.) *The Development of Language and Language Researchers: Essays in Honor of Roger Brown.* 373–92. Hillsdale, N.J.: Erlbaum.

Royster, J. F. 1918. The Causative Use of *hatan. Journal of English and Germanic Philology* 17: 82–93.

Rubba, Jo. 1994. Grammaticalization as Semantic Change: a Case Study of Preposition Development. In William Pagliuca (ed.). *Perspectives on Grammaticalization.* 81–101. Amsterdam and Philadelphia: Benjamins.

Rydén, Mats. 1983. The Emergence of *Who* as Relativizer. *Studia Linguistica* 37: 126–34.

Sanders, H. 1915. *Der syntaktische Gebrauch des Infinitivs im Frühmittelenglischen.* Heidelberg: Carl Winter.

Sauer, H. (ed.). 1978. *Theodulphi Capitula in England: Die altenglischen Übersetzungen, zusammen mit dem lateinischen Text.* Munich: Wilhelm Fink Verlag.

Scheler, M. 1961. Altenglische Lehnsyntax. Die syntaktischen Latinismen im Altenglischen. Dissertation, University of Berlin.

Schmidt, Deborah. 1980. A History of Inversion in English. Dissertation, Ohio State University.

Searle, A. (ed.) 1983. *Barrington Familiy Letters: 1628–1632.* Camden Fourth Series 28. London: Offices of the Royal Historical Society, University College London.

Shlonsky, Ur. 1997. Eyn-negation and What it Teaches us About Hebrew Clause Structure. In Jane Lecarme, Jean Lowenstamm and Ur Shlonsky (eds.) *Studies in Afroasiatic Grammar.* 392–409. The Hague: Holland Academic Graphics.

Sørensen, Knud. 1957. Latin Influence on English Syntax: a Survey with a Bibliography. *Travaux du Cercle Linguistique du Copenhague* 11: 131–55.

Spamer, James B. 1979. The Development of the Definite Article in English: a Case Study of Syntactic Change. *Glossa* 13: 241–50.

Stockwell, Robert P. 1977. Motivations for Exbraciation in Old English. In Ch. N. Li (ed.) *Mechanisms of Syntactic Change.* 291–314. Austin: University of Texas Press.

Stockwell, Robert P. and Donka Minkova. 1990. Verb Phrase Conjunction in Old English. In Henning Andersen and Konrad Koerner (eds.) *Historical Linguistics 1987*. 499–515. Amsterdam and Philadelphia: Benjamins.

1991. Subordination and Word Order Change in the History of English. In Kastovsky 1991. 367–408.

Stoett, Frederik A. 1923. *Middelnederlandsche spraakkunst: Syntaxis*. 3rd edn. The Hague: Nijhoff.

Stowell, Tim. 1981. Origins of Phrase Structure. Dissertation, MIT.

1983. Subjects across Categories. *Linguistic Review* 2: 285–312.

Swan, Toril. 1988. *Sentence Adverbials in English: a Synchronic and Diachronic Investigation*. Oslo: Novus.

Sweetser, Eve. 1990. *From Etymology to Pragmatics: Metaphorical and Cultural Aspects of Semantic Structure*. Cambridge: Cambridge University Press.

Thráinsson, H., S. D. Epstein and S. Peter (eds.). 1996. *Studies in Comparative Germanic Syntax*, vol. II. Dordrecht, Boston and London: Kluwer Academic.

Tieken-Boon van Ostade, Ingrid. 1987. *The Auxiliary* do *in Eighteenth-century English: a Sociohistorical-linguistic Approach*. Dordrecht: Foris.

Tieken-Boon van Ostade, Ingrid, G. Tottie and W. van der Wurff (eds.). 1999. *Negation in the History of English*. Berlin and New York: Mouton de Gruyter.

Toller, T. N. (ed.). 1921. *An Anglo-Saxon Dictionary: Supplement*. Oxford: Oxford University Press.

Tomaselli, Alessandra. 1995. Cases of Verb Third in Old High German. In Adrian Battye and Ian Roberts (eds.) *Clause Structure and Language Change*. 345–69. Oxford: Oxford University Press.

Toon, Thomas. 1983. *The Politics of Early Old English Sound Change*. New York: Academic Press.

Traugott, Elizabeth C. 1982. From Propositional to Textual and Expressive Meanings: some Semantic–Pragmatic Aspects of Grammaticalization. In Winfred P. Lehmann and Yakov Malkiel (eds.) *Perspectives on Historical Linguistics*. 245–71. Amsterdam and Philadelphia: Benjamins.

1992. Syntax. In Hogg 1992a. 168–289.

Traugott, Elizabeth C. and Bernd Heine (eds.) 1991a. *Approaches to Grammaticalization*, 2 vols. Amsterdam and Philadelphia: Benjamins.

1991b. Introduction. In Traugott and Heine 1991a. Vol. I. 1–14.

Vanden Wyngaerd, Guido. 1990. PRO-legomena, an Investigation into the Distribution and the Referential Properties of the Empty Category PRO. Dissertation, University of Antwerp.

Vikner, Sten. 1995. *Verb Movement and Expletive Subjects in the Germanic Languages*. New York and Oxford: Oxford University Press.

Vincent, Nigel. 1995. Exaptation and Grammaticalization. In Henning Andersen (ed.) *Historical Linguistics 1993*. 433–45. Amsterdam and Philadelphia: Benjamins.

1997. The Emergence of the D-system in Romance. In van Kemenade and Vincent 1997. 149–69.

Visser, F. Th. 1963–73. *An Historical Syntax of the English Language*. 3 parts. Leiden: Brill.

Wang, William. 1969. Competing Changes as a Cause of Residue. *Language* 45: 9–25.

Warner, Anthony. 1982. *Complementation in Middle English and the Methodology of Historical Linguistics.* London: Croom Helm.

1983. Review of Lightfoot 1979. *Journal of Linguistics* 19: 187–209.

1990. Reworking the History of English Auxiliaries. In Adamson et al. 1990. 537–58.

1993. *English Auxiliaries: Structure and History.* Cambridge: Cambridge University Press.

1997. The Structure of Parametric Change, and V-movement in the History of English. In van Kemenade and Vincent 1997. 380–93.

Weerman, Fred. 1989. *The Verb-Second Conspiracy: a Synchronic and a Diachronic Analysis.* Dordrecht: Foris.

1993. The Diachronic Consequences of First and Second Language Acquisition: the Change from OV to VO. *Linguistics* 31: 903–31.

Wilder, Christopher. 1991. Tough Movement Constructions. *Linguistische Berichte* 132: 115–32.

WNT 1882 – *Woordenboek der Nederlandsche taal*, M. de Vries et al. (eds.). The Hague and Leiden: Nijhoff, Sijthoff, Stemberg.

Wurff, Wim van der. 1987. Adjective plus Infinitive in Old English. In Frits Beukema and Peter Coopmans (eds.) *Linguistics in the Netherlands 1987.* 233–42. Dordrecht: Foris.

1990a. The *easy to please* Construction in Old and Middle English. In Adamson et al. 1990. 519–36.

1990b. Diffusion and Reanalysis in Syntax. Dissertation, University of Amsterdam.

1992a. Another Old English Impersonal: some Data. In Colman 1992. 211–48.

1992b. Syntactic Variability, Borrowing, and Innovation. *Diachronica* 9: 61–85.

1997a. Deriving Object–Verb Order in Late Middle English. *Journal of Linguistics* 33: 485–509.

1997b. OV-volgorde in vijftiende-eeuws Engels proza. In: A. van Santen, M. van der Wal (eds.) *Taal in Tijd en Ruimte.* 73–84. Leiden: Stichting Neerlandistiek Leiden.

1999. Objects and Verbs in Modern Icelandic and Fifteenth-Century English: a Word Order Parallel and its Causes. *Lingua* 109: 237–65.

Zeitlin, J. 1908. *The Accusative with Infinitive and some Kindred Constructions in English.* New York: Columbia University Press.

Zwart, Jan-Wouter. 1993. Dutch Syntax: a Minimalist Approach. Dissertation, University of Groningen.

Index